ARTHUR MERVYN

Volumes in the Bicentennial Edition

Wieland; or The Transformation. An American Tale with *Memoirs of Carwin the Biloquist*

Ormond; or The Secret Witness

Arthur Mervyn; or Memoirs of the Year 1793. First and Second Parts

Edgar Huntley; or, Memoirs of a Sleep-Walker

Clara Howard; In a Series of Letters with *Jane Talbot, A Novel*

Alcuin; A Dialogue (The Rights of Women) with *Memoirs of Stephen Calvert*

Available in Paperback

Wieland; or The Transformation. An American Tale with *Memoirs of Carwin the Biloquist*

Edgar Huntley; or, Memoirs of a Sleep-Walker

Arthur Mervyn; or Memoirs of the Year 1793. First and Second Parts

CHARLES BROCKDEN BROWN

ARTHUR MERVYN

or

MEMOIRS OF THE YEAR 1793

First and Second Parts

Edited by Sydney J. Krause and S. W. Reid

KENT STATE UNIVERSITY PRESS

Kent & London

The text of this edition reproduces that of Volume III of the Bicentennial
Edition of *The Novels and Related Works of Charles Brockden Brown,* published by
The Kent State University Press, 1980.

CENTER FOR EDITIONS OF
AMERICAN AUTHORS

AN APPROVED TEXT

MODERN LANGUAGE
ASSOCIATION OF AMERICA

© 1980, 2002 by The Kent State University Press, Kent, OH 44242
All rights reserved
ISBN 978-0-87338-738-5
Library of Congress Catalog Card Number 2002023364
Manufactured in the United States of America

Revised edition and first paperback edition, 2002

11 10 09 08 07   5 4 3 2

Library of Congress Cataloging-in-Publication Data
Brown, Charles Brockden, 1771–1810.
    Arthur Mervyn, or, Memoirs of the year 1793 : first and second parts /
    by Charles Brockden Brown ; edited by Sydney J. Krause and S. W.
    Reid.—Rev. ed., 1st pbk. ed.
        p. cm.
    Includes bibliographical references (p.   ).
    ISBN 0-87338-738-4 (alk. paper)
    1. Philadelphia (Pa.)—Fiction. 2. Yellow fever—Fiction. 3. Murderers—
Fiction. 4. Young men—Fiction. I. Title: Arthur Mervyn. II. Title: Memoirs
of the year 1793. III. Krause, Sydney J. (Sydney Joseph). IV. Reid, S. W.
V. Title.

PS1134 .A32 2002
813'.2—dc21   2002023364

British Library Cataloging-in-Publication data are available.

This edition of *Arthur Mervyn* commemorates
the distinguished career in early American literary studies
of Norman S. Grabo (1930–2001).

CONTENTS

ARTHUR MERVYN, FIRST PART   1

ARTHUR MERVYN, SECOND PART   217

Introduction to the Historical Essay   447

Historical Essay *by Norman S. Grabo*   449

Selected Bibliography   478

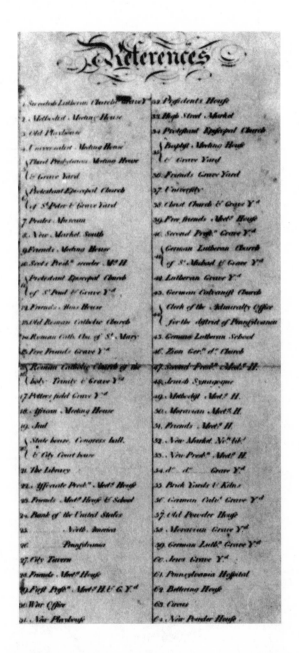

Overleaf: Plan of the City and Suburbs of Philadelphia (1794)
The "Davies" Map, engraved by R. Scot and S. Allardice
Key enlarged above
Courtesy of the Historical Society of Pennsylvania

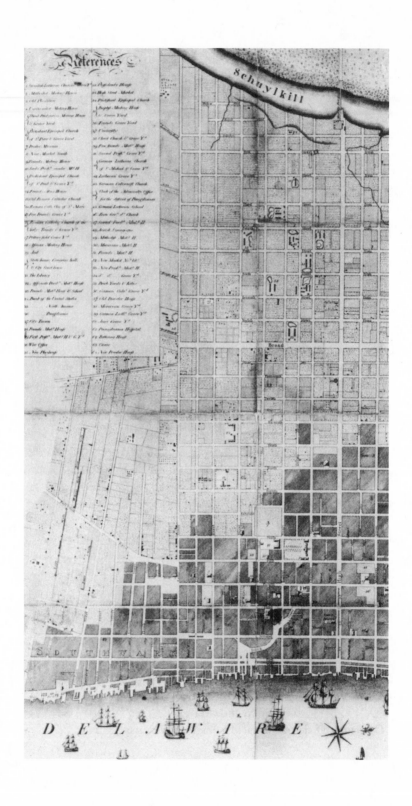

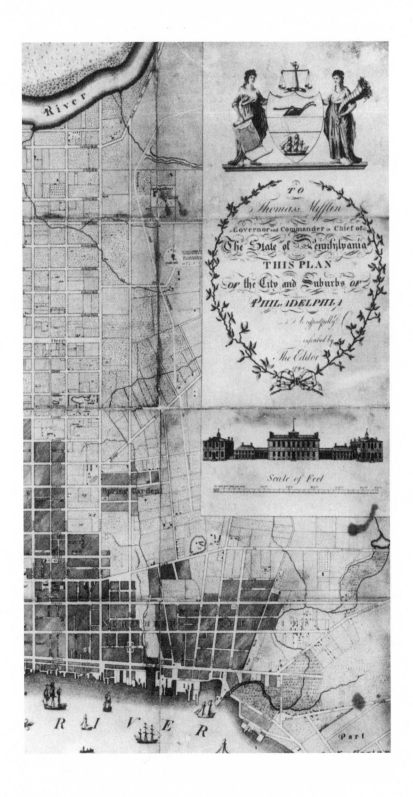

ARTHUR MERVYN;

or,

MEMOIRS OF THE YEAR 1793.

First Part

PREFACE

THE evils of pestilence by which this city has lately been afflicted will probably form an aera in its history. The schemes of reformation and improvement to which they will give birth, or, if no efforts of human wisdom can avail to avert the periodical visitations of this calamity, the change in manners and population which they will produce, will be, in the highest degree, memorable. They have already supplied new and copious materials for reflection to the physician and the political economist. They have not been less fertile of instruction to the moral observer, to whom they have furnished new displays of the influence of human passions and motives.

Amidst the medical and political discussions which are now afloat in the community relative to this topic, the author of these remarks has ventured to methodize his own reflections, and to weave into an humble narrative, such incidents as appeared to him most instructive and remarkable among those which came within the sphere of his own observation. It is every one's duty to profit by all opportunities of inculcating on mankind the lessons of justice and humanity. The influences of hope and fear, the trials of fortitude and constancy, which took place in this city, in the autumn of 1793, have, perhaps, never been exceeded in any age. It is but just to snatch some of these from oblivion, and to deliver to posterity a brief but faithful sketch of the condition of this metropolis during that calamitous period. Men only require to be made acquainted with distress for their compassion and their charity to be awakened. He that depicts, in lively colours, the evils of disease and poverty, performs an eminent service to the sufferers, by calling forth benevolence in those who are able to afford relief, and he who pourtrays examples of disinterestedness and intrepidity, confers on virtue the notoriety and homage that are due to it, and rouses in the spectators, the spirit of salutary emulation.

In the following tale a particular series of adventures is brought to a close; but these are necessarily connected with the events which happened subsequent to the period here described. These events are not less memorable than those which form the subject of the present volume, and may hereafter be published either separately or in addition to this.

C.B.B.

3

ARTHUR MERVYN;
OR, MEMOIRS OF THE YEAR 1793.
First Part

CHAPTER I

I WAS resident in this city during the year 1793. Many motives contributed to detain me, though departure was easy and commodious, and my friends were generally solicitous for me to go. It is not my purpose to enumerate these motives, or to dwell on my present concerns and transactions, but merely to compose a narrative of some incidents with which my situation made me acquainted.

Returning one evening, somewhat later than usual, to my own house, my attention was attracted, just as I entered the porch, by the figure of a man, reclining against the wall at a few paces distant. My sight was imperfectly assisted by a far-off lamp; but the posture in which he sat, the hour, and the place immediately suggested the idea of one disabled by sickness. It was obvious to conclude that his disease was pestilential. This did not deter me from approaching and examining him more closely.

He leaned his head against the wall, his eyes were shut, his hands clasped in each other, and his body seemed to be sustained in an upright position merely by the cellar door against which he rested his left shoulder. The lethargy into which he was sunk seemed scarcely interrupted by my feeling his hand and his forehead. His throbbing temples and burning skin indicated a fever, and his form, already emaciated, seemed to prove that it had not been of short duration.

There was only one circumstance that hindered me from forming an immediate determination in what manner this

5

person should be treated. My family consisted of my wife and a young child. Our servant maid had been seized three days before by the reigning malady, and, at her own request, had been conveyed to the hospital. We ourselves enjoyed good health, and were hopeful of escaping with our lives. Our measures for this end had been cautiously taken and carefully adhered to. They did not consist in avoiding the receptacles of infection, for my office required me to go daily into the midst of them; nor in filling the house with the exhalations of gun-powder, vinegar, or tar. They consisted in cleanliness, reasonable exercise, and wholesome diet. Custom had likewise blunted the edge of our apprehensions. To take this person into my house, and bestow upon him the requisite attendance was the scheme that first occurred to me. In this, however, the advice of my wife was to govern me.

I mentioned the incident to her. I pointed out the danger which was to be dreaded from such an inmate. I desired her to decide with caution and mentioned my resolution to conform myself implicitly to her decision. Should we refuse to harbour him, we must not forget that there was an hospital to which he would, perhaps, consent to be carried, and where he would be accommodated in the best manner the times would admit.

Nay, said she, talk not of hospitals. At least let him have his choice. I have no fear about me for my part, in a case where the injunctions of duty are so obvious. Let us take the poor unfortunate wretch into our protection and care, and leave the consequences to Heaven.

I expected and was pleased with this proposal. I returned to the sick man, and on rousing him from his stupor found him still in possession of his reason. With a candle near, I had opportunity of viewing him more accurately.

His garb was plain, careless, and denoted rusticity: His aspect was simple and ingenuous, and his decayed visage still retained traces of uncommon, but manlike beauty. He had all the appearances of mere youth, unspoiled by luxury and uninured to misfortune. I scarcely ever beheld an object which laid so powerful and sudden a claim to my affection and succour.

6

You are sick, said I, in as cheerful a tone as I could assume. Cold bricks and night airs are comfortless attendants for one in your condition. Rise, I pray you, and come into the house. We will try to supply you with accommodations a little more suitable.

At this address he fixed his languid eyes upon me. What would you have? said he. I am very well as I am. While I breathe, which will not be long, I shall breathe with more freedom here than elsewhere. Let me alone—I am very well as I am.

Nay, said I, this situation is unsuitable to a sick man. I only ask you to come into my house and receive all the kindness that it is in our power to bestow. Pluck up courage and I will answer for your recovery, provided you submit to directions, and do as we would have you. Rise, and come along with me. We will find you a physician and a nurse, and all we ask in return is good spirits and compliance.

Do you not know, he replied, what my disease is? Why should you risk your safety for the sake of one, whom your kindness cannot benefit, and who has nothing to give in return?

There was something in the style of this remark, that heightened my prepossession in his favour and made me pursue my purpose with more zeal. Let us try what we can do for you, I answered. If we save your life, we shall have done you some service, and as for recompence, we will look to that.

It was with considerable difficulty that he was persuaded to accept our invitation. He was conducted to a chamber, and the criticalness of his case requiring unusual attention, I spent the night at his bed-side.

My wife was encumbered with the care both of her infant and her family. The charming babe was in perfect health, but her mother's constitution was frail and delicate. We simplified the household duties as much as possible; but still these duties were considerably burthensome to one not used to the performance, and luxuriously educated. The addition of a sick man, was likely to be productive of much fatigue. My engagements would not allow me to be always at home, and the state of my patient and the remedies necessary to be prescribed were attended with many noxious and disgustful circumstances. My fortune would not allow me to hire assistance. My wife, with a feeble frame and a mind shrinking, on ordinary occasions, from such offices with fastidious scrupulousness, was to be his only or principal nurse.

My neighbours were fervent in their well-meant zeal, and loud in their remonstrances on the imprudence and rashness of my conduct. They called me presumptuous and cruel in exposing my wife and child as well as myself to such imminent hazard, for the sake of one too who most probably was worthless, and whose disease had doubtless been, by negligence or mistreatment, rendered incurable.

I did not turn a deaf ear to these censurers. I was aware of all the inconveniencies and perils to which I thus spontaneously exposed myself. No one knew better the value of that woman whom I called mine, or set an higher price upon her life, her health, and her ease. The virulence and activity of this contagion, the dangerous condition of my patient, and the dubiousness of his character, were not forgotten by me; but still my conduct in this affair received my own entire approbation. All objections on the score of my friend were removed by her own willingness and even solicitude to undertake the province. I had more confidence than others in the vincibility of this disease, and in the success of those measures which we had used for our defence against it. But, whatever were the evils to accrue to us, we were sure of one thing; namely, that the consciousness of having neglected this unfortunate person would be a source of more unhappiness than could possibly redound from the attendance and care that he would claim.

The more we saw of him, indeed, the more did we congratulate ourselves on our proceeding. His torments were acute and tedious, but in the midst even of delirium, his heart seemed to overflow with gratitude, and to be actuated by no wish but to alleviate our toil and our danger. He made prodigious exertions to perform necessary offices for himself. He suppressed his feelings and struggled to maintain a

8

cheerful tone and countenance, that he might prevent that anxiety which the sight of his sufferings produced in us. He was perpetually furnishing reasons why his nurse should leave him alone, and betrayed dissatisfaction whenever she entered his apartment.

In a few days there were reasons to conclude him out of danger; and in a fortnight, nothing but exercise and nourishment were wanting to complete his restoration. Meanwhile nothing was obtained from him but general information, that his place of abode was Chester County, and that some momentous engagement induced him to hazard his safety by coming to the city in the height of the epidemic.

He was far from being talkative. His silence seemed to be the joint result of modesty and unpleasing remembrances. His features were characterised by pathetic seriousness, and his deportment by a gravity very unusual at his age. According to his own representation, he was no more than eighteen years old, but the depth of his remarks indicated a much greater advance. His name was Arthur Mervyn. He described himself as having passed his life at the plough-tail and the threshing floor: as being destitute of all scholastic instruction; and as being long since bereft of the affectionate regards of parents and kinsmen.

When questioned as to the course of life which he meant to pursue, upon his recovery, he professed himself without any precise object. He was willing to be guided by the advice of others, and by the lights which experience should furnish. The country was open to him, and he supposed that there was no part of it in which food could not be purchased by his labour. He was unqualified, by his education, for any liberal profession. His poverty was likewise an insuperable impediment. He could afford to spend no time in the acquisition of a trade. He must labour not for future emolument but for immediate subsistence. The only pursuit which his present circumstances would allow him to adopt was that which, he was inclined to believe, was likewise the most eligible. Without doubt, his experience was slender,

9

and it seemed absurd to pronounce concerning that of which he had no direct knowledge; but so it was, he could not outroot from his mind the persuasion that to plow, to sow, and to reap were employments most befitting a reasonable creature, and from which the truest pleasure and the least pollution would flow. He contemplated no other scheme than to return as soon as his health should permit, into the country, seek employment where it was to be had, and acquit himself in his engagements with fidelity and diligence.

I pointed out to him various ways in which the city might furnish employment to one with his qualifications. He had said that he was somewhat accustomed to the pen. There were stations in which the possession of a legible hand was all that was requisite. He might add to this a knowledge of accompts and thereby procure himself a post in some mercantile or public office.

To this he objected, that experience had shewn him unfit for the life of a penman. This had been his chief occupation for a little while, and he found it wholly incompatible with his health. He must not sacrifice the end for the means. Starving was a disease preferable to consumption. Besides, he laboured merely for the sake of living, and he lived merely for the sake of pleasure. If his tasks should enable him to live, but at the same time, bereave him of all satisfaction, they inflicted injury and were to be shunned as worse evils than death.

I asked to what species of pleasure he alluded, with which the business of a clerk was inconsistent.

He answered, that he scarcely knew how to describe it. He read books when they came in his way. He had lighted upon few, and perhaps the pleasure they afforded him was owing to their fewness; yet he confessed that a mode of life which entirely forbade him to read, was by no means to his taste. But this was trivial. He knew how to value the thoughts of other people, but he could not part with the privilege of observing and thinking for himself. He wanted business which would suffer at least nine tenths of his attention to go free. If it afforded agreeable employment to that part of his attention which it applied to its own use, so much the better; but if it did not, he should not repine. He should be content with a life whose pleasures were to its pains as nine are to one. He had tried the trade of a copyist, and in circumstances more favourable than it was likely he should ever again have an opportunity of trying it, and he had found that it did not fulfil the requisite conditions. Whereas the trade of plowman was friendly to health, liberty, and pleasure.

The pestilence, if it may so be called, was now declining. The health of my young friend allowed him to breathe the fresh air and to walk. —A friend of mine, by name Wortley, who had spent two months from the city, and to whom, in the course of a familiar correspondence, I had mentioned the foregoing particulars, returned from his rural excursion. He was posting, on the evening of the day of his arrival, with a friendly expedition, to my house, when he overtook Mervyn going in the same direction. He was surprised to find him go before him into my dwelling, and to discover, which he speedily did, that this was the youth whom I had so frequently mentioned to him. I was present at their meeting.

There was a strange mixture in the countenance of Wortley, when they were presented to each other. His satisfaction was mingled with surprise, and his surprise with anger. Mervyn, in his turn, betrayed considerable embarrassment. Wortley's thoughts were too earnest on some topic to allow him to converse. He shortly made some excuse for taking leave and, rising, addressed himself to the youth with a request that he would walk home with him. This invitation, delivered in a tone which left it doubtful whether a compliment or menace were meant, augmented Mervyn's confusion. He complied without speaking, and they went out together; —my wife and I were left to comment upon the scene.

It could not fail to excite uneasiness. They were evidently no strangers to each other. The indignation that flashed from the eyes of Wortley, and the trembling consciousness of Mervyn were unwelcome tokens. The former was my

11

dearest friend, and venerable for his discernment and integrity: The latter appeared to have drawn upon himself the anger and disdain of this man. We already anticipated the shock which the discovery of his unworthiness would produce.

In an half hour Mervyn returned. His embarrassment had given place to dejection. He was always serious, but his features were now overcast by the deepest gloom. The anxiety which I felt would not allow me to hesitate long.

Arthur, said I, something is the matter with you. Will you not disclose it to us? Perhaps you have brought yourself into some dilemma out of which we may help you to escape. Has any thing of an unpleasant nature passed between you and Wortley?

The youth did not readily answer. He seemed at a loss for a suitable reply. At length he said, That something disagreeable had indeed passed between him and Wortley. He had had the misfortune to be connected with a man by whom Wortley, conceived himself to be injured. He had borne no part in inflicting this injury, but had nevertheless been threatened with ill treatment if he did not make disclosures which indeed it was in his power to make, but which he was bound by every sanction to withhold. This disclosure would be of no benefit to Wortley. It would rather operate injuriously than otherwise; yet it was endeavoured to be wrested from him by the heaviest menaces.—There he paused.

We were naturally inquisitive as to the scope of these menaces; but Mervyn intreated us to forbear any further discussion of this topic. He foresaw the difficulties to which his silence would subject him. One of its most fearful consequences would be the loss of our good opinion. He knew not what he had to dread from the enmity of Wortley. Mr. Wortley's violence was not without excuse. It was his mishap to be exposed to suspicions which could only be obviated by breaking his faith. But, indeed, he knew not, whether any degree of explicitness would confute the charges that were made against him; whether, by trampling on his sacred promise, he should not multiply his perils instead of lessening their number. A difficult part had been assigned to him: by much too difficult for one, young, improvident, and inexperienced as he was.

Sincerity, perhaps, was the best course. Perhaps, after having had an opportunity for deliberation, he should conclude to adopt it; meanwhile he intreated permission to retire to his chamber. He was unable to exclude from his mind ideas which yet could, with no propriety, at least at present, be made the theme of conversation.

These words were accompanied with simplicity and pathos, and with tokens of unaffected distress.

Arthur, said I, you are master of your actions and time in this house. Retire when you please; but you will naturally suppose us anxious to dispel this mystery. Whatever shall tend to obscure or malign your character will of course excite our solicitude. Wortley is not short-sighted or hasty to condemn. So great is my confidence in his integrity that I will not promise my esteem to one who has irrecoverably lost that of Wortley. I am not acquainted with your motives to concealment or what it is you conceal, but take the word of one who possesses that experience which you complain of wanting, that sincerity is always safest.

As soon as he had retired, my curiosity prompted me to pay an immediate visit to Wortley. I found him at home. He was no less desirous of an interview, and answered my enquiries with as much eagerness as they were made.

You know, said he, my disastrous connection with Thomas Welbeck. You recollect his sudden disappearance last July, by which I was reduced to the brink of ruin. Nay, I am, even now, far from certain that I shall survive that event. I spoke to you about the youth who lived with him, and by what means that youth was discovered to have crossed the river in his company on the night of his departure. This is that very youth.

This will account for my emotion at meeting him at your house: I brought him out with me. His confusion sufficiently indicated his knowledge of transactions between Welbeck and me. I questioned him as to the fate of that man. To own the truth, I expected some well digested lie;

but he merely said, that he had promised secrecy on that subject, and must therefore be excused from giving me any information. I asked him if he knew, that his master, or accomplice, or whatever was his relation to him, absconded in my debt? He answered that he knew it well; but still pleaded a promise of inviolable secrecy as to his hiding place. This conduct justly exasperated me and I treated him with the severity which he deserved. I am half ashamed to confess the excesses of my passion; I even went so far as to strike him. He bore my insults with the utmost patience. No doubt the young villain is well instructed in his lesson. He knows that he may safely defy my power.—From threats I descended to entreaties. I even endeavoured to wind the truth from him by artifice. I promised him a part of the debt if he would enable me to recover the whole. I offered him a considerable reward if he would merely afford me a clue by which I might trace him to his retreat; but all was insufficient. He merely put on an air of perplexity and shook his head in token of non-compliance.

Such was my friend's account of this interview. His suspicions were unquestionably plausible; but I was disposed to put a more favourable construction on Mervyn's behaviour. I recollected the desolate and pennyless condition in which I found him, and the uniform complacency and rectitude of his deportment for the period during which we had witnessed it. These ideas had considerable influence on my judgment, and indisposed me to follow the advice of my friend, which was to turn him forth from my doors that very night.

My wife's prepossessions were still more powerful advocates of this youth. She would vouch, she said, before any tribunal, for his innocence; but she willingly concurred with me in allowing him the continuance of our friendship, on no other condition than that of a disclosure of the truth. To entitle ourselves to this confidence we were willing to engage, in our turn, for the observance of secrecy, so far that no detriment should accrue from this disclosure to himself or his friend.

Next morning at breakfast, our guest appeared with a

countenance less expressive of embarrassment than on the last evening. His attention was chiefly engaged by his own thoughts, and little was said till the breakfast was removed. I then reminded him of the incidents of the former day, and mentioned that the uneasiness which thence arose to us had rather been encreased than diminished by time.

It is in your power, my young friend, continued I, to add still more to this uneasiness or to take it entirely away. I had no personal acquaintance with Thomas Welbeck. I have been informed by others that his character for a certain period was respectable, but that, at length, he contracted large debts and instead of paying them absconded. You, it seems, lived with him. On the night of his departure you are known to have accompanied him across the river, and this, it seems, is the first of your re-appearance on the stage. Welbeck's conduct was dishonest. He ought doubtless to be pursued to his asylum and be compelled to refund his winnings. You confess yourself to know his place of refuge, but urge a promise of secrecy. Know you not that to assist, or connive at, the escape of this man was wrong? To have promised to favour his concealment and impunity by silence was only an aggravation of this wrong. That, however, is past. Your youth, and circumstances, hitherto unexplained, may apologize for that misconduct, but it is certainly your duty to repair it to the utmost of your power. Think whether by disclosing what you know, you will not repair it.

I have spent most of last night, said the youth, in reflecting on this subject. I had come to a resolution, before you spoke, of confiding to you my simple tale. I perceive in what circumstances I am placed, and that I can keep my hold of your good opinion only by a candid deportment. I have indeed given a promise which it was wrong or rather absurd in another to exact and in me to give; yet none but considerations of the highest importance would persuade me to break my promise. No injury will accrue from my disclosure to Welbeck. If there should, dishonest as he was, that would be a sufficient reason for my silence. Wortley will not, in any degree, be benefited by any communication that I can

15

make. Whether I grant or withhold information my conduct will have influence only on my own happiness, and that influence will justify me in granting it.

I received your protection when I was friendless and forlorn. You have a right to know whom it is that you protected. My own fate is connected with the fate of Welbeck, and that connection, together with the interest you are pleased to take in my concerns because they are mine, will render a tale worthy of attention which will not be recommended by variety of facts or skill in the display of them.

Wortley, though passionate, and, with regard to me, unjust, may yet be a good man; but I have no desire to make him one of my auditors. You, Sir, may, if you think proper, relate to him afterwards what particulars concerning Welbeck it may be of importance for him to know; but at present it will be well if your indulgence shall support me to the end of a tedious but humble tale.

The eyes of my Eliza sparkled with delight at this proposal. She regarded this youth with a sisterly affection and considered his candour, in this respect, as an unerring test of his rectitude. She was prepared to hear and to forgive the errors of inexperience and precipitation. I did not fully participate in her satisfaction, but was nevertheless most zealously disposed to listen to his narrative.

My engagements obliged me to postpone this rehearsal till late in the evening. Collected then round a cheerful hearth, exempt from all likelihood of interruption from without, and our babe's unpractised senses shut up in the sweetest and profoundest sleep, Mervyn, after a pause of recollection, began.

CHAPTER II

MY natal soil is Chester County. My father had a small farm on which he has been able, by industry, to maintain himself and a numerous family. He has had many children, but some defect in the constitution of our mother has been fatal to all of them but me. They died successively as they attained the age of nineteen or twenty, and since I have not yet reached that age I may reasonably look for the same premature fate. In the spring of last year my mother followed her fifth child to the grave, and three months afterwards died herself.

My constitution has always been frail, and, till the death of my mother I enjoyed unlimited indulgence. I cheerfully sustained my portion of labour, for that necessity prescribed; but the intervals were always at my own disposal, and in whatever manner I thought proper to employ them, my plans were encouraged and assisted. Fond appellations, tones of mildness, solicitous attendance when I was sick, deference to my opinions, and veneration for my talents compose the image which I still retain of my mother. I had the thoughtlessness and presumption of youth, and now that she is gone my compunction is awakened by a thousand recollections of my treatment of her. I was indeed guilty of no flagrant acts of contempt or rebellion. Perhaps her deportment was inevitably calculated to instil into me a froward and refractory spirit. My faults, however, were speedily followed by repentance, and in the midst of impatience and passion, a look of tender upbraiding from her was always sufficient to melt me into tears and make me ductile to her will. If sorrow for her loss be any atonement for the offences which I committed during her life, ample atonement has been made.

My father is a man of slender capacity but of a temper easy and flexible. He was sober and industrious by habit. He was content to be guided by the superior intelligence of his wife. Under this guidance he prospered; but when that was withdrawn, his affairs soon began to betray marks of unskilfulness and negligence. My understanding, perhaps, qualified me to counsel and assist my father, but I was wholly unaccustomed to the task of superintendence. Besides, gentleness and fortitude did not descend to me from my mother, and these were indispensable attributes in a boy who desires to dictate to his grey-headed parent. Time perhaps might have conferred dexterity on me, or prudence on him, had not a most unexpected event given a different direction to my views.

Betty Lawrence was a wild girl from the pine forests of New Jersey. At the age of ten years she became a bond servant in this city, and, after the expiration of her time, came into my father's neighbourhood in search of employment. She was hired in our family as milk-maid and market woman. Her features were coarse, her frame robust, her mind totally unlettered, and her morals defective in that point in which female excellence is supposed chiefly to consist. She possessed superabundant health and good humour, and was quite a supportable companion in the hay-field or the barn-yard.

On the death of my mother, she was exalted to a somewhat higher station. The same tasks fell to her lot; but the time and manner of performing them were, in some degree, submitted to her own choice. The cows and the dairy were still her province; but in this no one interfered with her or pretended to prescribe her measures. For this province she seemed not unqualified, and as long as my father was pleased with her management, I had nothing to object.

This state of things continued, without material variation for several months. There were appearances in my father's deportment to Betty, which excited my reflections, but not my fears. The deference which was occasionally paid to the advice or the claims of this girl, was accounted for by that feebleness of mind which degraded my father, in whatever scene he should be placed, to be the tool of others. I had no conception that her claims extended beyond a temporary or superficial gratification.

At length, however, a visible change took place in her manners. A scornful affectation and awkward dignity began to be assumed. A greater attention was paid to dress, which was of gayer hues and more fashionable texture. I rallied her on these tokens of a sweetheart, and amused myself with expatiating to her on the qualifications of her lover. A clownish fellow was frequently her visitant. His attentions did not appear to be discouraged. He therefore was readily supposed to be the man. When pointed out as the favourite, great resentment was expressed, and obscure insinuations were made that her aim was not quite so low as that. These denials I supposed to be customary on such occasions, and considered the continuance of his visits as a sufficient confutation of them.

I frequently spoke of Betty, her newly acquired dignity, and of the probable cause of her change of manners to my father. When this theme was started, a certain coldness and reserve overspread his features. He dealt in monosyllables and either laboured to change the subject or made some excuse for leaving me. This behaviour, though it occasioned surprise, was never very deeply reflected on. My father was old, and the mournful impressions which were made upon him by the death of his wife, the lapse of almost half a year seemed scarcely to have weakened. Betty had chosen her partner and I was in daily expectation of receiving a summons to the wedding.

One afternoon this girl dressed herself in the gayest manner and seemed making preparations for some momentous ceremony. My father had directed me to put the horse to the chaise. On my enquiring whither he was going he answered me in general terms that he had some business at a few miles distance. I offered to go in his stead,

19

but he said that was impossible. I was proceeding to ascertain the possibility of this when he left me to go to a field where his workmen were busy, directing me to inform him when the chaise was ready, and to supply his place, while absent, in overlooking the workmen.

This office was performed; but before I called him from the field I exchanged a few words with the milk-maid, who sat on a bench, in all the primness of expectation and decked with the most gaudy plumage. I rated her imaginary lover for his tardiness, and vowed eternal hatred to them both for not making me a bride's attendant. She listened to me with an air in which embarrassment was mingled sometimes with exultation and sometimes with malice. I left her at length, and returned to the house not till a late hour. As soon as I entered, my father presented Betty to me as his wife, and desired she might receive that treatment from me which was due to a mother.

It was not till after repeated and solemn declarations from both of them that I was prevailed upon to credit this event. Its effect upon my feelings may be easily conceived. I knew the woman to be rude, ignorant, and licentious. Had I suspected this event I might have fortified my father's weakness and enabled him to shun the gulf to which he was tending; but my presumption had been careless of the danger. To think that such an one should take the place of my revered mother was intolerable.

To treat her in any way not squaring with her real merits; to hinder anger and scorn from rising at the sight of her in her new condition, was not in my power. To be degraded to the rank of her servant; to become the sport of her malice and her artifices was not to be endured. I had no independent provision; but I was the only child of my father, and had reasonably hoped to succeed to his patrimony. On this hope I had built a thousand agreeable visions. I had meditated innumerable projects which the possession of this estate would enable me to execute. I had no wish beyond the trade of agriculture, and beyond the opulence which an hundred acres would give.

These visions were now at an end. No doubt her own

interest would be to this woman the supreme law, and this interest would be considered as irreconcilably hostile to mine. My father would easily be moulded to her purpose and that act easily extorted from him which should reduce me to beggary. She had a gross and perverse taste. She had a numerous kindred, indigent and hungry. On these his substance would speedily be lavished. Me she hated because she was conscious of having injured me, because she knew that I held her in contempt, and because I had detected her in an illicit intercourse with the son of a neighbour.

The house in which I lived was no longer my own, nor even my father's. Hitherto I had thought and acted in it with the freedom of a master, but now I was become, in my own conceptions, an alien and an enemy to the roof under which I was born. Every tie which had bound me to it was dissolved or converted into something which repelled me to a distance from it. I was a guest whose presence was borne with anger and impatience.

I was fully impressed with the necessity of removal, but I knew not whither to go or what kind of subsistence to seek. My father had been a Scottish emigrant, and had no kindred on this side of the ocean. My mother's family lived in New Hampshire, and long separation had extinguished all the rights of relationship in her offspring. Tilling the earth was my only profession, and to profit by my skill in it, it would be necessary to become a day-labourer in the service of strangers; but this was a destiny to which I, who had so long enjoyed the pleasures of independence and command, could not suddenly reconcile myself. It occurred to me that the city might afford me an asylum. A short day's journey would transport me into it. I had been there twice or thrice in my life, but only for a few hours each time. I knew not an human face, and was a stranger to its modes and dangers. I was qualified for no employment, compatible with a town-life, but that of the pen. This indeed had ever been a favourite tool with me, and though it may appear somewhat strange, it is no less true that I had had nearly as much practice at the quill as at the mattock. But the sum of my skill lay in tracing distinct characters. I had

21

used it merely to transcribe what others had written, or to give form to my own conceptions. Whether the city would afford me employment, as a mere copyist, sufficiently lucrative, was a point on which I possessed no means of information.

My determination was hastened by the conduct of my new mother. My conjectures as to the course she would pursue with regard to me had not been erroneous. My father's deportment in a short time grew sullen and austere. Directions were given in a magisterial tone, and any remissness in the execution of his orders was rebuked with an air of authority. At length these rebukes were followed by certain intimations that I was now old enough to provide for myself; that it was time to think of some employment by which I might secure a livelihood; that it was a shame for me to spend my youth in idleness; that what he had gained was by his own labour; and I must be indebted for my living to the same source.

These hints were easily understood. At first, they excited indignation and grief. I knew the source whence they sprung and was merely able to suppress the utterance of my feelings in her presence. My looks, however, were abundantly significant, and my company became hourly more insupportable. Abstracted from these considerations, my father's remonstrances were not destitute of weight. He gave me being but sustenance ought surely to be my own gift. In the use of that for which he had been indebted to his own exertions, he might reasonably consult his own choice. He assumed no control over me; he merely did what he would with his own, and so far from fettering my liberty, he exhorted me to use it for my benefit and to make provision for myself.

I now reflected that there were other manual occupations besides that of the plough. Among these none had fewer disadvantages than that of carpenter or cabinet-maker. I had no knowledge of this art; but, neither custom, nor law, nor the impenetrableness of the mystery required me to serve a seven years' apprenticeship to it. A master in this trade might possibly be persuaded to take me under his tuition: two or three years would suffice to give me the requisite skill. Meanwhile my father would, perhaps, consent to bear the cost of my maintenance. Nobody could live upon less than I was willing to do.

I mentioned these ideas to my father; but he merely commended my intentions without offering to assist me in the execution of them. He had full employment, he said, for all the profits of his ground. No doubt if I would bind myself to serve four or five years, my master would be at the expence of my subsistence. Be that as it would, I must look for nothing from him. I had shewn very little regard for his happiness: I had refused all marks of respect to a woman who was entitled to it from her relation to him. He did not see why he should treat as a son one who refused what was due to him as a father. He thought it right that I should henceforth maintain myself. He did not want my services on the farm, and the sooner I quitted his house the better.

I retired from this conference with a resolution to follow the advice that was given. I saw that henceforth I must be my own protector, and wondered at the folly that detained me so long under this roof. To leave it was now become indispensable, and there could be no reason for delaying my departure for a single hour. I determined to bend my course to the city. The scheme foremost in my mind was to apprentice myself to some mechanical trade. I did not overlook the evils of constraint and the dubiousness as to the character of the master I should choose. I was not without hopes that accident would suggest a different expedient and enable me to procure an immediate subsistence without forfeiting my liberty.

I determined to commence my journey the next morning. No wonder the prospect of so considerable a change in my condition should deprive me of sleep. I spent the night ruminating on the future and in painting to my fancy the adventures which I should be likely to meet. The foresight of man is in proportion to his knowledge. No wonder that in my state of profound ignorance, not the faintest preconception should be formed of the events that really befel me. My temper was inquisitive, but there was nothing in the scene to which I was going from which my curiosity expected to derive gratification. Discords and evil smells, unsavoury food, unwholesome labour, and irksome companions, were, in my opinion, the unavoidable attendants of a city.

My best clothes were of the homeliest texture and shape. My whole stock of linen consisted of three check shirts. Part of my winter evening's employment since the death of my mother consisted in knitting my own stockings. Of these I had three pair, one of which I put on and the rest I formed, together with two shirts, into a bundle. Three quarter-dollar pieces composed my whole fortune in money.

CHAPTER III

I ROSE at the dawn, and without asking or bestowing a blessing, sallied forth into the high road to the city which passed near the house. I left nothing behind, the loss of which I regretted. I had purchased most of my own books with the product of my own separate industry, and their number being, of course, small, I had, by incessant application, gotten the whole of them by rote. They had ceased, therefore, to be of any further use. I left them, without reluctance, to the fate for which I knew them to be reserved, that of affording food and habitation to mice.

I trod this unwonted path with all the fearlessness of youth. In spite of the motives to despondency and apprehension, incident to my state, my heels were light and my heart joyous. Now, said I, I am mounted into man. I must build a name and a fortune for myself. Strange if this intellect and these hands will not supply me with an honest livelihood. I will try the city in the first place; but if that should fail, resources are still left to me. I will resume my post in the corn-field and threshing-floor, to which I shall always have access, and where I shall always be happy.

I had proceeded some miles on my journey, when I began to feel the inroads of hunger. I might have stopped at any farm house, and have breakfasted for nothing. It was prudent to husband, with the utmost care, my slender stock; but I felt reluctance to beg as long as I had the means of buying, and I imagined that coarse bread and a little milk would cost little even at a tavern, when any farmer was willing to bestow them for nothing. My resolution was farther influenced by the appearance of a sign-post. What excuse could I make for begging a breakfast with an inn at hand and silver in my pocket?

I stopped accordingly and breakfasted. The landlord was remarkably attentive and obliging, but his bread was stale, his milk sour, and his cheese the greenest imaginable. I disdained to animadvert on these defects, naturally supposing that his house could furnish no better.

Having finished my meal, I put, without speaking, one of my pieces into his hand. This deportment I conceived to be highly becoming, and to indicate a liberal and manly spirit. I always regarded with contempt a scrupulous maker of bargains. He received the money with a complaisant obeisance. Right, said he. *Just* the money, Sir. You are on foot, Sir. A pleasant way of travelling, Sir. I wish you a good day, Sir.—So saying he walked away.

This proceeding was wholly unexpected. I conceived myself entitled to at least three-fourths of it in change. The first impulse was to call him back, and contest the equity of his demand, but a moment's reflection shewed me the absurdity of such conduct. I resumed my journey with spirits somewhat depressed. I have heard of voyagers and wanderers in deserts who were willing to give a casket of gems for a cup of cold water. I had not supposed my own condition to be, in any respect, similar; yet I had just given one third of my estate for a breakfast.

I stopped at noon at another inn. I had counted on purchasing a dinner for the same price, since I meant to content myself with the same fare. A large company was just sitting down to a smoking banquet. The landlord invited me to join them. I took my place at the table, but was furnished with bread and milk. Being prepared to depart, I took him aside. What is to pay? said I.—Did you drink any thing, Sir?—Certainly. I drank the milk which was furnished.—But any liquors, Sir?—No.

He deliberated a moment and then assuming an air of disinterestedness, 'Tis our custom to charge dinner and club, but as you drank nothing, we'll let the club go. A mere dinner is half-a-dollar, Sir.

He had no leisure to attend to my fluctuations. After debating with myself on what was to be done, I concluded that compliance was best, and leaving the money at the bar, resumed my way.

I had not performed more than half my journey, yet my purse was entirely exhausted. This was a specimen of the cost incurred by living at an inn. If I entered the city, a tavern must, at least for some time, be my abode, but I had not a farthing remaining to defray my charges. My father had formerly entertained a boarder for a dollar per week, and, in a case of need, I was willing to subsist upon coarser fare, and lie on an harder bed than those with which our guest had been supplied. These facts had been the foundation of my negligence on this occasion.

What was now to be done? To return to my paternal mansion was impossible. To relinquish my design of entering the city and to seek a temporary asylum, if not permanent employment, at some one of the plantations, within view, was the most obvious expedient. These deliberations did not slacken my pace. I was almost unmindful of my way, when I found I had passed Schuylkill at the upper bridge. I was now within the precincts of the city and night was hastening. It behoved me to come to a speedy decision.

Suddenly I recollected that I had not paid the customary toll at the bridge: neither had I money wherewith to pay it. A demand of payment would have suddenly arrested my progress; and so slight an incident would have precluded that wonderful destiny to which I was reserved. The obstacle that would have hindered my advance, now prevented my return. Scrupulous honesty did not require me to turn back and awaken the vigilance of the toll-gatherer. I had nothing to pay, and by returning I should only double my debt. Let it stand, said I, where it does. All that honour enjoins is to pay when I am able.

I adhered to the cross ways, till I reached Market street. Night had fallen, and a triple row of lamps presented a spectacle enchanting and new. My personal cares were, for a time, lost in the tumultuous sensations with which I was now engrossed. I had never visited the city at this hour. When my last visit was paid I was a mere child. The novelty which environed every object was, therefore, nearly absolute. I proceeded with more cautious steps, but was still absorbed in attention to passing objects. I reached the market-house, and entering it, indulged myself in new delight and new wonder.

I need not remark that our ideas of magnificence and splendour are merely comparative; yet you may be prompted to smile when I tell you that, in walking through this avenue, I for a moment conceived myself transported to the hall "pendent with many a row of starry lamps and blazing crescents fed by naphtha and asphaltos." That this transition from my homely and quiet retreat, had been effected in so few hours, wore the aspect of miracle or magic.

I proceeded from one of these buildings to another, till I reached their termination in Front street. Here my progress was checked, and I sought repose to my weary limbs by seating myself on a stall. No wonder some fatigue was felt by me, accustomed as I was to strenuous exertions, since, exclusive of the minutes spent at breakfast and dinner, I had travelled fifteen hours and forty-five miles.

I began now to reflect, with some earnestness, on my condition. I was a stranger, friendless, and moneyless. I was unable to purchase food and shelter, and was wholly unused to the business of begging. Hunger was the only serious inconvenience to which I was immediately exposed. I had no objection to spend the night in the spot where I then sat. I had no fear that my visions would be troubled by the officers of police. It was no crime to be without a home; but how should I supply my present cravings and the cravings of to-morrow?

At length it occurred to me that one of our country neighbours was probably at this time in the city. He kept a store as well as cultivated a farm. He was a plain and well meaning man, and should I be so fortunate as to meet him, his superior knowledge of the city might be of essential benefit to me in my present forlorn circumstances. His generosity might likewise induce him to lend me so much as would purchase one meal. I had formed the resolution to leave the city next day and was astonished at the folly that had led me into it; but, meanwhile, my physical wants must be supplied.

Where should I look for this man? In the course of conversation I recollected him to have referred to the place of his temporary abode. It was an inn, but the sign or the name of the keeper, for some time withstood all my efforts to recall them.

At length I lighted on the last. It was Lesher's tavern. I immediately set out in search of it. After many enquiries I at last arrived at the door. I was preparing to enter the house when I perceived that my bundle was gone. I had left it on the stall where I had been sitting. People were perpetually passing to and fro. It was scarcely possible not to have been noticed. No one that observed it would fail to make it his prey. Yet it was of too much value to me, to allow me to be governed by a bare probability. I resolved to lose not a moment in returning.

With some difficulty I retraced my steps, but the bundle had disappeared. The clothes were, in themselves, of small value, but they constituted the whole of my wardrobe; and I now reflected that they were capable of being transmuted, by the pawn or sale of them, into food. There were other wretches as indigent as I was, and I consoled myself by thinking that my shirts and stockings might furnish a seasonable covering to their nakedness; but there was a relique concealed within this bundle, the loss of which could scarcely be endured by me. It was the portrait of a young man who died three years ago at my father's house, drawn by his own hand.

He was discovered one morning in the orchard with many marks of insanity upon him. His air and dress bespoke some elevation of rank and fortune. My mother's compassion was excited, and, as his singularities were harmless, an asylum was afforded him, though he was unable to pay for it. He was constantly declaiming in an incoherent manner, about some mistress who had proved faithless. His

29

speeches seemed, however, like the rantings of an actor, to be rehearsed by rote, or for the sake of exercise. He was totally careless of his person and health, and by repeated negligences of this kind, at last contracted a fever of which he speedily died. The name which he assumed was Clavering.

He gave no distinct account of his family, but stated in loose terms that they were residents in England, high born and wealthy. That they had denied him the woman whom he loved and banished him to America under penalty of death if he should dare to return, and that they had refused him all means of subsistence in a foreign land. He predicted, in his wild and declamatory way, his own death. He was very skilful at the pencil and drew this portrait a short time before his dissolution, presented it to me, and charged me to preserve it in remembrance of him. My mother loved the youth because he was amiable and unfortunate, and chiefly because she fancied a very powerful resemblance between his countenance and mine. I was too young to build affection on any rational foundation. I loved him, for whatever reason, with an ardour unusual at my age, and which this portrait had contributed to prolong and to cherish.

In thus finally leaving my home, I was careful not to leave this picture behind. I wrapt it in paper in which a few elegiac stanzas were inscribed in my own hand and with my utmost elegance of penmanship. I then placed it in a leathern case, which, for greater security, was deposited in the centre of my bundle. It will occur to you, perhaps, that it would be safer in some fold or pocket of the clothes which I wore. I was of a different opinion and was now to endure the penalty of my error.

It was in vain to heap execrations on my negligence, or to consume the little strength left to me in regrets. I returned once more to the tavern and made enquiries for Mr. Capper, the person whom I have just mentioned as my father's neighbour. I was informed that Capper was now in town; that he had lodged, on the last-night, at this house; that he had expected to do the same to-night, but a gentleman had called ten minutes ago, whose invitation to lodge with him to-night had been accepted. They had just gone out to-

gether. Who, I asked, was the gentleman? The landlord had
no knowledge of him: He knew neither his place of abode
nor his name. . . . Was Mr. Capper expected to return
hither in the morning?—No, he had heard the stranger
propose to Mr. Capper to go with him into the country
to-morrow, and Mr. Capper, he believed, had assented.

This disappointment was peculiarly severe. I had lost, by
my own negligence, the only opportunity that would offer
of meeting my friend. Had even the recollection of my loss
been postponed for three minutes, I should have entered
the house, and a meeting would have been secured. I could
discover no other expedient to obviate the present evil. My
heart began now, for the first time, to droop. I looked back,
with nameless emotions, on the days of my infancy. I called
up the image of my mother. I reflected on the infatuation of
my surviving parent, and the usurpation of the detestable
Betty with horror. I viewed myself as the most calamitous
and desolate of human beings.

At this time I was sitting in the common room. There
were others in the same apartment, lounging, or whistling,
or singing. I noticed them not, but leaning my head upon
my hand, I delivered myself up to painful and intense
meditation. From this I was roused by some one placing
himself on the bench near me and addressing me thus: Pray
Sir, if you will excuse me, who was the person whom you
were looking for just now? Perhaps I can give you the
information you want. If I can, you will be very welcome to
it.—I fixed my eyes with some eagerness on the person that
spoke. He was a young man, expensively and fashionably
dressed, whose mien was considerably prepossessing, and
whose countenance bespoke some portion of discernment.
I described to him the man whom I sought. I am in search of
the same man myself, said he, but I expect to meet him here.
He may lodge elsewhere, but he promised to meet me here
at half after nine. I have no doubt he will fulfil his promise,
so that you will meet the gentleman.

I was highly gratified by this information, and thanked
my informant with some degree of warmth. My gratitude
he did not notice but continued: In order to beguile expectation, I have ordered supper: Will you do me the favour to

partake with me, unless indeed you have supped already? I was obliged, somewhat awkwardly, to decline his invitation, conscious as I was that the means of payment were not in my power. He continued however to urge my compliance, till at length it was, though reluctantly, yielded. My chief motive was the certainty of seeing Capper.

My new acquaintance was exceedingly conversible, but his conversation was chiefly characterized by frankness and good humour. My reserves gradually diminished, and I ventured to inform him, in general terms, of my former condition and present views. He listened to my details with seeming attention, and commented on them with some judiciousness. His statements, however, tended to discourage me from remaining in the city.

Meanwhile the hour passed and Capper did not appear. I noticed this circumstance to him with no little solicitude. He said that possibly he might have forgotten or neglected his engagement. His affair was not of the highest importance, and might be readily postponed to a future opportunity. He perceived that my vivacity was greatly damped by this intelligence. He importuned me to disclose the cause. He made himself very merry with my distress, when it was at length discovered. As to the expence of supper, I had partaken of it at his invitation, he therefore should of course be charged with it. As to lodging, he had a chamber and a bed which he would insist upon my sharing with him.

My faculties were thus kept upon the stretch of wonder. Every new act of kindness in this man surpassed the fondest expectation that I had formed. I saw no reason why I should be treated with benevolence. I should have acted in the same manner if placed in the same circumstances; yet it appeared incongruous and inexplicable. I know not whence my ideas of human nature were derived. They certainly were not the offspring of my own feelings. These would have taught me that interest and duty were blended in every act of generosity.

I did not come into the world without my scruples and suspicions. I was more apt to impute kindnesses to sinister and hidden than to obvious and laudable motives. I paused to reflect upon the possible designs of this person. What end could be served by this behaviour? I was no subject of violence or fraud. I had neither trinket nor coin to stimulate the treachery of others. What was offered was merely lodging for the night. Was this an act of such transcendent disinterestedness as to be incredible? My garb was meaner than that of my companion, but my intellectual accomplishments were at least upon a level with his. Why should he be supposed to be insensible to my claims upon his kindness. I was a youth, destitute of experience, money, and friends; but I was not devoid of all mental and personal endowments. That my merit should be discovered, even on such slender intercourse, had surely nothing in it that shocked belief.

While I was thus deliberating, my new friend was earnest in his solicitations for my company. He remarked my hesitation but ascribed it to a wrong cause. Come, said he, I can guess your objections and can obviate them. You are afraid of being ushered into company; and people who have passed their lives like you have a wonderful antipathy to strange faces; but this is bed-time with our family, so that we can defer your introduction to them till to-morrow. We may go to our chamber without being seen by any but servants.

I had not been aware of this circumstance. My reluctance flowed from a different cause, but now that the inconveniences of ceremony were mentioned, they appeared to me of considerable weight. I was well pleased that they should thus be avoided, and consented to go along with him.

We passed several streets and turned several corners. At last we turned into a kind of court which seemed to be chiefly occupied by stables. We will go, said he, by the back way into the house. We shall thus save ourselves the necessity of entering the parlour, where some of the family may still be.

My companion was as talkative as ever, but said nothing from which I could gather any knowledge of the number, character, and condition of his family.

CHAPTER IV

WE arrived at a brick wall through which we passed by a gate into an extensive court or yard. The darkness would allow me to see nothing but outlines. Compared with the pigmy dimensions of my father's wooden hovel, the buildings before me were of gigantic loftiness. The horses were here far more magnificently accommodated than I had been. By a large door we entered an elevated hall. Stay here, said he, just while I fetch a light.

He returned, bearing a candle, before I had time to ponder on my present situation.

We now ascended a stair-case, covered with painted canvas. No one whose inexperience is less than mine, can imagine to himself the impressions made upon me by surrounding objects. The height to which this stair ascended, its dimensions, and its ornaments, appeared to me a combination of all that was pompous and superb.

We stopped not till we had reached the third story. Here my companion unlocked and led the way into a chamber. This, said he, is my room: Permit me to welcome you into it.

I had no time to examine this room before, by some accident, the candle was extinguished. Curse upon my carelessness, said he. I must go down again and light the candle. I will return in a twinkling. Meanwhile you may undress yourself and go to bed. He went out, and, as I afterwards recollected, locked the door behind him.

I was not indisposed to follow his advice, but my curiosity

would first be gratified by a survey of the room. Its height and spaciousness were imperfectly discernible by star-light, and by gleams from a street lamp. The floor was covered with a carpet, the walls with brilliant hangings; the bed and windows were shrouded by curtains of a rich texture and glossy hues. Hitherto I had merely read of these things. I knew them to be the decorations of opulence, and yet as I viewed them, and remembered where and what I was on the same hour the preceding day, I could scarcely believe myself awake or that my senses were not beguiled by some spell.

Where, said I, will this adventure terminate? I rise on the morrow with the dawn and speed into the country. When this night is remembered, how like a vision will it appear! If I tell the tale by a kitchen fire, my veracity will be disputed. I shall be ranked with the story tellers of Shirauz and Bagdad.

Though busied in these reflections, I was not inattentive to the progress of time. Methought my companion was remarkably dilatory. He went merely to re-light his candle, but certainly he might, during this time, have performed the operation ten times over. Some unforeseen accident might occasion his delay.

Another interval passed and no tokens of his coming. I began now to grow uneasy. I was unable to account for his detention. Was not some treachery designed? I went to the door and found that it was locked. This heightened my suspicions. I was alone, a stranger, in an upper room of the house. Should my conductor have disappeared, by design or by accident, and some one of the family should find me here, what would be the consequence? Should I not be arrested as a thief and conveyed to prison? My transition from the street to this chamber would not be more rapid than my passage hence to a gaol.

These ideas struck me with panick. I revolved them anew, but they only acquired greater plausibility. No doubt I had been the victim of malicious artifice. Inclination, however, conjured up opposite sentiments and my fears began to subside. What motive, I asked, could induce an human being to inflict wanton injury? I could not account for his

35

delay, but how numberless were the contingencies, that might occasion it?

I was somewhat comforted by these reflections, but the consolation they afforded was short-lived. I was listening with the utmost eagerness to catch the sound of a foot, when a noise was indeed heard, but totally unlike a step. It was human breath struggling, as it were, for passage. On the first effort of attention it appeared like a groan. Whence it arose I could not tell. He that uttered it was near; perhaps in the room.

Presently the same noise was again heard, and now I perceived that it came from the bed. It was accompanied with a motion like some one changing his posture. What I at first conceived to be a groan, appeared now to be nothing more than the expiration of a sleeping man. What should I infer from this incident? My companion did not apprize me that the apartment was inhabited. Was his imposture a jestful or a wicked one?

There was no need to deliberate. There were no means of concealment or escape. The person would sometime awaken and detect me. The interval would only be fraught with agony and it was wise to shorten it. Should I not withdraw the curtain, awake the person, and encounter at once all the consequences of my situation? I glided softly to the bed, when the thought occurred, May not the sleeper be a female?

I cannot describe the mixture of dread and of shame which glowed in my veins. The light in which such a visitant would be probably regarded by a woman's fears, the precipitate alarms that might be given, the injury which I might unknowingly inflict or undeservedly suffer, threw my thoughts into painful confusion. My presence might pollute a spotless reputation or furnish fuel to jealousy.

Still, though it were a female, would not least injury be done by gently interrupting her slumber? But the question of sex still remained to be decided. For this end I once more approached the bed and drew aside the silk. The sleeper was a babe. This I discovered by the glimmer of a street lamp.

36

Part of my solicitudes were now removed. It was plain that this chamber belonged to a nurse or a mother. She had not yet come to bed. Perhaps it was a married pair and their approach might be momently expected. I pictured to myself their entrance and my own detection. I could imagine no consequence that was not disastrous and horrible, and from which I would not, at any price, escape. I again examined the door, and found that exit by this avenue was impossible. There were other doors in this room. Any practicable expedient in this extremity was to be pursued. One of these was bolted. I unfastened it and found a considerable space within. Should I immure myself in this closet? I saw no benefit that would finally result from it. I discovered that there was a bolt on the inside which would somewhat contribute to security. This being drawn no one could enter without breaking the door.

I had scarcely paused when the long expected sound of footsteps were heard in the entry. Was it my companion or a stranger? If it were the latter, I had not yet mustered courage sufficient to meet him. I cannot applaud the magnanimity of my proceeding, but no one can expect intrepid or judicious measures from one in my circumstances. I stepped into the closet and closed the door. Some one immediately after, unlocked the chamber door. He was unattended with a light. The footsteps, as they moved along the carpet, could scarcely be heard.

I waited impatiently for some token by which I might be governed. I put my ear to the key-hole, and at length heard a voice, but not that of my companion, exclaim, somewhat above a whisper, Smiling cherub! safe and sound, I see. Would to God my experiment may succeed and that thou mayest find a mother where I have found a wife! There he stopped. He appeared to kiss the babe and presently retiring locked the door after him.

These words were capable of no consistent meaning. They served, at least, to assure me that I had been treacherously dealt with. This chamber it was manifest, did not belong to my companion. I put up prayers to my deity that he would deliver me from these toils. What a condition was

mine! Immersed in palpable darkness! shut up in this unknown recess! lurking like a robber!

My meditations were disturbed by new sounds. The door
was unlocked, more than one person entered the apartment, and light streamed through the key-hole. I looked;
but the aperture was too small and the figures passed too
quickly to permit me the sight of them. I bent my ear and
this imparted some more authentic information.

The man, as I judged by the voice, was the same who had
just departed. Rustling of silk denoted his companion to be
female. Some words being uttered by the man in too low a
key to be overheard, the lady burst into a passion of tears.
He strove to comfort her by soothing tones and tender
appellations. How can it be helped, said he. It is time to
resume your courage. Your duty to yourself and to me
requires you to subdue this unreasonable grief.

He spoke frequently in this strain, but all he said seemed
to have little influence in pacifying the lady. At length,
however, her sobs began to lessen in vehemence and frequency. He exhorted her to seek for some repose. Apparently she prepared to comply, and conversation was, for a
few minutes, intermitted.

I could not but advert to the possibility that some occasion
to examine the closet in which I was immured, might occur.
I knew not in what manner to demean myself if this should
take place. I had no option at present. By withdrawing
myself from view I had lost the privilege of an upright
deportment. Yet the thought of spending the night in this
spot was not to be endured.

Gradually I began to view the project of bursting from
the closet, and trusting to the energy of truth and of an
artless tale, with more complacency. More than once my
hand was placed upon the bolt, but withdrawn by a sudden
faltering of resolution. When one attempt failed, I recurred
once more to such reflections as were adapted to renew my
purpose.

I preconcerted the address which I should use. I resolved
to be perfectly explicit: To withhold no particular of my
adventures from the moment of my arrival. My description

must necessarily suit some person within their knowledge. All I should want was liberty to depart; but if this were not allowed, I might at least hope to escape any ill treatment, and to be confronted with my betrayer. In that case I did not fear to make him the attester of my innocence.

Influenced by these considerations, I once more touched the lock. At that moment the lady shrieked, and exclaimed Good God! What is here? An interesting conversation ensued. The object that excited her astonishment was the child. I collected from what passed that the discovery was wholly unexpected by her. Her husband acted as if equally unaware of this event. He joined in all her exclamations of wonder and all her wild conjectures. When these were somewhat exhausted he artfully insinuated the propriety of bestowing care upon the little foundling. I now found that her grief had been occasioned by the recent loss of her own offspring. She was, for some time, averse to her husband's proposal, but at length was persuaded to take the babe to her bosom and give it nourishment.

This incident had diverted my mind from its favourite project, and filled me with speculations on the nature of the scene. One explication was obvious, that the husband was the parent of this child and had used this singular expedient to procure for it the maternal protection of his wife. It would soon claim from her all the fondness which she entertained for her own progeny. No suspicion probably had yet, or would hereafter, occur with regard to its true parent. If her character be distinguished by the usual attributes of women, the knowledge of this truth may convert her love into hatred. I reflected with amazement on the slightness of that thread by which human passions are led from their true direction. With no less amazement did I remark the complexity of incidents by which I had been empowered to communicate to her this truth. How baseless are the structures of falsehood, which we build in opposition to the system of eternal nature. If I should escape undetected from this recess, it will be true that I never saw the face of either of these persons, and yet I am acquainted with the most secret transaction of their lives.

My own situation was now more critical than before. The lights were extinguished and the parties had sought repose. To issue from the closet now would be eminently dangerous. My councils were again at a stand and my designs frustrated. Meanwhile the persons did not drop their discourse, and I thought myself justified in listening. Many facts of the most secret and momentous nature were alluded to. Some allusions were unintelligible. To others I was able to affix a plausible meaning, and some were palpable enough. Every word that was uttered on that occasion is indelibly imprinted on my memory. Perhaps the singularity of my circumstances and my previous ignorance of what was passing in the world, contributed to render me a greedy listener. Most that was said I shall overlook, but one part of the conversation it will be necessary to repeat.

A large company had assembled that evening at their house. They criticised the character and manners of several. At last the husband said, What think you of the Nabob? Especially when he talked about riches? How artfully he encourages the notion of his poverty! Yet not a soul believes him. I cannot for my part account for that scheme of his. I half suspect that his wealth flows from a bad source, since he is so studious of concealing it.

Perhaps, after all, said the lady, you are mistaken as to his wealth.

Impossible, exclaimed the other. Mark how he lives. Have I not seen his bank account. His deposits, since he has been here, amount to not less than half a million.

Heaven grant that it be so, said the lady with a sigh. I shall think with less aversion of your scheme. If poor Tom's fortune be made, and he not the worse, or but little the worse on that account, I shall think it on the whole best.

That, replied he, is what reconciles me to the scheme. To him thirty thousand are nothing.

But will he not suspect you of some hand in it?

How can he? Will I not appear to lose as well as himself? Tom is my brother, but who can be supposed to answer for a brother's integrity: but he cannot suspect either of us. Nothing less than a miracle can bring our plot to light. Besides, this man is not what he ought to be. He will some time or other, come out to be a grand impostor. He makes money by other arts than bargain and sale. He has found his way, by some means, to the Portuguese treasury.

Here the conversation took a new direction, and, after some time, the silence of sleep ensued.

Who, thought I, is this nabob who counts his dollars by half millions, and on whom, it seems, as if some fraud was intended to be practised. Amidst their wariness and sub-tlety how little are they aware that their conversation has been overheard! By means as inscrutable as those which conducted me hither, I may hereafter be enabled to profit by this detection of a plot. But, meanwhile, what was I to do? How was I to effect my escape from this perilous asylum?

After much reflection it occurred to me that to gain the street without exciting their notice was not utterly impossi-ble. Sleep does not commonly end of itself, unless at a certain period. What impediments were there between me and liberty which I could not remove, and remove with so much caution as to escape notice. Motion and sound inevi-tably go together, but every sound is not attended to. The doors of the closet and the chamber did not creak upon their hinges. The latter might be locked. This I was able to ascertain only by experiment. If it were so, yet the key was probably in the lock and might be used without much noise.

I waited till their slow and hoarser inspirations shewed them to be both asleep. Just then, on changing my position, my head struck against some things which depended from the ceiling of the closet. They were implements of some kind which rattled against each other in consequence of this unlucky blow. I was fearful lest this noise should alarm, as the closet was little distant from the bed. The breathing of one instantly ceased, and a motion was made as if the head were lifted from the pillow. This motion, which was made by the husband, awaked his companion, who exclaimed, What is the matter?

Something, I believe, replied he, in the closet. If I was not dreaming, I heard the pistols strike against each other as if some one was taking them down.

This intimation was well suited to alarm the lady. She besought him to ascertain the matter. This to my utter dismay he at first consented to do, but presently observed that probably his ears had misinformed him. It was hardly possible that the sound proceeded from them. It might be a rat, or his own fancy might have fashioned it. —It is not easy to describe my trepidations while this conference was holding. I saw how easily their slumber was disturbed. The obstacles to my escape were less surmountable than I had imagined.

In a little time all was again still. I waited till the usual tokens of sleep were distinguishable. I once more resumed my attempt. The bolt was withdrawn with all possible slowness; but I could by no means prevent all sound. My state was full of inquietude and suspense; my attention being painfully divided between the bolt and the condition of the sleepers. The difficulty lay in giving that degree of force which was barely sufficient. Perhaps not less than fifteen minutes were consumed in this operation. At last it was happily effected and the door was cautiously opened.

Emerging as I did from utter darkness, the light admitted into three windows, produced, to my eyes, a considerable illumination. Objects which on my first entrance into this apartment were invisible, were now clearly discerned. The bed was shrouded by curtains, yet I shrunk back into my covert, fearful of being seen. To facilitate my escape I put off my shoes. My mind was so full of objects of more urgent moment that the propriety of taking them along with me never occurred. I left them in the closet.

I now glided across the apartment to the door. I was not a little discouraged by observing that the key was wanting. My whole hope depended on the omission to lock it. In my haste to ascertain this point, I made some noise which again roused one of the sleepers. He started and cried Who is there?

I now regarded my case as desperate and detection as inevitable. My apprehensions, rather than my caution, kept me mute. I shrunk to the wall, and waited in a kind of agony for the moment that should decide my fate.

The lady was again roused. In answer to her enquiries, her husband said that some one he believed was at the door, but there was no danger of their entering, for he had locked it and the key was in his pocket.

My courage was completely annihilated by this piece of intelligence. My resources were now at an end. I could only remain in this spot, till the morning light, which could be at no great distance, should discover me. My inexperience disabled me from estimating all the perils of my situation. Perhaps I had no more than temporary inconveniences to dread. My intention was innocent, and I had been betrayed into my present situation, not by my own wickedness but the wickedness of others.

I was deeply impressed with the ambiguousness which would necessarily rest upon my motives, and the scrutiny to which they would be subjected. I shuddered at the bare possibility of being ranked with thieves. These reflections again gave edge to my ingenuity in search of the means of escape. I had carefully attended to the circumstances of their entrance. Possibly the act of locking had been unnoticed; but was it not likewise possible that this person had been mistaken? The key was gone. Would this have been the case if the door were unlocked?

My fears rather than my hopes, impelled me to make the experiment. I drew back the latch and, to my unspeakable joy, the door opened.

I passed through and explored my way to the stair-case. I descended till I reached the bottom. I could not recollect with accuracy the position of the door leading into the court, but by carefully feeling along the wall with my hands, I at length, discovered it. It was fastened by several bolts and a lock. The bolts were easily withdrawn, but the key was removed. I knew not where it was deposited. I thought I had reached the threshold of liberty but here was an impediment that threatened to be insurmountable.

But if doors could not be passed, windows might be unbarred. I remembered that my companion had gone into a door on the left hand, in search of a light. I searched for this door. Fortunately it was fastened only by a bolt. It

43

admitted me into a room which I carefully explored till I reached a window. I will not dwell on my efforts to unbar this entrance. Suffice it to say that, after much exertion and frequent mistakes, I at length found my way into the yard, and thence passed into the court.

CHAPTER V

NOW I was once more on public ground. By so many anxious efforts had I disengaged myself from the perilous precincts of private property. As many stratagems as are usually made to enter an house, had been employed by me to get out of it. I was urged to the use of them by my fears; yet so far from carrying off spoil, I had escaped with the loss of an essential part of my dress.

I had now leisure to reflect. I seated myself on the ground and reviewed the scenes through which I had just passed. I began to think that my industry had been misemployed. Suppose I had met the person on his first entrance into his chamber. Was the truth so utterly wild as not to have found credit? Since the door was locked, and there was no other avenue; what other statement but the true one would account for my being found there? This deportment had been worthy of an honest purpose. My betrayer probably expected that this would be the issue of his jest. My rustic simplicity, he might think, would suggest no more ambiguous or elaborate expedient. He might likewise have predetermined to interfere if my safety had been really endangered.

On the morrow the two doors of the chamber and the window below would be found unclosed. They will suspect a design to pillage, but their searches will terminate in nothing but in the discovery of a pair of clumsy and dusty shoes in the closet. Now that I was safe I could not help smiling at the picture which my fancy drew of their anxiety and won-

der. These thoughts, however, gave place to more momentous considerations.

I could not image to myself a more perfect example of
indigence than I now exhibited. There was no being in the
city on whose kindness I had any claim. Money I had none
and what I then wore comprised my whole stock of move-
ables. I had just lost my shoes, and this loss rendered my
stockings of no use. My dignity remonstrated against a
barefoot pilgrimage, but to this, necessity now reconciled
me. I threw my stockings between the bars of a stable
window, belonging, as I thought, to the mansion I had just
left. These, together with my shoes, I left to pay the cost of
my entertainment.

I saw that the city was no place for *me*. The end that I had
had in view, of procuring some mechanical employment,
could only be obtained by the use of means, but what means
to pursue I knew not. This night's perils and deceptions
gave me a distaste to a city life, and my ancient occupations
rose to my view enhanced by a thousand imaginary charms.
I resolved forthwith to strike into the country.

The day began now to dawn. It was Sunday, and I was
desirous of eluding observation. I was somewhat recruited
by rest though the languors of sleeplessness oppressed me.
I meant to throw myself on the first lap of verdure I should
meet, and indulge in sleep that I so much wanted. I knew
not the direction of the streets; but followed that which I first
entered from the court, trusting that, by adhering steadily
to one course, I should sometime reach the fields. This
street, as I afterwards found, tended to Schuylkill, and soon
extricated me from houses. I could not cross this river
without payment of toll. It was requisite to cross it in order
to reach that part of the country whither I was desirous of
going, but how should I effect my passage? I knew of no
ford, and the smallest expence exceeded my capacity. Ten
thousand guineas and a farthing were equally remote from
nothing, and nothing was the portion allotted to me.

While my mind was thus occupied, I turned up one of the
streets which tend northward. It was, for some length,
uninhabited and unpaved. Presently I reached a pavement,

and a painted fence, along which a row of poplars was planted. It bounded a garden into which a knot hole permitted me to pry. The enclosure was a charming green, which I saw appended to an house of the loftiest and most stately order. It seemed like a recent erection, had all the gloss of novelty, and exhibited, to my unpracticed eyes, the magnificence of palaces. My father's dwelling did not equal the height of one story, and might be easily comprised in one fourth of those buildings which here were designed to accommodate the menials. My heart dictated the comparison between my own condition and that of the proprietors of this domain. How wide and how impassible was the gulf by which we were separated! This fair inheritance had fallen to one who, perhaps, would only abuse it to the purposes of luxury, while I, with intentions worthy of the friend of mankind, was doomed to wield the flail and the mattock.

I had been entirely unaccustomed to this strain of reflection. My books had taught me the dignity and safety of the middle path and my darling writer abounded with encomiums on rural life. At a distance from luxury and pomp I viewed them, perhaps, in a just light. A nearer scrutiny confirmed my early prepossessions, but at the distance at which I now stood, the lofty edifices, the splendid furniture, and the copious accommodations of the rich, excited my admiration and my envy.

I relinquished my station and proceeded, in an heartless mood, along the fence. I now came to the mansion itself. The principal door was entered by a stair-case of marble. I had never seen the stone of Carrara, and wildly supposed this to have been dug from Italian quarries. The beauty of the poplars, the coolness exhaled from the dew-besprent bricks, the commodiousness of the seat which these steps afforded, and the uncertainty into which I was plunged respecting my future conduct, all combined to make me pause. I sat down on the lower step and began to meditate.

By some transition it occurred to me that the supply of my most urgent wants, might be found in some inhabitant of this house. I needed at present a few cents; and what were a few cents to the tenant of a mansion like this. I had an invincible aversion to the calling of a beggar, but I regarded with still more antipathy the vocation of a thief; to this alternative, however, I was now reduced. I must either steal or beg; unless, indeed, assistance could be procured under the notion of a loan. Would a stranger refuse to lend the pittance that I wanted? Surely not, when the urgency of my wants were explained.

I recollected other obstacles. To summon the master of the house from his bed, perhaps, for the sake of such an application, would be preposterous. I should be in more danger of provoking his anger than exciting his benevolence. This request might, surely, with more propriety be preferred to a passenger. I should, probably, meet several before I should arrive at Schuylkill.

A servant just then appeared at the door, with bucket and brush. This obliged me, much sooner than I intended, to decamp. With some reluctance I rose and proceeded.— This house occupied the corner of the street, and I now turned this corner, towards the country. A person, at some distance before me, was approaching in an opposite direction.

Why, said I, may I not make my demand of the first man I meet? This person exhibits tokens of ability to lend. There is nothing chilling or austere in his demeanour.

The resolution to address this passenger was almost formed; but the nearer he advanced, my resolves grew less firm. He noticed me not till he came within a few paces. He seemed busy in reflection, and had not my figure caught his eye; or had he merely bestowed a passing glance upon me, I should not have been sufficiently courageous to have detained him. The event however was widely different.

He looked at me and started. For an instant, as it were, and till he had time to dart at me a second glance, he checked his pace. This behaviour decided mine, and he stopped on perceiving tokens of a desire to address him. I spoke, but my accents and air sufficiently denoted my embarrassments.

I am going to solicit a favour, which my situation makes of

48

the highest importance to me, and which I hope it will be easy for you, Sir, to grant. It is not an alms but a loan that I seek; a loan that I will repay the moment I am able to do it. I am going to the country, but have not wherewith to pay my passage over Schuylkill, or to buy a morsel of bread. May I venture to request of you, Sir, the loan of six pence? As I told you, it is my intention to repay it.

I delivered this address, not without some faltering, but with great earnestness. I laid particular stress upon my intention to refund the money. He listened with a most inquisitive air. His eye perused me from head to foot.

After some pause, he said, in a very emphatic manner. Why into the country? Have you family? Kindred? Friends?

No, answered I, I have neither. I go in search of the means of subsistence. I have passed my life upon a farm, and propose to die in the same condition.

Whence have you come?

I came yesterday from the country, with a view to earn my bread in some way, but have changed my plan and propose now to return.

Why have you changed it? In what way are you capable of earning your bread?

I hardly know, said I. I can, as yet, manage no tool, that can be managed in the city, but the pen. My habits have, in some small degree, qualified me for a writer. I would willingly accept employment of that kind.

He fixed his eyes upon the earth, and was silent for some minutes. At length, recovering himself, he said, Follow me to my house. Perhaps something may be done for you. If not, I will lend you six pence.

It may be supposed that I eagerly complied with the invitation. My companion said no more, his air bespeaking him to be absorbed by his own thoughts, till we reached his house, which proved to be that at the door of which I had been seated. We entered a parlour together.

Unless you can assume my ignorance and my simplicity, you will be unable to conceive the impressions that were made by the size and ornaments of this apartment. I shall omit these impressions, which, indeed, no descriptions could adequately convey, and dwell on incidents of greater moment. He asked me to give him a specimen of my penmanship. I told you that I had bestowed very great attention upon this art. Implements were brought and I sat down to the task. By some inexplicable connection a line in Shakspeare occurred to me, and I wrote

"My poverty, but not my will consents."

The sentiment conveyed in this line powerfully affected him, but in a way which I could not then comprehend. I collected from subsequent events that the inference was not unfavourable to my understanding or my morals. He questioned me as to my history. I related my origin and my inducements to desert my father's house. With respect to last night's adventures I was silent. I saw no useful purpose that could be answered by disclosure, and I half suspected that my companion would refuse credit to my tale.

There were frequent intervals of abstraction and reflection between his questions. My examination lasted not much less than an hour. At length he said, I want an amanuensis or copyist: On what terms will you live with me?

I answered that I knew not how to estimate the value of my services. I knew not whether these services were agreeable or healthful. My life had hitherto been active. My constitution was predisposed to diseases of the lungs and the change might be hurtful. I was willing however to try and to content myself for a month or a year, with so much as would furnish me with food, clothing, and lodging.

'Tis well, said he. You remain with me as long and no longer than both of us please. You shall lodge and eat in this house. I will supply you with clothing, and your task will be to write what I dictate. Your person, I see, has not shared much of your attention. It is in my power to equip you instantly in the manner which becomes a resident in this house. Come with me.

He led the way into the court behind and thence into a neat building, which contained large wooden vessels and a pump. There, said he, you may wash yourself, and when that is done, I will conduct you to your chamber and your wardrobe.

This was speedily performed and he accordingly led the way to the chamber. It was an apartment in the third story, finished and furnished in the same costly and superb style, with the rest of the house. He opened closets and drawers which overflowed with clothes and linen of all and of the best kinds. These are yours, said he, as long as you stay with me. Dress yourself as likes you best. Here is every thing your nakedness requires. When dressed you may descend to breakfast. With these words he left me.

The clothes were all in the French style, as I afterwards, by comparing my garb with that of others, discovered. They were fitted to my shape with the nicest precision. I bedecked myself with all my care. I remembered the style of dress, used by my beloved Clavering. My locks were of shining auburn, flowing and smooth like his. Having wrung the wet from them, and combed, I tied them carelessly in a black riband. Thus equipped I surveyed myself in a mirror.

You may imagine, if you can, the sensations which this instantaneous transformation produced. Appearances are wonderfully influenced by dress. Check shirt, buttoned at the neck, an awkward fustian coat, check trowsers, and bare feet were now supplanted by linen and muslin, nankeen coat, striped with green, a white silk waistcoat, elegantly needle-wrought, casimer pantaloons, stockings of varie-gated silk, and shoes that in their softness, pliancy, and polished surface vied with sattin. I could scarcely forbear looking back to see whether the image in the glass, so well proportioned, so galant, and so graceful, did not belong to another. I could scarcely recognize any lineaments of my own. I walked to the window. Twenty minutes ago, said I, I was traversing that path a barefoot beggar; now I am thus. Again I surveyed myself. Surely some insanity has fastened on my understanding. My senses are the sport of dreams. Some magic that disdains the cumbrousness of nature's progress, has wrought this change. I was roused from these doubts by a summons to breakfast, obsequiously delivered by a black servant.

I found Welbeck, (for I shall henceforth call him by his true name) at the breakfast table. A superb equipage of silver and china was before him. He was startled at my

51

entrance. The change in my dress seemed for a moment to have deceived him. His eye was frequently fixed upon me, with unusual steadfastness. At these times there was inquietude and wonder in his features.

I had now an opportunity of examining my host. There was nicety but no ornament in his dress. His form was of the middle height, spare, but vigorous and graceful. His face was cast, I thought, in a foreign mould. His forehead receded beyond the usual degree in visages which I had seen. His eyes large and prominent, but imparting no marks of benignity and habitual joy. The rest of his face forcibly suggested the idea of a convex edge. His whole figure impressed me with emotions of veneration and awe. A gravity that almost amounted to sadness invariably attended him when we were alone together.

He whispered the servant that waited, who immediately retired. He then said, turning to me, A lady will enter presently, whom your are to treat with the respect due to my daughter. You must not notice any emotion she may betray at the sight of you, nor expect her to converse with you; for she does not understand your language. He had scarcely spoken when she entered. I was seized with certain misgivings and flutterings which a clownish education may account for. I so far conquered my timidity, however, as to snatch a look at her. I was not born to execute her portrait. Perhaps the turban that wreathed her head, the brilliant texture and inimitable folds of her drapery, and nymphlike port, more than the essential attributes of her person, gave splendour to the celestial vision. Perhaps it was her snowy hues and the cast, rather than the position of her features, that were so prolific of enchantment: or perhaps the wonder originated only in my own ignorance.

She did not immediately notice me. When she did she almost shrieked with surprise. She held up her hands, and gazing upon me, uttered various exclamations which I could not understand. I could only remark that her accents were thrillingly musical. Her perturbations refused to be stilled. It was with difficulty that she withdrew her regards from me. Much conversation passed between her and Welbeck, but I could comprehend no part of it. I was at liberty to animadvert on the visible part of their intercourse. I diverted some part of my attention from my own embarrassments, and fixed it on their looks.

In this art, as in most others, I was an unpracticed simpleton. In the countenance of Welbeck, there was somewhat else than sympathy with the astonishment and distress of the lady; but I could not interpret these additional tokens. When her attention was engrossed by Welbeck, her eyes were frequently vagrant or downcast; her cheeks contracted a deeper hue; and her breathing was almost prolonged into a sigh. These were marks on which I made no comments at the time. My own situation was calculated to breed confusion in my thoughts and awkwardness in my gestures. Breakfast being finished, the lady apparently at the request of Welbeck, sat down to a piano forte.

Here again I must be silent. I was not wholly destitute of musical practice and musical taste. I had that degree of knowledge which enabled me to estimate the transcendent skill of this performer. As if the pathos of her touch were insufficient, I found after some time that the lawless jarrings of the keys were chastened by her own more liquid notes. She played without a book, and though her base might be preconcerted, it was plain that her right-hand notes were momentary and spontaneous inspirations. Meanwhile Welbeck stood, leaning his arms on the back of a chair near her, with his eyes fixed on her face. His features were fraught with a meaning which I was eager to interpret but unable.

I have read of transitions effected by magic: I have read of palaces and deserts which were subject to the dominion of spells: Poets may sport with their power, but I am certain that no transition was ever conceived more marvellous and more beyond the reach of foresight, than that which I had just experienced. Heaths vexed by a midnight storm may be changed into an hall of choral nymphs and regal banqueting; forest glades may give sudden place to colonnades and

53

carnivals, but he whose senses are deluded finds himself still on his natal earth. These miracles are contemptible when compared with that which placed me under this roof and gave me to partake in this audience. I know that my emotions are in danger of being regarded as ludicrous by those who cannot figure to themselves the consequences of a limited and rustic education.

CHAPTER VI

IN a short time the lady retired. I naturally expected that some comments would be made on her behaviour, and that the cause of her surprise and distress on seeing me, would be explained, but Welbeck said nothing on that subject. When she had gone, he went to the window and stood for some time occupied, as it seemed, with his own thoughts. Then he turned to me and, calling me by my name, desired me to accompany him up stairs. There was neither cheerfulness nor mildness in his address, but neither was there any thing domineering or arrogant.

We entered an apartment on the same floor with my chamber, but separated from it by a spacious entry. It was supplied with bureaus, cabinets, and book-cases. This, said he, is your room and mine; but we must enter it and leave it together. I mean to act not as your master but your friend. My maimed hand so saying he shewed me his right hand, the forefinger of which was wanting, will not allow me to write accurately or copiously. For this reason I have required your aid, in a work of some moment. Much haste will not be requisite, and as to the hours and duration of employment, these will be seasonable and short.

Your present situation is new to you and we will therefore defer entering on our business. Meanwhile you may amuse yourself in what manner you please. Consider this house as your home and make yourself familiar with it. Stay within or go out, be busy or be idle, as your fancy shall prompt: Only you will conform to our domestic system as to eating

55

and sleep: the servants will inform you of this. Next week we will enter on the task for which I designed you. You may now withdraw.

I obeyed this mandate with some awkwardness and hesitation. I went into my own chamber not displeased with an opportunity of loneliness. I threw myself on a chair and resigned myself to those thoughts which would naturally arise in this situation. I speculated on the character and views of Welbeck. I saw that he was embosomed in tranquility and grandeur. Riches, therefore, were his; but in what did his opulence consist, and whence did it arise? What were the limits by which it was confined, and what its degree of permanence? I was unhabituated to ideas of floating or transferable wealth. The rent of houses and lands was the only species of property which was, as yet, perfectly intelligible: My previous ideas led me to regard Welbeck as the proprietor of this dwelling and of numerous houses and farms. By the same cause I was fain to suppose him enriched by inheritance, and that his life had been uniform.

I next adverted to his social condition. This mansion appeared to have but two inhabitants beside servants. Who was the nymph who had hovered for a moment in my sight? Had he not called her his daughter? The apparent difference in their ages would justify this relation; but her guise, her features, and her accents were foreign. Her language I suspected strongly to be that of Italy. How should he be the father of an Italian? But were there not some foreign lineaments in his countenance?

This idea seemed to open a new world to my view. I had gained from my books, confused ideas of European governments and manners. I knew that the present was a period of revolution and hostility. Might not these be illustrious fugitives from Provence or the Milanese? Their portable wealth, which may reasonably be supposed to be great, they have transported hither. Thus may be explained the sorrow that veils their countenance. The loss of estates and honours; the untimely death of kindred, and perhaps of his wife, may furnish eternal food for regrets. Welbeck's utterance, though rapid and distinct, partook as I conceived, in some very slight degree of a foreign idiom.

Such was the dream that haunted my undisciplined and unenlightened imagination. The more I revolved it the more plausible it seemed. On this supposition every appearance that I had witnessed was easily solved—unless it were their treatment of me. This, at first, was a source of hopeless perplexity. Gradually, however, a clue seemed to be afforded. Welbeck had betrayed astonishment on my first appearance. The lady's wonder was mingled with distress. Perhaps they discovered a remarkable resemblance between me and one who stood in the relation of son to Welbeck and of brother to the lady. This youth might have perished on the scaffold or in war. These, no doubt were his clothes. This chamber might have been reserved for him, but his death left it to be appropriated to another.

I had hitherto been unable to guess at the reason why all this kindness had been lavished on me. Will not this conjecture sufficiently account for it? No wonder that this resemblance was enhanced by assuming his dress.

Taking all circumstances into view, these ideas were not, perhaps, destitute of probability. Appearances naturally suggested them to me. They were, also, powerfully enforced by inclination. They threw me into transports of wonder and hope. When I dwelt upon the incidents of my past life, and traced the chain of events from the death of my mother to the present moment, I almost acquiesced in the notion that some beneficent and ruling genius had prepared my path for me. Events which, when foreseen, would most ardently have been deprecated, and when they happened were accounted, in the highest degree luckless, were now seen to be propitious. Hence I inferred the infatuation of despair and the folly of precipitate conclusions.

But what was the fate reserved for me? Perhaps Welbeck would adopt me for his own son. Wealth has ever been capriciously distributed. The mere physical relation of birth is all that intitles us to manors and thrones. Identity itself frequently depends upon a casual likeness or an old nurse's imposture. Nations have risen in arms, as in the case of the Stewarts, in the cause of one, the genuineness of whose birth has been denied and can never be proved. But if the cause be trivial and fallacious, the effects are momentous and solid. It ascertains our portion of felicity and usefulness, and fixes our lot among peasants or princes.

Something may depend upon my own deportment. Will it not behove me to cultivate all my virtues and eradicate all my defects? I see that the abilities of this man are venerable. Perhaps he will not lightly or hastily decide in my favour. He will be governed by the proofs that I shall give of discernment and integrity. I had always been exempt from temptation and was therefore undepraved, but this view of things had a wonderful tendency to invigorate my virtuous resolutions. All within me was exhilaration and joy.

There was but one thing wanting to exalt me to a dizzy height and give me place among the stars of heaven. My resemblance to her brother had forcibly affected this lady: but I was not her brother. I was raised to a level with her and made a tenant of the same mansion. Some intercourse would take place between us: Time would lay level impediments and establish familiarity, and this intercourse might foster love and terminate in—*marriage!*

These images were of a nature too glowing and expansive to allow me to be longer inactive. I sallied forth into the open air. This tumult of delicious thoughts in some time subsided and gave way to images relative to my present situation. My curiosity was awake. As yet I had seen little of the city, and this opportunity for observation was not to be neglected. I therefore coursed through several streets, attentively examining the objects that successively presented themselves.

At length, it occurred to me to search out the house in which I had lately been immured. I was not without hopes that at some future period I should be able to comprehend the allusions and brighten the obscurities that hung about the dialogue of last night.

The house was easily discovered. I reconnoitred the court and gate through which I had passed. The mansion was of the first order in magnitude and decoration. This was not the bound of my present discovery, for I was gifted with that confidence which would make me set on foot inquiries in the neighbourhood. I looked around for a suitable medium of intelligence. The opposite and adjoining houses were small and apparently occupied by persons of an indigent class. At one of these was a sign denoting it to be the residence of a taylor. Seated on a bench at the door was a young man, with coarse, uncombed locks, breeches knee-unbound, stockings ungartered, shoes slip-shod and unbuckled, and a face unwashed, gazing stupidly from hollow eyes. His aspect was embellished with good nature though indicative of ignorance.

This was the only person in sight. He might be able to say something concerning his opulent neighbour. To him, therefore, I resolved to apply. I went up to him and, pointing to the house in question, asked him who lived there?

He answered, Mr. Mathews.

What is his profession: his way of life?

A gentleman. He does nothing but walk about.

How long has he been married?

Married! He is not married as I know on. He never has been married. He is a bachelor.

This intelligence was unexpected. It made me pause to reflect whether I had not mistaken the house. This, however, seemed impossible. I renewed my questions.

A bachelor, say you? Are you not mistaken?

No. It would be an odd thing if he was married. An old fellow, with one foot in the grave—Comical enough for him to *git* a *vife*.

An old man? Does he live alone? What is his family?

No he does not live alone. He has a niece that lives with him. She is married and her husband lives there too.

What is his name?

I don't know: I never heard it as I know on.

What is his trade?

He's a marchant: he keeps a store somewhere or other; but I don't know where.

How long has he been married?

About two years. They lost a child lately. The young woman was in a huge taking about it. They says she was quite crazy some days for the death of the child: And she is not quite out of *the dumps* yet. To be sure the child was a sweet little thing; but they need not make such a rout about it. I'll warn they'll have enough of them before they die.

What is the character of the young man? Where was he born and educated? Has he parents or brothers?

My companion was incapable of answering these questions, and I left him with little essential addition to the knowledge I already possessed.

CHAPTER VII

A FTER viewing various parts of the city; intruding into churches; and diving into alleys, I returned. The rest of the day I spent chiefly in my chamber, reflecting on my new condition; surveying my apartment, its presses and closets; and conjecturing the causes of appearances.

At dinner and supper I was alone. Venturing to inquire of the servant where his master and mistress were, I was answered that they were engaged. I did not question him as to the nature of their engagement, though it was a fertile source of curiosity.

Next morning, at breakfast, I again met Welbeck and the lady. The incidents were nearly those of the preceding morning, if it were not that the lady exhibited tokens of somewhat greater uneasiness. When she left us Welbeck sank into apparent meditation. I was at a loss whether to retire or remain where I was. At last, however, I was on the point of leaving the room, when he broke silence and began a conversation with me.

He put questions to me, the obvious scope of which was to know my sentiments on moral topics. I had no motives to conceal my opinions, and therefore delivered them with frankness. At length he introduced allusions to my own history, and made more particular inquiries on that head. Here I was not equally frank: yet I did not fain any thing, but merely dealt in generals. I had acquired notions of propriety on this head, perhaps somewhat fastidious. Min-

61

ute details, respecting our own concerns, are apt to weary all but the narrator himself. I said thus much and the truth of my remark was eagerly assented to.

With some marks of hesitation and after various preliminaries, my companion hinted that my own interest, as well as his, enjoined upon me silence to all but himself, on the subject of my birth and early adventures. It was not likely, that while in his service, my circle of acquaintance would be large or my intercourse with the world frequent; but in my communication with others he requested me to speak rather of others than of myself. This request, he said, might appear singular to me, but he had his reasons for making it, which it was not necessary, at present, to disclose, though, when I should know them, I should readily acknowledge their validity.

I scarcely knew what answer to make. I was willing to oblige him. I was far from expecting that any exigence would occur, making disclosure my duty. The employment was productive of pain more than of pleasure, and the curiosity that would uselessly seek a knowledge of my past life, was no less impertinent than the loquacity that would uselessly communicate that knowledge. I readily promised, therefore, to adhere to his advice.

This assurance afforded him evident satisfaction; yet it did not seem to amount to quite as much as he wished. He repeated, in stronger terms, the necessity there was for caution. He was far from suspecting me to possess an impertinent and talkative disposition, or that in my eagerness to expatiate on my own concerns, I should overstep the limits of politeness: But this was not enough. I was to govern myself by a persuasion that the interests of my friend and myself would be materially affected by my conduct.

Perhaps I ought to have allowed these insinuations to breed suspicion in my mind: but conscious as I was of the benefits which I had received from this man; prone, from my inexperience, to rely upon professions and confide in appearances; and unaware that I could be placed in any condition, in which mere silence respecting myself could be injurious or criminal, I made no scruple to promise compliance with his wishes. Nay, I went farther than this: I desired to be accurately informed as to what it was proper to conceal. He answered that my silence might extend to every thing anterior to my arrival in the city, and my being incorporated with his family. Here our conversation ended and I retired to ruminate on what had passed.

I derived little satisfaction from my reflections. I began now to perceive inconveniencies that might arise from this precipitate promise. Whatever should happen in consequence of my being immured in the chamber, and of the loss of my clothes and of the portrait of my friend, I had bound myself to silence. These inquietudes, however, were transient. I trusted that these events would operate auspiciously; but my curiosity was now awakened as to the motives which *Welbeck* could have for exacting from me this concealment? To act under the guidance of another, and to wander in the dark, ignorant whither my path tended, and what effects might flow from my agency was a new and irksome situation.

From these thoughts I was recalled by a message from Welbeck. He gave me a folded paper which he requested me to carry to No. . . . South Fourth Street. Inquire, said he, for Mrs. Wentworth, in order, merely to ascertain the house, for you need not ask to see her: merely give the letter to the servant and retire. Excuse me for imposing this service upon you. It is of too great moment to be trusted to a common messenger: I usually perform it myself, but am at present otherwise engaged.

I took the letter and set out to deliver it. This was a trifling circumstance, yet my mind was full of reflections on the consequences that might flow from it. I remembered the directions that were given, but construed them in a manner different, perhaps, from Welbeck's expectations or wishes. He had charged me to leave the billet with the servant who happened to answer my summons; but had he not said that the message was important, insomuch that it could not be intrusted to common hands? He had permitted, rather than enjoined, me to dispense with seeing the lady, and this permission I conceived to be dictated merely by regard to

63

my convenience. It was incumbent on me, therefore, to take some pains to deliver the script into her own hands.

I arrived at the house and knocked. A female servant appeared. Her mistress was up stairs: she would tell her if I wished to see her, and meanwhile invited me to enter the parlour: I did so; and the girl retired to inform her mistress that one waited for her.—I ought to mention that my departure from the directions which I had received was, in some degree, owing to an inquisitive temper: I was eager after knowledge, and was disposed to profit by every opportunity to survey the interior of dwellings and converse with their inhabitants.

I scanned the walls, the furniture, the pictures. Over the fire place was a portrait in oil of a female. She was elderly and matron-like. Perhaps she was the mistress of this habitation and the person to whom I should immediately be introduced. Was it a casual suggestion, or was there an actual resemblance between the strokes of the pencil which executed this portrait and that of Clavering? However that be, the sight of this picture revived the memory of my friend and called up a fugitive suspicion that this was the production of his skill.

I was busily revolving this idea when the lady herself entered. It was the same whose portrait I had been examining. She fixed scrutinizing and powerful eyes upon me. She looked at the superscription of the letter which I presented, and immediately resumed her examination of me. I was somewhat abashed by the closeness of her observation and gave tokens of this state of mind which did not pass unobserved. They seemed instantly to remind her that she behaved with too little regard to civility. She recovered herself and began to peruse the letter. Having done this, her attention was once more fixed upon me. She was evidently desirous of entering into some conversation, but seemed at a loss in what manner to begin. This situation was new to me and was productive of no small embarrassment. I was preparing to take my leave when she spoke, though not without considerable hesitation.

64

This letter is from Mr. Welbeck—you are his friend—I presume—perhaps—a relation?

I was conscious that I had no claim to either of these titles, and that I was no more than his servant. My pride would not allow me to acknowledge this, and I merely said—I live with him at present Madam.

I imagined that this answer did not perfectly satisfy her; yet she received it with a certain air of acquiescence. She was silent for a few minutes, and then, rising, said—Excuse me, Sir, for a few minutes. I will write a few words to Mr. Welbeck.—So saying she withdrew.

I returned to the contemplation of the picture. From this, however, my attention was quickly diverted by a paper that lay on the mantle. A single glance was sufficient to put my blood into motion. I started and laid my hand upon the well-known pacquet. It was that which inclosed the portrait of Clavering!

I unfolded and examined it with eagerness. By what miracle came it hither? It was found, together with my bundle, two nights before. I had despaired of ever seeing it again, and yet, here was the same portrait inclosed in the self-same paper! I have forborne to dwell upon the regret, amounting to grief, with which I was affected in consequence of the loss of this precious relique. My joy on thus speedily and unexpectedly regaining it, is not easily described.

For a time I did not reflect that to hold it thus in my hand was not sufficient to intitle me to repossession. I must acquaint this lady with the history of this picture, and convince her of my ownership. But how was this to be done? Was she connected in any way, by friendship or by consanguinity, with that unfortunate youth. If she were, some information as to his destiny would be anxiously sought. I did not, just then, perceive any impropriety in imparting it. If it came into her hands by accident still it will be necessary to relate the mode in which it was lost in order to prove my title to it.

I now heard her descending footsteps and hastily re-

placed the picture on the mantle. She entered and, presenting me a letter, desired me to deliver it to Mr. Welbeck. I
had no pretext for deferring my departure; but was unwilling to go without obtaining possession of the portrait. An
interval of silence and irresolution succeeded. I cast significant glances at the spot where it lay and at length, mustering
up my strength of mind, and pointing to the paper—
Madam, said I, *there* is something which I recognize to be
mine—I know not how it came into your possession, but so
lately as the day before yesterday, it was in mine. I lost it by a
strange accident, and as I deem it of inestimable value, I
hope you will have no objection to restore it. —

During this speech the lady's countenance exhibited
marks of the utmost perturbation—Your picture! she
exclaimed, You lost it! How? Where? Did you know that
person? What has become of him? —

I knew him well, said I. That picture was executed by
himself. He gave it to me with his own hands; and, till the
moment I unfortunately lost it, it was my dear and perpetual companion.

Good Heaven! she exclaimed with increasing vehemence, where did you meet with him? What has become of
him? Is he dead or alive?

These appearances sufficiently shewed me that Clavering and this lady were connected by some ties of tenderness.
I answered that he was dead; that my mother and myself
were his attendants and nurses, and that this portrait was
his legacy to me.

This intelligence melted her into tears, and it was some
time before she recovered strength enough to resume the
conversation. She then inquired When and where was it
that he died? How did you lose this portrait? It was found
wrapt in some coarse clothes, lying in a stall in the market
house, on Saturday evening. Two negro women, servants of
one of my friends, strolling through the market, found it
and brought it to their mistress, who, recognizing the portrait, sent it to me. To whom did that bundle belong? Was it
yours?

These questions reminded me of the painful predicament in which I now stood. I had promised Welbeck to conceal from every one my former condition: but to explain in what manner this bundle was lost, and how my intercourse with Clavering had taken place was to violate this promise. It was possible, perhaps, to escape the confession of the truth by equivocation. Falsehoods were easily invented, and might lead her far away from my true condition: but I was wholly unused to equivocation. Never yet had a lie polluted my lips. I was not weak enough to be ashamed of my origin. This lady had an interest in the fate of Clavering, and might justly claim all the information which I was able to impart. Yet to forget the compact which I had so lately made, and an adherence to which might possibly be in the highest degree, beneficial to me and to Welbeck—I was willing to adhere to it, provided falsehood could be avoided.

These thoughts rendered me silent. The pain of my embarrassment amounted almost to agony. I felt the keenest regret at my own precipitation in claiming the picture. Its value to me was altogether imaginary. The affection which this lady had borne the original, whatever was the source of that affection, would prompt her to cherish the copy, and, however precious it was in my eyes, I should cheerfully resign it to her.

In the confusion of my thoughts an expedient suggested itself sufficiently inartificial and bold—It is true, Madam; what I have said. I saw him breathe his last. This is his only legacy. If you wish it I willingly resign it; but this is all that I can now disclose. I am placed in circumstances which render it improper to say more.

These words were uttered not very distinctly, and the lady's vehemence hindered her from noticing them. She again repeated her interrogations, to which I returned the same answer.

At first she expressed the utmost surprise at my conduct. From this she descended to some degree of asperity. She made rapid allusions to the history of Clavering. He was the son of the gentleman who owned the house in which Welbeck resided. He was the object of immeasurable fondness and indulgence. He had sought permission to travel, and this being refused by the absurd timidity of his parents, he had twice been frustrated in attempting to embark for Europe clandestinely. They ascribed his disappearance to a third and successful attempt of this kind, and had exercised anxious and unwearied diligence in endeavouring to trace his footsteps. All their efforts had failed. One motive for their returning to Europe was the hope of discovering some traces of him, as they entertained no doubt of his having crossed the ocean. The vehemence of Mrs. Wentworth's curiosity as to those particulars of his life and death may be easily conceived. My refusal only heightened this passion.

Finding me refractory to all her efforts she at length dismissed me in anger.

CHAPTER VIII

THIS extraordinary interview was now passed. Pleasure as well as pain attended my reflections on it. I adhered to the promise I had improvidently given to Welbeck, but had excited displeasure, and perhaps suspicion in the lady. She would find it hard to account for my silence. She would probably impute it to perverseness, or imagine it to flow from some incident connected with the death of Clavering, calculated to give a new edge to her curiosity.

It was plain that some connection subsisted between her and Welbeck. Would she drop the subject at the point which it had now attained? Would she cease to exert herself to extract from me the desired information, or would she not rather make Welbeck a party in the cause, and prejudice my new friend against me? This was an evil proper, by all lawful means, to avoid. I knew of no other expedient than to confess to him the truth, with regard to Clavering, and explain to him the dilemma in which my adherence to my promise had involved me.

I found him on my return home and delivered him the letter with which I was charged. At the sight of it surprise, mingled with some uneasiness, appeared in his looks. What! said he, in a tone of disappointment, you then saw the lady?

I now remembered his directions to leave my message at the door, and apologized for my neglecting them by telling my reasons. His chagrin vanished, but not without an apparent effort, and he said that all was well; the affair was of no moment.

After a pause of preparation, I intreated his attention to something which I had to relate. I then detailed the history of Clavering and of my late embarrassments. As I went on his countenance betokened increasing solicitude. His emotion was particularly strong when I came to the interrogatories of Mrs. Wentworth in relation to Clavering; but this emotion gave way to profound surprise when I related the manner in which I had eluded her inquiries. I concluded with observing, that when I promised forbearance on the subject of my own adventures, I had not foreseen any exigence which would make an adherence to my promise difficult or inconvenient: that, if his interest was promoted by my silence, I was still willing to maintain it and requested his directions how to conduct myself on this occasion.

He appeared to ponder deeply and with much perplexity on what I had said. When he spoke there was hesitation in his manner and circuity in his expressions, that proved him to have something in his thoughts which he knew not how to communicate. He frequently paused; but my answers and remarks, occasionally given, appeared to deter him from the revelation of his purpose. Our discourse ended, for the present, by his desiring me to persist in my present plan; I should suffer no inconveniencies from it, since it would be my own fault if an interview again took place between the lady and me; meanwhile he should see her and effectually silence her inquiries.

I ruminated not superficially or briefly on this dialogue. By what means would he silence her inquiries? He surely meant not to mislead her by fallacious representations. Some inquietude now crept into my thoughts. I began to form conjectures as to the nature of the scheme to which my suppression of the truth was to be thus made subservient. It seemed as if I were walking in the dark and might rush into snares or drop into pits before I was aware of my danger. Each moment accumulated my doubts and I cherished a secret foreboding that the event would prove my new situation to be far less fortunate than I had, at first, fondly believed. The question now occurred with painful repetition, Who and what was Welbeck? What was his relation to this foreign lady? What was the service for which I was to be employed?

I could not be contented without a solution of these mysteries. Why should I not lay my soul open before my new friend? Considering my situation, would he regard my fears and my surmises as criminal? I felt that they originated in laudable habits and views. My peace of mind depended on the favourable verdict which conscience should pass on my proceedings. I saw the emptiness of fame and luxury when put in the balance against the recompense of virtue. Never would I purchase the blandishments of adulation and the glare of opulence at the price of my honesty.

Amidst these reflections the dinner-hour arrived. The lady and Welbeck were present. A new train of sentiments now occupied my mind. I regarded them both with inquisitive eyes. I cannot well account for the revolution which had taken place in my mind. Perhaps it was a proof of the capriciousness of my temper, or it was merely the fruit of my profound ignorance of life and manners. Whence ever it arose, certain it is that I contemplated the scene before me with altered eyes. Its order and pomp was no longer the parent of tranquility and awe. My wild reveries of inheriting this splendour and appropriating the affections of this nymph, I now regarded as lunatic hope and childish folly. Education and nature had qualified me for a different scene. This might be the mask of misery and the structure of vice.

My companions as well as myself were silent during the meal. The lady retired as soon as it was finished. My inexplicable melancholy increased. It did not pass unnoticed by Welbeck, who inquired, with an air of kindness, into the cause of my visible dejection. I am almost ashamed to relate to what extremes my folly transported me. Instead of answering him I was weak enough to shed tears.

This excited afresh his surprise and his sympathy. He renewed his inquiries: my heart was full, but how to disburthen it I knew not. At length, with some difficulty, I

71

expressed my wishes to leave his house and return into the country.

What, he asked, had occurred to suggest this new plan? What motive could incite me to bury myself in rustic obscurity? How did I purpose to dispose of myself? Had some new friend sprung up more able or more willing to benefit me than he had been?

No, I answered, I have no relation who would own me, or friend who would protect. If I went into the country it would be to the toilsome occupations of a day-labourer: but even that was better than my present situation.

This opinion, he observed, must be newly formed. What was there irksome or offensive in my present mode of life?

That this man condescended to expostulate with me; to dissuade me from my new plan; and to enumerate the benefits which he was willing to confer, penetrated my heart with gratitude. I could not but acknowledge that leisure and literature, copious and elegant accommodation were valuable for their own sake: that all the delights of sensation and refinements of intelligence were comprised within my present sphere; and would be nearly wanting in that to which I was going; I felt temporary compunction for my folly, and determined to adopt a different deportment. I could not prevail upon myself to unfold the true cause of my dejection and permitted him therefore to ascribe it to a kind of homesickness; to inexperience; and to that ignorance which, on being ushered into a new scene, is oppressed with a sensation of forlornness. He remarked that these chimeras would vanish before the influence of time, and company, and occupation. On the next week he would furnish me with employment; meanwhile he would introduce me into company where intelligence and vivacity would combine to dispel my glooms.

As soon as we separated, my disquietudes returned. I contended with them in vain and finally resolved to abandon my present situation. When and how this purpose was to be effected I knew not. That was to be the theme of future deliberation.

Evening having arrived, Welbeck proposed to me to accompany him on a visit to one of his friends. I cheerfully accepted the invitation and went with him to your friend Mr. Wortley's. A numerous party was assembled, chiefly of the female sex. I was introduced by Welbeck by the title of *a young friend of his*. Notwithstanding my embarrassment I did not fail to attend to what passed on this occasion. I remarked that the utmost deference was paid to my companion, on whom his entrance into this company appeared to operate like magic. His eye sparkled; his features expanded into a benign serenity; and his wonted reserve gave place to a torrent-like and overflowing elocution.

I marked this change in his deportment with the utmost astonishment. So great was it, that I could hardly persuade myself that it was the same person. A mind thus susceptible of new impressions must be, I conceived, of a wonderful texture. Nothing was further from my expectations than that this vivacity was mere dissimulation and would take its leave of him when he left the company: yet this I found to be the case. The door was no sooner closed after him than his accustomed solemnity returned. He spake little, and that little was delivered with emphatical and monosyllabic brevity.

We returned home at a late hour, and I immediately retired to my chamber, not so much from the desire of repose as in order to enjoy and pursue my own reflections without interruption.

The condition of my mind was considerably remote from happiness. I was placed in a scene that furnished fuel to my curiosity. This passion is a source of pleasure, provided its gratification be practicable. I had no reason, in my present circumstances, to despair of knowledge; yet suspicion and anxiety beset me. I thought upon the delay and toil which the removal of my ignorance would cost and reaped only pain and fear from the reflection.

The air was remarkably sultry. Lifted sashes and lofty ceilings were insufficient to attemper it. The perturbation of my thoughts affected my body, and the heat which oppressed me, was aggravated, by my restlessness, almost into fever. Some hours were thus painfully past, when I recollected that the bath, erected in the court below, contained a sufficient antidote to the scorching influence of the atmosphere.

I rose, and descended the stairs softly, that I might not alarm Welbeck and the lady, who occupied the two rooms on the second floor. I proceeded to the bath, and filling the reservoir with water, speedily dissipated the heat that incommoded me. Of all species of sensual gratification, that was the most delicious; and I continued for a long time, laving my limbs and moistening my hair. In the midst of this amusement, I noticed the approach of day, and immediately saw the propriety of returning to my chamber. I returned with the same caution which I had used in descending; my feet were bare, so that it was easy to proceed unattended by the smallest signal of my progress.

I had reached the carpetted stair-case, and was slowly ascending, when I heard, within the chamber that was occupied by the lady, a noise, as of some one moving. Though not conscious of having acted improperly, yet I felt reluctance to be seen. There was no reason to suppose that this sound was connected with the detection of me, in this situation; yet I acted as if this reason existed, and made haste to pass the door and gain the second flight of steps.

I was unable to accomplish my design, when the chamber door slowly opened, and Welbeck, with a light in his hand, came out. I was abashed and disconcerted at this interview. He started at seeing me; but discovering in an instant who it was, his face assumed an expression in which shame and anger were powerfully blended. He seemed on the point of opening his mouth to rebuke me; but suddenly checking himself, he said, in a tone of mildness, How is this?— Whence come you?

His emotion seemed to communicate itself, with an electrical rapidity, to my heart. My tongue faltered while I made some answer. I said, I had been seeking relief from the heat of the weather, in the bath. He heard my explanation in silence: and, after a moment's pause, passed into his own room, and shut himself in. I hastened to my chamber.

A different observer might have found in these circumstances no food for his suspicion or his wonder. To me, however, they suggested vague and tumultuous ideas.

As I strode across the room I repeated, This woman is his daughter. What proof have I of that? He once asserted it; and has frequently uttered allusions and hints from which no other inference could be drawn. The chamber from which he came, in an hour devoted to sleep, was hers. For what end could a visit like this be paid? A parent may visit his child at all seasons, without a crime. On seeing me, methought his features indicated more than surprise. A keen interpreter would be apt to suspect a consciousness of wrong. What if this woman be not his child! How shall their relationship be ascertained?

I was summoned at the customary hour to breakfast. My mind was full of ideas connected with this incident. I was not endowed with sufficient firmness to propose the cool and systematic observation of this man's deportment. I felt as if the state of my mind could not but be evident to him; and experienced in myself all the confusion which this discovery was calculated to produce in him. I would have willingly excused myself from meeting him; but that was impossible.

At breakfast, after the usual salutations, nothing was said. For a time I scarcely lifted my eyes from the table. Stealing a glance at Welbeck, I discovered in his features nothing but his wonted gravity. He appeared occupied with thoughts that had no relation to last night's adventure. This encouraged me; and I gradually recovered my composure. Their inattention to me allowed me occasionally to throw scrutinizing and comparing glances at the face of each.

The relationship of parent and child is commonly discoverable in the visage; but the child may resemble either of its parents, yet have no feature in common with both. Here outlines, surfaces, and hues were in absolute contrariety. That kindred subsisted between them was possible, notwithstanding this dissimilitude: but this circumstance contributed to envenom my suspicions.

Breakfast being finished, Welbeck cast an eye of invitation to the piano forte. The lady rose to comply with his request. My eye chanced to be, at that moment, fixed on her. In stepping to the instrument some motion or appearance awakened a thought in my mind, which affected my feelings like the shock of an earthquake.

I have too slight acquaintance with the history of the passions to truly explain the emotion which now throbbed in my veins. I had been a stranger to what is called love. From subsequent reflection, I have contracted a suspicion, that the sentiment with which I regarded this lady was not untinctured from this source, and that hence arose the turbulence of my feelings, on observing what I construed into marks of pregnancy. The evidence afforded me was slight; yet it exercised an absolute sway over my belief.

It was well that this suspicion had not been sooner excited. Now civility did not require my stay in the apartment, and nothing but flight could conceal the state of my mind. I hastened, therefore, to a distance, and shrouded myself in the friendly secrecy of my own chamber.

The constitution of my mind is doubtless singular and perverse; yet that opinion, perhaps, is the fruit of my ignorance. It may by no means be uncommon for men to *fashion* their conclusions in opposition to evidence and *probability,* and so as to feed their malice and subvert their happiness. Thus it was, in an eminent degree, in my case. The simple fact was connected, in my mind, with a train of the most hateful consequences. The depravity of Welbeck was inferred from it. The charms of this angelic woman were tarnished and withered. I had formerly surveyed her as a precious and perfect monument, but now it was a scene of ruin and blast.

This had been a source of sufficient anguish; but this was not all. I recollected that the claims of a parent had been urged. Will you believe that these claims were now admitted, and that they heightened the iniquity of Welbeck into the blackest and most stupendous of all crimes? These ideas were necessarily transient. Conclusions more conformable to appearances succeeded. This lady might have been lately reduced to widowhood. The recent loss of a beloved companion would sufficiently account for her dejection, and make her present situation compatible with duty.

By this new train of ideas I was somewhat comforted. I saw the folly of precipitate inferences, and the injustice of my atrocious imputations, and acquired some degree of patience in my present state of uncertainty. My heart was lightened of its wonted burthen, and I laboured to invent some harmless explication of the scene that I had witnessed the preceding night.

At dinner Welbeck appeared as usual, but not the lady. I ascribed her absence to some casual indisposition, and ventured to inquire into the state of her health. My companion said she was well, but that she had left the city for a month or two, finding the heat of summer inconvenient where she was. This was no unplausible reason for retirement. A candid mind would have acquiesced in this representation, and found in it nothing inconsistent with a supposition respecting the cause of appearances, favourable to her character; but otherwise was I affected. The uneasiness which had flown for a moment returned, and I sunk into gloomy silence.

From this I was roused by my patron, who requested me to deliver a billet, which he put into my hand, at the counting-house of Mr. Thetford, and to bring him an answer. This message was speedily performed. I entered a large building by the river side. A spacious apartment presented itself, well furnished with pipes and hogsheads. In one corner was a smaller room, in which a gentleman was busy at writing. I advanced to the door of the room, but was there met by a young person, who received my paper, and delivered it to him within. I stood still at the door; but was near enough to overhear what would pass between them.

The letter was laid upon the desk, and presently he that sat at it lifted his eyes, and glanced at the superscription. He scarcely spoke above a whisper, but his words, nevertheless, were clearly distinguishable. I did not call to mind the sound of his voice, but his words called up a train of recollections.

Lo! said he, carelessly, this from the *Nabob*!

An incident so slight as this was sufficient to open a spacious scene of meditation. This little word, half whispered in a thoughtless mood, was a key to unlock an extensive cabinet of secrets. Thetford was probably indifferent whether his exclamation were overheard. Little did he think on the inferences which would be built upon it.

The Nabob! By this appellation had some one been denoted in the chamber-dialogue, of which I had been an unsuspected auditor. The man who pretended poverty, and yet gave proofs of inordinate wealth; whom it was pardonable to defraud of thirty thousand dollars; first, because the loss of that sum would be trivial to one opulent as he; and secondly, because he was imagined to have acquired this opulence by other than honest methods. Instead of forthwith returning home, I wandered into the fields, to indulge myself in the new thoughts which were produced by this occurrence.

I entertained no doubt that the person alluded to was my patron. No new light was thrown upon his character; unless something were deducible from the charge vaguely made, that his wealth was the fruit of illicit practices. He was opulent, and the sources of his wealth were unknown, if not to the rest of the community, at least to Thetford. But here had a plot been laid. The fortune of Thetford's brother was to rise from the success of artifices, of which the credulity of Welbeck was to be the victim. To detect and to counterwork this plot was obviously my duty. My interference might now indeed be too late to be useful; but this was at least to be ascertained by experiment.

How should my intention be effected? I had hitherto concealed from Welbeck my adventures at Thetford's house. These it was now necessary to disclose, and to mention the recent occurrence. My deductions, in consequence of my ignorance, might be erroneous; but of their truth his knowledge of his own affairs would enable him to judge. It was possible that Thetford and he, whose chamber-conversation I had overheard, were different persons. I endeavoured in vain to ascertain their identity by a comparison of their voices. The words lately heard, my remembrance did not enable me certainly to pronounce to be uttered by the same organs.

This uncertainty was of little moment. It sufficed that Welbeck was designated by this appellation, and that therefore he was proved to be the subject of some fraudulent proceeding. The information that I possessed it was my duty to communicate as expeditiously as possible. I was resolved to employ the first opportunity that offered for this end.

My meditations had been ardently pursued, and, when I recalled my attention, I found myself bewildered among fields and fences. It was late before I extricated myself from unknown paths, and reached home.

I entered the parlour; but Welbeck was not there. A table, with tea-equipage for one person was set; from which I inferred that Welbeck was engaged abroad. This belief was confirmed by the report of the servant. He could not inform me where his master was, but merely that he should not take tea at home. This incident was a source of vexation and impatience. I knew not but that delay would be of the utmost moment to the safety of my friend. Wholly unacquainted as I was with the nature of his contracts with Thetford, I could not decide whether a single hour would not avail to obviate the evils that threatened him. Had I known whither to trace his footsteps, I should certainly have sought an immediate interview; but, as it was, I was obliged to wait with what patience I could collect for his return to his own house.

I waited hour after hour in vain. The sun declined, and the shades of evening descended; but Welbeck was still at a distance.

CHAPTER IX

WELBECK did not return tho' hour succeeded hour till the clock struck ten. I inquired of the servants, who informed me that their master was not accustomed to stay out so late. I seated myself at a table, in the parlour, on which there stood a light, and listened for the signal of his coming, either by the sound of steps on the pavement without, or by a peal from the bell. The silence was uninterrupted and profound, and each minute added to my sum of impatience and anxiety.

To relieve myself from the heat of the weather, which was aggravated by the condition of my thoughts, as well as to beguile this tormenting interval, it occurred to me to betake myself to the bath. I left the candle where it stood, and imagined that even in the bath, I should hear the sound of the bell which would be rung upon his arrival at the door.

No such signal occurred, and, after taking this refreshment, I prepared to return to my post. The parlour was still unoccupied, but this was not all: The candle I had left upon the table was gone. This was an inexplicable circumstance. On my promise to wait for their master, the servants had retired to bed. No signal of any one's entrance had been given. The street door was locked and the key hung at its customary place, upon the wall. What was I to think? It was obvious to suppose that the candle had been removed by a domestic; but their footsteps could not be traced, and I was not sufficiently acquainted with the house to find the way, especially immersed in darkness, to their chamber. One measure, however, it was evidently proper to take, which was to supply myself, anew, with a light. This was instantly performed; but what was next to be done?

I was weary of the perplexities in which I was embroiled. I saw no avenue to escape from them but that which led me to the bosom of nature and to my ancient occupations. For a moment I was tempted to resume my rustic garb, and, on that very hour, to desert this habitation. One thing only detained me; the desire to apprize my patron of the treachery of Thetford. For this end I was anxious to obtain an interview; but now I reflected that this information, could, by other means be imparted. Was it not sufficient to write him briefly these particulars, and leave him to profit by the knowledge? Thus, I might, likewise, acquaint him with my motives for thus abruptly and unseasonably deserting his service.

To the execution of this scheme pen and paper were necessary. The business of writing was performed in the chamber on the third story. I had been hitherto denied access to this room: In it was a show of papers and books. Here it was that the task, for which I had been retained, was to be performed; but I was to enter it and leave it only in company with Welbeck. For what reasons, I asked, was this procedure to be adopted?

The influence of prohibitions and an appearance of disguise in awakening curiosity, are well known. My mind fastened upon the idea of this room with an unusual degree of intenseness. I had seen it but for a moment. Many of Welbeck's hours were spent in it. It was not to be inferred that they were consumed in idleness: What then was the nature of his employment over which a veil of such impenetrable secrecy was cast?

Will you wonder that the design of entering this recess was insensibly formed? Possibly it was locked, but its accessibleness was likewise possible. I meant not the commission of any crime. My principal purpose was to procure the implements of writing, which were elsewhere not to be found. I should neither unseal papers nor open drawers. I would merely take a survey of the volumes and attend to the objects that spontaneously presented themselves to my view. In this there surely was nothing criminal or blameworthy. Meanwhile I was not unmindful of the sudden disappearance of the candle. This incident filled my bosom with the inquietudes of fear and the perturbations of wonder.

Once more I paused to catch any sound that might arise from without. All was still. I seized the candle and prepared to mount the stairs. I had not reached the first landing when I called to mind my midnight meeting with Welbeck at the door of his daughter's chamber. The chamber was now desolate: perhaps it was accessible: if so no injury was done by entering it. My curiosity was strong, but it pictured to itself no precise object. Three steps would bear me to the door. The trial, whether it was fastened, might be made in a moment; and I readily imagined that something might be found within to reward the trouble of examination. The door yielded to my hand and I entered.

No remarkable object was discoverable. The apartment was supplied with the usual furniture. I bent my steps towards a table over which a mirror was suspended. My glances which roved with swiftness from one object to another, shortly lighted on a miniature portrait that hung near. I scrutinized it with eagerness. It was impossible to overlook its resemblance to my own visage. This was so great that, for a moment, I imagined myself to have been the original from which it had been drawn. This flattering conception yielded place to a belief merely of similitude between me and the genuine original.

The thoughts which this opinion was fitted to produce were suspended by a new object. A small volume, that had, apparently, been much used, lay upon the toilet. I opened it, and found it to contain some of the Dramas of Apostolo Zeno. I turned over the leaves: a written paper saluted my sight. A single glance informed me that it was English. For the present I was insensible to all motives that would command me to forbear. I seized the paper with an intention to peruse it.

At that moment a stunning report was heard. It was loud enough to shake the walls of the apartment, and abrupt enough to throw me into tremours. I dropped the book and yielded for a moment to confusion and surprise. From what quarter it came, I was unable accurately to determine: but there could be no doubt, from its loudness, that it was near, and even in the house. It was no less manifest that the sound arose from the discharge of a pistol. Some hand must have drawn the trigger. I recollected the disappearance of the candle from the room below. Instantly a supposition darted into my mind which made my hair rise and my teeth chatter.

This, I said, is the deed of Welbeck. He entered while I was absent from the room; he hied to his chamber; and, prompted by some unknown instigation, has inflicted on himself death! This idea had a tendency to palsy my limbs and my thoughts. Some time past in painful and tumultuous fluctuation. My aversion to this catastrophe, rather than a belief of being, by that means, able to prevent or repair the evil, induced me to attempt to enter his chamber. It was possible that my conjectures were erroneous.

The door of his room was locked. I knocked: I demanded entrance in a low voice: I put my eye and my ear to the key-hole and the crevices: nothing could be heard or seen. It was unavoidable to conclude that no one was within; yet the effluvia of gun-powder was perceptible.

Perhaps the room above had been the scene of this catastrophe. I ascended the second flight of stairs. I approached the door. No sound could be caught by my most vigilant attention. I put out the light that I carried, and was then able to perceive that there was light within the room. I scarcely knew how to act. For some minutes I paused at the door. I spoke, and requested permission to enter. My words were succeeded by a death-like stillness. At length I ventured softly to withdraw the bolt; to open, and to advance within the room. Nothing could exceed the horror of my expectation; yet I was startled by the scene that I beheld.

In a chair, whose back was placed against the front wall, sat Welbeck. My entrance alarmed him not, nor roused him from the stupor into which he was plunged. He rested his hands upon his knees, and his eyes were rivetted to something that lay, at the distance of a few feet before him, on the floor. A second glance was sufficient to inform me of what nature this object was. It was the body of a man, bleeding, ghastly, and still exhibiting the marks of convulsion and agony!

I shall omit to describe the shock which a spectacle like this communicated to my unpractised senses. I was nearly as panic-struck and powerless as Welbeck himself. I gazed, without power of speech, at one time, at Welbeck: Then I fixed terrified eyes on the distorted features of the dead. At length, Welbeck, recovering from his reverie, looked up, as if to see who it was that had entered. No surprise, no alarm, was betrayed by him on seeing me. He manifested no desire or intention to interrupt the fearful silence.

My thoughts wandered in confusion and terror. The first impulse was to fly from the scene; but I could not be long insensible to the exigencies of the moment. I saw that affairs must not be suffered to remain in their present situation. The insensibility or despair of Welbeck required consolation and succour. How to communicate my thoughts, or offer my assistance, I knew not. What led to this murderous catastrophe; who it was whose breathless corpse was before me; what concern Welbeck had in producing his death; were as yet unknown.

At length he rose from his seat, and strode at first with faltering, and then with more steadfast steps, across the floor. This motion seemed to put him in possession of himself. He seemed now, for the first time, to recognize my presence. He turned to me and said, in a tone of severity:

How now! What brings you here?

This rebuke was unexpected. I stammered out in reply, that the report of the pistol had alarmed me, and that I came to discover the cause of it.

He noticed not my answer, but resumed his perturbed steps, and his anxious, but abstracted looks. Suddenly he checked himself, and glancing a furious eye at the corse, he muttered, Yes, the die is cast. This worthless and miserable scene shall last no longer. I will at once get rid of life and all its humiliations.

Here succeeded a new pause. The course of his thoughts

seemed now to become once more tranquil. Sadness, rather than fury, overspread his features; and his accent, when he spoke to me, was not faltering, but solemn.

Mervyn, said he, you comprehend not this scene. Your youth and inexperience make you a stranger to a deceitful and flagitious world. You know me not. It is time that this ignorance should vanish. The knowledge of me and of my actions may be of use to you. It may teach you to avoid the shoals on which my virtue and my peace have been wrecked; but to the rest of mankind it can be of no use. The ruin of my fame is, perhaps, irretrievable; but the height of my iniquity need not be known. I perceive in you a rectitude and firmness worthy to be trusted; promise me, therefore, that not a syllable of what I tell you shall ever pass your lips.

I had lately experienced the inconvenience of a promise; but I was now confused, embarrassed, ardently inquisitive as to the nature of this scene, and unapprized of the motives that might afterwards occur, persuading or compelling me to disclosure. The promise which he exacted was given. He resumed:

I have detained you in my service, partly for your own benefit, but chiefly for mine. I intended to inflict upon you injury, and to do you good. Neither of these ends can I now accomplish, unless the lessons which my example may inculcate shall inspire you with fortitude, and arm you with caution.

What it was that made me thus, I know not. I am not destitute of understanding. My thirst of knowledge, though irregular, is ardent. I can talk and can feel as virtue and justice prescribe; yet the tenor of my actions has been uniform. One tissue of iniquity and folly has been my life; while my thoughts have been familiar with enlightened and disinterested principles. Scorn and detestation I have heaped upon myself. Yesterday is remembered with remorse. To-morrow is contemplated with anguish and fear; yet every day is productive of the same crimes and of the same follies.

I was left, by the insolvency of my father (a trader of Liverpool), without any means of support, but such as labour should afford me. Whatever could generate pride, and the love of independence, was my portion. Whatever can incite to diligence was the growth of my condition; yet my indolence was a cureless disease; and there were no arts too sordid for me to practise.

I was content to live on the bounty of a kinsman. His family was numerous, and his revenue small. He forbore to upbraid me, or even to insinuate the propriety of providing for myself; but he empowered me to pursue any liberal or mechanical profession which might suit my taste. I was insensible to every generous motive. I laboured to forget my dependent and disgraceful condition, because the remembrance was a source of anguish, without being able to inspire me with a steady resolution to change it.

I contracted an acquaintance with a woman who was unchaste, perverse, and malignant. Me, however, she found it no difficult task to deceive. My uncle remonstrated against the union. He took infinite pain to unveil my error, and to convince me that wedlock was improper for one destitute, as I was, of the means of support, even if the object of my choice were personally unexceptionable.

His representations were listened to with anger. That he thwarted my will, in this respect, even by affectionate expostulation, cancelled all that debt of gratitude which I owed to him. I rewarded him for all his kindness by invective and disdain, and hastened to complete my ill-omened marriage. I had deceived the woman's father by assertions of possessing secret resources. To gratify my passion I descended to dissimulation and falsehood. He admitted me into his family, as the husband of his child; but the character of my wife and the fallacy of my assertions were quickly discovered. He denied me accommodation under his roof, and I was turned forth to the world to endure the penalty of my rashness and my indolence.

Temptation would have moulded me into any villainous shape. My virtuous theories and comprehensive erudition would not have saved me from the basest of crimes. Luckily for me, I was, for the present, exempted from temptation. I had formed an acquaintance with a young American captain. On being partially informed of my situation, he invited me to embark with him for his own country. My passage was gratuitous. I arrived, in a short time, at Charleston, which was the place of his abode.

He introduced me to his family, every member of which was, like himself, embued with affection and benevolence. I was treated like their son and brother. I was hospitably entertained until I should be able to select some path of lucrative industry. Such was my incurable depravity, that I made no haste to select my pursuit. An interval of inoccupation succeeded, which I applied to the worst purposes.

My friend had a sister, who was married; but, during the absence of her husband, resided with her family. Hence originated our acquaintance. The purest of human hearts and the most vigorous understanding were hers. She idolized her husband, who well deserved to be the object of her adoration. Her affection for him, and her general principles, appeared to be confirmed beyond the power to be shaken. I sought her intercourse without illicit views: I delighted in the effusions of her candour and the flashes of her intelligence: I conformed, by a kind of instinctive hypocrisy, to her views: I spoke and felt from the influence of immediate and momentary conviction. She imagined she had found in me a friend worthy to partake in all her sympathies, and forward all her wishes. We were mutually deceived. She was the victim of self-delusion; but I must charge myself with practising deceit both upon myself and her.

I reflect with astonishment and horror on the steps which led to her degradation and to my calamity. In the high career of passion all consequences were overlooked. She was the dupe of the most audacious sophistry and the grossest delusion. I was the slave of sensual impulses and voluntary blindness. The effect may be easily conceived. Not till symptoms of pregnancy began to appear were our eyes opened to the ruin which impended over us.

Then I began to revolve the consequences, which the mist of passion had hitherto concealed. I was tormented by the pangs of remorse, and pursued by the phantom of ingratitude. To complete my despair, this unfortunate lady was apprized of my marriage with another woman; a circumstance which I had anxiously concealed from her. She fled from her father's house at a time when her husband and brother were hourly expected. What became of her I knew not. She left behind her a letter to her father, in which the melancholy truth was told.

Shame and remorse had no power over my life. To elude the storm of invective and upbraiding; to quiet the uproar of my mind, I did not betake myself to voluntary death. My pusillanimity still clung to this wretched existence. I abruptly retired from the scene, and, repairing to the port, embarked in the first vessel which appeared. The ship chanced to belong to Wilmington, in Delaware, and here I sought out an obscure and cheap abode.

I possessed no means of subsistence. I was unknown to my neighbours, and desired to remain unknown. I was unqualified for manual labour by all the habits of my life; but there was no choice between penury and diligence — between honest labour and criminal inactivity. I mused incessantly on the forlornness of my condition. Hour after hour passed, and the horrors of want began to encompass me. I sought with eagerness for an avenue by which I might escape from it. The perverseness of my nature led me on from one guilty thought to another. I took refuge in my customary sophistries, and reconciled myself at length to a scheme of—*forgery!*

CHAPTER X

HAVING ascertained my purpose, it was requisite to search out the means by which I might effect it. These were not clearly or readily suggested. The more I contemplated my project, the more numerous and arduous its difficulties appeared. I had no associates in my undertaking. A due regard to my safety and the unextinguished sense of honour deterred me from seeking auxiliaries and co-agents. The esteem of mankind was the spring of all my activity, the parent of all my virtue and all my vice. To preserve this, it was necessary that my guilty projects should have neither witness nor partaker.

I quickly discovered that to execute this scheme demanded time, application and money, none of which my present situation would permit me to devote to it. At first, it appeared that an attainable degree of skill and circumspection would enable me to arrive, by means of counterfeit bills, to the pinnacle of affluence and honour. My error was detected by a closer scrutiny, and I, finally, saw nothing in this path but enormous perils and insurmountable impediments.

Yet what alternative was offered me. To maintain myself by the labour of my hands, to perform any toilsome or prescribed task, was incompatible with my nature. My habits debarred me from country occupations. My pride regarded as vile and ignominious drudgery any employment which the town could afford. Meanwhile, my wants were as urgent as ever and my funds were exhausted.

There are few, perhaps, whose external situation resembled mine, who would have found in it any thing but incitements to industry and invention. A thousand methods of subsistence, honest but laborious, were at my command, but to these I entertained an irreconcilable aversion. Ease and the respect attendant upon opulence I was willing to purchase at the price of ever-wakeful suspicion and eternal remorse; but, even at this price, the purchase was impossible.

The desperateness of my condition became hourly more apparent. The further I extended my view, the darker grew the clouds which hung over futurity. Anguish and infamy appeared to be the inseparable conditions of my existence. There was one mode of evading the evils that impended. To free myself from self-upbraiding and to shun the persecutions of my fortune was possible only by shaking off life itself.

One evening, as I traversed the bank of the creek, these dismal meditations were uncommonly intense. They at length terminated in a resolution to throw myself into the stream. The first impulse was to rush instantly to my death, but the remembrance of papers, lying at my lodgings, which might unfold more than I desired to the curiosity of survivors, induced me to postpone this catastrophe till the next morning.

My purpose being formed, I found my heart lightened of its usual weight. By you it will be thought strange, but it is nevertheless true, that I derived from this new prospect, not only tranquility but cheerfulness. I hastened home. As soon as I entered, my land-lord informed me that a person had been searching for me in my absence. This was an unexampled incident and forboded me no good. I was strongly persuaded that my visitant had been led hither not by friendly, but hostile purposes. This persuasion was confirmed by the description of the stranger's guize and demeanour given by my land-lord. My fears instantly recognized the image of Watson, the man by whom I had been so eminently benefitted, and whose kindness I had compensated by the ruin of his sister and the confusion of his family.

An interview with this man was less to be endured than to look upon the face of an avenging deity. I was determined to avoid this interview, and for this end, to execute my fatal purpose within the hour. My papers were collected with a tremulous hand, and consigned to the flames. I then bade my land-lord inform all visitants that I should not return till the next day, and once more hastened towards the river.

My way led past the Inn where one of the stages from Baltimore was accustomed to stop. I was not unaware that Watson had possibly been brought in the coach which had recently arrived, and which now stood before the door of the Inn. The danger of my being descried or encountered by him as I passed did not fail to occur. This was to be eluded by deviating from the main street.

Scarcely had I turned a corner for this purpose when I was accosted by a young man whom I knew to be an inhabitant of the town, but with whom I had hitherto had no intercourse but what consisted in a transient salutation. He apologized for the liberty of addressing me, and, at the same time, inquired if I understood the French language.

Being answered in the affirmative, he proceeded to tell me, that in the stage, just arrived, had come a passenger, a youth who appeared to be French, who was wholly unacquainted with our language, and who had been seized with a violent disease.

My informant had felt compassion for the forlorn condition of the stranger, and had just been seeking me at my lodgings, in hope that my knowledge of French would enable me to converse with the sick man, and obtain from him a knowledge of his situation and views.

The apprehensions I had precipitately formed, were thus removed and I readily consented to perform this service. The youth was, indeed, in a deplorable condition. Besides the pains of his disease, he was overpowered by dejection. The inn-keeper, was extremely anxious for the removal of his guest. He was by no means willing to sustain the trouble and expense of a sick or a dying man, for which it was, scarcely probable that he should ever be reimbursed. The traveller had no baggage and his dress betokened the pressure of many wants.

My compassion for this stranger was powerfully awakened. I was in possession of a suitable apartment, for which I had no power to pay the rent that was accruing, but my inability in this respect was unknown, and I might enjoy my lodgings unmolested for some weeks. The fate of this youth would be speedily decided, and I should be left at liberty to execute my first intentions before my embarrassments should be visibly increased.

After a moment's pause, I conducted the stranger to my home, placed him in my own bed, and became his nurse. His malady was such as is known in the tropical islands, by the name of the Yellow or Malignant Fever, and the physician who was called, speedily pronounced his case desperate.

It was my duty to warn him of the death that was hastening, and to promise the fulfillment of any of his wishes, not inconsistent with my present situation. He received my intelligence with fortitude, and appeared anxious to communicate some information respecting his own state. His pangs and his weakness scarcely allowed him to be intelligible. From his feeble efforts and broken narrative I collected thus much concerning his family and fortune.

His father's name was Vincentio Lodi. From a Merchant at Leghorn, he had changed himself into a planter in the Island of Guadaloupe. His Son, had been sent, at an early age, for the benefits of education to Europe. The young Vincentio was, at length, informed by his father, that, being weary of his present mode of existence, he had determined to sell his property, and transport himself to the United States. The son was directed to hasten home, that he might embark, with his father, on this voyage.

The summons was cheerfully obeyed. The youth on his arrival at the Island found preparation making for the funeral of his father. It appeared that the elder Lodi had flattered one of his slaves with the prospect of his freedom, but had, nevertheless, included this slave in the sale that he had made of his estate. Actuated by revenge, the slave assassinated Lodi in the open street and resigned himself, without a struggle, to the punishment which the law had provided for such a deed.

The property had been recently transferred, and the price was now presented to young Vincentio by the purchaser. He was, by no means, inclined to adopt his father's project, and was impatient, to return with his inheritance, to France. Before this could be done, the conduct of his father had rendered a voyage to the continent indispensable.

Lodi had a daughter, whom, a few weeks previous to his death, he had intrusted to an American Captain, for whom, he had contracted a friendship. The vessel was bound to Philadelphia, but the conduct she was to pursue, and the abode she was to select, on her arrival, were known only to the father, whose untimely death involved the son in considerable uncertainty, with regard to his sister's fate. His anxiety on this account induced him to seize the first conveyance that offered. In a short time he landed at Baltimore.

As soon as he recovered from the fatigues of his voyage, he prepared to go to Philadelphia. Thither his baggage was immediately sent under the protection of a passenger and countryman. His money consisted in Portuguese gold, which, in pursuance of advice, he had changed into Banknotes. He besought me, in pathetic terms, to search out his sister, whose youth and poverty and ignorance of the language and manners of the country might expose her to innumerable hardships. At the same time, he put a pocketbook and small volume into my hand, indicating, by his countenance and gestures, his desire that I would deliver them to his sister.

His obsequies being decently performed, I had leisure to reflect upon the change in my condition which this incident had produced. In the pocket-book were found bills to the amount of twenty thousand dollars. The volume proved to be a manuscript, written by the elder Lodi in Italian, and contained memoirs of the Ducal house of Visconti, from whom the writer believed himself to have lineally descended.

Thus had I arrived, by an avenue so much beyond my foresight, at the possession of wealth. The evil which impelled me to the brink of suicide, and which was the source, though not of all, yet of the larger portion of my anguish, was now removed. What claims to honour or to ease were consequent on riches, were, by an extraordinary fortune, now conferred upon me.

Such, for a time, were my new born but transitory raptures. I forgot that this money was not mine. That it had been received under every sanction of fidelity, for another's use. To retain it was equivalent to robbery. The sister of the deceased was the rightful claimant: it was my duty to search her out, and perform my tacit, but sacred obligations, by putting the whole into her possession.

This conclusion was too adverse to my wishes, not to be strenuously combatted. I asked, what it was that gave man the power of ascertaining the successor to his property? During his life, he might transfer the actual possession, but if vacant at his death, he, into whose hands accident should cast it, was the genuine proprietor. It is true, that the law had sometimes otherwise decreed, but in law, there was no validity, further than it was able by investigation and punishment, to enforce its decrees; But would the law extort this money from me?

It was rather by gesture than by words that the will of Lodi was imparted. It was the topic of remote inferences and vague conjecture rather than of explicit and unerring declarations. Besides if the lady were found, would not prudence dictate the reservation of her fortune to be administered by me, for her benefit? Of this her age and education had disqualified herself. It was sufficient for the maintenance of both. She would regard me as her benefactor and protector. By supplying all her wants and watching over her safety without apprizing her of the means, by which I shall be enabled to do this, I shall lay irresistible claims to her love and her gratitude.

Such were the sophistries by which reason was seduced and my integrity annihilated. I hastened away from my present abode. I easily traced the baggage of the deceased to an inn, and gained possession of it. It contained nothing but clothes and books. I then instituted the most diligent search after the young lady. For a time, my exertions were fruitless.

Meanwhile, the possessor of this house thought proper to embark with his family for Europe. The sum which he demanded for his furniture, though enormous, was precipitately paid by me. His servants were continued in their former stations, and in the day, at which he relinquished the mansion, I entered on possession.

There was no difficulty in persuading the world that Welbeck was a personage of opulence and rank. My birth and previous adventures it was proper to conceal. The facility with which mankind are misled in their estimate of characters, their proneness to multiply inferences and conjectures will not be readily conceived by one destitute of my experience. My sudden appearance on the stage, my stately reserve, my splendid habitation and my circumspect deportment were sufficient to intitle me to homage. The artifices that were used to unveil the truth, and the guesses that were current respecting me, were adapted to gratify my ruling passion.

I did not remit my diligence to discover the retreat of Mademoiselle Lodi; I found her, at length, in the family of a kinsman of the Captain under whose care she had come to America. Her situation was irksome and perilous. She had already experienced the evils of being protectorless and indigent, and my seasonable interference snatched her from impending and less supportable ills.

I could safely unfold all that I knew of her brother's history, except the legacy which he had left. I ascribed the diligence with which I had sought her to his death-bed injunctions, and prevailed upon her to accept from me the treatment which she would have received from her brother, if he had continued to live, and if his power to benefit had been equal to my own.

Though less can be said in praise of the understanding, than of the sensibilities of this woman, she is one, whom, no one could refrain from loving, though placed in situations far less favourable to the generation of that sentiment, than mine. In habits of domestic and incessant intercourse, in the perpetual contemplation of features animated by boundless gratitude and ineffable sympathies, it could not be expected that either she or I should escape enchantment.

The poison was too sweet not to be swallowed with avidity by me. Too late I remembered that I was already enslaved by inextricable obligations. It was easy to have hidden this impediment from the eyes of my companion, but here my integrity refused to yield. I can, indeed, lay claim to little merit on account of this forbearance. If there had been no alternative between deceit and the frustration of my hopes, I should doubtless have dissembled the truth with as little scruple on this, as on a different occasion, but I could not be blind to the weakness of her with whom I had to contend.

CHAPTER XI

MEANWHILE large deductions had been made from my stock of money, and the remnant would be speedily consumed by my present mode of life. My expences far exceeded my previous expectations. In no long time I should be reduced to my ancient poverty, which the luxurious existence that I now enjoyed, and the regard due to my beloved and helpless companion, would render more irksome than ever. Some scheme to rescue me from this fate, was indispensable; but my aversion to labour, to any pursuit, the end of which was merely gain, and which would require application and attention continued undiminished.

I was plunged anew into dejection and perplexity. From this I was somewhat relieved by a plan suggested by Mr. Thetford. I thought I had experience of his knowledge and integrity, and the scheme that he proposed seemed liable to no possibility of miscarriage. A ship was to be purchased, supplied with a suitable cargo, and dispatched to a port in the West-Indies. Loss from storms and enemies was to be precluded by insurance. Every hazard was to be enumerated, and the ship and cargo valued at the highest rate. Should the voyage be safely performed, the profits would be double the original expense. Should the ship be taken or wrecked, the insurers would have bound themselves to make ample, speedy, and certain indemnification— Thetford's brother, a wary and experienced trader, was to be the supercargo.

All my money was laid out upon this scheme. Scarcely

enough was reserved to supply domestic and personal wants. Large debts were likewise incurred. Our caution had, as we conceived, annihilated every chance of failure. Too much could not be expended on a project so infallible; and the vessel, amply fitted and freighted, departed on her voyage.

An interval, not devoid of suspense and anxiety, succeeded. My mercantile inexperience made me distrust the clearness of my own discernment, and I could not but remember, that my utter and irretrievable destruction was connected with the failure of my scheme. Time added to my distrust and apprehensions. The time, at which tidings of the ship were to be expected, elapsed without affording any information of her destiny. My anxieties, however, were to be carefully hidden from the world. I had taught mankind to believe, that this project had been adopted more for amusement than gain; and the debts which I had contracted, seemed to arise from willingness to adhere to established maxims, more than from the pressure of necessity.

Month succeeded month, and intelligence was still withheld. The notes which I had given for one third of the cargo, and for the premium of insurance, would shortly become due. For the payment of the former, and the cancelling of the latter, I had relied upon the expeditious return, or the demonstrated loss of the vessel. Neither of these events had taken place.

My cares were augmented from another quarter. My companion's situation now appeared to be such, as, if our intercourse had been sanctified by wedlock, would have been regarded with delight. As it was, no symptoms were equally to be deplored. Consequences, as long as they were involved in uncertainty, were extenuated or overlooked; but now, when they became apparent and inevitable, were fertile of distress and upbraiding.

Indefinable fears, and a desire to monopolize all the meditations and affections of this being, had induced me to perpetuate her ignorance of any but her native language, and debar her from all intercourse with the world. My friends were of course inquisitive respecting her character, adventures, and particularly her relation to me. The consciousness how much the truth redounded to my dishonour, made me solicitous to lead conjecture astray. For this purpose I did not discountenance the conclusion that was adopted by some, that she was my daughter. I reflected, that all dangerous surmizes would be effectually precluded by this belief.

These precautions afforded me some consolation in my present difficulties. It was requisite to conceal the lady's condition from the world. If this should be ineffectual, it would not be difficult to divert suspicion from my person. The secrecy that I had practised would be justified, in the apprehension of those to whom the personal condition of Clemenza should be disclosed, by the feelings of a father.

Meanwhile, it was an obvious expedient to remove the unhappy lady to a distance from impertinent observers. A rural retreat, lonely, and sequestered, was easily procured, and hither she consented to repair. This arrangement being concerted, I had leisure to reflect upon the evils which every hour brought nearer, and which threatened to exterminate me.

My inquietudes forbade me to sleep, and I was accustomed to rise before day, and seek some respite in the fields. Returning from one of these unseasonable rambles, I chanced to meet you. Your resemblance to the deceased Lodi, in person and visage, is remarkable. When you first met my eye, this similitude startled me. Your subsequent appeal to my compassion was cloathed in such terms, as formed a powerful contrast with your dress, and prepossessed me greatly in favour of your education and capacity.

In my present hopeless condition, every incident, however trivial, was attentively considered, with a view to extract from it some means of escaping from my difficulties. My love for the Italian girl, in spite of all my efforts to keep it alive, had begun to languish. Marriage was impossible; and had now, in some degree, ceased to be desirable. We are apt to judge of others by ourselves. The passion, I now found myself disposed to ascribe chiefly to fortuitous circumstances; to the impulse of gratitude, and the exclusion of competitors; and believed that your resemblance to her brother, your age, and personal accomplishments, might, after a certain time, and in consequence of suitable contrivances, on my part, give a new direction to her feelings. To gain your concurrence, I relied upon your simplicity, your gratitude, and your susceptibility to the charms of this bewitching creature.

I contemplated, likewise, another end. Mrs. Wentworth is rich. A youth who was once her favourite, and designed to inherit her fortunes, has disappeared, for some years, from the scene. His death is most probable, but of that there is no satisfactory information. The life of this person, whose name is Clavering, is an obstacle to some designs which had occurred to me in relation to this woman. My purposes were crude and scarcely formed. I need not swell the catalogue of my errors by expatiating upon them. Suffice it to say, that the peculiar circumstances of your introduction to me, led me to reflections on the use that might be made of your agency, in procuring this lady's acquiescence in my schemes. You were to be ultimately persuaded to confirm in her the belief that her nephew was dead. To this consummation it was indispensible to lead you by slow degrees, and circuitous paths. Meanwhile, a profound silence, with regard to your genuine history, was to be observed; and to this forbearance, your consent was obtained with more readiness than I expected.

There was an additional motive for the treatment you received from me. My personal projects and cares had hitherto prevented me from reading Lodi's manuscript; a slight inspection, however, was sufficient to prove that the work was profound and eloquent. My ambition has panted, with equal avidity, after the reputation of literature and opulence. To claim the authorship of this work was too harmless and specious a stratagem, not to be readily suggested. I meant to translate it into English, and to enlarge it by enterprising incidents of my own invention. My scruples to assume the merit of the original composer, might thus be removed. For this end, your assistance as an amanuensis would be necessary.

100

You will perceive, that all these projects depended on the seasonable arrival of intelligence from . . . . The delay of another week would seal my destruction. The silence might arise from the foundering of the ship, and the destruction of all on board. In this case, the insurance was not forfeited, but payment could not be obtained within a year. Meanwhile, the premium and other debts must be immediately discharged, and this was beyond my power. Meanwhile I was to live in a manner that would not belie my pretensions; but my coffers were empty.

I cannot adequately paint the anxieties with which I have been haunted. Each hour has added to the burthen of my existence, till, in consequence of the events of this day, it has become altogether insupportable. Some hours ago, I was summoned by Thetford to his house. The messenger informed me that tidings had been received of my ship. In answer to my eager interrogations, he could give no other information than that she had been captured by the British. He was unable to relate particulars.

News of her safe return would, indeed, have been far more acceptable; but even this information was a source of infinite congratulation. It precluded the demand of my insurers. The payment of other debts might be postponed for a month, and my situation be the same as before the adoption of this successless scheme. Hope and joy were reinstated in my bosom, and I hasted to Thetford's compting house.

He received me with an air of gloomy dissatisfaction. I accounted for his sadness by supposing him averse to communicate information, which was less favourable than our wishes had dictated. He confirmed, with visible reluctance, the news of her capture. He had just received letters from his brother, acquainting him with all particulars, and containing the official documents of this transaction.

This had no tendency to damp my satisfaction, and I proceeded to peruse with eagerness, the papers which he put into my hand. I had not proceeded far when my joyous hopes vanished. Two French mulattoes had, after much solicitation, and the most solemn promises to carry with them no articles which the laws of war decree to be contraband, obtained a passage in the vessel. She was speedily encountered by a privateer, by whom every receptacle was ransacked. In a chest, belonging to the Frenchmen, and which they had affirmed to contain nothing but their clothes, were found two sabres, and other accoutrements of an officer of cavalry. Under this pretence, the vessel was captured and condemned, and this was a cause of forfeiture, which had not been provided against in the contract of insurance.

By this untoward event my hopes were irreparably blasted. The utmost efforts were demanded to conceal my thoughts from my companion. The anguish that preyed upon my heart was endeavoured to be masked by looks of indifference. I pretended to have been previously informed by the messenger, not only of the capture, but of the cause that led to it, and forbore to expatiate upon my loss, or to execrate the authors of my disappointment. My mind, however, was the theatre of discord and agony, and I waited with impatience for an opportunity to leave him.

For want of other topics, I asked by whom this information had been brought. He answered, that the bearer was Captain Amos Watson, whose vessel had been forfeited, at the same time, under a different pretence. He added, that my name being mentioned, accidentally, to Watson, the latter had betrayed marks of great surprise, and been very earnest in his inquiries respecting my situation. Having obtained what knowledge Thetford was able to communicate, the captain had departed, avowing a former acquaintance with me, and declaring his intention of paying me a visit.

These words operated on my frame like lightning. All within me was tumult and terror, and I rushed precipitately out of the house. I went forward with unequal steps, and at random. Some instinct led me into the fields, and I was not apprized of the direction of my steps, till, looking up, I found myself upon the shore of Schuylkill.

Thus was I, a second time, overborne by hopeless and

incurable evils. An interval of motley feelings, of specious artifice, and contemptible imposture, had elapsed since my meeting with the stranger at Wilmington. Then my forlorn state had led me to the brink of suicide. A brief and feverish respite had been afforded me, but now was I transported to the verge of the same abyss.

Amos Watson was the brother of the angel whom I had degraded and destroyed. What but fiery indignation and unappeasable vengeance, could lead him into my presence? With what heart could I listen to his invectives? How could I endure to look upon the face of one, whom I had loaded with such atrocious and intolerable injuries?

I was acquainted with his loftiness of mind: his detestation of injustice, and the whirl-wind passions that ingratitude and villainy like mine were qualified to awaken in his bosom. I dreaded not his violence. The death that he might be prompted to inflict, was no object of aversion. It was poverty and disgrace, the detection of my crimes, the looks and voice of malediction and upbraiding, from which my cowardice shrunk.

Why should I live? I must vanish from that stage which I had lately trodden. My flight must be instant and precipitate. To be a fugitive from exasperated creditors, and from the industrious revenge of Watson, was an easy undertaking; but whither could I fly, where I should not be pursued by the phantoms of remorse, by the dread of hourly detection, by the necessities of hunger and thirst? In what scene should I be exempt from servitude and drudgery? Was my existence embellished with enjoyments that would justify my holding it, encumbered with hardships, and immersed in obscurity?

There was no room for hesitation. To rush into the stream before me, and to put an end at once to my life and the miseries inseparably linked with it, was the only proceeding which fate had left to my choice. My muscles were already exerted for this end, when the helpless condition of Clemenza was remembered. What provision could I make against the evils that threatened her? Should I leave her utterly forlorn and friendless? Mrs. Wentworth's temper was forgiving and compassionate. Adversity had taught her to participate, and her wealth enabled her to relieve distress. Who was there by whom such powerful claims to succour and protection could be urged as by this desolate girl? Might I not state her situation in a letter to this lady, and urge irresistible pleas for the extension of her kindness to this object?

These thoughts made me suspend my steps. I determined to seek my habitation once more, and having written and deposited this letter, to return to the execution of my fatal purpose. I had scarcely reached my own door, when some one approached along the pavement. The form, at first, was undistinguishable, but by coming, at length, within the illumination of a lamp, it was perfectly recognized.

To avoid this detested interview was now impossible. Watson approached and accosted me. In this conflict of tumultuous feelings I was still able to maintain an air of intrepidity. His demeanour was that of a man who struggles with his rage. His accents were hurried, and scarcely articulate. I have ten words to say to you, said he: lead into the house, and to some private room. My business with you will be dispatched in a breath.

I made him no answer, but led the way into my house, and to my study. On entering this room, I put the light upon the table, and turning to my visitant, prepared, silently to hear, what he had to unfold. He struck his clenched hand against the table with violence. His motion was of that tempestuous kind, as to overwhelm the power of utterance, and found it easier to vent itself in gesticulations than in words. At length, he exclaimed,

It is well. Now has the hour, so long, and so impatiently demanded by my vengeance, arrived. Welbeck! Would that my first words could strike thee dead! They will so, if thou hast any title to the name of man.

My sister is dead: dead of anguish and a broken heart. Remote from her friends; in a hovel; the abode of indigence and misery.

Her husband is no more. He returned after long absence, a tedious navigation, and vicissitudes of hardships. He flew to the bosom of his love; of his wife. She was gone; lost to him, and to virtue. In a fit of desperation, he retired to his chamber, and dispatched himself. This is the instrument with which the deed was performed.

Saying this, Watson took a pistol from his pocket, and held it to my head. I lifted not my hand to turn aside the weapon. I did not shudder at the spectacle, or shrink from his approaching hand. With fingers clasped together, and eyes fixed upon the floor, I waited till his fury was exhausted. He continued:

All passed in a few hours. The elopement of his daughter—the death of his son. O! my father! Most loved, and most venerable of men! To see thee changed into a maniac! Haggard and wild! Deterred from outrage on thyself and those around thee, by fetters and stripes! What was it that saved me from a like fate? To view this hideous ruin, and to think by whom it was occasioned! Yet not to become frantic like thee, my father; or not destroy myself like thee, my brother! My friend!—

No. For this hour was I reserved: to avenge your wrongs and mine in the blood of this ungrateful villain.

There, continued he, producing a second pistol, and tendering it to me, there is thy defence. Take we opposite sides of this table, and fire at the same instant.

During this address I was motionless. He tendered the pistol, but I unclasped not my hands to receive it.

Why do you hesitate? resumed he. Let the chance between us be equal, or fire you first.

No, said I, I am ready to die by your hand. I wish it. It will preclude the necessity of performing the office for myself. I have injured you, and merit all that your vengeance can inflict. I know your nature too well, to believe that my death will be perfect expiation. When the gust of indignation is past, the remembrance of your deed will only add to your sum of misery: yet I do not love you well enough to wish that you would forbear. I desire to die, and to die by another's hand rather than my own.

105

Coward! exclaimed Watson, with augmented vehemence. You know me too well, to believe me capable of assassination. Vile subterfuge! Contemptible plea! Take the pistol and defend yourself. You want not the power or the will; but, knowing that I spurn at murder, you think your safety will be found in passiveness. Your refusal will avail you little. Your fame, if not your life, is at my mercy. If you faulter now, I will allow you to live, but only till I have stabbed your reputation.

I now fixed my eyes stedfastly upon him, and spoke: How much a stranger are you to the feelings of Welbeck! How poor a judge of his cowardice! I take your pistol, and consent to your conditions.

We took opposite sides of the table. Are you ready? he cried, fire!

Both triggers were drawn at the same instant. Both pistols were discharged. Mine was negligently raised. Such is the untoward chance that presides over human affairs: such is the malignant destiny by which my steps have ever been pursued. The bullet whistled harmlessly by me. Levelled by an eye that never before failed, and with so small an interval between us. I escaped, but my blind and random shot took place in his heart.

There is the fruit of this disastrous meeting. The catalogue of death is thus completed. Thou sleepest Watson! Thy sister is at rest, and so art thou. Thy vows of vengeance are at an end. It was not reserved for thee to be thy own and thy sister's avenger. Welbeck's measure of transgressions is now full, and his own hand must execute the justice that is due to him.

CHAPTER XII

S UCH was Welbeck's tale listened to by me with an eagerness in which every faculty was absorbed. How adverse to my dreams were the incidents that had just been related! The curtain was lifted, and a scene of guilt and ignominy disclosed where my rash and inexperienced youth had suspected nothing but loftiness and magnanimity.

For a while the wondrousness of this tale kept me from contemplating the consequences that awaited us. My unfledged fancy had not hitherto soared to this pitch. All was astounding by its novelty, or terrific by its horror. The very scene of these offences partook, to my rustic apprehension, of fairy splendour, and magical abruptness. My understanding was bemazed, and my senses were taught to distrust their own testimony.

From this musing state I was recalled by my companion, who said to me in solemn accents. Mervyn! I have but two requests to make. Assist me to bury these remains, and then accompany me across the river. I have no power to compel your silence on the acts that you have witnessed. I have meditated to benefit, as well as to injure you; but I do not desire that your demeanour should conform to any other standard than justice. You have promised, and to that promise I trust.

If you chuse to fly from this scene, to withdraw yourself from what you may conceive to be a theatre of guilt or peril, the avenues are open; retire unmolested and in silence. If you have a man-like spirit, if you are grateful for the benefits bestowed upon you, if your discernment enables you to see that compliance with my request will intangle you in no guilt, and betray you into no danger, stay, and aid me in hiding these remains from human scrutiny.

Watson is beyond the reach of further injury. I never intended him harm, though I have torn from him his sister and friend, and have brought his life to an untimely close. To provide him a grave, is a duty that I owe to the dead and to the living. I shall quickly place myself beyond the reach of inquisitors and judges, but would willingly rescue from molestation or suspicion those whom I shall leave behind.

What would have been the fruit of deliberation, if I had had the time or power to deliberate, I know not. My thoughts flowed with tumult and rapidity. To shut this spectacle from my view was the first impulse; but to desert this man, in a time of so much need, appeared a thankless and dastardly deportment. To remain where I was, to conform implicitly to his direction, required no effort. Some fear was connected with his presence, and with that of the dead; but, in the tremulous confusion of my present thoughts, solitude would conjure up a thousand phantoms.

I made no preparation to depart. I did not verbally assent to his proposal. He interpreted my silence into acquiescence. He wrapt the body in the carpet, and then lifting one end, cast at me a look which indicated his expectations, that I would aid him in lifting this ghastly burthen. During this process, the silence was unbroken.

I knew not whither he intended to convey the corpse. He had talked of burial, but no receptacle had been provided. How far safety might depend upon his conduct in this particular, I was unable to estimate. I was in too heartless a mood to utter my doubts. I followed his example in raising the corpse from the floor.

He led the way into the passage and down stairs. Having reached the first floor, he unbolted a door which led into the cellar. The stairs and passage were illuminated by lamps, that hung from the ceiling, and were accustomed to

108

burn during the night. Now, however, we were entering darksome and murky recesses.

Return, said he, in a tone of command, and fetch the light. I will wait for you.

I obeyed. As I returned with the light, a suspicion stole into my mind, that Welbeck had taken this opportunity to fly; and that on regaining the foot of the stairs, I should find the spot deserted by all but the dead. My blood was chilled by this image. The momentary resolution it inspired was to follow the example of the fugitive, and leave the persons, whom the ensuing day might convene on this spot, to form their own conjectures as to the cause of this catastrophe.

Meanwhile, I cast anxious eyes forward. Welbeck was discovered in the same place and posture in which he had been left; lifting the corpse and its shroud in his arms he directed me to follow him. The vaults beneath were lofty and spacious. He passed from one to the other till we reached a small and remote cell. Here he cast his burthen on the ground. In the fall, the face of Watson chanced to be disengaged from its covering. Its closed eyes and sunken muscles were rendered, in a tenfold degree, ghastly and rueful by the feeble light which the candle shed upon it.

This object did not escape the attention of Welbeck. He leaned against the wall and folding his arms resigned himself to reverie. He gazed upon the countenance of Watson but his looks denoted his attention to be elsewhere employed.

As to me, my state will not be easily described. My eye roved fearfully from one object to another. By turns it was fixed upon the murdered person and the murderer. The narrow cell in which we stood, its rudely fashioned walls and arches, destitute of communication with the external air, and its palpable dark scarcely penetrated by the rays of a solitary candle, added to the silence which was deep and universal, produced an impression on my fancy which no time will obliterate.

Perhaps my imagination was distempered by terror. The incident which I am going to relate may appear to have existed only in my fancy. Be that as it may, I experienced all the effects which the fullest belief is adapted to produce. Glancing vaguely at the countenance of Watson, my attention was arrested by a convulsive motion in the eye-lids. This motion increased, till, at length the eyes opened, and a glance, languid but wild, was thrown around. Instantly they closed, and the tremulous appearance vanished.

I started from my place and was on the point of uttering some involuntary exclamation. At the same moment, Welbeck seemed to recover from his reverie.

How is this! said he. Why do we linger here? Every moment is precious. We cannot dig for him a grave with our hands. Wait here, while I go in search of a spade.

Saying this, he snatched the candle from my hand, and hasted away. My eye followed the light as its gleams shifted their place upon the walls and ceilings, and gradually vanishing, gave place to unrespited gloom. This proceeding was so unexpected and abrupt, that I had no time to remonstrate against it. Before I retrieved the power of reflection, the light had disappeared and the foot-steps were no longer to be heard.

I was not, on ordinary occasions, destitute of equanimity, but, perhaps the imagination of man is naturally abhorrent of death, until tutored into indifference by habit. Every circumstance combined to fill me with shuddering and panick. For a while, I was enabled to endure my situation by the exertions of my reason. That the lifeless remains of an human being are powerless to injure or benefit, I was thoroughly persuaded. I summoned this belief to my aid, and was able, if not to subdue, yet to curb my fears. I listened to catch the sound of the returning foot-steps of Welbeck, and hoped that every new moment would terminate my solitude.

No signal of his coming was afforded. At length it occurred to me that Welbeck had gone with no intention to return: That his malice had seduced me hither, to encounter the consequences of his deed. He had fled and barred every door behind him. This suspicion may well be supposed to overpower my courage, and to call forth desperate efforts for my deliverance.

I extended my hands and went forward. I had been too little attentive to the situation and direction of these vaults and passages, to go forward with undeviating accuracy. My fears likewise tended to confuse my perceptions and bewilder my steps. Notwithstanding the danger of encountering obstructions, I rushed towards the entrance with precipitation.

My temerity was quickly punished. In a moment, I was repelled by a jutting angle of the wall, with such force that I staggered backward and fell. The blow was stunning, and when I recovered my senses, I perceived that a torrent of blood was gushing from my nostrils. My clothes were moistened with this unwelcome effusion, and I could not but reflect on the hazard which I should incur by being detected in this recess, covered by these accusing stains.

This reflection once more set me on my feet, and incited my exertions. I now proceeded with greater wariness and caution. I had lost all distinct notions of my way. My motions were at random. All my labour was to shun obstructions and to advance whenever the vacuity would permit. By this means, the entrance was at length found, and after various efforts, I arrived, beyond my hopes, at the foot of the stair-case.

I ascended, but quickly encountered an insuperable impediment. The door at the stair-head, was closed and barred. My utmost strength was exerted in vain, to break the lock or the hinges. Thus were my direst apprehensions fulfilled. Welbeck had left me to sustain the charge of murder: to obviate suspicions the most atrocious and plausible that the course of human events is capable of producing.

Here I must remain till the morrow: till some one can be made to overhear my calls and come to my deliverance. What effects will my appearance produce on the spectator! Terrified by phantoms and stained with blood shall I not exhibit the tokens of a maniac as well as an assassin?

The corpse of Watson will quickly be discovered. If previous to this disclosure I should change my blood-stained garments and withdraw into the country, shall I not be pursued by the most vehement suspicions and, perhaps, hunted to my obscurest retreat by the ministers of justice? I am innocent, but my tale however circumstantial or true, will scarcely suffice for my vindication. My flight will be construed into a proof of incontestable guilt.

While harassed by these thoughts my attention was attracted by a faint gleam cast upon the bottom of the staircase. It grew stronger, hovered for a moment in my sight, and then disappeared. That it proceeded from a lamp or candle, borne by some one along the passages was no untenable opinion, but was far less probable than that the effulgence was meteorous. I confided in the latter supposition and fortified myself anew against the dread of preternatural dangers. My thoughts reverted to the contemplation of the hazards and suspicions which flowed from my continuance in this spot.

In the midst of my perturbed musing, my attention was again recalled by an illumination like the former. Instead of hovering and vanishing, it was permanent. No ray could be more feeble, but the tangible obscurity to which it succeeded rendered it conspicuous as an electrical flash. For a while I eyed it without moving from my place, and in momentary expectation of its disappearance.

Remarking its stability, the propriety of scrutinizing it more nearly, and of ascertaining the source whence it flowed, was at length suggested. Hope, as well as curiosity, was the parent of my conduct. Though utterly at a loss to assign the cause of this appearance, I was willing to believe some connection between that cause and the means of my deliverance.

I had scarcely formed the resolution of descending the stair, when my hope was extinguished by the recollection that the cellar had narrow and grated windows, through which light from the street might possibly have found access. A second recollection supplanted this belief, for in my way to this stair-case, my attention would have been solicited, and my steps, in some degree, been guided by light coming through these avenues.

Having returned to the bottom of the stair, I perceived every part of the long drawn passage illuminated. I threw a glance forward, to the quarter whence the rays seemed to proceed, and beheld, at a considerable distance, Welbeck in the cell which I had left, turning up the earth with a spade.

After a pause of astonishment, the nature of the error which I had committed, rushed upon apprehension. I now perceived that the darkness had misled me to a different stair-case from that which I had originally descended. It was apparent that Welbeck intended me no evil, but had really gone in search of the instrument which he had mentioned.

This discovery overwhelmed me with contrition and shame, though it freed from the terrors of imprisonment and accusation. To return to the cell which I had left, and where Welbeck was employed in his disastrous office, was the expedient which regards to my own safety unavoidably suggested.

Welbeck paused at my approach, and betrayed a momentary consternation at the sight of my ensanguined visage. The blood, by some inexplicable process of nature, perhaps by the counteracting influence of fear, had quickly ceased to flow. Whether the cause of my evasion, and of my flux of blood, was guessed, or whether his attention was withdrawn, by more momentous objects, from my condition, he proceeded in his task in silence. .

A shallow bed, and a slight covering of clay was provided for the hapless Watson. Welbeck's movements were hurried and tremulous. His countenance betokened a mind engrossed by a single purpose, in some degree, foreign to the scene before him. An intensity and fixedness of features, that were conspicuous, led me to suspect the subversion of his reason.

Having finished the task, he threw aside his impliment. He then put into my hand a pocket-book, saying it belonged to Watson, and might contain something serviceable to the living. I might make what use of it I thought proper. He then remounted the stairs and, placing the candle on a table in the hall, opened the principal door and went forth. I was driven, by a sort of mechanical impulse, in his foot-steps. I followed him because it was agreeable to him and because I knew not whither else to direct my steps.

113

The streets were desolate and silent. The watchman's call remotely and faintly heard, added to the general solemnity. I followed my companion in a state of mind not easily described. I had no spirit even to inquire whither he was going. It was not till we arrived at the water's edge that I persuaded myself to break silence. I then began to reflect on the degree in which his present schemes might endanger Welbeck or myself. I had acted long enough a servile and mechanical part; and been guided by blind and foreign impulses. It was time to lay aside my fetters, and demand to know whither the path tended in which I was importuned to walk.

Meanwhile I found myself intangled among boats and shipping. I am unable to describe the spot by any indisputable tokens. I know merely that it was the termination of one of the principal streets. Here Welbeck selected a boat and prepared to enter it. For a moment I hesitated to comply with his apparent invitation. I stammered out an interrogation. Why is this? Why should we cross the river? What service can I do for you? I ought to know the purpose of my voyage before I enter it.

He checked himself and surveyed me for a minute in silence. What do you fear? said he. Have I not explained my wishes? Merely cross the river with me, for I cannot navigate a boat by myself. Is there any thing arduous or mysterious in this undertaking? We part on the Jersey shore, and I shall leave you to your destiny. All I shall ask from you will be silence, and to hide from mankind what you know concerning me.

He now entered the boat and urged me to follow his example. I reluctantly complied. I perceived that the boat contained but one oar and that was a small one. He seemed startled and thrown into great perplexity by this discovery. It will be impossible, said he, in a tone of panic and vexation, to procure another at this hour; what is to be done?

This impediment was by no means insuperable. I had sinewy arms and knew well how to use an oar for the double purpose of oar and rudder. I took my station at the stern, and quickly extricated the boat from its neighbours and from the wharves. I was wholly unacquainted with the river.

114

The bar, by which it was incumbered, I knew to exist, but in what direction and to what extent it existed, and how it might be avoided in the present state of the tide I knew not. It was probable, therefore, unknowing as I was of the proper tract, that our boat would speedily have grounded.

My attention, meanwhile, was fixed upon the oar. My companion sat at the prow and was in a considerable degree unnoticed. I cast eyes occasionally at the scene which I had left. Its novelty, joined with the incidents of my condition, threw me into a state of suspense and wonder which frequently slackened my hand, and left the vessel to be driven by the downward current. Lights were sparingly seen, and these were perpetually fluctuating, as masts, yards, and hulls were interposed, and passed before them. In proportion as we receded from the shore, the clamours seemed to multiply, and the suggestion that the city was involved in confusion and uproar, did not easily give way to maturer thoughts. *Twelve* was the hour cried, and this ascended at once from all quarters, and was mingled with the baying of dogs, so as to produce trepidation and alarm.

From this state of magnificent and awful feeling, I was suddenly called by the conduct of Welbeck. We had scarcely moved two hundred yards from the shore, when he plunged into the water. The first conception was that some implement or part of the boat had fallen overboard. I looked back and perceived that his seat was vacant. In my first astonishment I loosened my hold of the oar, and it floated away. The surface was smooth as glass and the eddy occasioned by his sinking was scarcely visible. I had not time to determine whether this was designed or accidental. Its suddenness deprived me of the power to exert myself for his succour. I wildly gazed around me in hopes of seeing him rise. After some time my attention was drawn, by the sound of agitation in the water, to a considerable distance.

It was too dark for any thing to be distinctly seen. There was no cry for help. The noise was like that of one vigorously struggling for a moment, and then sinking to the bottom. I listened with painful eagerness, but was unable to distinguish a third signal. He sunk to rise no more.

I was, for a time, inattentive to my own situation. The

dreadfulness, and unexpectedness of this catastrophe occupied me wholly. The quick motion of the lights upon the shore, shewed me that I was borne rapidly along with the tide. How to help myself, how to impede my course, or to regain either shore, since I had lost the oar, I was unable to tell. I was no less at a loss to conjecture whither the current, if suffered to control my vehicle, would finally transport me.

The disappearance of lights and buildings, and the diminution of the noises, acquainted me that I had passed the town. It was impossible longer to hesitate. The shore was to be regained by one way only, which was swimming. To any exploit of this kind, my strength and my skill were adequate. I threw away my loose gown; put the pocket-book of the unfortunate Watson in my mouth, to preserve it from being injured by moisture; and committed myself to the stream.

I landed in a spot incommoded with mud and reeds. I sunk knee-deep into the former, and was exhausted by the fatigue of extricating myself. At length I recovered firm ground, and threw myself on the turf to repair my wasted strength, and to reflect on the measures which my future welfare enjoined me to pursue.

What condition was ever parallel to mine? The transactions of the last three days, resembled the monstrous creations of delirium. They were painted with vivid hues on my memory; but so rapid and incongruous were these transitions, that I almost denied belief to their reality. They exercised a bewildering and stupifying influence on my mind, from which the meditations of an hour were scarcely sufficient to relieve me. Gradually I recovered the power of arranging my ideas, and forming conclusions.

Welbeck was dead. His property was swallowed up, and his creditors left to wonder at his disappearance. All that was left, was the furniture of his house, to which Mrs. Wentworth would lay claim, in discharge of the unpaid rent. What now was the destiny that awaited the lost and friendless Mademoiselle Lodi. Where was she concealed?

116

Welbeck had dropped no intimation by which I might be led to suspect the place of her abode. If my power, in other respects, could have contributed aught to her relief, my ignorance of her asylum had utterly disabled me.

But what of the murdered person? He had suddenly vanished from the face of the earth. His fate and the place of his interment would probably be suspected and ascertained. Was I sure to escape from the consequences of this deed? Watson had relatives and friends. What influence on their state and happiness his untimely and mysterious fate would possess, it was obvious to inquire. This idea led me to the recollection of his pocket-book. Some papers might be there explanatory of his situation.

I resumed my feet. I knew not where to direct my steps. I was dropping with wet, and shivering with the cold. I was destitute of habitation and friend. I had neither money, nor any valuable thing in my possession. I moved forward, mechanically and at random. Where I landed was at no great distance from the verge of the town. In a short time I discovered the glimmering of a distant lamp. To this I directed my steps, and here I paused to examine the contents of the pocket-book.

I found three bank-notes, each of fifty dollars, inclosed in a piece of blank paper. Beside these were three letters, apparently written by his wife, and dated at Baltimore. They were brief, but composed in a strain of great tenderness, and containing affecting allusions to their child. I could gather from their date and tenor, that they were received during his absence on his recent voyage; that her condition was considerably necessitous, and surrounded by wants which their prolonged separation had increased.

The fourth letter was open, and seemed to have been very lately written. It was directed to Mrs. Mary Watson. He informed her in it of his arrival at Philadelphia from St. Domingo; of the loss of his ship and cargo; and of his intention to hasten home with all possible expedition. He told her that all was lost but one hundred and fifty dollars, the greater part of which he should bring with him, to

117

relieve her more pressing wants. The letter was signed, and folded, and superscribed, but unsealed.

A little consideration shewed me, in what manner it became me, on this occasion, to demean myself. I put the bank-notes in the letter, and sealed it with a wafer, a few of which were found in the pocket-book. I hesitated sometime whether I should add any thing to the information which the letter contained, by means of a pencil which offered itself to my view; but I concluded to forbear. I could select no suitable terms in which to communicate the mournful truth. I resolved to deposit this letter at the post-office, where I knew letters could be left at all hours.

My reflections at length, reverted to my own condition. What was the fate reserved for me? How far my safety might be affected by remaining in the city, in consequence of the disappearance of Welbeck, and my known connection with the fugitive, it was impossible to foresee. My fears readily suggested innumerable embarrassments and inconveniences which would flow from this source. Besides, on what pretence should I remain? To whom could I apply for protection or employment? All avenues, even to subsistence, were shut against me. The country was my sole asylum. Here, in exchange for my labour, I could at least purchase food, safety, and repose. But if my choice pointed to the country, there was no reason for a moment's delay. It would be prudent to regain the fields, and be far from this detested city before the rising of the sun.

Meanwhile I was chilled and chaffed by the clothes that I wore. To change them for others, was absolutely necessary to my ease. The clothes which I wore were not my own, and were extremely unsuitable to my new condition. My rustic and homely garb was deposited in my chamber at Welbeck's. These thoughts suggested the design of returning thither. I considered, that, probably, the servants had not been alarmed. That the door was unfastened, and the house was accessible. It would be easy to enter and retire without notice; and this, not without some waverings and misgivings, I presently determined to do.

Having deposited my letter at the office, I proceeded to

my late abode. I approached, and lifted the latch with caution. There were no appearances of any one having been disturbed. I procured a light in the kitchen, and hied softly and with dubious foot-steps to my chamber. There I disrobed, and resumed my check shirt, and trowsers, and fustian coat. This change being accomplished, nothing remained but that I should strike into the country with the utmost expedition.

In a momentary review which I took of the past, the design for which Welbeck professed to have originally detained me in his service, occurred to my mind. I knew the danger of reasoning loosely on the subject of property. To any trinket, or piece of furniture in this house, I did not allow myself to question the right of Mrs. Wentworth; a right accruing to her in consequence of Welbeck's failure in the payment of his rent; but there was one thing which I felt an irresistible desire, and no scruples which should forbid me, to possess, and that was, the manuscript to which Welbeck had alluded, as having been written by the deceased Lodi.

I was well instructed in Latin, and knew the Tuscan language to be nearly akin to it. I despaired not of being at sometime able to cultivate this language, and believed that the possession of this manuscript might essentially contribute to this end, as well as to many others equally beneficial. It was easy to conjecture that the volume was to be found among his printed books, and it was scarcely less easy to ascertain the truth of this conjecture. I entered, not without tremulous sensations, into the apartment which had been the scene of the disastrous interview between Watson and Welbeck. At every step I almost dreaded to behold the spectre of the former rise before me.

Numerous and splendid volumes were arranged on mahogany shelves, and screened by doors of glass. I ran swiftly over their names, and was at length so fortunate as to light upon the book of which I was in search. I immediately secured it, and leaving the candle extinguished on a table in the parlour, I once more issued forth into the street. With light steps and palpitating heart I turned my face towards the country. My necessitous condition I believed would justify me in passing without payment the Schuylkill bridge, and the eastern sky began to brighten with the dawn of morning not till I had gained the distance of nine miles from the city.

Such is the tale which I proposed to relate to you. Such are the memorable incidents of five days of my life; from which I have gathered more instruction than from the whole tissue of my previous existence. Such are the particulars of my knowledge respecting the crimes and misfortunes of Welbeck; which the insinuations of Wortley, and my desire to retain your good opinion, have induced me to unfold.

CHAPTER XIII

MERVYN's pause allowed his auditors to reflect on the particulars of his narration, and to compare them with the facts, with a knowledge of which, their own observation had supplied them. My profession introduced me to the friendship of Mrs. Wentworth, by whom, after the disappearance of Welbeck, many circumstances respecting him had been mentioned. She particularly dwelt upon the deportment and appearance of this youth, at the single interview which took place between them, and her representations were perfectly conformable to those which Mervyn had himself delivered.

Previously to this interview Welbeck had insinuated to her that a recent event had put him in possession of the truth respecting the destiny of Clavering. A kinsman of his, had arrived from Portugal, by whom this intelligence had been brought. He dexterously eluded her intreaties to be furnished with minuter information, or to introduce this kinsman to her acquaintance. As soon as Mervyn was ushered into her presence, she suspected him to be the person to whom Welbeck had alluded, and this suspicion his conversation had confirmed. She was at a loss to comprehend the reasons of the silence which he so pertinaciously maintained.

Her uneasiness, however, prompted her to renew her solicitations. On the day, subsequent to the catastrophe related by Mervyn, she sent a messenger to Welbeck, with a request to see him. Gabriel, the black servant, informed the messenger that his master had gone into the country for a week. At the end of the week, a messenger was again dispatched with the same errand. He called and knocked, but no one answered his signals. He examined the entrance by the kitchen, but every avenue was closed. It appeared that the house was wholly deserted.

These appearances naturally gave birth to curiosity and suspicion. The house was repeatedly examined, but the solitude and silence within continued the same. The creditors of Welbeck were alarmed by these appearances, and their claims to the property remaining in the house were precluded by Mrs. Wentworth, who, as owner of the mansion, was legally entitled to the furniture, in place of the rent which Welbeck had suffered to accumulate.

On examining the dwelling, all that was valuable and portable, particularly linen and plate, was removed. The remainder was distrained, but the tumults of pestilence succeeded, and hindered it from being sold. Things were allowed to continue in their former situation, and the house was carefully secured. We had no leisure to form conjectures on the causes of this desertion. An explanation was afforded us by the narrative of this youth. It is probable that the servants, finding their master's absence continue, had pillaged the house and fled.

Meanwhile, though our curiosity with regard to Welbeck was appeased, it was obvious to inquire by what series of inducements and events Mervyn was reconducted to the city and led to the spot where I first met with him. We intimated our wishes in this respect, and our young friend readily consented to take up the thread of his story and bring it down to the point that was desired. For this purpose, the ensuing evening was selected. Having, at an early hour, shut ourselves up from all intruders and visitors, he continued as follows:

I have mentioned that, by sun-rise, I had gained the distance of many miles from the city. My purpose was to stop at the first farm-house, and seek employment as a day-labourer. The first person whom I observed was a man of placid mien and plain garb. Habitual benevolence was apparent amidst the wrinkles of age. He was traversing his buck-wheat field and measuring, as it seemed, the harvest that was now nearly ripe.

I accosted him with diffidence, and explained my wishes. He listened to my tale with complacency, inquired into my name and family, and into my qualifications for the office to which I aspired. My answers were candid and full.

Why, said he, I believe thou and I can make a bargain. We will, at least, try each other for a week or two. If it does not suit our mutual convenience we can change. The morning is damp and cool, and thy plight does not appear the most comfortable that can be imagined. Come to the house and eat some breakfast.

The behaviour of this good man filled me with gratitude and joy. Methought I could embrace him as a father, and entrance into his house, appeared like return to a long-lost and much-loved home. My desolate and lonely condition appeared to be changed for paternal regards and the tenderness of friendship.

These emotions were confirmed and heightened by every object that presented itself under this roof. The family consisted of Mrs. Hadwin, two simple and affectionate girls, his daughters, and servants. The manners of this family, quiet, artless, and cordial, the occupations allotted me, the land by which the dwelling was surrounded, its pure airs, romantic walks, and exhaustless fertility, constituted a powerful contrast to the scenes which I had left behind, and were congenial with every dictate of my understanding and every sentiment that glowed in my heart.

My youth, mental cultivation, and circumspect deportment entitled me to deference and confidence. Each hour confirmed me in the good opinion of Mr. Hadwin, and in the affections of his daughters. In the mind of my employer, the simplicity of the husbandman and the devotion of the Quaker, were blended with humanity and intelligence. The sisters, Susan and Eliza, were unacquainted with calamity and vice, through the medium of either observation or books. They were strangers to the benefits of an elaborate education, but they were endowed with curiosity

123

and discernment, and had not suffered their slender means of instruction to remain unimproved.

The sedateness of the elder formed an amusing contrast with the laughing eye and untamable vivacity of the younger: but they smiled and they wept in unison. They thought and acted in different but not discordant keys. On all momentous occasions, they reasoned and felt alike. In ordinary cases, they separated, as it were, into different tracks; but this diversity was productive, not of jarring, but of harmony.

A romantic and untutored disposition like mine, may be supposed liable to strong impressions from perpetual converse with persons of their age and sex. The elder was soon discovered to have already disposed of her affections. The younger was free, and somewhat that is more easily conceived than named, stole insensibly upon my heart. The images that haunted me at home and abroad, in her absence and her presence, gradually coalesced into one shape, and gave birth to an incessant train of latent palpitations and indefinable hopes. My days were little else than uninterrupted reveries, and night only called up phantoms more vivid and equally enchanting.

The memorable incidents which had lately happened scarcely counterpoised my new sensations or diverted my contemplations from the present. My views were gradually led to rest upon futurity, and in that I quickly found cause of circumspection and dread. My present labours were light and were sufficient for my subsistence in a single state; but wedlock was the parent of new wants and of new cares. Mr. Hadwin's possessions were adequate to his own frugal maintenance, but divided between his children would be too scanty for either. Besides this division could only take place at his death, and that was an event whose speedy occurrence was neither desirable nor probable.

Another obstacle was now remembered. Hadwin was the consciencious member of a sect, which forbade the marriage of its votaries with those of a different communion. I had been trained in an opposite creed, and imagined it impossible that I should ever become a proselyte to

Quakerism. It only remained for me to feign conversion, or to root out the opinions of my friend, and win her consent to a secret marriage. Whether hypocrisy was eligible was no subject of deliberation. If the possession of all that ambition can conceive, were added to the transports of union with Eliza Hadwin, and offered as the price of dissimulation, it would have been instantly rejected. My external goods were not abundant nor numerous, but the consciousness of rectitude was mine, and, in competition with this, the luxury of the heart and of the senses, the gratifications of boundless ambition and inexhaustible wealth were contemptible and frivolous.

The conquest of Eliza's errors was easy; but to introduce discord and sorrow into this family, was an act of the utmost ingratitude and profligacy. It was only requisite for my understanding clearly to discern, to be convinced of the insuperability of this obstacle. It was manifest, therefore, that the point to which my wishes tended was placed beyond my reach.

To foster my passion, was to foster a disease destructive either of my integrity or my existence. It was indispensable to fix my thoughts upon a different object, and to debar myself even from her intercourse. To ponder on themes foreign to my darling image, and to seclude myself from her society, at hours which had usually been spent with her, were difficult tasks. The latter was the least practicable. I had to contend with eyes, which alternately wondered at, and upbraided me for my unkindness. She was wholly unaware of the nature of her own feelings, and this ignorance made her less scrupulous in the expression of her sentiments.

Hitherto I had needed not employment beyond myself and my companions. Now my new motives made me eager to discover some means of controlling and beguiling my thoughts. In this state, the manuscript of Lodi occurred to me. In my way hither, I had resolved to make the study of the language of this book, and the translation of its contents into English, the business and solace of my leisure. Now this resolution was revived with new force.

My project was perhaps singular. The ancient language of Italy possessed a strong affinity with the modern. My knowledge of the former, was my only means of gaining the latter. I had no grammar or vocabulary to explain how far the meanings and inflections of Tuscan words varied from the Roman dialect. I was to ponder on each sentence and phrase; to select among different conjectures the most plausible, and to ascertain the true, by patient and repeated scrutiny.

This undertaking, phantastic and impracticable as it may seem, proved upon experiment, to be within the compass of my powers. The detail of my progress would be curious and instructive. What impediments, in the attainment of a darling purpose, human ingenuity and patience are able to surmount; how much may be done by strenuous and solitary efforts; how the mind, unassisted, may draw forth the principles of inflection and arrangement; may profit by remote, analogous, and latent similitudes, would be forcibly illustrated by my example; but the theme, however attractive, must, for the present, be omitted.

My progress was slow; but the perception of hourly improvement afforded me unspeakable pleasure. Having arrived near the last pages, I was able to pursue, with little interruption, the thread of an eloquent narration. The triumph of a leader of out-laws over the popular enthusiasm of the Milanese, and the claims of neighbouring potentates, were about to be depicted. The *Condottiere* Sforza, had taken refuge from his enemies in a tomb, accidentally discovered amidst the ruins of a Roman fortress in the Apennine. He had sought this recess for the sake of concealment, but found in it a treasure, by which he would be enabled to secure the wavering and venal faith of that crew of ruffians that followed his standard, provided he fell not into the hands of the enemies who were now in search of him.

My tumultuous curiosity was suddenly checked by the following leaves being glewed together at the edges. To dissever them without injury to the written spaces, was by no means easy. I proceeded to the task, not without precipitation. The edges were torn away, and the leaves parted.

It may be thought that I took up the thread where it had been broken; but no. The object that my eyes encountered, and which the cemented leaves had so long concealed, was beyond the power of the most capricious or lawless fancy to have prefigured; yet it bore a shadowy resemblance to the images with which my imagination was previously occupied. I opened, and beheld—*a bank-note!*

To the first transports of surprise, the conjecture succeeded that the remaining leaves, cemented together in the same manner, might inclose similar bills. They were hastily separated, and the conjecture was verified. My sensations, at this discovery, were of an inexplicable kind. I gazed at the notes in silence. I moved my finger over them; held them in different positions; read and re-read the name of each sum, and the signature; added them together, and repeated to myself—*Twenty thousand dollars!* They are mine, and by such means!

This sum would have redeemed the falling fortunes of Welbeck. The dying Lodi was unable to communicate all the contents of this inestimable volume. He had divided his treasure, with a view to its greater safety, between this volume and his pocket-book. Death hasted upon him too suddenly to allow him to explain his precautions. Welbeck had placed the book in his collection, purposing sometime to peruse it; but deterred by anxieties, which the perusal would have dissipated, he rushed to desperation and suicide, from which some evanescent contingency, by unfolding this treasure to his view, would have effectually rescued him.

But was this event to be regretted? This sum, like the former, would probably have been expended in the same pernicious prodigality. His career would have continued sometime longer, but his inveterate habits would have finally conducted his existence to the same criminal and ignominious close.

But the destiny of Welbeck was accomplished. The money was placed, without guilt or artifice, in my possession. My fortune had been thus unexpectedly and wonderously propitious. How was I to profit by her favour? Would

127

not this sum enable me to gather round me all the instruments of pleasure? Equipage, and palace, and a multitude of servants; polished mirrors, splendid hangings, banquets, and flatterers, were equally abhorrent to my taste, and my principles. The accumulation of knowledge, and the diffusion of happiness, in which riches may be rendered eminently instrumental, were the only precepts of duty, and the only avenues to genuine felicity.

But what, said I, is my title to this money? By retaining it, shall I not be as culpable as Welbeck? It came into his possession as it came into mine, without a crime; but my knowledge of the true proprietor is equally certain, and the claims of the unfortunate stranger are as valid as ever. Indeed, if utility, and not law, be the measure of justice, her claim, desolate and indigent as she is, unfitted, by her past life, by the softness and the prejudices of her education, for contending with calamity, is incontestible.

As to me, health and diligence will give me, not only the competence which I seek, but the power of enjoying it. If my present condition be unchangeable, I shall not be unhappy. My occupations are salutary and meritorious; I am a stranger to the cares as well as to the enjoyment of riches; abundant means of knowledge are possessed by me, as long as I have eyes to gaze at man and at nature, as they are exhibited in their original forms or in books. The precepts of my duty cannot be mistaken. The lady must be sought and the money be restored to her.

Certain obstacles existed to the immediate execution of this scheme. How should I conduct my search? What apology should I make for withdrawing thus abruptly, and contrary to the terms of an agreement into which I had lately entered, from the family and service of my friend and benefactor, Hadwin?

My thoughts were called away from pursuing these inquiries by a rumour, which had gradually swelled to formidable dimensions; and which, at length, reached us in our quiet retreats. The city, we were told, was involved in confusion and panick, for a pestilential disease had begun its destructive progress. Magistrates and citizens were flying to the country. The numbers of the sick multiplied beyond all example; even in the pest affected cities of the Levant. The malady was malignant, and unsparing.

The usual occupations and amusements of life were at an end. Terror had exterminated all the sentiments of nature. Wives were deserted by husbands, and children by parents. Some had shut themselves in their houses, and debarred themselves from all communication with the rest of mankind. The consternation of others had destroyed their understanding, and their misguided steps hurried them into the midst of the danger which they had previously laboured to shun. Men were seized by this disease in the streets; passengers fled from them; entrance into their own dwellings was denied to them; they perished in the public ways.

The chambers of disease were deserted, and the sick left to die of negligence. None could be found to remove the lifeless bodies. Their remains, suffered to decay by piecemeal, filled the air with deadly exhalations, and added tenfold to the devastation.

Such was the tale, distorted and diversified a thousand ways, by the credulity and exaggeration of the tellers. At first I listened to the story with indifference or mirth. Methought it was confuted by its own extravagance. The enormity and variety of such an evil made it unworthy to be believed. I expected that every new day would detect the absurdity and fallacy of such representations. Every new day, however, added to the number of witnesses, and the consistency of the tale, till, at length, it was not possible to withhold my faith.

CHAPTER XIV

THIS rumour was of a nature to absorb and suspend the whole soul. A certain sublimity is connected with enormous dangers, that imparts to our consternation or our pity, a tincture of the pleasing. This, at least, may be experienced by those who are beyond the verge of peril. My own person was exposed to no hazard. I had leisure to conjure up terrific images, and to personate the witnesses and sufferers of this calamity. This employment was not enjoined upon me by necessity, but was ardently pursued, and must therefore have been recommended by some nameless charm.

Others were very differently affected. As often as the tale was embellished with new incidents, or inforced by new testimony, the hearer grew pale, his breath was stifled by inquietudes, his blood was chilled and his stomach was bereaved of its usual energies. A temporary indisposition was produced in many. Some were haunted by a melancholy bordering upon madness, and some, in consequence of sleepless panics, for which no cause could be assigned, and for which no opiates could be found, were attacked by lingering or mortal diseases.

Mr. Hadwin was superior to groundless apprehensions. His daughters, however, partook in all the consternation which surrounded them. The eldest had, indeed, abundant reason for her terror. The youth to whom she was betrothed, resided in the city. A year previous to this, he had left the house of Mr. Hadwin, who was his uncle, and had removed to Philadelphia, in pursuit of fortune.

130

He made himself clerk to a merchant, and by some mercantile adventures in which he had successfully engaged, began to flatter himself with being able, in no long time, to support a family. Meanwhile, a tender and constant correspondence was maintained between him and his beloved Susan. This girl was a soft enthusiast, in whose bosom devotion and love glowed with an ardour that has seldom been exceeded.

The first tidings of the *yellow fever*, was heard by her with unspeakable perturbation. Wallace was interrogated, by letter, respecting its truth. For a time, he treated it as a vague report. At length, a confession was extorted from him that there existed a pestilential disease in the city, but, he added, that it was hitherto confined to one quarter, distant from the place of his abode.

The most pathetic intreaties, were urged by her that he would withdraw into the country. He declared his resolution to comply when the street in which he lived should become infected, and his stay should be attended with real danger. He stated how much his interests depended upon the favour of his present employer, who had used the most powerful arguments to detain him, but declared that, when his situation should become, in the least degree, perillous, he would slight every consideration of gratitude and interest, and fly to *Malverton*. Meanwhile, he promised to communicate tidings of his safety, by every opportunity.

Belding, Mr. Hadwin's next neighbour, though not uninfected by the general panic, persisted to visit the city daily with his *market-cart*. He set out by sun-rise, and usually returned by noon. By him a letter was punctually received by Susan. As the hour of Belding's return approached, her impatience and anxiety increased. The daily epistle was received and read, in a transport of eagerness. For a while, her emotion subsided, but returned with augmented vehemence at noon on the ensuing day.

These agitations were too vehement for a feeble constitution like her's. She renewed her supplications to Wallace to quit the city. He repeated his assertions of being, hitherto, secure, and his promise of coming when the danger should be imminent. When Belding returned, and, instead of being accompanied by Wallace, merely brought a letter from him, the unhappy Susan would sink into fits of lamentation and weeping, and repel every effort to console her with an obstinacy that partook of madness. It was, at length, manifest, that Wallace's delays would be fatally injurious to the health of his mistress.

Mr. Hadwin had hitherto been passive. He conceived that the intreaties and remonstrances of his daughter were more likely to influence the conduct of Wallace, than any representations which he could make. Now, however, he wrote the contumacious Wallace a letter, in which he laid his commands upon him to return in company with Belding, and declared that by a longer delay, the youth would forfeit his favour.

The malady had, at this time, made considerable progress. Belding's interest at length yielded to his fears, and this was the last journey which he proposed to make. Hence our impatience for the return of Wallace was augmented; since, if this opportunity were lost, no suitable conveyance might again be offered him.

Belding set out, as usual, at the dawn of day. The customary interval between his departure and return, was spent by Susan, in a tumult of hopes and fears. As noon approached her suspense arose to a pitch of wildness and agony. She could scarcely be restrained from running along the road, many miles, towards the city; that she might, by meeting Belding half way, the sooner ascertain the fate of her lover. She stationed herself at a window which overlooked the road along which Belding was to pass.

Her sister, and her father, though less impatient, marked, with painful eagerness, the first sound of the approaching vehicle. They snatched a look at it as soon as it appeared in sight. Belding was without a companion.

This confirmation of her fears, overwhelmed the unhappy Susan. She sunk into a fit, from which, for a long time, her recovery was hopeless. This was succeeded by paroxysms of a furious insanity, in which she attempted to snatch any pointed implement which lay within her reach, with a view to destroy herself. These being carefully removed, or forcibly wrested from her, she resigned herself to sobs and exclamations.

Having interrogated Belding, he informed us that he occupied his usual post in the market place; that heretofore, Wallace had duly sought him out, and exchanged letters; but, that on this morning, the young man had not made his appearance; though Belding had been induced, by his wish to see him, to prolong his stay in the city, much beyond the usual period.

That some other cause than sickness had occasioned this omission, was barely possible. There was scarcely room for the most sanguine temper to indulge an hope. Wallace was without kindred, and probably without friends, in the city. The merchant, in whose service he had placed himself, was connected with him by no consideration but that of interest. What then must be his situation when seized with a malady which all believed to be contagious; and the fear of which, was able to dissolve the strongest ties that bind human beings together?

I was personally a stranger to this youth. I had seen his letters, and they bespoke, not indeed any great refinement or elevation of intelligence, but a frank and generous spirit, to which I could not refuse my esteem; but his chief claim to my affection consisted in his consanguinity to Mr. Hadwin, and his place in the affections of Susan. His welfare was essential to the happiness of those, whose happiness had become essential to mine. I witnessed the outrages of despair in the daughter, and the symptoms of a deep, but less violent grief, in the sister and parent. Was it not possible for me to alleviate their pangs? Could not the fate of Wallace be ascertained?

This disease assailed men with different degrees of malignity. In its worst form perhaps it was incurable; but in some of its modes, it was doubtless conquerable by the skill of physicians, and the fidelity of nurses. In its least formidable symptoms, negligence and solitude would render it fatal.

133

Wallace might, perhaps, experience this pest in its most lenient degree: but the desertion of all mankind; the want, not only of medicines, but of food, would irrevocably seal his doom. My imagination was incessantly pursued by the image of this youth, perishing alone, and in obscurity; calling on the name of distant friends, or invoking, ineffectually, the succour of those who were near.

Hitherto distress had been contemplated at a distance, and through the medium of a fancy delighting to be startled by the wonderful, or transported by sublimity. Now the calamity had entered my own doors, imaginary evils were supplanted by real, and my heart was the seat of commiseration and horror.

I found myself unfit for recreation or employment. I shrouded myself in the gloom of the neighbouring forest, or lost myself in the maze of rocks and dells. I endeavoured, in vain, to shut out the phantoms of the dying Wallace, and to forget the spectacle of domestic woes. At length, it occurred to me to ask, May not this evil be obviated, and the felicity of the Hadwins re-established? Wallace is friendless and succourless; but cannot I supply to him the place of protector and nurse? Why not hasten to the city, search out his abode, and ascertain whether he be living or dead? If he still retain life, may I not, by consolation and attendance, contribute to the restoration of his health, and conduct him once more to the bosom of his family?

With what transports will his arrival be hailed! How amply will their impatience and their sorrow be compensated by his return! In the spectacle of their joys, how rapturous and pure will be my delight! Do the benefits which I have received from the Hadwins demand a less retribution than this?

It is true, that my own life will be endangered; but my danger will be proportioned to the duration of my stay in this seat of infection. The death or the flight of Wallace may absolve me from the necessity of spending one night in the city. The rustics who daily frequent the market are, as experience proves, exempt from this disease; in consequence, perhaps, of limiting their continuance in the city to a few hours. May I not, in this respect, conform to their example, and enjoy a similar exemption?

My stay, however, may be longer than the day. I may be condemned to share in the common destiny. What then? Life is dependent on a thousand contingencies, not to be computed or foreseen. The seeds of an early and lingering death are sown in my constitution. It is vain to hope to escape the malady by which my mother and my brothers have died. We are a race, whose existence some inherent property has limited to the short space of twenty years. We are exposed, in common with the rest of mankind, to innumerable casualities; but if these be shunned, we are unalterably fated to perish by *consumption*. Why then should I scruple to lay down my life in the cause of virtue and humanity? It is better to die, in the consciousness of having offered an heroic sacrifice; to die by a speedy stroke, than by the perverseness of nature, in ignominious inactivity, and lingering agonies.

These considerations determined me to hasten to the city. To mention my purpose to the Hadwins would be useless or pernicious. It would only augment the sum of their present anxieties. I should meet with a thousand obstacles in the tenderness and terror of Eliza, and in the prudent affection of her father. Their arguments I should be condemned to hear, but should not be able to confute; and should only load myself with imputations of perverseness and temerity.

But how else should I explain my absence? I had hitherto preserved my lips untainted by prevarication or falsehood. Perhaps there was no occasion which would justify an untruth; but here, at least, it was superfluous or hurtful. My disappearance, if effected without notice or warning, will give birth to speculation and conjecture; but my true motives will never be suspected, and therefore will excite no fears. My conduct will not be charged with guilt. It will merely be thought upon with some regret, which will be alleviated by the opinion of my safety, and the daily expectation of my return.

But, since my purpose was to search out Wallace, I must

be previously furnished with directions to the place of his abode, and a description of his person. Satisfaction on this head was easily obtained from Mr. Hadwin; who was prevented from suspecting the motives of my curiosity, by my questions being put in a manner apparently casual. He mentioned the street, and the number of the house.

I listened with surprise. It was an house with which I was already familiar. He resided, it seems, with a merchant. Was it possible for me to be mistaken?

What, I asked, was the merchant's name?

Thetford.

This was a confirmation of my first conjecture. I recollected the extraordinary means by which I had gained access to the house and bed-chamber of this gentleman. I recalled the person and appearance of the youth by whose artifices I had been intangled in the snare. These artifices implied some domestic or confidential connection between Thetford and my guide. Wallace was a member of the family. Could it be he by whom I was betrayed?

Suitable questions easily obtained from Hadwin a description of the person and carriage of his nephew. Every circumstance evinced the identity of their persons. Wallace, then, was the engaging and sprightly youth whom I had encountered at Lesher's; and who, for purposes not hitherto discoverable, had led me into a situation so romantic and perilous.

I was far from suspecting that these purposes were criminal. It was easy to infer that his conduct proceeded from juvenile wantonness, and a love of sport. My resolution was unaltered by this disclosure; and having obtained all the information which I needed, I secretly began my journey.

My reflections, on the way, were sufficiently employed in tracing the consequences of my project; in computing the inconveniences and dangers to which I was preparing to subject myself; in fortifying my courage against the influence of rueful sights and abrupt transitions; and in imagining the measures which it would be proper to pursue in every emergency.

Connected as these views were with the family and character of Thetford, I could not but sometimes advert to

136

those incidents which formerly happened. The mercantile alliance between him and Welbeck was remembered; the allusions which were made to the condition of the latter in the chamber conversation, of which I was an unsuspected auditor; and the relation which these allusions might possess with subsequent occurrences. Welbeck's property was forfeited. It had been confided to the care of Thetford's brother. Had the case of this forfeiture been truly or thoroughly explained? Might not contraband articles have been admitted through the management, or under the connivance of the brothers; and might not the younger Thetford be furnished with the means of purchasing the captured vessel and her cargo; which, as usual, would be sold by auction at a fifth or tenth of its real value?

Welbeck was not alive to profit by the detection of this artifice, admitting these conclusions to be just. My knowledge will be useless to the world; for by what motives can I be influenced to publish the truth; or by whom will my single testimony be believed, in opposition to that plausible exterior, and, perhaps, to that general integrity which Thetford has maintained? To myself it will not be unprofitable. It is a lesson on the principles of human nature; on the delusiveness of appearances; on the perviousness of fraud; and on the power with which nature has invested human beings over the thoughts and actions of each other.

Thetford and his frauds were dismissed from my thoughts, to give place to considerations relative to Clemenza Lodi, and the money which chance had thrown into my possession. Time had only confirmed my purpose to restore these bills to the rightful proprietor, and heightened my impatience to discover her retreat. I reflected, that the means of doing this were more likely to suggest themselves at the place to which I was going than elsewhere. I might, indeed, perish before my views, in this respect, could be accomplished. Against these evils, I had at present no power to provide. While I lived, I would bear perpetually about me the volume and its precious contents. If I died, a superior power must direct the course of this as of all other events.

137

CHAPTER XV

THESE meditations did not enfeeble my resolution, or slacken my pace. In proportion as I drew near the city, the tokens of its calamitous condition became more apparent. Every farm-house was filled with supernumerary tenants; fugitives from home, and haunting the skirts of the road, eager to detain every passenger with inquiries after news. The passengers were numerous; for the tide of emigration was by no means exhausted. Some were on foot, bearing in their countenances the tokens of their recent terror, and filled with mournful reflections on the forlornness of their state. Few had secured to themselves an asylum; some were without the means of paying for victuals or lodging for the coming night; others, who were not thus destitute, yet knew not whither to apply for entertainment, every house being already over-stocked with inhabitants, or barring its inhospitable doors at their approach.

Families of weeping mothers, and dismayed children, attended with a few pieces of indispensable furniture, were carried in vehicles of every form. The parent or husband had perished; and the price of some moveable, or the pittance handed forth by public charity, had been expended to purchase the means of retiring from this theatre of disasters; though uncertain and hopeless of accommodation in the neighbouring districts.

Between these and the fugitives whom curiosity had led to the road, dialogues frequently took place, to which I was suffered to listen. From every mouth the tale of sorrow was repeated with new aggravations. Pictures of their own distress, or of that of their neighbours, were exhibited in all the hues which imagination can annex to pestilence and poverty.

My preconceptions of the evil now appeared to have fallen short of the truth. The dangers into which I was rushing, seemed more numerous and imminent than I had previously imagined. I wavered not in my purpose. A panick crept to my heart, which more vehement exertions were necessary to subdue or control; but I harboured not a momentary doubt that the course which I had taken was prescribed by duty. There was no difficulty or reluctance in proceeding. All for which my efforts were demanded, was to walk in this path without tumult or alarm.

Various circumstances had hindered me from setting out upon this journey as early as was proper. My frequent pauses to listen to the narratives of travellers, contributed likewise to procrastination. The sun had nearly set before I reached the precincts of the city. I pursued the track which I had formerly taken, and entered High-street after night-fall. Instead of equipages and a throng of passengers, the voice of levity and glee, which I had formerly observed, and which the mildness of the season would, at other times, have produced, I found nothing but a dreary solitude.

The market-place, and each side of this magnificent avenue were illuminated, as before, by lamps; but between the verge of Schuylkill and the heart of the city, I met not more than a dozen figures; and these were ghost-like, wrapt in cloaks, from behind which they cast upon me glances of wonder and suspicion; and, as I approached, changed their course, to avoid touching me. Their clothes were sprinkled with vinegar; and their nostrils defended from contagion by some powerful perfume.

I cast a look upon the houses, which I recollected to have formerly been, at this hour, brilliant with lights, resounding with lively voices, and thronged with busy faces. Now they were closed, above and below; dark, and without tokens of being inhabited. From the upper windows of some, a gleam sometimes fell upon the pavement I was traversing, and shewed that their tenants had not fled, but were secluded or disabled.

These tokens were new, and awakened all my panicks. Death seemed to hover over this scene, and I dreaded that the floating pestilence had already lighted on my frame. I had scarcely overcome these tremors, when I approached an house, the door of which was open, and before which stood a vehicle, which I presently recognized to be an *hearse.*

The driver was seated on it. I stood still to mark his visage, and to observe the course which he proposed to take. Presently a coffin, borne by two men, issued from the house. The driver was a negro, but his companions were white. Their features were marked by ferocious indifference to danger or pity. One of them as he assisted in thrusting the coffin into the cavity provided for it, said, I'll be damned if I think the poor dog was quite dead. It wasn't the *fever* that ailed him, but the sight of the girl and her mother on the floor. I wonder how they all got into that room. What carried them there?

The other surlily muttered, Their legs to be sure.

But what should they hug together in one room for?

To save us trouble to be sure.

And I thank them with all my heart; but damn it, it wasn't right to put him in his coffin before the breath was fairly gone. I thought the last look he gave me, told me to stay a few minutes.

Pshaw! He could not live. The sooner dead the better for him; as well as for us. Did you mark how he eyed us, when we carried away his wife and daughter? I never cried in my life, since I was knee-high, but curse me if I ever felt in better tune for the business than just then. Hey! continued he, looking up, and observing me standing a few paces distant, and listening to their discourse, What's wanted? Any body dead?

I stayed not to answer or parly, but hurried forward. My joints trembled, and cold drops stood on my forehead. I was ashamed of my own infirmity; and by vigorous efforts of my reason, regained some degree of composure. The evening had now advanced, and it behoved me to procure accommodation at some of the inns.

These were easily distinguished by their *signs,* but many were without inhabitants. At length, I lighted upon one, the hall of which was open, and the windows lifted. After knocking for some time, a young girl appeared, with many marks of distress. In answer to my question, she answered that both her parents were sick, and that they could receive no one. I inquired, in vain, for any other tavern at which strangers might be accommodated. She knew of none such; and left me, on some one's calling to her from above, in the midst of my embarrassment. After a moment's pause, I returned, discomforted and perplexed, to the street.

I proceeded, in a considerable degree, at random. At length, I reached a spacious building, in Fourth-street, which the sign-post shewed me to be an inn. I knocked loudly and often at the door. At length, a female opened the window of the second story, and, in a tone of peevishness, demanded what I wanted? I told her that I wanted lodging.

Go hunt for it somewhere else, said she; you'll find none here. I began to expostulate; but she shut the window with quickness, and left me to my own reflections.

I began now to feel some regret at the journey I had taken. Never, in the depth of caverns or forests, was I equally conscious of loneliness. I was surrounded by the habitations of men; but I was destitute of associate or friend. I had money, but an horse shelter, or a morsel of food, could not be purchased. I came for the purpose of relieving others, but stood in the utmost need myself. Even in health my condition was helpless and forlorn; but what would become of me, should this fatal malady be contracted. To hope that an asylum would be afforded to a sick man, which was denied to one in health, was unreasonable.

The first impulse which flowed from these reflections, was to hasten back to *Malverton*; which, with sufficient diligence, I might hope to regain before the morning light. I could not, methought, return upon my steps with too much

141

speed. I was prompted to run, as if the pest was rushing upon me, and could be eluded only by the most precipitate flight.

This impulse was quickly counteracted by new ideas. I thought with indignation and shame on the imbecility of my proceeding. I called up the images of Susan Hadwin, and of Wallace. I reviewed the motives which had led me to the undertaking of this journey. Time had, by no means, diminished their force. I had, indeed, nearly arrived at the accomplishment of what I had intended. A few steps would carry me to Thetford's habitation. This might be the critical moment, when succour was most needed, and would be most efficacious.

I had previously concluded to defer going thither till the ensuing morning; but why should I allow myself a moment's delay? I might at least gain an external view of the house, and circumstances might arise, which would absolve me from the obligation of remaining an hour longer in the city. All for which I came might be performed; the destiny of Wallace be ascertained; and I be once more safe within the precincts of *Malverton* before the return of day.

I immediately directed my steps towards the habitation of Thetford. Carriages bearing the dead were frequently discovered. A few passengers likewise occurred, whose hasty and perturbed steps, denoted their participation in the common distress. The house, of which I was in quest, quickly appeared. Light, from an upper window, indicated that it was still inhabited.

I paused a moment to reflect in what manner it became me to proceed. To ascertain the existence and condition of Wallace was the purpose of my journey. He had inhabited this house; and whether he remained in it, was now to be known. I felt repugnance to enter, since my safety might, by entering, be unawares and uselessly endangered. Most of the neighbouring houses were apparently deserted. In some there were various tokens of people being within. Might I not inquire, at one of these, respecting the condition of Thetford's family? Yet why should I disturb them by inquiries so impertinent, at this unseasonable hour? To knock at Thetford's door, and put my questions to him who should obey the signal, was the obvious method.

I knocked dubiously and lightly. No one came. I knocked again, and more loudly; I likewise drew the bell. I distinctly heard its distant peals. If any were within, my signal could not fail to be noticed. I paused, and listened, but neither voice nor foot-steps could be heard. The light, though obscured by window curtains, which seemed to be drawn close, was still perceptible.

I ruminated on the causes that might hinder my summons from being obeyed. I figured to myself nothing but the helplessness of disease, or the insensibility of death. These images only urged me to persist in endeavouring to obtain admission. Without weighing the consequences of my act, I involuntarily lifted the latch. The door yielded to my hand, and I put my feet within the passage.

Once more I paused. The passage was of considerable extent, and at the end of it I perceived light as from a lamp or candle. This impelled me to go forward, till I reached the foot of a stair-case. A candle stood upon the lowest step.

This was a new proof that the house was not deserted. I struck my heel against the floor with some violence; but this, like my former signals, was unnoticed. Having proceeded thus far, it would have been absurd to retire with my purpose uneffected. Taking the candle in my hand, I opened a door that was near. It led into a spacious parlour, furnished with profusion and splendour. I walked to and fro, gazing at the objects which presented themselves; and involved in perplexity, I knocked with my heel louder than ever; but no less ineffectually.

Notwithstanding the lights which I had seen, it was possible that the house was uninhabited. This I was resolved to ascertain, by proceeding to the chamber which I had observed, from without, to be illuminated. This chamber, as far as the comparison of circumstances would permit me to decide, I believed to be the same in which I had passed the first night of my late abode in the city. Now was I, a second

143

time, in almost equal ignorance of my situation, and of the consequences which impended exploring my way to the same recess.

I mounted the stair. As I approached the door of which I was in search, a vapour, infectious and deadly, assailed my senses. It resembled nothing of which I had ever before been sensible. Many odours had been met with, even since my arrival in the city, less insupportable than this. I seemed not so much to smell as to taste the element that now encompassed me. I felt as if I had inhaled a poisonous and subtle fluid, whose power instantly bereft my stomach of all vigour. Some fatal influence appeared to seize upon my vitals; and the work of corrosion and decomposition to be busily begun.

For a moment, I doubted whether imagination had not some share in producing my sensation; but I had not been previously panick-struck; and even now I attended to my own sensations without mental discomposure. That I had imbibed this disease was not to be questioned. So far the chances in my favour were annihilated. The lot of sickness was drawn.

Whether my case would be lenient or malignant; whether I should recover or perish, was to be left to the decision of the future. This incident, instead of appalling me, tended rather to invigorate my courage. The danger which I feared had come. I might enter with indifference, on this theatre of pestilence. I might execute without faultering, the duties that my circumstances might create. My state was no longer hazardous; and my destiny would be totally uninfluenced by my future conduct.

The pang with which I was first seized, and the momentary inclination to vomit, which it produced, presently subsided. My wholesome feelings, indeed, did not revisit me, but strength to proceed was restored to me. The effluvia became more sensible as I approached the door of the chamber. The door was ajar; and the light within was perceived. My belief, that those within were dead, was presently confuted by a sound, which I first supposed to be that

144

of steps moving quickly and timorously across the floor. This ceased, and was succeeded by sounds of different, but inexplicable import.

Having entered the apartment, I saw a candle on the hearth. A table was covered with vials and other apparatus of a sick chamber. A bed stood on one side, the curtain of which was dropped at the foot, so as to conceal any one within. I fixed my eyes upon this object. There were sufficient tokens that some one lay upon the bed. Breath, drawn at long intervals; mutterings scarcely audible; and a tremulous motion in the bedstead, were fearful and intelligible indications.

If my heart faultered, it must not be supposed that my trepidations arose from any selfish considerations. Wallace only, the object of my search, was present to my fancy. Pervaded with remembrance of the Hadwins; of the agonies which they had already endured; of the despair which would overwhelm the unhappy Susan, when the death of her lover should be ascertained; observant of the lonely condition of this house, whence I could only infer that the sick had been denied suitable attendance; and reminded by the symptoms that appeared, that this being was struggling with the agonies of death; a sickness of the heart, more insupportable than that which I had just experienced stole upon me.

My fancy readily depicted the progress and completion of this tragedy. Wallace was the first of the family on whom the pestilence had seized. Thetford had fled from his habitation. Perhaps, as a father and husband, to shun the danger attending his stay, was the injunction of his duty. It was questionless the conduct which selfish regards would dictate. Wallace was left to perish alone; or, perhaps, which indeed was a supposition somewhat justified by appearances, he had been left to the tendence of mercenary wretches; by whom, at this desperate moment he had been abandoned.

I was not mindless of the possibility that these forebodings, specious as they were, might be false. The dying person might be some other than Wallace. The whispers of my hope were, indeed, faint; but they, at least, prompted me to snatch a look at the expiring man. For this purpose, I advanced and thrust my head within the curtain.

CHAPTER XVI

THE features of one whom I had seen so transiently as Wallace, may be imagined to be not easily recognized, especially when those features were tremulous and deathful. Here, however, the differences were too conspicuous to mislead me. I beheld one to whom I could recollect none that bore resemblance. Though ghastly and livid, the traces of intelligence and beauty were undefaced. The life of Wallace was of more value to a feeble individual, but surely the being that was stretched before me and who was hastening to his last breath was precious to thousands.

Was he not one in whose place I would willingly have died? The offering was too late. His extremities were already cold. A vapour, noisome and contagious, hovered over him. The flutterings of his pulse had ceased. His existence was about to close amidst convulsion and pangs.

I withdrew my gaze from this object, and walked to a table. I was nearly unconscious of my movements. My thoughts were occupied with contemplations of the train of horrors and disasters that pursue the race of man. My musings were quickly interrupted by the sight of a small cabinet the hinges of which were broken and the lid half-raised. In the present state of my thoughts, I was prone to suspect the worst. Here were traces of pillage. Some casual or mercenary attendant, had not only contributed to hasten the death of the patient, but had rifled his property and fled.

This suspicion would, perhaps, have yielded to mature

147

reflections, if I had been suffered to reflect. A moment scarcely elapsed, when some appearance in the mirror, which hung over the table, called my attention. It was a human figure, nothing could be briefer than the glance that I fixed upon this apparition, yet there was room enough for the vague conception to suggest itself, that the dying man had started from his bed and was approaching me. This belief was, at the same instant, confuted, by the survey of his form and garb. One eye, a scar upon his cheek, a tawny skin, a form grotesquely misproportioned, brawny as Hercules, and habited in livery, composed, as it were, the parts of one view.

To perceive, to fear, and to confront this apparition were blended into one sentiment. I turned towards him with the swiftness of lightning, but my speed was useless to my safety. A blow upon my temple was succeeded by an utter oblivion of thought and of feeling. I sunk upon the floor prostrate and senseless.

My insensibility might be mistaken by observers for death, yet some part of this interval was haunted by a fearful dream. I conceived myself lying on the brink of a pit whose bottom the eye could not reach. My hands and legs were fettered, so as to disable me from resisting two grim and gigantic figures, who stooped to lift me from the earth. Their purpose methought was to cast me into this abyss. My terrors were unspeakable, and I struggled with such force, that my bonds snapt and I found myself at liberty. At this moment my senses returned and I opened my eyes.

The memory of recent events was, for a time, effaced by my visionary horrors. I was conscious of transition from one state of being to another, but my imagination was still filled with images of danger. The bottomless gulf and my gigantic persecutors were still dreaded. I looked up with eagerness. Beside me I discovered three figures, whose character or office were explained by a coffin of pine-boards which lay upon the floor. One stood with hammer and nails in his hand, as ready to replace and fasten the lid of the coffin, as soon as its burthen should be received.

I attempted to rise from the floor, but my head was dizzy and my sight confused. Perceiving me revive, one of the men, assisted me to regain my feet. The mist and confusion presently vanished, so as to allow me to stand unsupported and to move. I once more gazed at my attendants, and recognized the three men, whom I had met in High-street, and whose conversation I have mentioned that I overheard. I looked again upon the coffin. A wavering recollection of the incidents that led me hither and of the stunning blow which I had received, occurred to me. I saw into what error, appearances had misled these men, and shuddered to reflect, by what hair-breadth means I had escaped being buried alive.

Before the men had time to interrogate me, or to comment upon my situation, one entered the apartment whose habit and mein tended to incourage me. The stranger was characterised by an aspect full of composure and benignity, a face in which the serious lines of age were blended with the ruddiness and smoothness of youth, and a garb that bespoke that religious profession, with whose benevolent doctrines the example of Hadwin had rendered me familiar.

On observing me on my feet, he betrayed marks of surprise and satisfaction. He addressed me in a tone of mildness.

Young man, said he, what is thy condition? Art thou sick? If thou art, thou must consent to receive the best treatment which the times will afford. These men will convey thee to the hospital at Bush-Hill.

The mention of that contagious and abhorred receptacle, inspired me with some degree of energy. No, said I, I am not sick, a violent blow reduced me to this situation. I shall presently recover strength enough to leave this spot, without assistance.

He looked at me, with an incredulous but compassionate air: I fear thou dost deceive thyself or me. The necessity of going to the hospital is much to be regretted, but on the whole it is best. Perhaps, indeed, thou hast kindred or friends who will take care of thee.

No, said I; neither kindred nor friends. I am a stranger in the city. I do not even know a single being.

Alas! returned the stranger with a sigh, thy state is

149

sorrowful—but how camest thou hither? continued he, looking around him, and whence comest thou?

I came from the country. I reached the city, a few hours ago. I was in search of a friend who lived in this house.

Thy undertaking was strangely hazardous and rash: but who is the friend thou seekest? Was it he who died in that bed, and whose corpse has just been removed?

The men now betrayed some impatience; and inquired of the last comer, whom they called Mr. Estwick, what they were to do. He turned to me, and asked if I were willing to be conducted to the hospital?

I assured him that I was free from disease, and stood in no need of assistance; adding, that my feebleness was owing to a stunning blow received from a ruffian on my temple. The marks of this blow were conspicuous, and after some hesitation he dismissed the men; who, lifting the empty coffin on their shoulders, disappeared.

He now invited me to descend into the parlour: for, said he, the air of this room is deadly. I feel already as if I should have reason to repent of having entered it.

He now inquired into the cause of those appearances which he had witnessed. I explained my situation as clearly and succinctly as I was able.

After pondering, in silence, on my story:—I see how it is, said he: the person whom thou sawest in the agonies of death was a stranger. He was attended by his servant and an hired nurse. His master's death being certain, the nurse was dispatched by the servant to procure a coffin. He probably chose that opportunity to rifle his master's trunk, that stood upon the table. Thy unseasonable entrance interrupted him; and he designed, by the blow which he gave thee, to secure his retreat before the arrival of an hearse. I know the man, and the apparition thou hast so well described, was his. Thou sayest that a friend of thine lived in this house— Thou hast come too late to be of service. The whole family have perished—Not one was suffered to escape.

This intelligence was fatal to my hopes. It required some efforts to subdue my rising emotions. Compassion not only for Wallace, but for Thetford, his father, his wife and his

150

child, caused a passionate effusion of tears. I was ashamed of this useless and child-like sensibility; and attempted to apologize to my companion. The sympathy, however, had proved contagious, and the stranger turned away his face to hide his own tears.

Nay, said he, in answer to my excuses, there is no need to be ashamed of thy emotion. Merely to have known this family, and to have witnessed their deplorable fate, is sufficient to melt the most obdurate heart. I suspect that thou wast united to some one of this family, by ties of tenderness like those which led the unfortunate *Maravegli* hither.

This suggestion was attended, in relation to myself, with some degree of obscurity; but my curiosity was somewhat excited by the name that he had mentioned. I inquired into the character and situation of this person, and particularly respecting his connection with this family.

Maravegli, answered he, was the lover of the eldest daughter and already betrothed to her. The whole family, consisting of helpless females, had placed themselves under his peculiar guardianship. Mary Walpole and her children enjoyed in him an husband and a father.

The name of Walpole, to which I was a stranger, suggested doubts which I hastened to communicate. I am in search, said I, not of a female friend, though not devoid of interest in the welfare of Thetford and his family. My principal concern is for a youth, by name, Wallace.

He looked at me with surprise. Thetford! this is not his abode. He changed his habitation some weeks previous to the *fever*. Those who last dwelt under this roof were an English woman, and seven daughters.

This detection of my error somewhat consoled me. It was still possible that Wallace was alive and in safety. I eagerly inquired whither Thetford had removed, and whether he had any knowledge of his present condition.

They had removed to number . . ., in Market-street. Concerning their state he knew nothing. His acquaintance with Thetford was imperfect. Whether he had left the city or had remained, he was wholly uninformed.

It became me to ascertain the truth in these respects. I was

151

preparing to offer my parting thanks to the person by whom I had been so highly benefitted; since, as he now informed, it was by his interposition that I was hindered from being inclosed alive in a coffin. He was dubious of my true condition, and peremptorily commanded the followers of the hearse to desist. A delay of twenty minutes, and some medical application, would, he believed, determine whether my life was extinguished or suspended. At the end of this time, happily, my senses were recovered.

Seeing my intention to depart he inquired why, and whither I was going? Having heard my answer, Thy design resumed he, is highly indiscrete and rash. Nothing will sooner generate this fever than fatigue and anxiety. Thou hast scarcely recovered from the blow so lately received. Instead of being useful to others this precipitation will only disable thyself. Instead of roaming the streets and inhaling this unwholesome air, thou hadst better betake thyself to bed and try to obtain some sleep. In the morning, thou wilt be better qualified to ascertain the fate of thy friend, and afford him the relief which he shall want.

I could not but admit the reasonableness of these remonstrances, but where should a chamber and bed be sought? It was not likely that a new attempt to procure accommodation at the Inns would succeed better than the former.

Thy state, replied he, is sorrowful. I have no house to which I can lead thee. I divide my chamber and even my bed with another, and my landlady could not be prevailed upon to admit a stranger. What thou wilt do, I know not. This house has no one to defend it. It was purchased and furnished by the last possessor, but the whole family, including mistress, children and servants, were cut off in a single week. Perhaps, no one in America can claim the property. Meanwhile plunderers are numerous and active. An house thus totally deserted, and replenished with valuable furniture will, I fear, become their prey. To night, nothing can be done towards rendering it secure, but staying in it. Art thou willing to remain here till the morrow?

152

Every bed in the house has probably sustained a dead person. It would not be proper, therefore, to lie in any one of them. Perhaps, thou mayest find some repose upon this carpet. It is, at least, better than the harder pavement, and the open air.

This proposal, after some hesitation, I embraced. He was preparing to leave me, promising, if life were spared to him, to return early in the morning. My curiosity respecting the person whose dying agonies I had witnessed, prompted me to detain him a few minutes.

Ah! said he, this perhaps, is the only one of many victims to this pestilence whose loss the remotest generations may have reason to deplore. He was the only descendent of an illustrious house of Venice. He has been devoted from his childhood to the acquisition of knowledge and the practice of virtue. He came hither, as an enlightened observer, and after traversing the country, conversing with all the men in it eminent for their talents or their office; and collecting a fund of observations, whose solidity and justice have seldom been paralleled, he embarked, three months ago, for Europe.

Previously to his departure, he formed a tender connection with the eldest daughter of this family. The mother and her children had recently arrived from England. So many faultless women, both mentally and personally considered, it was not my fortune to meet with before. This youth well deserved to be adopted into this family. He proposed to return with the utmost expedition to his native country, and after the settlement of his affairs, to hasten back to America, and ratify his contract with Fanny Walpole.

The ship in which he embarked, had scarcely gone twenty leagues to sea, before she was disabled by a storm, and obliged to return to port. He posted to New-York, to gain a passage in a packet shortly to sail. Meanwhile this malady prevailed among us. Mary Walpole was hindered by her ignorance of the nature of that evil which assailed us, and the counsel of injudicious friends, from taking the due precautions for her safety. She hesitated to fly till flight was

153

rendered impracticable. Her death added to the helplessness and distraction of the family. They were successively
seized and destroyed by the same pest.

Maravegli was apprised of their danger. He allowed the
packet to depart without him, and hastened to the rescue of
the Walpoles from the perils which encompassed them. He
arrived in this city time enough to witness the interment of
the last survivor. In the same hour he was seized himself by
this disease: the catastrophe is known to thee.

I will now leave thee to thy repose. Sleep is no less needful
to myself than to thee: for this is the second night which has
past without it—Saying this, my companion took his leave.

I now enjoyed leisure to review my situation. I experienced no inclination to sleep. I lay down for a moment, but
my comfortless sensations and restless contemplations
would not permit me to rest. Before I entered this roof, I
was tormented with hunger, but my craving had given place
to inquietude and loathing. I paced, in thoughtful and
anxious mood, across the floor of the apartment.

I mused upon the incidents related by Estwick, upon the
exterminating nature of this pestilence, and on the horrors
of which it was productive. I compared the experience of
the last hours, with those pictures which my imagination
had drawn in the retirements of *Malverton*. I wondered at
the contrariety that exists between the scenes of the city and
the country; and fostered with more zeal than ever, the
resolution to avoid those seats of depravity and danger.

Concerning my own destiny, however, I entertained no
doubt. My new sensations assured me that my stomach had
received this corrosive poison. Whether I should die or live
was easily decided. The sickness which assiduous attendance and powerful prescriptions might remove, would, by
negligence and solitude, be rendered fatal: but from whom
could I expect medical or friendly treatment?

I had indeed a roof over my head. I should not perish in
the public way: but what was my ground for hoping to
continue under this roof? My sickness being suspected, I
should be dragged in a cart to the hospital; where I should,
indeed die; but not with the consolation of loneliness and

154

silence. Dying groans were the only music, and livid corpses were the only spectacle to which I should there be introduced.

Immured in these dreary meditations, the night passed away. The light glancing through the window awakened in my bosom a gleam of cheerfulness. Contrary to my expectations, my feelings were not more distempered, notwithstanding my want of sleep, than on the last evening. This was a token that my state was far from being so desperate as I suspected. It was possible, I thought, that this was the worst indisposition to which I was liable.

Meanwhile the coming of Estwick was impatiently expected. The sun arose, and the morning advanced, but he came not. I remembered that he talked of having reason to repent his visit to this house. Perhaps, he likewise, was sick, and that this was the cause of his delay. This man's kindness had even my love. If I had known the way to his dwelling, I should have hastened thither, to inquire into his condition, and to perform for him every office that humanity might enjoin, but he had not afforded me any information on that head.

CHAPTER XVII

I T was now incumbent on me to seek the habitation of Thetford. To leave this house accessible to every passenger appeared to be imprudent. I had no key by which I might lock the principal door. I therefore bolted it on the inside, and passed through a window, the shutters of which I closed, though I could not fasten, after me. This led me into a spacious court, at the end of which was a brick wall, over which I leaped into the street. This was the means by which I had formerly escaped from the same precincts.

The streets, as I passed, were desolate and silent. The largest computation made the number of fugitives two-thirds of the whole people; yet, judging by the universal desolation, it seemed, as if the solitude were nearly absolute. That so many of the houses were closed, I was obliged to ascribe to the cessation of traffic, which made the opening of their windows useless, and the terror of infection, which made the inhabitants seclude themselves from the observation of each other.

I proceeded to search out the house to which Estwick had directed me, as the abode of Thetford. What was my consternation when I found it to be the same, at the door of which the conversation took place, of which I had been an auditor on the last evening.

I recalled the scene, of which a rude sketch had been given by the *hearse-men*. If such were the fate of the master of the family, abounding with money and friends, what could be hoped for the moneyless and friendless Wallace? The house appeared to be vacant and silent; but these tokens might deceive. There was little room for hope; but certainty was wanting, and might, perhaps, be obtained by entering the house. In some of the upper rooms a wretched being might be immured; by whom the information, so earnestly desired, might be imparted, and to whom my presence might bring relief; not only from pestilence, but famine. For a moment, I forgot my own necessitous condition; and reflected not that abstinence had already undermined my strength.

I proceeded to knock at the door. That my signal was unnoticed, produced no surprise. The door was unlocked, and I opened. At this moment my attention was attracted by the opening of another door near me. I looked, and perceived a man issuing forth from an house at a small distance.

It now occurred to me, that the information which I sought might possibly be gained from one of Thetford's neighbours. This person was aged, but seemed to have lost neither cheerfulness nor vigour. He had an air of intrepidity and calmness. It soon appeared that I was the object of his curiosity. He had, probably, marked my deportment through some window of his dwelling, and had come forth to make inquiries into the motives of my conduct.

He courteously saluted me. You seem, said he, to be in search of some one. If I can afford you the information you want, you will be welcome to it.

Encouraged by this address, I mentioned the name of Thetford; and added my fears that he had not escaped the general calamity.

It is true, said he. Yesterday himself, his wife, and his child were in an hopeless condition. I saw them in the evening, and expected not to find them alive this morning. As soon as it was light, however, I visited the house again; but found it empty. I suppose they must have died, and been removed in the night.

Though anxious to ascertain the destiny of Wallace, I was

157

unwilling to put direct questions. I shuddered, while I longed to know the truth.

Why, said I, falteringly, did he not seasonably withdraw from the city? Surely he had the means of purchasing an asylum in the country.

I can scarcely tell you, he answered. Some infatuation appeared to have seized him. No one was more timorous; but he seemed to think himself safe, as long as he avoided contact with infected persons. He was likewise, I believe, detained by a regard to his interest. His flight would not have been more injurious to his affairs, than it was to those of others; but gain was, in his eyes, the supreme good. He intended ultimately to withdraw; but his escape to-day, gave him new courage to encounter the perils of to-morrow. He deferred his departure from day to day, till it ceased to be practicable.

His family, said I, was numerous. It consisted of more than his wife and children. Perhaps these retired in sufficient season.

Yes, said he; his father left the house at an early period. One or two of the servants likewise forsook him. One girl, more faithful and heroic than the rest, resisted the remonstrances of her parents and friends, and resolved to adhere to him in every fortune. She was anxious that the family should fly from danger, and would willingly have fled in their company; but while they stayed, it was her immovable resolution not to abandon them.

Alas, poor girl! She knew not of what stuff the heart of Thetford was made. Unhappily, she was the first to become sick. I question much whether her disease was pestilential. It was, probably, a slight indisposition; which, in a few days, would have vanished of itself, or have readily yielded to suitable treatment.

Thetford was transfixed with terror. Instead of summoning a physician, to ascertain the nature of her symptoms, he called a negro and his cart from Bush-hill. In vain the neighbours interceded for this unhappy victim. In vain she implored his clemency, and asserted the lightness of her indisposition. She besought him to allow her to send to her mother, who resided a few miles in the country, who would hasten to her succour, and relieve him and his family from the danger and trouble of nursing her.

The man was lunatic with apprehension. He rejected her intreaties, though urged in a manner that would have subdued an heart of flint. The girl was innocent, and amiable, and courageous, but entertained an unconquerable dread of the hospital. Finding intreaties ineffectual, she exerted all her strength in opposition to the man who lifted her into the cart.

Finding that her struggles availed nothing, she resigned herself to despair. In going to the hospital, she believed herself led to certain death, and to the sufferance of every evil which the known inhumanity of its attendants could inflict. This state of mind, added to exposure to a noon-day sun, in an open vehicle, moving, for a mile, over a rugged pavement, was sufficient to destroy her. I was not surprised to hear that she died the next day.

This proceeding was sufficiently iniquitous; yet it was not the worst act of this man. The rank and education of the young woman, might be some apology for negligence; but his clerk, a youth who seemed to enjoy his confidence, and to be treated by his family, on the footing of a brother or son, fell sick on the next night, and was treated in the same manner.

These tidings struck me to the heart. A burst of indignation and sorrow filled my eyes. I could scarcely stifle my emotion sufficiently to ask, Of whom, sir, do you speak? Was the name of the youth—his name—was—

His name was Wallace. I see that you have some interest in his fate. He was one whom I loved. I would have given half my fortune to procure him accommodation under some hospitable roof. His attack was violent; but still, his recovery, if he had been suitably attended, was possible. That he should survive removal to the hospital, and the treatment he must receive when there, was not to be hoped.

The conduct of Thetford was as absurd as it was wicked. To imagine this disease to be contagious was the height of folly; to suppose himself secure, merely by not permitting a sick man to remain under his roof, was no less stupid; but Thetford's fears had subverted his understanding. He did not listen to arguments or supplications. His attention was incapable of straying from one object. To influence him by words was equivalent to reasoning with the deaf.

Perhaps the wretch was more to be pitied than hated. The victims of his implacable caution, could scarcely have endured agonies greater than those which his pusillanimity inflicted on himself. Whatever be the amount of his guilt, the retribution has been adequate. He witnessed the death of his wife and child, and last night was the close of his own existence. Their sole attendant was a black woman; whom, by frequent visits, I endeavoured, with little success, to make diligent in the performance of her duty.

Such, then, was the catastrophe of Wallace. The end for which I journeyed hither was accomplished. His destiny was ascertained; and all that remained was to fulfil the gloomy predictions of the lovely, but unhappy Susan. To tell them all the truth, would be needlesly to exasperate her sorrow. Time, aided by the tenderness and sympathy of friendship, may banish her despair, and relieve her from all but the witcheries of melancholy.

Having disengaged my mind from these reflections, I explained to my companion in general terms, my reasons for visiting the city, and my curiosity respecting Thetford. He inquired into the particulars of my journey, and the time of my arrival. When informed that I had come in the preceding evening, and had passed the subsequent hours without sleep or food, he expressed astonishment and compassion.

Your undertaking, said he, has certainly been hazardous. There is poison in every breath which you draw, but this hazard has been greatly increased by abstaining from food and sleep. My advice is to hasten back into the country; but you must first take some repose and some victuals. If you pass Schuylkill before night-fall, it will be sufficient.

I mentioned the difficulty of procuring accommodation on the road. It would be most prudent to set out upon my journey so as to reach *Malverton* at night. As to food and sleep they were not to be purchased in this city.

True, answered my companion, with quickness, they are

not to be bought, but I will furnish you with as much as you desire of both for nothing. That is my abode, continued he, pointing to the house, which he had lately left. I reside with a widow lady and her daughter, who took my counsel, and fled in due season. I remain to moralize upon the scene, with only a faithful black, who makes my bed, prepares my coffee, and bakes my loaf. If I am sick, all that a physician can do, I will do for myself, and all that a nurse can perform, I expect to be performed by *Austin.*

Come with me, drink some coffee, rest a while on my matrass, and then fly, with my benedictions on your head.

These words were accompanied by features disembarrassed and benevolent. My temper is alive to social impulses, and I accepted his invitation, not so much because I wished to eat or to sleep, but because I felt reluctance to part so soon with a being, who possessed so much fortitude and virtue.

He was surrounded by neatness and plenty. Austin added dexterity to submissiveness. My companion, whose name I now found to be Medlicote, was prone to converse, and commented on the state of the city like one whose reading had been extensive and experience large. He combatted an opinion which I had casually formed, respecting the origin of this epidemic, and imputed it, not to infected substances imported from the east or west, but to a morbid constitution of the atmosphere, owing wholly, or in part to filthy streets, airless habitations and squalid persons.

As I talked with this man, the sense of danger was obliterated, I felt confidence revive in my heart, and energy revisit my stomach. Though far from my wonted health, my sensation grew less comfortless, and I found myself to stand in no need of repose.

Breakfast being finished, my friend pleaded his daily engagements as reasons for leaving me. He counselled me to strive for some repose, but I was conscious of incapacity to sleep. I was desirous of escaping, as soon as possible, from this tainted atmosphere and reflected whether any thing remained to be done respecting Wallace.

It now occurred to me that this youth must have left some

clothes and papers, and, perhaps, books. The property of these was now vested in the Hadwins. I might deem myself, without presumtion, their representative or agent. Might I not take some measures for obtaining possession, or at least, for the security of these articles?

The house and its furniture was tenantless and unprotected. It was liable to be ransacked and pillaged by those desperate ruffians, of whom many were said to be hunting for spoil, even at a time like this. If these should overlook this dwelling, Thetford's unknown successor or heir might appropriate the whole. Numberless accidents might happen to occasion the destruction or embezzlement of what belonged to Wallace, which might be prevented by the conduct which I should now pursue.

Immersed in these perplexities, I remained bewildered and motionless. I was at length roused by some one knocking at the door. Austin obeyed the signal, and instantly returned, leading in—Mr. Hadwin!

I know not whether this unlooked-for interview excited on my part, most grief or surprize. The motive of his coming was easily divined. His journey was on two accounts superfluous. He whom he sought was dead. The duty of ascertaining his condition, I had assigned to myself.

I now perceived and deplored the error of which I had been guilty, in concealing my intended journey from my patron. Ignorant of the part I had acted, he had rushed into the jaws of this pest, and endangered a life unspeakably valuable to his children and friends. I should doubtless have obtained his grateful consent to the project which I had conceived; but my wretched policy had led me into this clandestine path. Secrecy may seldom be a crime. A virtuous intention may produce it; but surely it is always erroneous and pernicious.

My friend's astonishment at the sight of me, was not inferior to my own. The causes which led to this unexpected interview were mutually explained. To soothe the agonies of his child, he consented to approach the city, and endeavour to procure intelligence of Wallace. When he left his house, he intended to stop in the environs, and hire some

162

emissary, whom an ample reward might tempt to enter the city, and procure the information which was needed.

No one could be prevailed upon to execute so dangerous a service. Averse to return without performing his commission, he concluded to examine for himself. Thetford's removal to this street was known to him; but, being ignorant of my purpose, he had not mentioned this circumstance to me, during our last conversation.

I was sensible of the danger which Hadwin had incurred by entering the city. Perhaps, my knowledge or the inexpressible importance of his life, to the happiness of his daughters, made me aggravate his danger. I knew that the longer he lingered in this tainted air, the hazard was increased. A moment's delay was unnecessary. Neither Wallace nor myself were capable of being benefitted by his presence.

I mentioned the death of his nephew, as a reason for hastening his departure. I urged him in the most vehement terms to remount his horse and to fly; I endeavoured to preclude all inquiries respecting myself or Wallace; promising to follow him immediately, and answer all his questions at *Malverton*. My importunities were inforced by his own fears, and after a moment's hesitation, he rode away.

The emotions produced by this incident, were, in the present critical state of my frame, eminently hurtful. My morbid indications suddenly returned. I had reason to ascribe my condition to my visit to the chamber of Maravegli, but this, and its consequences, to myself, as well as the journey of Hadwin, were the fruits of my unhappy secrecy.

I had always been accustomed to perform my journeys on foot. This, on ordinary occasions, was the preferable method, but now I ought to have adopted the easiest and swiftest means. If Hadwin had been acquainted with my purpose he would not only have approved, but would have allowed me the use of an horse. These reflections were rendered less pungent by the recollection that my motives were benevolent, and that I had endeavoured the benefit of others by means, which appeared to me most suitable.

Meanwhile, how was I to proceed? What hindered me

163

from pursuing the foot-steps of Hadwin with all the expedition which my uneasiness, of brain and stomach would allow? I conceived that to leave any thing undone, with regard to Wallace, would be absurd. His property might be put under the care of my new friend. But how was it to be distinguished from the property of others? It was, probably, contained in trunks, which was designated by some label or mark. I was unacquainted with his chamber, but, by passing from one to the other, I might finally discover it. Some token, directing my foot-steps, might occur, though at present unforeseen.

Actuated by these considerations, I once more entered Thetford's habitation. I regretted that I had not procured the counsel or attendance of my new friend, but some engagements, the nature of which he did not explain, occasioned him to leave me as soon as breakfast was finished.

CHAPTER XVIII

I WANDERED over this deserted mansion, in a considerable degree, at random. Effluvia of a pestilential nature, assailed me from every corner. In the front room of the second story, I imagined that I discovered vestiges of that catastrophe which the past night had produced. The bed appeared as if some one had recently been dragged from it. The sheets were tinged with yellow, and with that substance which is said to be characteristic of this disease, the gangrenous or black vomit. The floor exhibited similar stains.

There are many, who will regard my conduct as the last refinement of temerity, or of heroism. Nothing, indeed, more perplexes me than a review of my own conduct. Not, indeed, that death is an object always to be dreaded, or that my motive did not justify my actions; but of all dangers, those allied to pestilence, by being mysterious and unseen, are the most formidable. To disarm them of their terrors, requires the longest familiarity. Nurses and physicians soonest become intrepid or indifferent; but the rest of mankind recoil from the scene with unconquerable loathing.

I was sustained, not by confidence of safety, and a belief of exemption from this malady, or by the influence of habit, which inures us to all that is detestable or perilous, but by a belief that this was as eligible an avenue to death as any other; and that life is a trivial sacrifice in the cause of duty.

I passed from one room to the other. A portmanteau,

165

marked with the initials of Wallace's name, at length attracted my notice. From this circumstance I inferred, that this apartment had been occupied by him. The room was neatly arranged, and appeared as if no one had lately used it. There were trunks and drawers. That which I have mentioned, was the only one that bore marks of Wallace's ownership. This I lifted in my arms with a view to remove it to Medlicote's house.

At that moment, methought I heard a foot-step slowly and lingeringly ascending the stair. I was disconcerted at this incident. The foot-step had in it a ghost-like solemnity and tardiness. This phantom vanished in a moment, and yielded place to more humble conjectures. A human being approached, whose office and commission were inscrutable. That we were strangers to each other was easily imagined; but how would my appearance, in this remote chamber, and loaded with another's property, be interpreted? Did he enter the house after me, or was he the tenant of some chamber hitherto unvisited; whom my entrance had awakened from his trance and called from his couch?

In the confusion of my mind, I still held my burthen uplifted. To have placed it on the floor, and encountered this visitant, without this equivocal token about me, was the obvious proceeding. Indeed, time only could decide whether these foot-steps tended to this, or to some other apartment.

My doubts were quickly dispelled. The door opened, and a figure glided in. The portmanteau dropped from my arms, and my heart's-blood was chilled. If an apparition of the dead were possible, and that possibility I could not deny, this was such an apparition. A hue, yellowish and livid; bones, uncovered with flesh; eyes, ghastly, hollow, woebegone, and fixed in an agony of wonder upon me; and locks, matted and negligent, constituted the image which I now beheld. My belief of somewhat preternatural in this appearance, was confirmed by recollection of resemblances between these features and those of one who was dead. In this shape and visage, shadowy and death-like as they were, the lineaments of Wallace, of him who had misled my rustic simplicity on my first visit to this city, and whose death I had conceived to be incontestably ascertained, were forcibly recognized.

This recognition, which at first alarmed my superstition, speedily led to more rational inferences. Wallace had been dragged to the hospital. Nothing was less to be suspected than that he would return alive from that hideous receptacle, but this was by no means impossible. The figure that stood before me, had just risen from the bed of sickness, and from the brink of the grave. The crisis of his malady had passed, and he was once more entitled to be ranked among the living.

This event, and the consequences which my imagination connected with it, filled me with the liveliest joy. I thought not of his ignorance of the causes of my satisfaction, of the doubts to which the circumstances of our interview would give birth, respecting the integrity of my purpose. I forgot the artifices by which I had formerly been betrayed, and the embarrassments which a meeting with the victim of his artifices would excite in him; I thought only of the happiness which his recovery would confer upon his uncle and his cousins.

I advanced towards him with an air of congratulation, and offered him my hand. He shrunk back, and exclaimed in a feeble voice, Who are you? What business have you here?

I am the friend of Wallace, if he will allow me to be so. I am a messenger from your uncle and cousins at *Malverton*. I came to know the cause of your silence, and to afford you any assistance in my power.

He continued to regard me with an air of suspicion and doubt. These I endeavoured to remove by explaining the motives that led me hither. It was with difficulty that he seemed to credit my representations. When thoroughly convinced of the truth of my assertions, he inquired with great anxiety and tenderness concerning his relations; and expressed his hope that they were ignorant of what had befallen him.

I could not encourage his hopes. I regretted my own precipitation in adopting the belief of his death. This belief, had been uttered with confidence, and without stating my reasons for embracing it, to Mr. Hadwin. These tidings would be borne to his daughters, and their grief would be exasperated to a deplorable, and, perhaps, to a fatal degree.

There was but one method of repairing or eluding this mischief. Intelligence ought to be conveyed to them of his recovery. But where was the messenger to be found? No one's attention could be found disengaged from his own concerns. Those who were able or willing to leave the city had sufficient motives for departure, in relation to themselves. If vehicle or horse were procurable for money, ought it not to be secured for the use of Wallace himself, whose health required the easiest and speediest conveyance from this theatre of death?

My companion was powerless in mind as in limbs. He seemed unable to consult upon the means of escaping from the inconveniences by which he was surrounded. As soon as sufficient strength was regained, he had left the hospital. To repair to *Malverton* was the measure which prudence obviously dictated; but he was hopeless of effecting it. The city was close at hand; this was his usual home; and hither his tottering, and almost involuntary steps had conducted him.

He listened to my representations and councils, and acknowledged their propriety. He put himself under my protection and guidance, and promised to conform implicitly to my directions. His strength had sufficed to bring him thus far, but was now utterly exhausted. The task of searching for a carriage and horse devolved upon me.

In effecting this purpose, I was obliged to rely upon my own ingenuity and diligence. Wallace, though so long a resident in the city, knew not to whom I could apply, or by whom carriages were let to hire. My own reflections taught me, that this accommodation was most likely to be furnished by innkeepers, or that some of those might at least inform me of the best measures to be taken. I resolved to set out immediately on this search. Meanwhile, Wallace was persuaded to take refuge in Medlicote's apartments; and to make, by the assistance of Austin, the necessary preparation for his journey.

The morning had now advanced. The rays of a sultry sun had a sickening and enfeebling influence, beyond any which I had ever experienced. The drought of unusual duration had bereft the air and the earth of every particle of moisture. The element which I breathed appeared to have stagnated into noxiousness and putrifaction. I was astonished at observing the enormous diminution of my strength. My brows were heavy, my intellects benumbed, my sinews enfeebled, and my sensations universally unquiet.

These prognostics were easily interpreted. What I chiefly dreaded was, that they would disable me from executing the task which I had undertaken. I summoned up all my resolution, and cherished a disdain of yielding to this ignoble destiny. I reflected that the source of all energy, and even of life, is seated in thought; that nothing is arduous to human efforts; that the external frame will seldom languish, while actuated by an unconquerable soul.

I fought against my dreary feelings, which pulled me to the earth. I quickened my pace, raised my drooping eyelids, and hummed a cheerful and favourite air. For all that I accomplished during this day, I believe myself indebted to the strenuousness and ardour of my resolutions.

I went from one tavern to another. One was deserted; in another the people were sick, and their attendants refused to hearken to my inquiries or offers; at a third, their horses were engaged. I was determined to prosecute my search as long as an inn or a livery-stable remained unexamined, and my strength would permit.

To detail the events of this expedition, the arguments and supplications which I used to overcome the dictates of avarice and fear, the fluctuation of my hopes and my incessant disappointments, would be useless. Having exhausted all my expedients ineffectually, I was compelled to turn my weary steps once more to Medlicote's lodgings.

My meditations were deeply engaged by the present circumstances of my situation. Since the means which were first suggested, were impracticable, I endeavoured to investigate others. Wallace's debility made it impossible for him to perform this journey on foot: but would not his strength and his resolution suffice to carry him beyond Schuylkill? A carriage or horse, though not to be obtained in the city, could, without difficulty, be procured, in the country. Every farmer had beasts for burthen and draught. One of these might be hired at no immoderate expense, for half a day.

This project appeared so practicable and so specious, that I deeply regretted the time and the efforts which had already been so fruitlessly expended. If my project, however, had been mischievous, to review it with regret, was only to prolong and to multiply its mischiefs. I trusted that time and strength would not be wanting to the execution of this new design.

On entering Medlicote's house, my looks, which, in spite of my languors, were sprightly and confident, flattered Wallace with the belief that my exertions had succeeded. When acquainted with their failure, he sunk as quickly into hopelessness. My new expedient was heard by him with no marks of satisfaction. It was impossible, he said, to move from this spot by his own strength. All his powers were exhausted by his walk from Bush-hill.

I endeavoured, by arguments and railleries, to revive his courage. The pure air of the country would exhilirate him into new life. He might stop at every fifty yards, and rest upon the green sod. If overtaken by the night, we would procure a lodging, by address and importunity; but if every door should be shut against us, we should at least, enjoy the shelter of some barn, and might diet wholsomely upon the new-laid eggs that we should find there. The worst treatment we could meet with, was better than continuance in the city.

These remonstrances had some influence, and he at length consented to put his ability to the test. First, however, it was necessary to invigorate himself by a few hours rest. To this, though with infinite reluctance, I consented.

This interval allowed him to reflect upon the past, and to

inquire into the fate of Thetford and his family. The intelligence, which Medlicote had enabled me to afford him, was heard with more satisfaction than regret. The ingratitude and cruelty with which he had been treated, seemed to have extinguished every sentiment, but hatred and vengeance. I was willing to profit by this interval to know more of Thetford, than I already possessed. I inquired why Wallace, had so perversely neglected the advice of his uncle and cousin, and persisted to brave so many dangers when flight was so easy.

I cannot justify my conduct, answered he. It was in the highest degree, thoughtless and perverse. I was confident and unconcerned as long as our neighbourhood was free from disease, and as long as I forbore any communication with the sick; yet I should have withdrawn to Malverton, merely to gratify my friends, if Thetford had not used the most powerful arguments to detain me. He laboured to extenuate the danger.

Why not stay, said he, as long as I and my family stay? Do you think that we would linger here, if the danger were imminent. As soon as it becomes so, we will fly. You know that we have a country-house prepared for our reception. When we go, you shall accompany us. Your services at this time are indispensable to my affairs. If you will not desert me, your salary next year shall be double; and that will enable you to marry your cousin immediately. Nothing is more improbable than that any of us should be sick, but if this should happen to you, I plight my honour that you shall be carefully and faithfully attended.

These assurances were solemn and generous. To make Susan Hadwin my wife, was the scope of all my wishes and labours. By staying I should hasten this desirable event, and incur little hazard. By going, I should alienate the affections of Thetford; by whom, it is but justice to acknowledge, that I had hitherto been treated with unexampled generosity and kindness; and blast all the schemes I had formed for rising into wealth.

My resolution was by no means stedfast. As often as a letter from *Malverton* arrived, I felt myself disposed to hasten away, but this inclination was combated by new arguments and new intreaties of Thetford.

In this state of suspense, the girl by whom Mrs. Thetford's infant was nursed, fell sick. She was an excellent creature, and merited better treatment than she received. Like me, she resisted the persuasions of her friends, but her motives for remaining were disinterested and heroic.

No sooner did her indisposition appear, than she was hurried to the hospital. I saw that no reliance could be placed upon the assurances of Thetford. Every consideration gave way to his fear of death. After the girl's departure, though he knew that she was led by his means to execution,—yet he consoled himself with repeating and believing her assertions, that her disease was not *the fever*.

I was now greatly alarmed for my own safety. I was determined to encounter his anger and repel his persuasions; and to depart with the market-man, next morning. That night, however, I was seized with a violent fever. I knew in what manner patients were treated at the hospital, and removal thither was to the last degree abhorred.

The morning arrived, and my situation was discovered. At the first intimation, Thetford rushed out of the house, and refused to re-enter it till I was removed. I knew not my fate, till three ruffians made their appearance at my bedside, and communicated their commission.

I called on the name of Thetford and his wife. I intreated a moment's delay, till I had seen these persons, and endeavoured to procure a respite from my sentence. They were deaf to my intreaties, and prepared to execute their office by force. I was delirious with rage and with terror. I heaped the bitterest execrations on my murderer; and by turns, invoked the compassion, and poured a torrent of reproaches on, the wretches whom he had selected for his ministers. My struggles and outcries were vain.

I have no perfect recollection of what passed till my arrival at the hospital. My passions combined with my disease, to make me frantic and wild. In a state like mine, the slightest motion could not be indured without agony. What then must I have felt, scorched and dazled by the sun,

sustained by hard boards, and borne for miles over a rugged pavement?

I cannot make you comprehend the anguish of my feelings. To be disjointed and torn piece-meal by the rack, was a
torment inexpressibly inferior to this. Nothing excites my
wonder, but that I did not expire before the cart had moved
three paces.

I knew not how, or by whom I was moved from this
vehicle. Insensibility came at length to my relief. After a
time I opened my eyes, and slowly gained some knowledge
of my situation. I lay upon a mattress, whose condition
proved that an half-decayed corpse had recently been
dragged from it. The room was large, but it was covered
with beds like my own. Between each, there was scarcely the
interval of three feet. Each sustained a wretch, whose
groans and distortions, bespoke the desperateness of his
condition.

The atmosphere was loaded by mortal stenches. A vapour, suffocating and malignant, scarcely allowed me to
breathe. No suitable receptacle was provided for the evacu-
ations produced by medicine or disease. My nearest
neighbour was struggling with death, and my bed, casually
extended, was moist with the detestable matter which had
flowed from his stomach.

You will scarcely believe that, in this scene of horrors, the
sound of laughter should be overheard. While the upper
rooms of this building, are filled with the sick and the dying,
the lower apartments are the scene of carrousals and mirth.
The wretches who are hired, at enormous wages, to tend
the sick and convey away the dead, neglect their duty and
consume the cordials, which are provided for the patients,
in debauchery and riot.

A female visage, bloated with malignity and drunkenness, occasionally looked in. Dying eyes were cast upon her,
invoking the boon, perhaps, of a drop of cold water, or her
assistance to change a posture which compelled him to
behold the ghastly writhings or deathful *smile* of his
neighbour.

The visitant had left the banquet for a moment, only to

see who was dead. If she entered the room, blinking eyes and reeling steps, shewed her to be totally unqualified for ministering the aid that was needed. Presently, she disappeared and others ascended the stair-case, a coffin was deposited at the door, the wretch, whose heart still quivered, was seized by rude hands, and dragged along the floor into the passage.

O! how poor are the conceptions which are formed, by the fortunate few, of the sufferings to which millions of their fellow beings are condemned. This misery was more frightful, because it was seen to flow from the depravity of the attendants. My own eyes only would make me credit the existence of wickedness so enormous. No wonder that to die in garrets and cellars and stables, unvisited and unknown, had, by so many, been preferred to being brought hither.

A physician cast an eye upon my state. He gave some directions to the person who attended him. I did not comprehend them, they were never executed by the nurses, and if the attempt had been made, I should probably have refused to receive what was offered. Recovery was equally beyond my expectations and my wishes. The scene which was hourly displayed before me, the entrance of the sick, most of whom perished in a few hours, and their departure to the graves prepared for them, reminded me of the fate to which I, also, was reserved.

Three days passed away, in which every hour was expected to be the last. That, amidst an atmosphere so contagious and deadly, amidst causes of distruction hourly accumulating, I should yet survive, appears to me nothing less than miraculous. That of so many conducted to this house, the only one who passed out of it alive, should be myself, almost surpasses my belief.

Some inexplicable principle rendered harmless those potent enemies of human life. My fever subsided and vanished. My strength was revived, and the first use that I made of my limbs, was to bear me far from the contemplation and sufferance of those evils.

174

CHAPTER XIX

AVING gratified my curiosity in this respect, Wallace proceeded to remind me of the circumstances of our first interview. He had entertained doubts whether I was the person, whom he had met at Lesher's. I acknowledged myself to be the same, and inquired, in my turn, into the motives of his conduct on that occasion.

I confess, said he, with some hesitation, I meant only to sport with your simplicity and ignorance. You must not imagine, however, that my stratagem was deep-laid and deliberately executed. My professions at the tavern were sincere. I meant not to injure but to serve you. It was not till I reached the head of the stair-case, that the mischievous contrivance occurred. I foresaw nothing, at the moment, but ludicrous mistakes and embarrassment. The scheme was executed almost at the very moment it occurred.

After I had returned to the parlour, Thetford charged me with the delivery of a message in a distant quarter of the city. It was not till I had performed this commission, and had set out on my return, that I fully revolved the consequences likely to flow from my project.

That Thetford and his wife would detect you in their bed-chamber was unquestionable. Perhaps, weary of my long delay, you would have fairly undressed and gone to bed. The married couple would have made preparation to follow you, and when the curtain was undrawn, would discover a robust youth, fast asleep, in their place. These images, which had just before excited my laughter, now produced a very different emotion. I dreaded some fatal

175

catastrophe from the fiery passions of Thetford. In the first transports of his fury he might pistol you, or, at least, might command you to be dragged to prison.

I now heartily repented of my jest and hastened home that I might prevent, as far as possible, the evil effects that might flow from it. The acknowledgment of my own agency in this affair, would at least, transfer Thetford's indignation to myself to whom it was equitably due.

The married couple had retired to their chamber, and no alarm or confusion had followed. This was an inexplicable circumstance. I waited with impatience till the morning should furnish a solution of the difficulty. The morning arrived. A strange event, had, indeed, taken place in their bed-chamber. They found an infant asleep in their bed. Thetford had been roused twice in the night, once by a noise in the closet and, afterwards, by a noise at the door.

Some connection between these sounds and the foundling, was naturally suspected. In the morning the closet was examined, and a coarse pair of shoes was found on the floor. The chamber door, which Thetford had locked in the evening, was discovered to be open, as likewise a window in the kitchen.

These appearances were a source of wonder and doubt to others, but were perfectly intelligible to me. I rejoiced that my stratagem had no more dangerous consequence, and admired the ingenuity and perseverance with which you had extricated yourself from so critical a state.

This narrative was only the verification of my own guesses. Its facts were quickly supplanted in my thoughts by the disastrous picture he had drawn of the state of the hospital. I was confounded and shocked by the magnitude of this evil. The cause of it was obvious. The wretches whom money could purchase, were of course, licentious and unprincipled; superintended and controlled they might be useful instruments, but that superintendence could not be bought.

What qualities were requisite in the governor of such an institution? He must have zeal, diligence and perseverance. He must act from lofty and pure motives. He must be mild and firm, intrepid and compliant. One perfectly qualified for the office it is desirable, but not possible, to find. A dispassionate and honest zeal in the cause of duty and humanity, may be of eminent utility. Am I not endowed with this zeal? Cannot my feeble efforts obviate some portion of this evil?

No one has hitherto claimed this disgustful and perillous situation. My powers and discernment are small, but if they be honestly exerted they cannot fail to be somewhat beneficial.

The impulse, produced by these reflections, was to hasten to the City-hall, and make known my wishes. This impulse was controlled by recollections of my own indisposition, and of the state of Wallace. To deliver this youth to his friends was the strongest obligation. When this was discharged, I might return to the city, and acquit myself of more comprehensive duties.

Wallace had now enjoyed a few hours rest, and was persuaded to begin the journey. It was now noon-day, and the sun darted insupportable rays. Wallace was more sensible than I of their unwholesome influence. We had not reached the suburbs, when his strength was wholly exhausted, and had I not supported him, he would have sunk upon the pavement.

My limbs were scarcely less weak, but my resolutions were much more strenuous than his. I made light of his indisposition, and endeavoured to persuade him that his vigour would return in proportion to his distance from the city. The moment we should reach a shade, a short respite would restore us to health and cheerfulness.

Nothing could revive his courage or induce him to go on. To return or to proceed was equally impracticable. But, should he be able to return, where should he find a retreat! The danger of relapse was imminent: his own chamber at Thetford's was unoccupied. If he could regain this house, might I not procure him a physician and perform for him the part of nurse.

His present situation was critical and mournful. To remain in the street, exposed to the malignant fervours of the sun, was not to be endured. To carry him in my arms, exceeded my strength. Should I not claim the assistance of the first passenger that appeared?

At that moment a horse and chaise passed us. The vehicle proceeded at a quick pace. He that rode in it might afford us the succour that we needed. He might be persuaded to deviate from his course and convey the helpless Wallace to the house we had just left.

This thought instantly impelled me forward. Feeble as I was, I even ran with speed, in order to overtake the vehicle. My purpose was effected with the utmost difficulty. It fortunately happened that the carriage contained but one person, who stopped at my request. His countenance and guise was mild and encouraging.

Good friend, I exclaimed, here is a young man too indisposed to walk. I want him carried to his lodgings. Will you, for money or for charity, allow him a place in your chaise, and set him down where I shall direct? Observing tokens of hesitation, I continued, you need have no fears to perform this office. He is not sick, but merely feeble. I will not ask twenty minutes, and you may ask what reward you think proper.

Still he hesitated to comply. His business, he said, had not led him into the city. He merely passed along the skirts of it, whence he conceived that no danger would arise. He was desirous of helping the unfortunate, but he could not think of risqueing his own life, in the cause of a stranger, when he had a wife and children depending on his existence and exertions, for bread. It gave him pain to refuse, but he thought his duty to himself and to others required that he should not hazard his safety by compliance.

This plea was irresistable. The mildness of his manner shewed, that he might have been overpowered by persuasion or tempted by reward. I would not take advantage of his tractability; but should have declined his assistance, even if it had been spontaneously offered. I turned away from him in silence, and prepared to return to the spot where I had left my friend. The man prepared to resume his way.

In this perplexity, the thought occurred to me, that, since

this person was going into the country, he might, possibly, consent to carry Wallace along with him. I confided greatly in the salutary influence of rural airs. I believed that debility constituted the whole of his complaint; that continuance in the city might occasion his relapse, or, at least, procrastinate his restoration.

I once more addressed myself to the traveller, and inquired in what direction, and how far he was going. To my unspeakable satisfaction, his answer informed me, that his home lay beyond Mr. Hadwin's, and that his road carried him directly past that gentleman's door. He was willing to receive Wallace into his chaise, and to leave him at his uncle's.

This joyous and auspicious occurrence surpassed my fondest hopes. I hurried with the pleasing tidings to Wallace, who eagerly consented to enter the carriage. I thought not at the moment of myself, or how far the same means of escaping from my danger might be used. The stranger could not be anxious on my account; and Wallace's dejection and weakness may apologize for his not soliciting my company, or expressing his fears for my safety. He was no sooner seated, than the traveller hurried away. I gazed after them, motionless and mute, till the carriage turning a corner, passed beyond my sight.

I had now leisure to revert to my own condition, and to ruminate on that series of abrupt and diversified events that had happened, during the few hours which had been passed in the city: the end of my coming was thus speedily and satisfactorily accomplished. My hopes and fears had rapidly fluctuated; but, respecting this young man, had now subsided into calm and propitious certainty. Before the decline of the sun, he would enter his paternal roof, and diffuse ineffable joy throughout that peaceful and chaste asylum.

This contemplation, though rapturous and soothing speedily gave way to reflections on the conduct which my duty required, and the safe departure of Wallace, afforded me liberty to pursue. To offer myself as a superintendent of the hospital was still my purpose. The languors of my frame might terminate in sickness, but this event it was useless to anticipate. The lofty scite and pure airs of Bush-hill might tend to dissipate my languors and restore me to health. At least, while I had power, I was bound to exert it to the wisest purposes. I resolved to seek the City-hall immediately, and, for that end, crossed the intermediate fields which separated Sassafras from Chesnut-street.

More urgent considerations had diverted my attention from the money which I bore about me, and from the image of the desolate lady to whom it belonged. My intentions, with regard to her, were the same as ever; but now it occurred to me, with new force, that my death might preclude an interview between us, and that it was prudent to dispose, in some useful way, of the money which would otherwise be left to the sport of chance.

The evils which had befallen this city were obvious and enormous. Hunger and negligence had exasperated the malignity and facilitated the progress of the pestilence. Could this money be more usefully employed than in alleviating these evils? During my life, I had no power over it, but my death would justify me in prescribing the course which it should take.

How was this course to be pointed out? How might I place it, so that I should effect my intentions without relinquishing the possession during my life.

These thoughts were superseded by a tide of new sensations. The weight that incommoded my brows and my stomach was suddenly increased. My brain was usurped by some benumbing power, and my limbs refused to support me. My pulsations were quickened, and the prevalence of fever could no longer be doubted.

Till now, I had entertained a faint hope, that my indisposition would vanish of itself. This hope was at an end. The grave was before me, and my projects of curiosity or benevolence were to sink into oblivion. I was not bereaved of the powers of reflection. The consequences of lying in the road, friendless and unprotected, were sure. The first passenger would notice me, and hasten to summon one of those carriages which are busy night and day, in transporting its victims to the hospital.

This fate was, beyond all others, abhorrent to my imagination. To hide me under some roof, where my existence would be unknown and unsuspected, and where I might perish unmolested and in quiet, was my present wish. Thetford's or Medlicote's might afford me such an asylum, if it were possible to reach it.

I made the most strenuous exertions; but they could not carry me forward more than an hundred paces. Here I rested on steps, which, on looking up, I perceived to belong to Welbeck's house.

This incident was unexpected. It led my reflections into a new train. To go farther, in the present condition of my frame, was impossible. I was well acquainted with this dwelling. All its avenues were closed. Whether it had remained unoccupied since my flight from it, I could not decide. It was evident that, at present, it was without inhabitants. Possibly it might have continued in the same condition in which Welbeck had left it. Beds or sofas might be found, on which a sick man might rest, and be fearless of intrusion.

This inference was quickly overturned by the obvious supposition, that every avenue was bolted and locked. This, however, might not be the condition of the bath-house, in which there was nothing that required to be guarded with unusual precautions. I was suffocated by inward, and scorched by external heat; and the relief of bathing and drinking, appeared inestimable.

The value of this prize, in addition to my desire to avoid the observation of passengers, made me exert all my remnant of strength. Repeated efforts at length enabled me to mount the wall; and placed me, as I imagined, in security. I swallowed large draughts of water as soon as I could reach the well.

The effect was, for a time, salutary and delicious. My fervours were abated, and my faculties relieved from the weight which had lately oppressed them. My present condition was unspeakably more advantageous than the former. I did not believe that it could be improved, till, casting my eye vaguely over the building, I happened to observe the shutters of a lower window partly opened.

Whether this was occasioned by design or by accident

there was no means of deciding. Perhaps, in the precipitation of the latest possessor, this window had been overlooked. Perhaps it had been unclosed by violence, and afforded entrance to a robber. By what means soever it had happened, it undoubtedly afforded ingress to me. I felt no scruple in profiting by this circumstance. My purposes were not dishonest. I should not injure or purloin any thing. It was laudable to seek a refuge from the well-meant persecutions of those who governed the city. All I sought was the privilege of dying alone.

Having gotten in at the window, I could not but remark that the furniture and its arrangements had undergone no alteration in my absence. I moved softly from one apartment to another, till at length I entered, that which had formerly been Welbeck's bed-chamber.

The bed was naked of covering. The cabinets and closets exhibited their fastenings broken. Their contents were gone. Whether these appearances had been produced by midnight robbers or by the ministers of law, and the rage of the creditors of Welbeck, was a topic of fruitless conjecture.

My design was now effected. This chamber should be the scene of my disease and my refuge from the charitable cruelty of my neighbours. My new sensations, conjured up the hope that my indisposition might prove a temporary evil. Instead of pestilential or malignant fever it might be an harmless intermittent. Time would ascertain its true nature; meanwhile I would turn the carpet into a coverlet, supplying my pitcher with water, and administer without sparing, and without fear, that remedy which was placed within my reach.

CHAPTER XX

I LAID myself on the bed and wrapped my limbs in the folds of the carpet. My thoughts were restless and perturbed. I was once more busy in reflecting on the conduct which I ought to pursue, with regard to the bank-bills. I weighed with scrupulous attention, every circumstance that might influence my decision. I could not conceive any more beneficial application of this property, than to the service of the indigent, at this season of multiplied distress, but I considered that if my death were unknown, the house would not be opened or examined till the pestilence had ceased, and the benefits of this application would thus be partly or wholly precluded.

This season of disease, however, would give place to a season of scarcity. The number and wants of the poor, during the ensuing winter, would be deplorably aggravated. What multitudes might be rescued from famine and nakedness by the judicious application of this sum?

But how should I secure this application? To inclose the bills in a letter, directed to some eminent citizen or public officer, was the obvious proceeding. Both of these conditions were fulfilled in the person of the present chief magistrate. To him, therefore, the packet was to be sent.

Paper and the implements of writing were necessary for this end. Would they be found, I asked, in the upper room? If that apartment, like the rest which I had seen, and its furniture had remained untouched, my task would be practicable, but if the means of writing were not to be immediately procured, my purpose, momentous and dear as it was, must be relinquished.

The truth, in this respect, was easily, and ought immediately to be ascertained. I rose from the bed which I had lately taken, and proceeded to the *study*. The entries and stair cases were illuminated by a pretty strong twilight. The rooms, in consequence of every ray being excluded by the closed shutters, were nearly as dark as if it had been midnight. The rooms into which I had already passed, were locked, but its key was in each lock. I flattered myself that the entrance into the *study* would be found in the same condition. The door was shut but no key was to be seen. My hopes were considerably damped by this appearance, but I conceived it to be still possible to enter, since, by chance or by design, the door might be unlocked.

My fingers touched the lock, when a sound was heard as if a bolt, appending to the door on the inside, had been drawn. I was startled by this incident. It betokened that the room was already occupied by some other, who desired to exclude a visitor. The unbarred shutter below was remembered, and associated itself with this circumstance. That this house should be entered by the same avenue, at the same time, and this room should be sought, by two persons was a mysterious concurrence.

I began to question whether I had heard distinctly. Numberless inexplicable noises are apt to assail the ear in an empty dwelling. The very echoes of our steps are unwonted and new. This perhaps was some such sound. Resuming courage, I once more applied to the lock. The door, in spite of my repeated efforts, would not open.

My design was too momentous to be readily relinquished. My curiosity and my fears likewise were awakened. The marks of violence, which I had seen on the closets and cabinets below, seemed to indicate the presence of plunderers. Here was one who laboured for seclusion and concealment.

The pillage was not made upon my property. My weakness would disable me from encountering or mastering a man of violence. To solicit admission into this room would be useless. To attempt to force my way would be absurd. These reflections prompted me to withdraw from the door, but the uncertainty of the conclusions I had drawn, and the importance of gaining access to this apartment, combined to check my steps.

Perplexed as to the means I should employ, I once more tried the lock. This attempt was as fruitless as the former. Though hopeless of any information to be gained by that means, I put my eye to the key-hole. I discovered a light different from what was usually met with at this hour. It was not the twilight which the sun, imperfectly excluded, produces, but gleams, as from a lamp; yet gleams were fainter and obscurer than a lamp generally imparts.

Was this a confirmation of my first conjecture? Lamp-light at noon-day, in a mansion thus deserted, and in a room which had been the scene of memorable and disastrous events, was ominous. Hitherto no direct proof had been given of the presence of an human being. How to ascertain his presence, or whether it were eligible by any means, to ascertain it, were points on which I had not deliberated.

I had no power to deliberate. My curiosity, impelled me to call—Is there any one within? Speak.

These words were scarcely uttered, when some one exclaimed, in a voice, vehement but half-smothered— Good God!—

A deep pause succeeded. I waited for an answer: for somewhat to which this emphatic invocation might be a prelude. Whether the tones were expressive of surprise or pain, or grief, was, for a moment dubious. Perhaps the motives which led me to this house, suggested the suspicion, which, presently succeeded to my doubts, that the person within was disabled by sickness. The circumstances of my own condition took away the improbability from this belief. Why might not another be induced like me to hide himself in this desolate retreat? Might not a servant, left to take care of the house, a measure usually adopted by the opulent at this time, be seized by the reigning malady? Incapacitated for exertion, or fearing to be dragged to the hospital, he has shut himself in this apartment. The robber, it may be,

185

who came to pillage, was overtaken and detained by disease. In either case, detection or intrusion would be hateful, and would be assiduously eluded.

These thoughts had no tendency to weaken or divert my efforts to obtain access to this room. The person was a brother in calamity, whom it was my duty to succour and cherish to the utmost of my power. Once more I spoke:—

Who is within? I beseech you answer me. Whatever you be, I desire to do you good and not injury. Open the door and let me know your condition. I will try to be of use to you.

I was answered by a deep groan, and by a sob counteracted and devoured as it were by a mighty effort. This token of distress thrilled to my heart. My terrors wholly disappeared, and gave place to unlimited compassion. I again intreated to be admitted, promising all the succour or consolation which my situation allowed me to afford.

Answers were made in tones of anger and impatience, blended with those of grief—I want no succour—vex me not with your entreaties and offers. Fly from this spot: Linger not a moment lest you participate my destiny and rush upon your death.

These, I considered merely as the effusions of delirium, or the dictates of despair. The style and articulation denoted the speaker to be superior to the class of servants. Hence my anxiety to see and to aid him was increased. My remonstrances were sternly and pertinaciously repelled. For a time, incoherent and impassioned exclamations flowed from him. At length, I was only permitted to hear strong aspirations and sobs, more eloquent and more indicative of grief than any language.

This deportment filled me with no less wonder than commiseration. By what views this person was led hither, by what motives induced to deny himself to my intreaties, was wholly incomprehensible. Again, though hopeless of success, I repeated my request to be admitted.

My perseverance seemed now to have exhausted all his patience, and he exclaimed, in a voice of thunder—Arthur Mervyn! Begone. Linger but a moment and my rage, tyger-like, will rush upon you and rend you limb from limb.

186

This address petrified me. The voice that uttered this sanguinary menace, was strange to my ears. It suggested no suspicion of ever having heard it before. Yet my accents had betrayed me to him. He was familiar with my name. Notwithstanding the improbability of my entrance into this dwelling, I was clearly recognized and unhesitatingly named!

My curiosity and compassion were in no wise diminished, but I found myself compelled to give up my purpose—I withdrew reluctantly from the door, and once more threw myself upon my bed. Nothing was more necessary in the present condition of my frame, than sleep; and sleep had, perhaps, been possible, if the scene around me had been less pregnant with causes of wonder and panic.

Once more I tasked my memory in order to discover, in the persons with whom I had hitherto conversed, some resemblance in voice or tones, to him whom I had just heard. This process was effectual. Gradually my imagination called up an image, which now, that it was clearly seen, I was astonished had not instantly occurred. Three years ago, a man, by name Colvill, came on foot, and with a knapsack on his back, into the district where my father resided. He had learning and genius, and readily obtained the station for which only he deemed himself qualified; that of a schoolmaster.

His demeanour was gentle and modest; his habits, as to sleep, food, and exercise, abstemious and regular. Meditation in the forest, or reading in his closet, seemed to constitute, together with attention to his scholars, his sole amusement and employment. He estranged himself from company, not because society afforded no pleasure, but because studious seclusion afforded him chief satisfaction.

No one was more idolized by his unsuspecting neighbours. His scholars revered him as a father, and made under his tuition a remarkable proficiency. His character seemed open to boundless inspection, and his conduct was pronounced by all to be faultless.

At the end of a year the scene was changed. A daughter of one of his patrons, young, artless and beautiful, appeared

187

to have fallen a prey to the arts of some detestable seducer. The betrayer was gradually detected, and successive discoveries shewed that the same artifices had been practised, with the same success upon many others. Colvill was the arch-villain. He retired from the storm of vengeance that was gathering over him, and had not been heard of since that period.

I saw him rarely, and for a short time, and I was a mere boy. Hence, the failure to recollect his voice, and to perceive that the voice of him, immured in the room above, was the same with that of Colvill. Though I had slight reasons for recognizing his features, or accents, I had abundant cause to think of him with detestation, and pursue him with implacable revenge, for the victim of his arts, she whose ruin was first detected, was—*my sister*.

This unhappy girl, escaped from the upbraidings of her parents, from the contumelies of the world, from the goadings of remorse, and the anguish flowing from the perfidy and desertion of Colvill, in a voluntary death. She was innocent and lovely. Previous to this evil, my soul was linked with her's by a thousand resemblances and sympathies, as well as by perpetual intercourse from infancy, and by the fraternal relation. She was my sister, my preceptress and friend, but she died—her end was violent, untimely, and criminal!—I cannot think of her without heart-bursting grief, of her destroyer, without a rancour which I know to be wrong, but which I cannot subdue.

When the image of Colvill rushed, upon this occasion, on my thought, I almost started on my feet. To meet him, after so long a separation, here, and in these circumstances, was so unlooked-for and abrupt an event, and revived a tribe of such hateful impulses and agonizing recollections, that a total revolution seemed to have been effected in my frame. His recognition of my person, his aversion to be seen, his ejaculation of terror and surprise on first hearing my voice, all contributed to strengthen my belief.

How was I to act? My feeble frame could but illy second my vengeful purposes; but vengeance, though it sometimes occupied my thoughts, was hindered by my reason, from leading me in any instance, to outrage or even to upbraiding.

All my wishes with regard to this man, were limited to expelling his image from my memory, and to shunning a meeting with him. That he had not opened the door at my bidding, was now a topic of joy. To look upon some bottomless pit, into which I was about to be cast headlong, and alive, was less to be abhorred than to look upon the face of Colvill. Had I known that he had taken refuge in this house, no power should have compelled me to enter it. To be immersed in the infection of the hospital, and to be hurried, yet breathing and observant, to my grave, was a more supportable fate.

I dwell, with self-condemnation and shame, upon this part of my story. To feel extraordinary indignation at vice, merely because we have partaken in an extraordinary degree, of its mischiefs, is unjustifiable. To regard the wicked with no emotion but pity, to be active in reclaiming them, in controlling their malevolence, and preventing or repairing the ills which they produce, is the only province of duty. This lesson, as well as a thousand others, I have yet to learn; but I despair of living long enough for that or any beneficial purpose.

My emotions with regard to Colvill, were erroneous, but omnipotent. I started from my bed, and prepared to rush into the street. I was careless of the lot that should befal me, since no fate could be worse than that of abiding under the same roof with a wretch spotted with so many crimes.

I had not set my feet upon the floor before my precipitation was checked by a sound from above. The door of the study was cautiously and slowly opened. This incident admitted only of one construction, supposing all obstructions removed. Colvill was creeping from his hiding place, and would probably fly with speed from the house. My belief of his sickness was now confuted. An illicit design was congenial with his character and congruous with those appearances already observed.

I had no power or wish to obstruct his flight. I thought of it with transport and once more threw myself upon the bed, and wrapped my averted face in the carpet. He would probably pass this door, unobservant of me, and my muffled face would save me from the agonies connected with the sight of him.

The foot-steps above were distinguishable, though it was manifest that they moved with lightsomeness and circumspection. They reached the stair and descended. The room in which I lay, was, like the rest, obscured by the closed shutters. This obscurity now gave way to a light, resembling that glimmering and pale reflection which I had noticed in the study. My eyes, though averted from the door, were disengaged from the folds which covered the rest of my head, and observed these tokens of Colvill's approach, flitting on the wall.

My feverish perturbations increased as he drew nearer. He reached the door, and stopped. The light rested for a moment. Presently he entered the apartment. My emotions suddenly rose to an height that would not be controlled. I imagined that he approached the bed, and was gazing upon me. At the same moment, by an involuntary impulse, I threw off my covering, and, turning my face, fixed my eyes upon my visitant.

It was as I suspected. The figure, lifting in his right hand a candle, and gazing at the bed, with lineaments and attitude, bespeaking fearful expectation and tormenting doubts, was now beheld. One glance communicated to my senses all the parts of this terrific vision. A sinking at my heart, as if it had been penetrated by a dagger, seized me. This was not enough. I uttered a shriek, too rueful and loud not to have startled the attention of the passengers, if any had, at that moment been passing the street.

Heaven seemed to have decreed that this period should be filled with trials of my equanimity and fortitude. The test of my courage was once more employed to cover me with humiliation and remorse. This second time, my fancy conjured up a spectre, and I shuddered as if the grave were forsaken and the unquiet dead haunted my pillow.

The visage and the shape had indeed preternatural attitudes, but they belonged, not to Colvill, but to— WELBECK.

190

CHAPTER XXI

H E whom I had accompanied to the midst of the
river; whom I had imagined that I saw sink to rise
no more, was now before me. Though incapable
of precluding the groundless belief of preternatural visitations, I was able to banish the phantom almost at the same
instant at which it appeared. Welbeck had escaped from the
stream alive; or had, by some inconceivable means, been
restored to life.

The first was the most plausible conclusion. It instantly
engendered a suspicion, that his plunging into the water
was an artifice, intended to establish a belief of his death.
His own tale had shewn him to be versed in frauds, and
flexible to evil. But was he not associated with Colvill; and
what, but a compact in iniquity, could bind together such
men?

While thus musing, Welbeck's countenance and gesture
displayed emotions too vehement for speech. The glances
that he fixed upon me were unstedfast and wild. He walked
along the floor, stopping at each moment, and darting looks
of eagerness upon me. A conflict of passions kept him mute.
At length, advancing to the bed, on the side of which I was
now sitting, he addressed me.

What is this? Are you here? In defiance of pestilence, are
you actuated by some demon to haunt me, like the ghost of
my offences, and cover me with shame? What have I to do
with that dauntless, yet guileless front? With that foolishly,
confiding, and obsequious, yet erect and unconquerable

191

spirit? Is there no means of evading your pursuit? Must I dip my hands, a second time, in blood; and dig for you a grave by the side of Watson?

These words were listened to with calmness. I suspected and pitied the man, but I did not fear him. His words and his looks were indicative less of cruelty than madness. I looked at him with an air compassionate and wistful. I spoke with mildness and composure.

Mr. Welbeck, you are unfortunate and criminal. Would to God I could restore you to happiness and virtue; but though my desire be strong, I have no power to change your habits or rescue you from misery.

I believed you to be dead. I rejoice to find myself mistaken. While you live, there is room to hope that your errors will be cured; and the turmoils, and inquietudes that have hitherto beset your guilty progress, will vanish by your reverting into better paths.

From me you have nothing to fear. If your welfare will be promoted by my silence on the subject of your history, my silence shall be inviolate. I deem not lightly of my promises. They are given and shall not be recalled.

This meeting was casual. Since I believed you to be dead, it could not be otherwise. You err, if you suppose that any injury will accrue to you from my life; but you need not discard that error. Since my death is coming, I am not averse to your adopting the belief that the event is fortunate to you.

Death is the inevitable and universal lot. When or how it comes, is of little moment. To stand, when so many thousands are falling around me, is not to be expected. I have acted an humble and obscure part in the world, and my career has been short; but I murmur not at the decree that makes it so.

The pestilence is now upon me. The chances of recovery are too slender to deserve my confidence. I came hither to die unmolested, and at peace. All I ask of you is to consult your own safety by immediate flight; and not to disappoint my hopes of concealment, by disclosing my condition to the agents of the hospital.

Welbeck listened with the deepest attention. The wildness of his air disappeared, and gave place to perplexity and apprehension.

You are sick, said he, in a tremulous tone, in which terror was mingled with affection. You know this, and expect not to recover. No mother, nor sister, nor friend will be near to administer food, or medicine, or comfort; yet you can talk calmly; can be thus considerate of others—of me; whose guilt has been so deep, and who has merited so little at your hands!

Wretched coward! Thus miserable as I am, and expect to be, I cling to life. To comply with your heroic counsel, and to fly; to leave you thus desolate and helpless, is the strongest impulse. Fain would I resist it but cannot.

To desert you would be flagitious and dastardly beyond all former acts, yet to stay with you is to contract the disease and to perish after you.

Life, burthened as it is, with guilt and ignominy, is still dear—yet you exhort me to go; you dispense with my assistance. Indeed, I could be of no use, I should injure myself and profit you nothing. I cannot go into the city and procure a physician or attendant. I must never more appear in the streets of this city. I must leave you then—He hurried to the door. Again, he hesitated. I renewed my intreaties that he would leave me; and encouraged his belief that his presence might endanger himself without conferring the slightest benefit upon me.

Whither should I fly? The wide world contains no asylum for me. I lived but on one condition. I came hither to find what would save me from ruin—from death. I find it not. It has vanished. Some audacious and fortunate hand has snatched it from its place, and now my ruin is complete. My last hope is extinct.

Yes. Mervyn! I will stay with you. I will hold your head. I will put water to your lips. I will watch night and day by your side. When you die, I will carry you by night to the neighbouring field: will bury you, and water your grave with those tears that are due to your incomparable worth and untimely destiny. Then I will lay myself in your bed and wait for the same oblivion.

Welbeck seemed now no longer to be fluctuating between

opposite purposes. His tempestuous features subsided into calm. He put the candle, still lighted on the table, and paced the floor with less disorder than at his first entrance.

His resolution was seen to be the dictate of despair. I hoped that it would not prove invincible to my remonstrances. I was conscious that his attendance might preclude, in some degree, my own exertions, and alleviate the pangs of death; but these consolations might be purchased too dear. To receive them at the hazard of his life would be to make them odious.

But if he should remain, what conduct would his companion pursue? Why did he continue in the study when Welbeck had departed? By what motives were those men led hither? I addressed myself to Welbeck.

Your resolution to remain is hasty and rash. By persisting in it, you will add to the miseries of my condition; you will take away the only hope that I cherished. But, however you may act, Colvill or I must be banished from this roof. What is the league between you? Break it, I conjure you; before his frauds have involved you in inextricable destruction.

Welbeck looked at me with some expression of doubt.

I mean, continued I, the man whose voice I heard above. He is a villain and betrayer. I have manifold proofs of his guilt. Why does he linger behind you? However you may decide, it is fitting that he should vanish.

Alas! said Welbeck, I have no companion; none to partake with me in good or evil. I came hither alone.

How? exclaimed I. Whom did I hear in the room above? Some one answered my interrogations and intreaties, whom I too certainly recognized. Why does he remain?

You heard no one but myself. The design that brought me hither, was to be accomplished without a witness. I desired to escape detection, and repelled your solicitations for admission in a counterfeited voice.

That voice belonged to one from whom I had lately parted. What his merits or demerits are, I know not. He found me wandering in the forests of New-Jersey. He took me to his home. When seized by a lingering malady, he nursed me with fidelity, and tenderness. When somewhat recovered, I speeded hither; but our ignorance of each other's character and views was mutual and profound.

I deemed it useful to assume a voice different from my own. This was the last which I had heard, and this arbitrary and casual circumstance decided my choice.

This imitation was too perfect, and had influenced my fears too strongly, to be easily credited. I suspected Welbeck of some new artifice to baffle my conclusions and mislead my judgment. This suspicion, however, yielded to his earnest and repeated declarations. If Colvill were not here, where had he made his abode? How came friendship and intercourse between Welbeck and him? By what miracle escaped the former from the river, into which I had imagined him forever sunk?

I will answer you, said he, with candour. You know already too much for me to have any interest in concealing any part of my life. You have discovered my existence, and the causes that rescued me from destruction may be told without detriment to my person or fame.

When I leaped into the river, I intended to perish. I harboured no previous doubts of my ability to execute my fatal purpose. In this respect I was deceived. Suffocation would not come at my bidding. My muscles and limbs rebelled against my will. There was a mechanical repugnance to the loss of life which I could not vanquish. My struggles might thrust me below the surface, but my lips were spontaneously shut and excluded the torrent from my lungs. When my breath was exhausted, the efforts that kept me at the bottom were involuntarily remitted, and I rose to the surface.

I cursed my own pusillanimity. Thrice I plunged to the bottom and as often rose again. My aversion to life swiftly diminished, and at length, I consented to make use of my skill in swimming, which has seldom been exceeded, to prolong my existence. I landed in a few minutes on the Jersey shore.

This scheme being frustrated, I sunk into dreariness and

inactivity. I felt as if no dependence could be placed upon my courage, as if any effort I should make for self-destruction would be fruitless; yet existence was as void as ever of enjoyment and embellishment. My means of living were annihilated. I saw no path before me. To shun the presence of mankind was my sovereign wish. Since I could not die, by my own hands, I must be content to crawl upon the surface, till a superior fate should permit me to perish.

I wandered into the centre of the wood. I stretched myself on the mossy verge of a brook, and gazed at the stars till they disappeared. The next day was spent with little variation. The cravings of hunger were felt, and the sensation was a joyous one, since it afforded me the practicable means of death. To refrain from food was easy, since some efforts would be needful to procure it, and these efforts should not be made. Thus was the sweet oblivion for which I so earnestly panted, placed within my reach.

Three days of abstinence, and reverie, and solitude succeeded. On the evening of the fourth, I was seated on a rock, with my face buried in my hands. Some one laid his hand upon my shoulder. I started and looked up. I beheld a face, beaming with compassion and benignity. He endeavoured to extort from me the cause of my solitude and sorrow. I disregarded his intreaties, and was obstinately silent.

Finding me invincible in this respect, he invited me to his cottage, which was hard by. I repelled him at first, with impatience and anger, but he was not to be discouraged or intimidated. To elude his persuasions I was obliged to comply. My strength was gone and the vital fabric was crumbling into pieces. A fever raged in my veins, and I was consoled by reflecting that my life was at once assailed by famine and disease.

Meanwhile, my gloomy meditations experienced no respite. I incessantly ruminated on the events of my past life. The long series of my crimes arose daily and afresh to my imagination. The image of Lodi was recalled, his expiring looks and the directions which were mutually given respecting his sister and his property.

As I perpetually revolved these incidents, they assumed

new forms, and were linked with new assocations. The volume written by his father, and transferred to me by tokens, which were now remembered to be more emphatic than the nature of the composition seemed to justify, was likewise remembered. It came attended by recollections respecting a volume which I filled, when a youth, with extracts from the Roman and Greek poets. Besides this literary purpose I likewise used to preserve the bank-bills, with the keeping or carriage of which I chanced to be intrusted. This image led me back to the leather-case containing Lodi's property, which was put into my hands at the same time with the volume.

These images now gave birth to a third conception, which darted on my benighted understanding like an electrical flash. Was it possible that part of Lodi's property might be inclosed within the leaves of this volume? In hastily turning it over, I recollected to have noticed leaves whose edges by accident or design adhered to each other. Lodi, in speaking of the sale of his father's West-Indian property, mentioned that the sum obtained for it, was forty thousand dollars. Half only of this sum had been discovered by me. How had the remainder been appropriated? Surely this volume contained it.

The influence of this thought was like the infusion of a new soul into my frame. From torpid and desperate, from inflexible aversion to medicine and food, I was changed in a moment into vivacity and hope, into ravenous avidity for whatever could contribute to my restoration to health.

I was not without pungent regrets and racking fears. That this volume would be ravished away by creditors or plunderers, was possible. Every hour might be that which decided my fate. The first impulse was to seek my dwelling and search for this precious deposit.

Meanwhile, my perturbations and impatience only exasperated my disease. While chained to my bed, the rumour of pestilence was spread abroad. This event, however generally calamitous, was propitious to me, and was hailed with satisfaction. It multiplied the chances that my house and its furniture would be unmolested.

My friend was assiduous and indefatigable in his kind-

197

ness. My deportment, before and subsequent to the revival of my hopes, was incomprehensible, and argued nothing less than insanity. My thoughts were carefully concealed from him, and all that he witnessed was contradictory and unintelligible.

At length, my strength was sufficiently restored. I resisted all my protector's importunities, to postpone my departure till the perfect confirmation of my health. I designed to enter the city at midnight, that prying eyes might be eluded; to bear with me a candle and the means of lighting it, to explore my way to my ancient study, and to ascertain my future claim to existence and felicity.

I crossed the river this morning. My impatience would not suffer me to wait till evening. Considering the desolation of the city, I thought I might venture to approach thus near, without hazard of detection. The house, at all its avenues was closed. I stole into the back-court. A window-shutter proved to be unfastened. I entered, and discovered closets and cabinets, unfastened and emptied of all their contents. At this spectacle my heart sunk. My books, doubtless, had shared the common destiny. My blood throbbed with painful vehemence as I approached the study and opened the door.

My hopes, that languished for a moment, were revived by the sight of my shelves, furnished as formerly. I had lighted my candle below, for I desired not to awaken observation and suspicion, by unclosing the windows. My eye eagerly sought the spot where I remembered to have left the volume. Its place was empty. The object of all my hopes had eluded my grasp, and disappeared forever.

To paint my confusion, to repeat my execrations on the infatuation, which had rendered, during so long a time, that it was in my possession, this treasure useless to me, and my curses of the fatal interference which had snatched away this prize, would be only aggravations of my disappointment and my sorrow. You found me in this state, and know what followed.

CHAPTER XXII

THIS narrative threw new light on the character of Welbeck. If accident had given him possession of this treasure, it was easy to predict on what schemes of luxury and selfishness it would have been expended. The same dependence on the world's erroneous estimation, the same devotion to imposture, and thoughtlessness of futurity, would have constituted the picture of his future life, as had distinguished the past.

This money was another's. To retain it for his own use was criminal. Of this crime he appeared to be as insensible as ever. His own gratification was the supreme law of his actions. To be subjected to the necessity of honest labour, was the heaviest of all evils, and one from which he was willing to escape by the commission of suicide.

The volume which he sought was mine. It was my duty to restore it to the rightful owner, or, if the legal claimant could not be found, to employ it in the promotion of virtue and happiness. To give it to Welbeck was to consecrate it to the purpose of selfishness and misery. My right, legally considered, was as valid as his.

But if I intended not to resign it to him, was it proper to disclose the truth, and explain by whom the volume was purloined from the shelf? The first impulse was to hide this truth: but my understanding had been taught, by recent occurrences, to question the justice, and deny the usefulness of secrecy in any case. My principles were true; my motives were pure: Why should I scruple to avow my principles, and vindicate my actions?

Welbeck had ceased to be dreaded or revered. That awe which was once created by his superiority of age, refinement of manners and dignity of garb, had vanished. I was a boy in years, an indigent and uneducated rustic, but I was able to discern the illusions of power and riches, and abjured every claim to esteem that was not founded on integrity. There was no tribunal before which I should faulter in asserting the truth, and no species of martyrdom which I would not cheerfully embrace in its cause.

After some pause, I said: cannot you conjecture in what way this volume has disappeared?

No: he answered with a sigh. Why, of all his volumes, this only should have vanished, was an inexplicable enigma.

Perhaps, said I, it is less important to know how it was removed, than by whom it is now possessed.

Unquestionably: and yet, unless that knowledge enables me to regain the possession it will be useless.

Useless then it will be, for the present possessor will never return it to you.

Indeed, replied he, in a tone of dejection, your conjecture is most probable. Such a prize is of too much value to be given up.

What I have said, flows not from conjecture, but from knowledge. I know that it will never be restored to you.

At these words, Welbeck looked at me with anxiety and doubt—You *know* that it will not! Have you any knowledge of the book? Can you tell me what has become of it?

Yes, after our separation on the river, I returned to this house. I found this volume and secured it; you rightly suspected its contents. The money was there.

Welbeck started as if he had trodden on a mine of gold. His first emotion was rapturous, but was immediately chastised by some degree of doubt. What has become of it? Have you got it? Is it entire? Have you it with you?

It is unimpaired. I have got it, and shall hold it as a sacred trust for the rightful proprietor.

The tone with which this declaration was accompanied, shook the new born confidence of Welbeck. The rightful

200

Proprietor! true, but I am he. To me only it belongs and to me, you are, doubtless, willing to restore it.

Mr. Welbeck! It is not my desire to give you perplexity or anguish; to sport with your passions. On the supposition of your death, I deemed it no infraction of justice to take this manuscript. Accident unfolded its contents. I could not hesitate to chuse my path. The natural and legal successor of Vincentio Lodi is his sister. To her, therefore, this property belongs, and to her only will I give it.

Presumptuous boy! And this is your sage decision. I tell you that I am the owner, and to me you shall render it. Who is this girl! childish and ignorant! Unable to consult and to act for herself on the most trivial occasion. Am I not, by the appointment of her dying brother, her protector and guardian? Her age produces a legal incapacity of property. Do you imagine that so obvious an expedient, as that of procuring my legal appointment as her guardian, was overlooked by me? If it were neglected, still my title to provide her subsistance and enjoyment is unquestionable.

Did I not rescue her from poverty and prostitution and infamy? Have I not supplied all her wants with incessant solicitude? Whatever her condition required has been plenteously supplied. This dwelling and its furniture, was hers, as far as a rigid jurisprudence would permit. To prescribe her expences and govern her family, was the province of her guardian.

You have heard the tale of my anguish and despair. Whence did they flow but from the frustration of schemes, projected for her benefit, as they were executed with her money and by means which the authority of her guardian fully justified. Why have I encountered this contagious atmosphere, and explored my way, like a thief, to this recess, but with a view to rescue her from poverty and restore to her, her own?

Your scruples are ridiculous and criminal. I treat them with less severity, because your youth is raw and your conceptions crude. But if, after this proof of the justice of my claim, you hesitate to restore the money, I shall treat you as a robber, who has plundered my cabinet and refused to refund his spoil.

These reasonings were powerful and new. I was acquainted with the rights of guardianship. Welbeck had, in some respects, acted as the friend of this lady. To vest himself with this office, was the conduct which her youth and helplessness prescribed to her friend. His title to this money, as her guardian, could not be denied.

But how was this statement compatible with former representations? No mention had then been made of guardianship. By thus acting, he would have thwarted all his schemes for winning the esteem of mankind, and fostering the belief which the world entertained of his opulence and independence.

I was thrown, by these thoughts, into considerable perplexity. If his statement were true, his claim to this money was established, but I questioned its truth. To intimate my doubts of his veracity, would be to provoke abhorrence and outrage.

His last insinuation was peculiarly momentous. Suppose him the fraudulent possessor of this money, shall I be justified in taking it away by violence under pretence of restoring it to the genuine proprietor, who, for aught I know, may be dead, or with whom, at least, I may never procure a meeting? But will not my behaviour on this occasion, be deemed illicit? I entered Welbeck's habitation at midnight, proceeded to his closet, possessed myself of portable property, and retired unobserved. Is not guilt imputable to an action like this?

Welbeck waited with impatience for a conclusion to my pause. My perplexity and indecision did not abate, and my silence continued. At length, he repeated his demands, with new vehemence. I was compelled to answer. I told him, in few words, that his reasonings had not convinced me of the equity of his claim, and that my determination was unaltered.

He had not expected this inflexibility from one in my situation. The folly of opposition, when my feebleness and loneliness were contrasted with his activity and resources, appeared to him monstrous and glaring, but his contempt

was converted into rage and fear when he reflected that this
folly might finally defeat his hopes. He had probably determined to obtain the money, let the purchase cost what it
would, but was willing to exhaust pacific expedients before
he should resort to force. He might likewise question
whether the money was within his reach: I had told him that
I had it, but whether it was now about me, was somewhat
dubious; yet, though he used no direct inquiries, he chose to
proceed on the supposition of its being at hand. His angry
tones were now changed into those of remonstrance and
persuasion.

Your present behaviour, Mervyn, does not justify the
expectation I had formed of you. You have been guilty of a
base theft. To this you have added the deeper crime of
ingratitude, but your infatuation and folly are, at least, as
glaring as your guilt. Do you think I can credit your assertions that you keep this money for another, when I recollect
that six weeks have passed since you carried it off? Why
have you not sought the owner and restored it to her? If
your intentions had been honest, would you have suffered
so long a time to elapse without doing this? It is plain, that
you designed to keep it for your own use.

But whether this were your purpose or not, you have no
longer power to restore it or retain it. You say that you came
hither to die. If so, what is to be the fate of the money? In
your present situation you cannot gain access to the lady.
Some other must inherit this wealth. Next to *Signora Lodi*,
whose right can be put in competition with mine? But if you
will not give it to me, on my own account, let it be given in
trust for her. Let me be the bearer of it to her own hands. I
have already shewn you that my claim to it, as her guardian,
is legal and incontrovertible, but this claim, I wave. I will
merely be the executor of your will. I will bind myself to
comply with your directions by any oath, however solemn
and tremendous, which you shall prescribe.

As long as my own heart acquitted me, these imputations
of dishonesty affected me but little. They excited no anger,
because they originated in ignorance, and were rendered

203

plausible to Welbeck, by such facts as were known to him. It was needless to confute the charge by elaborate and circumstantial details.

It was true that my recovery was, in the highest degree, improbable, and that my death would put an end to my power over this money; but had I not determined to secure its useful application, in case of my death? This project was obstructed by the presence of Welbeck, but I hoped that his love of life would induce him to fly. He might wrest this volume from me by violence, or he might wait till my death should give him peaceable possession. But these, though probable events, were not certain, and would, by no means, justify the voluntary surrender. His strength, if employed for this end, could not be resisted; but then it would be a sacrifice, not to choice, but necessity.

Promises were easily given, but were surely not to be confided in. Welbeck's own tale, in which it could not be imagined that he had aggravated his defects, attested the frailty of his virtue. To put into his hands, a sum like this, in expectation of his delivering it to another, when my death would cover the transaction with impenetrable secrecy, would be, indeed, a proof of that infatuation which he thought proper to impute to me.

These thoughts influenced my resolutions, but they were revolved in silence. To state them verbally was useless. They would not justify my conduct in his eyes. They would only exasperate dispute, and impel him to those acts of violence which I was desirous of preventing. The sooner this controversy should end, and my measure be freed from the obstruction of his company, the better.

Mr. Welbeck, said I, my regard to your safety compels me to wish that this interview should terminate. At a different time, I should not be unwilling to discuss this matter. Now it will be fruitless. My conscience points out to me too clearly the path I should pursue for me to mistake it. As long as I have power over this money I shall keep it for the use of the unfortunate lady, whom I have seen in this house. I shall exert myself to find her, but if that be impossible, I shall appropriate it in a way, in which you shall have no participation.

I will not repeat the contest that succeeded between my forbearance and his passions. I listened to the dictates of his rage and his avarice in silence. Astonishment, at my inflexibility, was blended with his anger. By turns he commented on the guilt and on the folly of my resolutions. Sometimes his emotions would mount into fury, and he would approach me in a menacing attitude, and lift his hand as if he would exterminate me at a blow. My languid eyes, my cheeks glowing, and my temples throbbing with fever, and my total passiveness, attracted his attention and arrested his stroke. Compassion would take place of rage, and the belief be revived that remonstrances and arguments would answer his purpose.

CHAPTER XXIII

THIS scene lasted, I know not how long. Insensibly the passions and reasonings of Welbeck assumed a new form. A grief, mingled with perplexity, overspread his countenance. He ceased to contend or to speak. His regards were withdrawn from me, on whom they had hitherto been fixed; and wandering or vacant, testified a conflict of mind, terrible beyond any that my young imagination had ever conceived.

For a time, he appeared to be unconscious of my presence. He moved to and fro with unequal steps, and with gesticulations, that possessed an horrible but indistinct significance. Occasionally he struggled for breath, and his efforts were directed to remove some choaking impediment.

No test of my fortitude had hitherto occurred equal to that to which it was now subjected. The suspicion which this deportment suggested was vague and formless. The tempest which I witnessed was the prelude of horror. These were throes which would terminate in the birth of some gigantic and sanguinary purpose. Did he meditate to offer a bloody sacrifice? Was his own death or was mine to attest the magnitude of his despair, or the impetuosity of his vengeance?

Suicide was familiar to his thoughts. He had consented to live but on one condition: that of regaining possession of this money. Should I be justified in driving him, by my obstinate refusal, to this fatal consummation of his crimes?

Yet my fear of this catastrophe was groundless. Hitherto he had argued and persuaded, but this method was pursued because it was more eligible than the employment of force, or than procrastination.

No. These were tokens that pointed to me. Some unknown instigation was at work within him, to tear away his remnant of humanity, and fit him for the office of my murderer. I knew not how the accumulation of guilt could contribute to his gratification or security. His actions had been partially exhibited and vaguely seen. What extenuations or omissions had vitiated his former or recent narrative; how far his actual performances were congenial with the deed which was now to be perpetrated, I knew not.

These thoughts lent new rapidity to my blood. I raised my head from the pillow, and watched the deportment of this man, with deeper attention. The paroxysm which controlled him, at length, in some degree subsided. He muttered, Yes. It must come. My last humiliation must cover me. My last confession must be made. To die, and leave behind me this train of enormous perils, must not be.

O Clemenza! O Mervyn! Ye have not merited that I should leave you a legacy of persecution and death. Your safety must be purchased at what price my malignant destiny will set upon it. The cord of the executioner, the note of everlasting infamy, is better than to leave you beset by the consequences of my guilt. It must not be.

Saying this, Welbeck cast fearful glances at the windows and door. He examined every avenue and listened. Thrice he repeated this scrutiny. Having, as it seemed, ascertained that no one lurked within audience, he approached the bed. He put his mouth close to my face. He attempted to speak, but once more examined the apartment with suspicious glances.

He drew closer, and at length, in a tone, scarcely articulate and suffocated with emotion, he spoke: Excellent but fatally obstinate youth! Know at least the cause of my importunity. Know at least the depth of my infatuation and the enormity of my guilt.

The bills—Surrender them to me, and save yourself

207

from persecution and disgrace. Save the woman whom you wish to benefit, from the blackest imputations; from hazard to her life and her fame; from languishing in dungeons; from expiring on the gallows!—

The bills—O save me from the bitterness of death. Let the evils, to which my miserable life has given birth terminate here and in myself. Surrender them to me, for—

There he stopped. His utterance was choaked by terror. Rapid glances were again darted at the windows and door. The silence was uninterrupted except by far-off sounds, produced by some moving carriage. Once more, he summoned resolution, and spoke:

Surrender them to me, for—*they are forged.*

Formerly I told you, that a scheme of forgery had been conceived. Shame would not suffer me to add, that my scheme was carried into execution. The bills were fashioned, but my fears contended against my necessities, and forbade me to attempt to exchange them. The interview with Lodi saved me from the dangerous experiment. I enclosed them in that volume, as the means of future opulence, to be used when all other, and less hazardous resources should fail.

In the agonies of my remorse, at the death of Watson, they were forgotten. They afterwards recurred to recollection. My wishes pointed to the grave; but the stroke that should deliver me from life, was suspended only till I could hasten hither, get possession of these papers, and destroy them.

When I thought upon the chances that should give them an owner; bring them into circulation; load the innocent with suspicion; and lead them to trial, and, perhaps, to death, my sensations were fraught with agony: earnestly as I panted for death, it was necessarily deferred till I had gained possession of and destroyed these papers.

What now remains? You have found them. Happily they have not been used. Give them, therefore, to me, that I may crush at once the brood of mischiefs which they could not but generate.

This disclosure was strange. It was accompanied with

every token of sincerity. How had I tottered on the brink of destruction! If I had made use of this money, in what a labyrinth of misery might I not have been involved! My innocence could never have been proved. An alliance with Welbeck could not have failed to be inferred. My career would have found an ignominious close; or, if my punishment had been transmuted into slavery and toil, would the testimony of my conscience have supported me?

I shuddered at the view of those disasters from which I was rescued by the miraculous chance which led me to this house. Welbeck's request was salutary to me, and honourable to himself. I could not hestitate a moment in compliance. The notes were enclosed in paper, and deposited in a fold of my clothes. I put my hand upon them.

My motion and attention was arrested at the instant, by a noise which arose in the street. Foot-steps were heard upon the pavement before the door, and voices, as if busy in discourse. This incident was adapted to infuse the deepest alarm into myself and my companion. The motives of our trepidation were, indeed, different, and were infinitely more powerful in my case than in his. It portended to me nothing less than the loss of my asylum, and condemnation to an hospital.

Welbeck hurried to the door, to listen to the conversation below. This interval was pregnant with thought. That impulse which led my reflections from Welbeck to my own state, past away in a moment, and suffered me to meditate anew upon the terms of that confession which had just been made.

Horror at the fate which this interview had enabled me to shun, was uppermost in my conceptions. I was eager to surrender these fatal bills. I held them for that purpose in my hand, and was impatient for Welbeck's return. He continued at the door; stooping, with his face averted, and eagerly attentive to the conversation in the street.

All the circumstances of my present situation tended to arrest the progress of thought, and chain my contemplations to one image; but even now there was room for foresight and deliberation. Welbeck intended to destroy these bills. Perhaps he had not been sincere; or, if his purpose had been honestly disclosed, this purpose might change when the bills were in his possession. His poverty and sanguineness of temper, might prompt him to use them.

That this conduct was evil and would only multiply his miseries, could not be questioned. Why should I subject his frailty to this temptation? The destruction of these bills was the loudest injunction of my duty; was demanded by every sanction which bound me to promote the welfare of mankind.

The means of destruction were easy. A lighted candle stood on a table, at the distance of a few yards. Why should I hesitate a moment to annihilate so powerful a cause of error and guilt? A passing instant was sufficient. A momentary lingering might change the circumstances that surrounded me, and frustrate my project.

My languors were suspended by the urgencies of this occasion. I started from my bed and glided to the table. Seizing the notes with my right hand, I held them in the flame of the candle, and then threw them, blazing, on the floor.

The sudden illumination was perceived by Welbeck. The cause of it appeared to suggest itself as soon. He turned, and marking the paper where it lay, leaped to the spot, and extinguished the fire with his foot. His interposition was too late. Only enough of them remained to inform him of the nature of the sacrifice.

Welbeck now stood, with limbs trembling, features aghast, and eyes glaring upon me. For a time he was without speech. The storm was gathering in silence, and at length burst upon me. In a tone menacing and loud, he exclaimed:

Wretch! What have you done?

I have done justly. These notes were false. You desired to destroy them that they might not betray the innocent. I applauded your purpose, and have saved you from the danger of temptation by destroying them myself.

Maniac! Miscreant! To be fooled by so gross an artifice! The notes were genuine. The tale of their forgery was false, and meant only to wrest them from you. Execrable and perverse idiot! Your deed has sealed my perdition. It has sealed your own. You shall pay for it with your blood. I will slay you by inches. I will stretch you as you have stretched me, on the rack.

During this speech, all was frenzy and storm in the countenance and features of Welbeck. Nothing less could be expected than that the scene would terminate in some bloody catastrophe. I bitterly regretted the facility with which I had been deceived, and the precipitation of my sacrifice. The act, however lamentable, could not be revoked. What remained, but to encounter or endure its consequences with unshrinking firmness?

The contest was too unequal. It is possible that the frenzy which actuated Welbeck might have speedily subsided. It is more likely that his passions would have been satiated with nothing but my death. This event was precluded by loud knocks at the street-door, and calls by some one on the pavement without, of—Who is within? Is any one within?

These noises gave a new direction to Welbeck's thoughts. They are coming, said he. They will treat you as a sick man and a theif. I cannot desire you to suffer a worse evil than they will inflict. I leave you to your fate. So saying, he rushed out of the room.

Though confounded and stunned by this rapid succession of events, I was yet able to pursue measures for eluding these detested visitants. I first extinguished the light, and then, observing that the parley in the street continued and grew louder, I sought an asylum in the remotest corner of the house. During my former abode here, I noticed, that a trap door opened in the ceiling of the third story, to which you were conducted by a movable stair or ladder. I considered that this, probably, was an opening into a narrow and darksome nook, formed by the angle of the roof. By ascending, drawing after me the ladder, and closing the door, I should escape the most vigilant search.

Enfeebled as I was by my disease, my resolution rendered me strenuous. I gained the uppermost room, and mounting the ladder, found myself at a sufficient distance from suspicion. The stair was hastily drawn up, and the door closed. In a few minutes, however, my new retreat proved to be worse than any for which it was possible to change it. The air was musty, stagnant, and scorchingly hot. My breathing became difficult, and I saw that to remain here ten minutes, would unavoidably produce suffocation.

My terror of intruders had rendered me blind to the consequences of immuring myself in this chearless recess. It was incumbent on me to extricate myself as speedily as possible. I attempted to lift the door. My first effort was successless. Every inspiration was quicker, and more difficult than the former. As my terror, so my strength and my exertions increased. Finally my trembling hand lighted on a nail that was imperfectly driven into the wood, and which by affording me a firmer hold, enabled me at length to raise it, and to inhale the air from beneath.

Relieved from my new peril, by this situation, I bent an attentive ear through the opening with a view to ascertain if the house had been entered or if the outer door was still beset, but could hear nothing. Hence I was authorized to conclude, that the people had departed, and that I might resume my former station without hazard.

Before I descended, however, I cast a curious eye over this recess—It was large enough to accommodate an human being. The means by which it was entered were easily concealed. Though narrow and low, it was long, and were it possible to contrive some inlet for the air, one studious of concealment, might rely on its protection with unbounded confidence.

My scrutiny was imperfect by reason of the faint light which found its way through the opening, yet it was sufficient to set me afloat on a sea of new wonders and subject my fortitude to a new test—

Here Mervyn paused in his narrative. A minute passed in silence and seeming indecision. His perplexities gradually disappeared, and he continued.

I have promised to relate the momentous incidents of my life, and have hitherto been faithful in my enumeration. There is nothing which I more detest than equivocation and mystery. Perhaps, however, I shall now incur some imputation of that kind. I would willingly escape the accusation, but confess that I am hopeless of escaping it.

I might indeed have precluded your guesses and surmises by omitting to relate what befel me from the time of my leaving my chamber till I regained it. I might deceive you by asserting that nothing remarkable occurred, but this would be false, and every sacrifice is trivial which is made upon the altar of sincerity. Beside, the time may come when no inconvenience will arise from minute descriptions of the objects which I now saw and of the reasonings and inferences which they suggested to my understanding. At present, it appears to be my duty to pass them over in silence, but it would be needless to conceal from you that the interval, though short, and the scrutiny, though hasty, furnished matter which my curiosity devoured with unspeakable eagerness, and from which consequences may hereafter flow, deciding on my peace and my life.

Nothing however occurred which could detain me long in this spot. I once more sought the lower story and threw myself on the bed which I had left. My mind was thronged with the images flowing from my late adventures. My fever had gradually increased, and my thoughts were deformed by inaccuracy and confusion.

My heart did not sink when I reverted to my own condition. That I should quickly be disabled from moving, was readily perceived. The fore-sight of my destiny was stedfast and clear. To linger for days in this comfortless solitude; to ask in vain, not for powerful restoratives or alleviating cordials, but for water to moisten my burning lips, and abate the torments of thirst; ultimately, to expire in torpor or phrenzy, was the fate to which I looked forward, yet I was not terrified. I seemed to be sustained by a preternatural energy. I felt as if the opportunity of combating such evils was an enviable privilege, and though none would witness my victorious magnanimity, yet to be conscious that praise was my due, was all that my ambition required.

These sentiments were doubtless tokens of delirium. The excruciating agonies which now seized upon my head, and the cord which seemed to be drawn across my breast, and which, as my fancy imagined, was tightened by some forcible hand, with a view to strangle me, were incompatible with sober and coherent views.

Thirst was the evil which chiefly oppressed me. The means of relief were pointed out by nature and habit. I rose and determined to replenish my pitcher at the well. It was easier, however, to descend than to return. My limbs refused to bear me, and I sat down upon the lower step of the stair-case. Several hours had elapsed since my entrance into this dwelling, and it was now night.

My imagination now suggested a new expedient. Medlicote was a generous and fearless spirit. To put myself under his protection, if I could walk as far as his lodgings, was the wisest proceeding which I could adopt. From this design, my incapacity to walk thus far, and the consequences of being discovered in the street, had hitherto deterred me. These impediments were now, in the confusion of my understanding, overlooked or despised, and I forthwith set out upon this hopeless expedition.

The doors communicating with the court, and through the court, with the street, were fastened by inside bolts. These were easily withdrawn, and I issued forth with alacrity and confidence. My perturbed senses and the darkness hindered me from discerning the right way. I was conscious of this difficulty, but was not disheartened. I proceeded, as I have since discovered, in a direction different from the true, but hesitated not, till my powers were exhausted, and I sunk upon the ground. I closed my eyes, and dismissed all fear, and all fore-sight of futurity. In this situation I remained some hours, and should probably have expired on this spot, had not I attracted your notice, and been provided under this roof, with all that medical skill, and the tenderest humanity could suggest.

In consequence of your care, I have been restored to life and to health. Your conduct was not influenced by the prospect of pecuniary recompence, of service, or of gratitude. It is only in one way that I am able to heighten the gratification which must flow from reflection on your conduct—by shewing that the being whose life you have prolonged, though uneducated, ignorant and poor, is not profligate and worthless, and will not dedicate that life which your bounty has given, to mischievous or contempt-ible purposes.

ARTHUR MERVYN;

or,

MEMOIRS OF THE YEAR 1793.

Second Part

ARTHUR MERVYN;
OR, MEMOIRS OF THE YEAR 1793.
Second Part

CHAPTER I

HERE ended the narrative of Mervyn. Surely its incidents were of no common kind. During this season of pestilence, my opportunities of observation had been numerous, and I had not suffered them to pass unimproved. The occurrences which fell within my own experience bore a general resemblance to those which had just been related, but they did not hinder the latter from striking on my mind with all the force of novelty. They served no end, but as vouchers for the truth of the tale.

Surely the youth had displayed inimitable and heroic qualities. His courage was the growth of benevolence and reason, and not the child of insensibility and the nursling of habit. He had been qualified for the encounter of gigantic dangers by no laborious education. He stept forth upon the stage, unfurnished, by anticipation or experience, with the means of security against fraud; and yet, by the aid of pure intentions, had frustrated the wiles of an accomplished and veteran deceiver.

I blessed the chance which placed the youth under my protection. When I reflected on that tissue of nice contingences which led him to my door, and enabled me to save from death a being of such rare endowments, my heart overflowed with joy, not unmingled with regrets and trepidation. How many have been cut off by this disease, in their career of virtue and their blossom-time of genius! How many deeds of heroism and self-devotion are ravished from existence, and consigned to hopeless oblivion!

I had saved the life of this youth. This was not the limit of my duty or my power. Could I not render that life profitable to himself and to mankind? The gains of my profession were slender; but these gains were sufficient for his maintainance as well as my own. By residing with me, partaking my instructions, and reading my books, he would, in a few years, be fitted for the practice of physic. A science, whose truths are so conducive to the welfare of mankind, and which comprehends the whole system of nature, could not but gratify a mind so beneficent and strenuous as his.

This scheme occurred to me as soon as the conclusion of his tale allowed me to think. I did not immediately mention it; since the approbation of my wife, of whose concurrence, however, I entertained no doubt, was previously to be obtained. Dismissing it, for the present, from my thoughts, I reverted to the incidents of his tale.

The lady whom Welbeck had betrayed and deserted, was not unknown to me. I was but too well acquainted with her fate. If she had been single in calamity, her tale would have been listened to with insupportable sympathy; but the frequency of the spectacle of distress, seems to lessen the compassion with which it is reviewed. Now that those scenes are only remembered, my anguish is greater than when they were witnessed. Then every new day was only a repetition of the disasters of the foregoing. My sensibility, if not extinguished, was blunted; and I gazed upon the complicated ills of poverty and sickness with a degree of unconcern, on which I should once have reflected with astonishment.

The fate of Clemenza Lodi was not, perhaps, more signal than many which have occurred. It threw detestable light upon the character of Welbeck, and showed him to be more inhuman than the tale of Mervyn had evinced him to be. That man, indeed, was hitherto imperfectly seen. The time had not come which should fully unfold the enormity of his transgressions and the complexity of his frauds.

There lived in a remote quarter of the city a woman, by name Villars, who passed for the widow of an English officer. Her manners and mode of living were specious. She had three daughters, well trained in the school of fashion, and elegant in person, manners and dress. They had lately arrived from Europe, and for a time, received from their neighbors that respect to which their education and fortune appeared to lay claim.

The fallacy of their pretensions slowly appeared. It began to be suspected that their subsistence was derived not from pension or patrimony, but from the wages of pollution. Their habitation was clandestinely frequented by men who were unfaithful to their secret; one of these was allied to me by ties, which authorized me in watching his steps and detecting his errors, with a view to his reformation. From him I obtained a knowledge of the genuine character of these women.

A man like Welbeck, who was the slave of depraved appetites, could not fail of being quickly satiated with innocence and beauty. Some accident introduced him to the knowledge of this family, and the youngest daughter found him a proper subject on which to exercise her artifices. It was to the frequent demands made upon his purse, by this woman, that part of the embarrassments in which Mervyn found him involved, are to be ascribed.

To this circumstance must likewise be imputed his anxiety to transfer to some other the possession of the unhappy stranger. Why he concealed from Mervyn his connection with Lucy Villars, may be easily imagined. His silence, with regard to Clemenza's asylum, will not create surprise, when it is told that she was placed with Mrs. Villars. On what conditions she was received under this roof, cannot be so readily conjectured. It is obvious, however, to suppose, that advantage was to be taken of her ignorance and weakness, and that they hoped, in time, to make her an associate in their profligate schemes.

The appearance of pestilence, meanwhile, threw them into panick, and they hastened to remove from danger. Mrs. Villars appears to have been a woman of no ordinary views. She stooped to the vilest means of amassing money;

but this money was employed to secure to herself and her daughters the benefits of independence. She purchased the house which she occupied in the city, and a mansion in the environs, well built and splendidly furnished. To the latter, she and her family, of which the Italian girl was now a member, retired at the close of July.

I have mentioned that the source of my intelligence was a kinsman, who had been drawn from the paths of sobriety and rectitude, by the impetuosity of youthful passions. He had power to confess and deplore, but none to repair his errors. One of these women held him by a spell which he struggled in vain to dissolve, and by which, in spite of resolutions and remorses, he was drawn to her feet, and made to sacrifice to her pleasure, his reputation and his fortune.

My house was his customary abode during those intervals in which he was persuaded to pursue his profession. Some time before the infection began its progress, he had disappeared. No tidings was received of him, till a messenger arrived intreating my assistance. I was conducted to the house of Mrs. Villars, in which I found no one but my kinsman. Here it seems he had immured himself from my enquiries, and on being seized by the reigning malady, had been deserted by the family, who, ere they departed, informed me by a messenger of his condition.

Despondency combined with his disease to destroy him. Before he died, he informed me fully of the character of his betrayers. The late arrival, name and personal condition of Clemenza Lodi were related. Welbeck was not named, but was described in terms, which, combined with the narrative of Mervyn, enabled me to recognize the paramour of Lucy Villars in the man whose crimes had been the principal theme of our discourse.

Mervyn's curiosity was greatly roused when I intimated my acquaintance with the fate of Clemenza. In answer to his eager interrogations, I related what I knew. The tale plunged him into reverie. Recovering, at length, from his thoughtfulness, he spoke.

Her condition is perilous. The poverty of Welbeck will

222

drive him far from her abode. Her profligate protectors will entice her or abandon her to ruin. Cannot she be saved?

I know not, answered I, by what means.

The means are obvious. Let her remove to some other dwelling. Let her be apprized of the vices of those who surround her. Let her be intreated to fly. The will need only be inspired, the danger need only be shown, and she is safe, for she will remove beyond its reach.

Thou art an adventurous youth. Who wilt thou find to undertake the office? Who will be persuaded to enter the house of a stranger, seek without an introduction the presence of this girl, tell her that the house she inhabits is an house of prostitution, prevail on her to believe the tale, and persuade her to accompany him? Who will open his house to the fugitive? Whom will you convince that her illicit intercourse with Welbeck, of which the opprobrious tokens cannot be concealed, has not fitted her for the company of prostitutes, and made her unworthy of protection? Who will adopt into their family, a stranger, whose conduct has incurred infamy, and whose present associates have, no doubt, made her worthy of the curse?

True. These are difficulties which I did not foresee. Must she then perish! Shall not something be done to rescue her from infamy and guilt?

It is neither in your power nor in mine to do any thing.

The lateness of the hour put an end to our conversation and summoned us to repose. I seized the first opportunity of imparting to my wife the scheme which had occurred, relative to our guest; with which, as I expected, she readily concurred. In the morning, I mentioned it to Mervyn. I dwelt upon the benefits that adhered to the medical profession, the power which it confers of lightening the distresses of our neighbors, the dignity which popular opinion annexes to it, the avenue which it opens to the acquisition of competence, the freedom from servile cares which attends it, and the means of intellectual gratification with which it supplies us.

As I spoke, his eyes sparkled with joy. Yes, said he with vehemence, I willingly embrace your offer. I accept this benefit, because I know that if my pride should refuse it, I should prove myself less worthy than you think, and give you pain, instead of that pleasure which I am bound to confer. I would enter on the duties and studies of my new profession immediately, but somewhat is due to Mr. Hadwin and his daughters. I cannot vanquish my inquietudes respecting them, but by returning to Malverton and ascertaining their state with my own eyes. You know in what circumstances I parted with Wallace and Mr. Hadwin. I am not sure, that either of them ever reached home, or that they did not carry the infection along with them. I now find myself sufficiently strong to perform the journey, and proposed to have acquainted you, at this interview, with my intentions. An hour's delay is superfluous, and I hope you will consent to my setting out immediately. Rural exercise and air, for a week or fortnight, will greatly contribute to my health.

No objection could be made to this scheme. His narrative had excited no common affection in our bosoms for the Hadwins. His visit could not only inform us of their true state, but would dispel that anxiety which they could not but entertain respecting our guest. It was a topic of some surprize that neither Wallace nor Hadwin had returned to the city, with a view to obtain some tidings of their friend. It was more easy to suppose them to have been detained by some misfortune, than by insensibility or indolence. In a few minutes Mervyn bade us adieu, and set out upon his journey, promising to acquaint us with the state of affairs, as soon as possible after his arrival. We parted from him with reluctance, and found no consolation but in the prospect of his speedy return.

During his absence, conversation naturally turned upon those topics which were suggested by the narrative and deportment of this youth. Different conclusions were formed by his two auditors. They had both contracted a deep interest in his welfare, and an ardent curiosity as to those particulars which his unfinished story had left in obscurity. The true character and actual condition of Welbeck, were themes of much speculation. Whether he were dead or alive, near or distant from his ancient abode, was a point on which neither Mervyn, nor any of those with whom I had means of intercourse, afforded any information. Whether he had shared the common fate, and had been carried by the collectors of the dead from the highway or the hovel to the pits opened alike for the rich and the poor, the known and the unknown; whether he had escaped to a foreign shore, or were destined to re-appear upon this stage, were questions involved in uncertainty.

The disappearance of Watson would, at a different time, have excited much enquiry and suspicion; but as this had taken place on the eve of the epidemic, his kindred and friends would acquiesce, without scruple, in the belief that he had been involved in the general calamity, and was to be numbered among the earliest victims. Those of his profession usually resided in the street where the infection began, and where its ravages had been most destructive; and this circumstance would corroborate the conclusions of his friends.

I did not perceive any immediate advantage to flow from imparting the knowledge I had lately gained to others. Shortly after Mervyn's departure to Malverton, I was visited by Wortley. Enquiring for my guest, I told him that, having recovered his health, he had left my house. He repeated his invectives against the villainy of Welbeck, his suspicions of Mervyn, and his wishes for another interview with the youth. Why had I suffered him to depart, and whither had he gone?

He has gone for a short time into the country. I expect him to return in less than a week, when you will meet with him here as often as you please, for I expect him to take up his abode in this house.

Much astonishment and disapprobation were expressed by my friend. I hinted that the lad had made disclosures to me, which justified my confidence in his integrity. These proofs of his honesty were not of a nature to be indiscriminately unfolded. Mervyn had authorized me to communicate so much of his story to Wortley, as would serve to vindicate him from the charge of being Welbeck's copartner in fraud; but this end would only be counteracted by an imperfect tale, and the full recital, though it might

225

exculpate Mervyn, might produce inconveniences by which this advantage would be outweighed.

Wortley, as might be naturally expected, was by no means satisfied with this statement. He suspected that Mervyn was a wily imposter; that he had been trained in the arts of fraud, under an accomplished teacher; that the tale which he had told to me, was a tissue of ingenious and plausible lies; that the mere assertions, however plausible and solemn, of one like him, whose conduct had incurred such strong suspicions, were unworthy of the least credit.

It cannot be denied, continued my friend, that he lived with Welbeck at the time of his elopement; that they disappeared together; that they entered a boat, at Pine-street wharf, at midnight; that this boat was discovered by the owner in the possession of a fisherman at Red-bank, who affirmed that he had found it stranded near his door, the day succeeding that on which they disappeared. Of all this, I can supply you with incontestible proof. If, after this proof, you can give credit to his story, I shall think you made of very perverse and credulous materials.

The proof you mention, said I, will only enhance his credibility. All the facts which you have stated, have been admitted by him. They constitute an essential portion of his narrative.

What then is the inference? Are not these evidences of a compact between them? Has he not acknowledged this compact in confessing that he knew Welbeck was my debtor; that he was apprized of his flight, but that, (what matchless effrontery!) he had promised secrecy, and would, by no means, betray him? You say he means to return; but of that I doubt. You will never see his face more. He is too wise to thrust himself again into the noose: but I do not utterly despair of lighting upon Welbeck. Old Thetford, Jamieson and I, have sworn to hunt him through the world. I have strong hopes that he has not strayed far. Some intelligence has lately been received, which has enabled us to place our hounds upon the scent. He may double and skulk; but if he does not fall into our toils at last, he will have the agility and cunning, as well as the malignity of devils.

The vengeful disposition thus betrayed by Wortley, was not without excuse. The vigor of his days had been spent in acquiring a slender capital: his diligence and honesty had succeeded, and he had lately thought his situation such as to justify marriage with an excellent woman, to whom he had for years been betrothed, but from whom his poverty had hitherto compelled him to live separate. Scarcely had this alliance taken place, and the full career of nuptial enjoyments begun, when his ill fate exposed him to the frauds of Welbeck, and brought him, in one evil hour, to the brink of insolvency.

Jamieson and Thetford, however, were rich, and I had not till now been informed that they had reasons for pursuing Welbeck with peculiar animosity. The latter was the uncle of him whose fate had been related by Mervyn, and was one of those who employed money, not as the medium of traffic, but as in itself a commodity. He had neither wines nor cloths, to transmute into silver. He thought it a tedious process to exchange to day, one hundred dollars for a cask or bale, and to-morrow exchange the bale or cask for an hundred *and ten* dollars. It was better to give the hundred for a piece of paper, which, carried forthwith to the money changers, he could procure an hundred twenty-three and three-fourths. In short, this man's coffers were supplied by the despair of honest men and the stratagems of rogues. I did not immediately suspect how this man's prudence and indefatigable attention to his own interest should allow him to become the dupe of Welbeck.

What, said I, is old Thetford's claim upon Welbeck?

It is a claim, he replied, that, if it ever be made good, will doom Welbeck to imprisonment and wholsome labor for life.

How? Surely it is nothing more than debt.

Have you not heard? But that is no wonder. Happily you are a stranger to mercantile anxieties and revolutions. Your fortune does not rest on a basis which an untoward blast may sweep away, or four strokes of a pen may demolish. That hoary dealer in suspicions was persuaded to put his hand to three notes for eight hundred dollars each. The

227

eight was then dextrously prolonged to eigh*teen*; they were duly deposited in time and place, and the next day Welbeck was credited for fifty-three hundred and seventy-three, which an hour after, were *told out* to his messenger. Hard to say whether the old man's grief, shame or rage be uppermost. He disdains all comfort but revenge, and that he will procure at any price. Jamieson, who deals in the same *stuff* with Thetford, was outwitted in the same manner, to the same amount, and on the same day.

This Welbeck must have powers above the common rate of mortals. Grown grey in studying the follies and the stratagems of men, these veterans were overreached. No one pities them. 'Twere well if his artifices had been limited to such, and he had spared the honest and the poor. It is for his injuries to men who have earned their scanty subsistence without forfeiting their probity, that I hate him, and shall exult to see him suffer all the rigors of the law. Here Wortley's engagements compelled him to take his leave.

CHAPTER II

WHILE musing upon these facts, I could not but reflect with astonishment on the narrow escapes which Mervyn's virtue had experienced. I was by no means certain that his fame or his life was exempt from all danger, or that the suspicions which had already been formed respecting him, could possibly be wiped away. Nothing but his own narrative, repeated with that simple but nervous eloquence, which we had witnessed, could rescue him from the most heinous charges. Was there any tribunal that would not acquit him on merely hearing his defence?

Surely the youth was honest. His tale could not be the fruit of invention; and yet, what are the bounds of fraud? Nature has set no limits to the combinations of fancy. A smooth exterior, a show of virtue, and a specious tale, are, a thousand times, exhibited in human intercourse by craft and subtlety. Motives are endlessly varied, while actions continue the same; and an acute penetration may not find it hard to select and arrange motives, suited to exempt from censure any action that an human being can commit.

Had I heard Mervyn's story from another, or read it in a book, I might, perhaps, have found it possible to suspect the truth; but, as long as the impression, made by his tones, gestures and looks, remained in my memory, this suspicion was impossible. Wickedness may sometimes be ambiguous, its mask may puzzle the observer; our judgment may be made to faulter and fluctuate, but the face of Mervyn is the

229

index of an honest mind. Calm or vehement, doubting or confident, it is full of benevolence and candor. He that listens to his words may question their truth, but he that looks upon his countenance when speaking, cannot withhold his faith.

It was possible, however, to find evidence, supporting or confuting his story. I chanced to be acquainted with a family, by name Althorpe, who were natives of that part of the country where his father resided. I paid them a visit, and, after a few preliminaries, mentioned, as if by accident, the name of Mervyn. They immediately recognized this name as belonging to one of their ancient neighbors. The death of the wife and sons, and the seduction of the only daughter by Colvil, with many pathetic incidents connected with the fate of this daughter, were mentioned.

This intelligence induced me to inquire of Mrs. Althorpe, a sensible and candid woman, if she were acquainted with the recent or present situation of this family.

I cannot say much, she answered, of my own knowledge. Since my marriage, I am used to spend a few weeks of summer, at my father's, but am less inquisitive than I once was into the concerns of my old neighbors. I recollect, however, when there, last year, during *the fever,* to have heard that Sawny Mervyn had taken a second wife; that his only son, a youth of eighteen, had thought proper to be highly offended with his father's conduct, and treated the new mistress of the house with insult and contempt. I should not much wonder at this, seeing children are so apt to deem themselves unjustly treated by a second marriage of their parent, but it was hinted that the boy's jealousy and discontent was excited by no common cause. The new mother was not much older than himself, had been a servant of the family, and a criminal intimacy had subsisted between her, while in that condition, and the son. Her marriage with his father was justly accounted by their neighbors, a most profligate and odious transaction. The son, perhaps, had, in such a case, a right to scold, but he ought not to have carried his anger to such extremes as have been imputed to him. He is said to have grinned upon her with contempt, and even to have called her *strumpet* in the presence of his father and of strangers.

It was impossible for such a family to keep together. Arthur took leave one night to possess himself of all his father's cash, mount the best horse in his meadow, and elope. For a time, no one knew whither he had gone. At last, one was said to have met with him in the streets of this city, metamorphosed from a rustic lad into a fine gentleman. Nothing could be quicker than this change, for he left the country on a Saturday morning, and was seen in a French frock and silk stockings, going into Christ's Church the next day. I suppose he kept it up with an high hand, as long as his money lasted.

My father paid us a visit last week, and among other country news, told us that Sawny Mervyn had sold his place. His wife had persuaded him to try his fortune in the Western Country. The price of his hundred acres here would purchase a thousand there, and the man being very gross and ignorant, and withall, quite a simpleton, found no difficulty in perceiving that a thousand are ten times more than an hundred. He was not aware that a rood of ground upon Schuylkill is ten fold better than an acre on the Tenessee.

The woman turned out to be an artful profligate. Having sold his ground and gotten his money, he placed it in her keeping, and she, to enjoy it with the more security, ran away to the city; leaving him to prosecute his journey to Kentucky, moneyless and alone. Sometime after, Mr. Althorpe and I were at the play, when he pointed out to me a groupe of females in an upper box, one of whom was no other than Betty Laurence. It was not easy to recognize, in her present gaudy trim, all flaunting with ribbons and shining with trinkets, the same Betty who used to deal out pecks of potatoes and superintend her basket of cantilopes in the Jersey market, in paste-board bonnet and linsey petticoat. Her companions were of the infamous class. If Arthur were still in the city, there is no doubt that the mother and son might renew the ancient terms of their acquaintance.

The old man, thus robbed and betrayed, sought consolation in the bottle, of which he had been at all times over-fond. He wandered from one tavern to another till his credit was exhausted, and then was sent to jail, where, I believe, he is likely to continue till his death. Such, my friend, is the history of the Mervyns.

What proof, said I, have you of the immoral conduct of the son? of his mistreatment of his mother, and his elopement with his father's horse and money?

I have no proof but the unanimous report of Mervyn's neighbors. Respectable and honest men have affirmed, in my hearing, that they have been present when the boy treated his mother in the way that I have described. I was, besides, once in company with the old man, and heard him bitterly inveigh against his son, and charge him with the fact of stealing his horse and money. I well remember that tears rolled from his eyes while talking on the subject. As to his being seen in the city the next day after his elopement, dressed in a most costly and fashionable manner, I can doubt that as little as the rest, for he that saw him was my father, and you who know my father, know what credit is due to his eyes and his word. He had seen Arthur often enough not to be mistaken, and described his appearance with great exactness. The boy is extremely handsome, give him his due; has dark hazle eyes, auburn hair, and very elegant proportions. His air and gate have nothing of the clown in them. Take away his jacket and trowsers, and you have as spruce a fellow as ever came from dancing-school or college. He is the exact picture of his mother, and the most perfect contrast to the sturdy legs, squat figure, and broad, unthinking, sheepish face of the father that can be imagined. You must confess that his appearance here is a pretty strong proof of the father's assertions. The money given for these clothes could not possibly have been honestly acquired. It is to be presumed that they were bought or stolen, for how else should they have been gotten?

What was this lad's personal deportment during the life of his mother, and before his father's second marriage?

Very little to the credit of his heart or his intellects. Being the youngest son, the only one who at length survived, and having a powerful resemblance to herself, he became the mother's favorite. His constitution was feeble, and he loved to stroll in the woods more than to plow or sow. This idleness was much against the father's inclination and judgment; and, indeed, it was the foundation of all his vices. When he could be prevailed upon to do any thing it was in a bungling manner, and so as to prove that his thoughts were fixed on any thing except his business. When his assistance was wanted he was never to be found at hand. They were compelled to search for him among the rocks and bushes, and he was generally discovered sauntering along the bank of the river, or lolling in the shade of a tree. This disposition to inactivity and laziness, in so young a man, was very strange. Persons of his age are rarely fond of work, but then they are addicted to company, and sports, and exercises. They ride, or shoot, or frolic; but this being moped away his time in solitude, never associated with other young people, never mounted an horse but when he could not help it, and never fired a gun or angled for a fish in his life. Some people supposed him to be half an idiot, or, at least, not to be in his right mind; and, indeed, his conduct was so very perverse and singular, that I do not wonder at those who accounted for it in this way.

But, surely, said I, he had some object of pursuit. Perhaps he was addicted to books.

Far from it. On the contrary, his aversion to school was as great as his hatred of the plough. He never could get his lessons or bear the least constraint. He was so much indulged by his mother at home, that tasks and discipline of any kind were intolerable. He was a perpetual truant; till the master one day attempting to strike him, he ran out of the room and never entered it more. The mother excused and countenanced his frowardness, and the foolish father was obliged to give way. I do not believe he had two months' schooling in his life.

Perhaps, said I, he preferred studying by himself, and at liberty. I have known boys endowed with great curiosity and aptitude to learning, who never could endure set tasks, and spurned at the pedagogue and his rod.

I have known such likewise, but this was not one of them. I know not whence he could derive his love of knowledge or the means of acquiring it. The family were totally illiterate. The father was a Scotch peasant, whose ignorance was so great that he could not sign his name. His wife, I believe, could read, and might sometimes decypher the figures in an almanac, but that was all. I am apt to think, that the son's ability was not much greater. You might as well look for silver platters or marble tables in his house, as for a book or a pen.

I remember calling at their house one evening in the winter before last. It was intensely cold; and my father, who rode with me, having business with Sawney Mervyn, we stopped a minute at his gate; and, while the two old men were engaged in conversation, I begged leave to warm myself by the kitchen fire. Here, in the chimney-corner, seated on a block, I found Arthur busily engaged in *knitting stockings*! I thought this a whimsical employment for a young active man. I told him so, for I wanted to put him to the blush; but he smiled in my face, and answered, without the least discomposure, just as whimsical a business for a young active woman. Pray, did you never knit a stocking?

Yes; but that was from necessity. Were I of a different sex, or did I possess the strength of a man, I should rather work in my field or study my book.

Rejoice that you are a woman, then, and are at liberty to pursue that which costs least labor and demands most skill. You see, though a man, I use your privilege, and prefer knitting yarn to threshing my brain with a book or the barn-floor with a flail.

I wonder, said I contemptuously, you do not put on the petticoat as well as handle the needle.

Do not wonder, he replied: it is because I hate a petticoat incumbrance as much as I love warm feet. Look there (offering the stocking to my inspection) is it not well done?

I did not touch it, but sneeringly said, excellent! I wonder you do not apprentice yourself to a taylor.

He looked at me with an air of ridiculous simplicity and said, how prone the woman is to *wonder*. You call the work

234

excellent, and yet *wonder* that I do not make myself a slave to improve my skill! Did you learn needle-work from seven years' squatting on a taylor's board? Had you come to me, I would have taught you in a day.

I was taught at school.

And paid your instructor?

To be sure.

'Twas liberty and money thrown away. Send your sister, if you have one, to me, and I will teach her without either rod or wages. Will you?

You have an old and a violent antipathy, I believe, to any thing like a school.

True. It was early and violent. Had not you?

No. I went to school with pleasure; for I thought to read and write were accomplishments of some value.

Indeed? Then I misunderstood you just now. I thought you said, that, had you the strength of a man, you should prefer the plough and the book to the needle. Whence, supposing you a female, I inferred that you had a woman's love for the needle and a fool's hatred of books.

My father calling me from without, I now made a motion to go. Stay, continued he with great earnestness, throwing aside his knitting apparatus, and beginning in great haste to pull off his stockings. Draw these stockings over your shoes. They will save your feet from the snow while walking to your horse.

Half angry, and half laughing, I declined the offer. He had drawn them off, however, and holding them in his hand, be persuaded, said he; only lift your feet, and I will slip them on in a trice.

Finding me positive in my refusal, he dropped the stockings; and, without more ado, caught me up in his arms, rushed out of the room, and, running barefoot through the snow, set me fairly on my horse. All was done in a moment, and before I had time to reflect on his intentions. He then seized my hand, and, kissing it with great fervor, exclaimed, a thousand thanks to you for not accepting my stockings. You have thereby saved yourself and me the time and toil of drawing on and drawing off. Since you have taught me to wonder, let me practice the lesson in wondering at your folly, in wearing worsted shoes and silk stockings at a season like this. Take my counsel, and turn your silk to worsted and your worsted to leather. Then may you hope for warm feet and dry. What! Leave the gate without a blessing on your counsellor?

I spurred my horse into a gallop, glad to escape from so strange a being. I could give you many instances of behaviour equally singular, and which betrayed a mixture of shrewdness and folly, of kindness and impudence, which justified, perhaps, the common notion that his intellects were unsound. Nothing was more remarkable than his impenetrability to ridicule and censure. You might revile him for hours, and he would listen to you with invincible composure. To awaken anger or shame in him was impossible. He would answer, but in such a way as to show him totally unaware of your true meaning. He would afterwards talk to you with all the smiling affability and freedom of an old friend. Every one despised him for his idleness and folly, no less conspicuous in his words than his actions; but no one feared him, and few were angry with him, till after the detection of his commerce with *Betty*, and his inhuman treatment of his father.

Have you good reasons for supposing him to have been illicitly connected with that girl?

Yes. Such as cannot be discredited. It would not be proper for me to state these proofs. Nay, he never denied it. When reminded, on one occasion, of the inference which every impartial person would draw from appearances, he acknowledged, with his usual placid effrontery, that the inference was unavoidable. He even mentioned other concurring and contemporary incidents, which had eluded the observation of his censurer, and which added still more force to the conclusion. He was studious to palliate the vices of this woman as long as he was her only paramour; but after her marriage with his father, the tone was changed. He confessed that she was tidy, notable, industrious; but, then, she was a prostitute. When charged with being instrumental in making her such, and when his companions

236

dwelt upon the depravity of reviling her for vices which she owed to him: True, he would say, there is depravity and folly in the conduct you describe. Make me out, if you please, to be a villain. What then? I was talking not of myself, but of Betty. Still this woman is a prostitute. If it were I that made her such, with more confidence may I make the charge. But think not that I blame Betty. Place me in her situation, and I should have acted just so. I should have formed just such notions of my interest, and pursued it by the same means. Still, say I, I would fain have a different woman for my father's wife, and the mistress of this family.

CHAPTER III

THIS conversation was interrupted by a messenger from my wife, who desired my return immediately. I had some hopes of meeting with Mervyn, some days having now elapsed since his parting from us, and not being conscious of any extraordinary motives for delay. It was Wortley, however, and not Mervyn, to whom I was called.

My friend came to share with me his suspicions and inquietudes respecting Welbeck and Mervyn. An accident had newly happened which had awakened these suspicions afresh. He desired a patient audience while he explained them to me. These were his words.

To-day a person presented me a letter from a mercantile friend at Baltimore. I easily discerned the bearer to be a sea captain. He was a man of sensible and pleasing aspect, and was recommended to my friendship and counsel in the letter which he brought. The letter stated, that a man, by name Amos Watson, by profession a mariner, and a resident at Baltimore, had disappeared in the summer of last year, in a mysterious and incomprehensible manner. He was known to have arrived in this city from Jamaica, and to have intended an immediate journey to his family, who lived at Baltimore; but he never arrived there, and no trace of his existence has since been discovered. The bearer had come to investigate, if possible, the secret of his fate, and I was earnestly intreated to afford him all the assistance and advice in my power, in the prosecution of his search. I

238

expressed my willingness to serve the stranger, whose name was Williams; and, after offering him entertainment at my house, which was thankfully accepted, he proceeded to unfold to me the particulars of this affair. His story was this.

On the 20th of last June, I arrived, said he, from the West-Indies, in company with captain Watson. I commanded the ship in which he came as a passenger, his own ship being taken and confiscated by the English. We had long lived in habits of strict friendship, and I loved him for his own sake, as well as because he had married my sister. We landed in the morning, and went to dine with Mr. Keysler, since dead, but who then lived in Water-street. He was extremely anxious to visit his family, and having a few commissions to perform in the city, which would not demand more than a couple of hours, he determined to set out next morning in the stage. Meanwhile, I had engagements which required me to repair with the utmost expedition to New-York. I was scarcely less anxious than my brother to reach Baltimore, where my friends also reside, but there was an absolute necessity of going eastward. I expected, however, to return hither in three days, and then to follow Watson home. Shortly after dinner we parted; he to execute his commissions, and I to embark in the mail-stage.

In the time prefixed I returned. I arrived early in the morning, and prepared to depart again at noon. Meanwhile, I called at Keysler's. This is an old acquaintance of Watson's and mine; and, in the course of talk, he expressed some surprize that Watson had so precipitately deserted his house. I stated the necessity there was for Watson's immediate departure *southward*, and added, that no doubt my brother had explained this necessity.

Why, said Keysler, it is true, Captain Watson mentioned his intention of leaving town early next day; but then he gave me reason to expect that he would sup and lodge with me that night, whereas he has not made his appearance since. Beside his trunk was brought to my house. This, no doubt, he intended to carry home with him, but here it remains still. It is not likely that in the hurry of departure his baggage was forgotten. Hence, I inferred that he was still in town, and have been puzzling myself these three days with conjectures, as to what is become of him. What surprizes me more is, that, on enquiring among the few friends which he has in this city, I find them as ignorant of his motions as myself. I have not, indeed, been wholly without apprehensions that some accident or other has befallen him.

I was not a little alarmed by this intimation. I went myself, agreeably to Keysler's directions, to Watson's friends, and made anxious enquiries, but none of them had seen my brother since his arrival. I endeavored to recollect the commissions which he designed to execute, and, if possible, to trace him to the spot where he last appeared. He had several packets to deliver, one of which was addressed to Walter Thetford. Him, after some enquiry, I found out, but unluckily he chanced to be in the country. I found, by questioning a clerk who transacted his business in his absence, that a person, who answered the minute description which I gave of Watson, had been there on the day on which I parted with him, and had left papers relative to the capture of one of Thetford's vessels by the English. This was the sum of the information he was able to afford me.

I then applied to three merchants for whom my brother had letters. They all acknowledged the receipt of these letters, but they were delivered through the medium of the post-office.

I was extremely anxious to reach home. Urgent engagements compelled me to go on without delay. I had already exhausted all the means of enquiry within my reach, and was obliged to acquiesce in the belief, that Watson had proceeded homeward at the time appointed, and left, by forgetfulness or accident, his trunk behind him. On examining the books kept at the stage offices, his name no where appeared, and no conveyance by water had occurred during the last week. Still the only conjecture I could form, was that he had gone homeward.

Arriving at Baltimore, I found that Watson had not yet made his appearance. His wife produced a letter, which, by the post mark, appeared to have been put into the office at

Philadelphia, on the morning after our arrival, and on which he had designed to commence his journey. This letter had been written by my brother, in my presence, but I had dissuaded him from sending it, since the same coach that should bear the letter, was likewise to carry himself. I had seen him put it unwafered in his pocket-book, but this letter, unaltered in any part, and containing money which he had at first intended to enclose in it, was now conveyed to his wife's hand. In this letter he mentioned his design of setting out for Baltimore, on the *twenty-first*, yet, on that day the letter itself had been put into the office.

We hoped that a short time would clear up this mystery, and bring the fugitive home, but from that day till the present, no atom of intelligence has been received concerning him. The yellow-fever, which quickly followed, in this city, and my own engagements, have hindered me, till now, from coming hither and resuming the search.

My brother was one of the most excellent of men. His wife loved him to distraction, and, together with his children, depended for subsistence upon his efforts. You will not, therefore, be surprized that his disappearance excited, in us, the deepest consternation and distress; but I have other, and peculiar reasons for wishing to know his fate. I gave him several bills of exchange on merchants of Baltimore, which I had received in payment of my cargo, in order that they might, as soon as possible, be presented and accepted. These have disappeared with the bearer. There is likewise another circumstance that makes his existence of no small value.

There is an English family, who formerly resided in Jamaica, and possessed an estate of great value, but who, for some years, have lived in the neighborhood of Baltimore. The head of this family died a year ago, and left a widow and three daughters. The lady tho't it eligible to sell her husband's property in Jamaica, the Island becoming hourly more exposed to the chances of war and revolution, and transfer it to the United States, where she purposes henceforth to reside. Watson had been her husband's friend, and his probity and disinterestedness being well known, she

241

entrusted him with legal powers to sell this estate. This commission was punctually performed, and the purchase money was received. In order to confer on it the utmost possible security, he rolled up four bills of exchange, drawn upon opulent merchants of London, in a thin sheet of lead, and depositing this roll in a leathern girdle, fastened it round his waist, and under his clothes; a second set he gave to me, and a third he dispatched to Mr. Keysler, by a vessel which sailed a few days before him. On our arrival in this city, we found that Keysler had received those transmitted to him, and which he had been charged to keep till our arrival. They were now produced, and, together with those which I had carried, were delivered to Watson. By him they were joined to those in the girdle, which he still wore, conceiving this method of conveyance to be safer than any other, and, at the same time, imagining it needless, in so short a journey as remained to be performed, to resort to other expedients.

The sum which he thus bore about him, was no less than ten thousand pounds sterling. It constituted the whole patrimony of a worthy and excellent family, and the loss of it reduces them to beggary. It is gone with Watson, and whither Watson has gone, it is impossible even to guess.

You may now easily conceive, Sir, the dreadful disasters which may be connected with this man's fate, and with what immeasurable anxiety his family and friends have regarded his disappearance. That he is alive, can scarcely be believed, for in what situation could he be placed in which he would not be able and willing to communicate some tidings of his fate to his family?

Our grief has been unspeakably aggravated by the suspicions which Mrs. Maurice and her friends have allowed themselves to admit. They do not scruple to insinuate, that Watson, tempted by so great a prize, has secretly embarked for England, in order to obtain payment for these bills, and retain the money for his own use.

No man was more impatient of poverty than Watson, but no man's honesty was more inflexible. He murmured at the destiny that compelled him to sacrifice his ease, and risk his life upon the ocean in order to procure the means of subsistence; and all the property which he had spent the best part of his life in collecting, had just been ravished away from him by the English; but if he had yielded to this temptation at any time, it would have been on receiving these bills at Jamaica. Instead of coming hither, it would have been infinitely more easy and convenient to have embarked directly for London; but none, who thoroughly knew him, can, for a moment, harbor a suspicion of his truth.

If he be dead, and if the bills are not to be recovered, yet, to ascertain this, will, at last, serve to vindicate his character. As long as his fate is unknown, his fame will be loaded with the most flagrant imputations, and if these bills be ever paid in London, these imputations will appear to be justified. If he has been robbed, the robber will make haste to secure the payment, and the Maurices may not unreasonably conclude that the robber was Watson himself. Many other particulars were added by the stranger, to show the extent of the evils flowing from the death of his brother, and the loss of the papers which he carried with him.

I was greatly at a loss, continued Wortley, what directions or advice to afford this man. Keysler, as you know, died early of the pestilence; but Keysler was the only resident in this city with whom Williams had any acquaintance. On mentioning the propriety of preventing the sale of these bills in America, by some public notice, he told me that this caution had been early taken; and I now remembered seeing the advertisement, in which the bills had been represented as having been lost or stolen in this city, and a reward of a thousand dollars was offered to any one who should restore them. This caution had been published in September, in all the trading towns from Portsmouth to Savannah, but had produced no satisfaction.

I accompanied Williams to the mayor's office, in hopes of finding in the records of his proceedings, during the last six months, some traces of Watson, but neither these records nor the memory of the magistrate, afforded us any satisfaction. Watson's friends had drawn up, likewise, a description of the person and dress of the fugitive, an account of the incidents attending his disappearance, and of the papers which he had in his possession, with the manner in which these papers had been secured. These had been already published in the Southern newspapers, and have been just re-printed in our own. As the former notice had availed nothing, this second expedient was thought necessary to be employed.

After some reflection, it occurred to me that it might be proper to renew the attempt which Williams had made to trace the footsteps of his friend to the moment of his final disappearance. He had pursued Watson to Thetford's, but Thetford himself had not been seen, and he had been contented with the vague information of his clerk. Thetford and his family, including his clerk, had perished, and it seemed as if this source of information was dried up. It was possible, however, that old Thetford might have some knowledge of his nephew's transactions, by which some light might chance to be thrown upon this obscurity. I therefore called on him, but found him utterly unable to afford me the light that I wished. My mention of the packet which Watson had brought to Thetford, containing documents respecting the capture of a certain ship, reminded him of the injuries which he had received from Welbeck, and excited him to renew his menaces and imputations on that wretch. Having somewhat exhausted this rhetoric, he proceeded to tell me what connection there was between the remembrance of his injuries and the capture of this vessel.

This vessel and its cargo were, in fact, the property of Welbeck. They had been sent to a good market and had been secured by an adequate insurance. The value of this ship and cargo, and the validity of the policy he had taken care to ascertain by means of his two nephews, one of whom had gone out supercargo. This had formed his inducement to lend his three notes to Welbeck, in exchange for three other notes, the whole amount of which included the *equitable interest* of *five per cent. per month* on his own loan. For the payment of these notes, he by no means relied, as the world foolishly imagined, on the seeming opulence and secret funds of Welbeck. These were illusions too gross to have

244

any influence on him. He was too old a bird to be decoyed into the net by *such* chaff. No; his nephew, the supercargo, would of course receive the produce of the voyage, and so much of this produce as would pay his debt. He had procured the owner's authority to intercept its passage from the pocket of his nephew to that of Welbeck. In case of loss, he had obtained a similar security upon the policy. Jamieson's proceedings had been the same with his own, and no affair in which he had ever engaged, had appeared to be more free from hazard than this. Their calculations, however, though plausible, were defeated. The ship was taken and condemned, for a cause which rendered the insurance ineffectual.

I bestowed no time in reflecting on this tissue of extortions and frauds, and on that course of events which so often disconcerts the stratagems of cunning. The names of Welbeck and Watson were thus associated together, and filled my thoughts with restlessness and suspicion. Welbeck was capable of any wickedness. It was possible an interview had happened between these men, and that the fugitive had been someway instrumental in Watson's fate. These thoughts were mentioned to Williams, whom the name of Welbeck threw into the utmost perturbation. On finding that one of this name had dwelt in this city, and, that he had proved a villain, he instantly admitted the most dreary forebodings.

I have heard, said Williams, the history of this Welbeck a score of times from my brother. There formerly subsisted a very intimate connection between them. My brother had conferred upon one whom he thought honest, innumerable benefits, but all his benefits had been repaid by the blackest treachery. Welbeck's character and guilt had often been made the subject of talk between us, but, on these occasions, my brother's placid and patient temper forsook him. His grief for the calamities which had sprung from this man, and his desire of revenge, burst all bounds, and transported him to a pitch of temporary frenzy. I often enquired in what manner he intended to act, if a meeting should take place between them. He answered, that doubtless he should act like a maniac, in defiance of his sober principles, and of the duty which he owed his family.

What, said I, would you stab or pistol him?

No! I was not born for an assassin. I would upbraid him in such terms as the furious moment might suggest, and then challenge him to a meeting, from which either he or I should not part with life. I would allow time for him to make his peace with Heaven, and for me to blast his reputation upon earth, and to make such provision for my possible death, as duty and discretion would prescribe.

Now, nothing is more probable than that Welbeck and my brother have met. Thetford would of course mention his name and interest in the captured ship, and hence the residence of this detested being in this city, would be made known. Their meeting could not take place without some dreadful consequence. I am fearful that to that meeting we must impute the disappearance of my brother.

CHAPTER IV

HERE was new light thrown upon the character of Welbeck, and new food administered to my suspicions. No conclusion could be more plausible than that which Williams had drawn; but how should it be rendered certain? Walter Thetford, or some of his family, had possibly been witnesses of something, which, added to our previous knowledge, might strengthen or prolong that clue, one end of which seemed now to be put into our hands; but Thetford's father-in-law was the only one of his family, who, by seasonable flight from the city, had escaped the pestilence. To him, who still resided in the country, I repaired with all speed, accompanied by Williams.

The old man being reminded, by a variety of circumstances, of the incidents of that eventful period, was, at length, enabled to relate that he had been present at the meeting which took place between Watson and his son Walter, when certain packets were delivered by the former, relative, as he quickly understood, to the condemnation of a ship in which Thomas Thetford had gone supercargo. He had noticed some emotion of the stranger, occasioned by his son's mentioning the concern which Welbeck had in the vessel. He likewise remembered the stranger's declaring his intention of visiting Welbeck, and requesting Walter to afford him directions to his house.

Next morning at the breakfast table, continued the old man, I adverted to yesterday's incidents, and asked my son how Welbeck had borne the news of the loss of his ship. He bore it, says Walter, as a man of his wealth ought to bear so trivial a loss. But there was something very strange in his behaviour, says my son, when I mentioned the name of the captain who brought the papers; and when I mentioned the captain's design of paying him a visit, he stared upon me, for a moment, as if he were frighted out of his wits, and then, snatching up his hat, ran furiously out of the house. This was all my son said upon that occasion; but, as I have since heard, it was on that very night, that Welbeck absconded from his creditors.

I have this moment returned from this interview with old Thetford. I come to you, because I thought it possible that Mervyn, agreeably to your expectations, had returned, and I wanted to see the lad once more. My suspicions with regard to him have been confirmed, and a warrant was this day issued for apprehending him as Welbeck's accomplice.

I was startled by this news. My friend, said I, be cautious how you act, I beseech you. You know not in what evils you may involve the innocent. Mervyn I know to be blameless; but Welbeck is indeed, a villain. The latter I shall not be sorry to see brought to justice, but the former, instead of meriting punishment, is entitled to rewards.

So you believe, on the mere assertion of the boy; perhaps, his plausible lies might produce the same effect upon me, but I must stay till he thinks proper to exert his skill. The suspicions to which he is exposed will not easily be obviated; but if he has any thing to say in his defence, his judicial examination will afford him the suitable opportunity. Why are you so much afraid to subject his innocence to this test? It was not till you heard his tale, that your own suspicions were removed. Allow me the same privilege of unbelief.

But you do me wrong, in deeming me the cause of his apprehension. It is Jamieson and Thetford's work, and they have not proceeded on shadowy surmises and the impulses of mere revenge. Facts have come to light of which you are wholly unaware, and which, when known to you, will conquer even your incredulity as to the guilt of Mervyn.

Facts? Let me know them, I beseech you. If Mervyn has deceived me, there is an end to my confidence in human

248

nature. All limits to dissimulation, and all distinctions between vice and virtue will be effaced. No man's word, no force of collateral evidence shall weigh with me an hair.

It was time, replied my friend, that your confidence in smooth features and fluent accents should have ended long ago. Till I gained from my present profession, some knowledge of the world, a knowledge which was not gained in a moment, and has not cost a trifle, I was equally wise in my own conceit; and, in order to decide upon the truth of any one's pretensions, needed only a clear view of his face and a distinct hearing of his words. My folly, in that respect, was only to be cured, however, by my own experience, and I suppose your credulity will yield to no other remedy. These are the facts.

Mrs. Wentworth, the proprietor of the house in which Welbeck lived, has furnished some intelligence respecting Mervyn, whose truth cannot be doubted, and which furnishes the strongest evidence of a conspiracy between this lad and his employer. It seems, that, some years since, a nephew of this lady left his father's family clandestinely, and has not been heard of since. This nephew was intended to inherit her fortunes, and her anxieties and enquiries respecting him have been endless and incessant. These, however, have been fruitless. Welbeck, knowing these circumstances, and being desirous of substituting a girl whom he had moulded for his purpose, in place of the lost youth, in the affections of the lady while living, and in her testament when dead, endeavored to persuade her that the youth had died in some foreign country. For this end, Mervyn was to personate a kinsman of Welbeck who had just arrived from Europe, and who had been a witness of her nephew's death. A story was, no doubt, to be contrived, where truth should be copied with the most exquisite dexterity, and the lady, being prevailed upon to believe the story, the way was cleared for accomplishing the remainder of the plot.

In due time, and after the lady's mind had been artfully prepared by Welbeck, the pupil made his appearance; and, in a conversation full of studied ambiguities, assured the lady, that her nephew was dead. For the present he declined relating the particulars of his death, and displayed a constancy and intrepidity in resisting her intreaties, that would have been admirable in a better cause. Before she had time to fathom this painful mystery, Welbeck's frauds were in danger of detection, and he and his pupil suddenly disappeared.

While the plot was going forward, there occurred an incident which the plotters had not foreseen or precluded, and which possibly might have created some confusion or impediment in their designs. A bundle was found one night in the street, consisting of some coarse clothes, and containing, in the midst of it, the miniature portrait of Mrs. Wentworth's nephew. It fell into the hands of one of that lady's friends, who immediately dispatched the bundle to her. Mervyn, in his interview with this lady, spied the portrait on the mantle-piece. Led by some freak of fancy, or some web of artifice, he introduced the talk respecting her nephew, by boldly claiming it as his; but, when the mode in which it had been found was mentioned, he was disconcerted and confounded, and precipitately withdrew.

This conduct, and the subsequent flight of the lad, afforded ground enough to question the truth of his intelligence respecting her nephew; but it has since been confuted, in a letter just received from her brother in England. In this letter she is informed, that her nephew had been seen by one who knew him well, in Charleston; that some intercourse took place between the youth and the bearer of the news, in the course of which the latter had persuaded the nephew to return to his family, and that the youth had given some tokens of compliance. The letter-writer, who was father to the fugitive, had written to certain friends at Charleston, intreating them to use their influence with the runaway to the same end, and, at any rate, to cherish and protect him. Thus, I hope you will admit that the duplicity of Mervyn is demonstrated.

The facts which you have mentioned, said I, after some pause, partly correspond with Mervyn's story; but the last particular is irreconcileably repugnant to it. Now, for the

250

first time, I begin to feel that my confidence is shaken. I feel my mind bewildered and distracted by the multitude of new discoveries which have just taken place. I want time to revolve them slowly, to weigh them accurately, and to estimate their consequences fully. I am afraid to speak; fearing, that, in the present trouble of my thoughts, I may say something which I may afterwards regret. I want a counsellor; but you, Wortley, are unfit for the office. Your judgment is unfurnished with the same materials; your sufferings have soured your humanity and biassed your candor. The only one qualified to divide with me these cares, and aid in selecting the best mode of action, is my wife. She is mistress of Mervyn's history; an observer of his conduct during his abode with us; and is hindered, by her education and temper, from deviating into rigor and malevolence. Will you pardon me, therefore, if I defer commenting on your narrative till I have had an opportunity of reviewing it and comparing it with my knowledge of the lad, collected from himself and from my own observation.

Wortley could not but admit the justice of my request, and after some desultory conversation we parted. I hastened to communicate to my wife the various intelligence which I had lately received. Mrs. Althorpe's portrait of the Mervyns contained lineaments which the summary detail of Arthur did not enable us fully to comprehend. The treatment which the youth is said to have given to his father; the illicit commerce that subsisted between him and his father's wife; the pillage of money and his father's horse, but ill accorded with the tale which we had heard, and disquieted our minds with doubts, though far from dictating our belief.

What, however, more deeply absorbed our attention, was the testimony of Williams and of Mrs. Wentworth. That which was mysterious and inscrutable to Wortley and the friends of Watson, was luminous to us. The coincidence between the vague hints, laboriously collected by these enquirers, and the narrative of Mervyn, afforded the most cogent attestation of the truth of that narrative.

Watson had vanished from all eyes, but the spot where

rested his remains was known to us. The girdle spoken of by Williams, would not be suspected to exist by his murderer. It was unmolested, and was doubtless buried with him. That which was so earnestly sought, and which constituted the subsistence of the Maurices, would probably be found adhering to his body. What conduct was incumbent upon me who possessed this knowledge?

It was just to restore these bills to their true owner; but how could this be done without hazardous processes and tedious disclosures? To whom ought these disclosures to be made? By what authority or agency could these half-decayed limbs be dug up, and the lost treasure be taken from amidst the horrible corruption in which it was immersed?

This ought not to be the act of a single individual. This act would entangle him in a maze of perils and suspicions, of concealments and evasions, from which he could not hope to escape with his reputation inviolate. The proper method was through the agency of the law. It is to this that Mervyn must submit his conduct. The story which he told to me he must tell to the world. Suspicions have fixed themselves upon him, which allow him not the privilege of silence and obscurity. While he continued unknown and unthought of, the publication of his story would only give unnecessary birth to dangers; but now dangers are incurred which it may probably contribute to lessen, if not to remove.

Meanwhile the return of Mervyn to the city was anxiously expected. Day after day passed and no tidings were received. I had business of an urgent nature which required my presence in Jersey, but which, in the daily expectation of the return of my young friend, I postponed a week longer than rigid discretion allowed. At length I was obliged to comply with the exigence, and left the city, but made such arrangements that I should be apprized by my wife of Mervyn's return with all practicable expedition.

These arrangements were superfluous, for my business was dispatched, and my absence at an end, before the youth had given us any tokens of his approach. I now remembered the warnings of Wortley, and his assertions that Mervyn had withdrawn himself forever from our view. The event had hitherto unwelcomely coincided with these predictions, and a thousand doubts and misgivings were awakened.

One evening, while preparing to shake off gloomy thoughts by a visit to a friend, some one knocked at my door, and left a billet containing these words:

"Dr. Stevens is requested to come immediately to the Debtors' Apartments in Prune Street."

This billet was without signature. The hand writing was unknown, and the precipitate departure of the bearer, left me wholly at a loss with respect to the person of the writer, or the end for which my presence was required. This uncertainty only hastened my compliance with the summons.

The evening was approaching—a time when the prison doors are accustomed to be shut and strangers to be excluded. This furnished an additional reason for dispatch. As I walked swiftly along, I revolved the possible motives that might have prompted this message. A conjecture was soon formed, which led to apprehension and inquietude.

One of my friends, by name Carlton, was embarrassed with debts which he was unable to discharge. He had lately been menaced with arrest, by a creditor not accustomed to remit any of his claims. I dreaded that this catastrophe had now happened, and called to mind the anguish with which this untoward incident would overwhelm his family. I knew his incapacity to take away the claim of his creditor by payment, or to soothe him into clemency by supplication.

So prone is the human mind to create for itself distress, that I was not aware of the uncertainty of this evil till I arrived at the prison. I checked myself at the moment when I opened my lips to utter the name of my friend, and was admitted without particular enquiries. I supposed that he by whom I had been summoned hither would meet me in the common room.

The apartment was filled with pale faces and withered forms. The marks of negligence and poverty were visible in

253

all; but few betrayed, in their features or gestures, any symptoms of concern on account of their condition. Ferocious gaiety, or stupid indifference, seemed to sit upon every brow. The vapour from an heated stove, mingled with the fumes of beer and tallow that were spilled upon it, and with the tainted breath of so promiscuous a crowd, loaded the stagnant atmosphere. At my first transition from the cold and pure air without, to this noxious element, I found it difficult to breathe. A moment, however, reconciled me to my situation, and I looked anxiously round to discover some face which I knew.

Almost every mouth was furnished with a segar, and every hand with a glass of porter. Conversation, carried on with much emphasis of tone and gesture, was not wanting. Sundry groupes, in different corners, were beguiling the tedious hours at whist. Others, unemployed, were strolling to and fro, and testified their vacancy of thought and care by humming or whistling a tune.

I fostered the hope, that my prognostics had deceived me. This hope was strengthened by reflecting that the billet received was written in a different hand from that of my friend. Meanwhile I continued my search. Seated on a bench, silent and aloof from the crowd, his eyes fixed upon the floor, and his face half concealed by his hand, a form was at length discovered which verified all my conjectures and fears. Carlton was he.

My heart drooped, and my tongue faultered, at this sight. I surveyed him for some minutes in silence. At length, approaching the bench on which he sat, I touched his hand and awakened him from his reverie. He looked up. A momentary gleam of joy and surprize was succeeded by a gloom deeper than before.

It was plain that my friend needed consolation. He was governed by an exquisite sensibility to disgrace. He was impatient of constraint. He shrunk, with fastidious abhorrence, from the contact of the vulgar and the profligate. His constitution was delicate and feeble. Impure airs, restraint from exercise, unusual aliment, unwholesome or incommodious accommodations, and perturbed thoughts, were, at any time, sufficient to generate disease and to deprive him of life.

To these evils he was now subjected. He had no money wherewith to purchase food. He had been dragged hither in the morning. He had not tasted a morsel since his entrance. He had not provided a bed on which to lie; or enquired in what room, or with what companions, the night was to be spent.

Fortitude was not among my friend's qualities. He was more prone to shrink from danger than encounter it, and to yield to the flood rather than sustain it; but it is just to observe, that his anguish, on the present occasion, arose not wholly from selfish considerations. His parents were dead, and two sisters were dependent on him for support. One of these was nearly of his own age. The other was scarcely emerged from childhood. There was an intellectual as well as a personal resemblance between my friend and his sisters. They possessed his physical infirmities, his vehement passions, and refinements of taste; and the misery of his condition was tenfold increased, by reflecting on the feelings which would be awakened in them by the knowledge of his state, and the hardships to which the loss of his succour would expose them.

CHAPTER V

IT was not in my power to release my friend by the payment of his debt; but, by contracting with the keeper of the prison for his board, I could save him from famine; and, by suitable exertions, could procure him lodging as convenient as the time would admit. I could promise to console and protect his sisters, and, by cheerful tones and frequent visits, dispel some part of the evil which encompassed him.

After the first surprize had subsided, he enquired by what accident this meeting had been produced. Conscious of my incapacity to do him any essential service, and unwilling to make me a partaker in his miseries, he had forborne to inform me of his condition.

This assurance was listened to with some wonder. I showed him the billet. It had not been written by him. He was a stranger to the penmanship. None but the attorney and officer were apprized of his fate. It was obvious to conclude, that this was the interposition of some friend, who, knowing my affection for Carlton, had taken this mysterious method of calling me to his succour.

Conjectures, as to the author and motives of this interposition, were suspended by more urgent considerations. I requested an interview with the keeper, and enquired how Carlton could be best accommodated.

He said, that all his rooms were full but one, which, in consequence of the dismission of three persons in the morning, had at present but one tenant. This person had lately arrived, was sick, and had with him, at this time, one of his friends. Carlton might divide the chamber with this person. No doubt his consent would be readily given; though this arrangement, being the best, must take place whether he consented or not.

This consent I resolved immediately to seek, and, for that purpose, desired to be led to the chamber. The door of the apartment was shut. I knocked for admission. It was instantly opened, and I entered. The first person who met my view was—Arthur Mervyn.

I started with astonishment. Mervyn's countenance betrayed nothing but satisfaction at the interview. The traces of fatigue and anxiety gave place to tenderness and joy. It readily occurred to me that Mervyn was the writer of the note which I had lately received. To meet him within these walls, and at this time, was the most remote and undesirable of all contingences. The same hour had thus made me acquainted with the kindred and unwelcome fate of two beings whom I most loved.

I had scarcely time to return his embrace, when, taking my hand, he led me to a bed that stood in one corner. There was stretched upon it one whom a second glance enabled me to call by his name, though I had never before seen him. The vivid portrait which Mervyn had drawn was conspicuous in the sunken and haggard visage before me. This face had, indeed, proportions and lines which could never be forgotten or mistaken. Welbeck, when once seen or described, was easily distinguished from the rest of mankind. He had stronger motives than other men for abstaining from guilt, the difficulty of concealment or disguise being tenfold greater in him than in others, by reason of the indelible and eye-attracting marks which nature had set upon him.

He was pallid and emaciated. He did not open his eyes on my entrance. He seemed to be asleep; but, before I had time to exchange glances with Mervyn, or to enquire into the nature of the scene, he awoke. On seeing me he started, and cast a look of upbraiding on my companion. The latter comprehended his emotion and endeavored to appease him.

This person, said he, is my friend. He is likewise a physician; and, perceiving your state to require medical assistance, I ventured to send for him.

Welbeck replied, in a contemptuous and indignant tone, thou mistakest my condition, boy. My disease lies deeper than his scrutiny will ever reach. I had hoped thou wert gone. Thy importunities are well meant, but they aggravate my miseries.

He now rose from the bed, and continued, in a firm and resolute tone, you are intruders into this apartment. It is mine, and I desire to be left alone.

Mervyn returned, at first, no answer to this address. He was immersed in perplexity. At length, raising his eyes from the floor, he said, my intentions are indeed honest, and I am grieved that I want the power of persuasion. To-morrow, perhaps, I may reason more cogently with your despair, or your present mood may be changed. To aid my own weakness I will entreat the assistance of this friend.

These words roused a new spirit in Welbeck. His confusion and anger encreased. His tongue faultered as he exclaimed, good God! what mean you? Headlong and rash as you are, you will not share with this person your knowledge of me?—Here he checked himself, conscious that the words he had already uttered tended to the very end which he dreaded. This consciousness, added to the terror of more ample disclosures, which the simplicity and rectitude of Mervyn might prompt him to make, chained up his tongue, and covered him with dismay.

Mervyn was not long in answering—I comprehend your fears and your wishes. I am bound to tell you the truth. To this person your story has already been told. Whatever I have witnessed under your roof, whatever I have heard from your lips, have been faithfully disclosed to him.

The countenance of Welbeck now betrayed a mixture of incredulity and horror. For a time his utterance was stifled by his complicated feelings.

It cannot be. So enormous a deed is beyond thy power. Thy qualities are marvellous. Every new act of thine out-

strips the last, and belies the newest calculations. But this—
this perfidy exceeds—This outrage upon promises, this
violation of faith, this blindness to the future is incredible.
There he stopped; while his looks seemed to call upon
Mervyn for a contradiction of his first assertion.

I know full well how inexpiably stupid or wicked my act
will appear to you, but I will not prevaricate or lie. I repeat,
that every thing is known to him. Your birth; your early
fortunes; the incidents at Charleston and Wilmington; your
treatment of the brother and sister; your interview with
Watson, and the fatal issue of that interview—I have told
him all, just as it was told to me.

Here the shock that was felt by Welbeck overpowered his
caution and his strength. He sunk upon the side of the bed.
His air was still incredulous, and he continued to gaze upon
Mervyn. He spoke in a tone less vehement.

And hast thou then betrayed me? Hast thou shut every
avenue to my return to honor? Am I known to be a seducer
and assassin? To have meditated all crimes, and to have
perpetrated the worst?

Infamy and death are my portion. I know they are reserved for me; but I did not think to receive them at thy
hands, that under that innocent guise there lurked a heart
treacherous and cruel. But go; leave me to myself. This
stroke has exterminated my remnant of hope. Leave me to
prepare my neck for the halter, and my lips for this last, and
bitterest cup.

Mervyn struggled with his tears and replied, all this was
foreseen, and all this I was prepared to endure. My friend
and I will withdraw, as you wish; but to-morrow I return;
not to vindicate my faith or my humanity; not to make you
recant your charges, or forgive the faults which I seem to
have committed, but to extricate you from your present
evil, or to arm you with fortitude.

So saying he led the way out of the room. I followed him
in silence. The strangeness and abruptness of this scene left
me no power to assume a part in it. I looked on with new and
indescribable sensations. I reached the street before my

259

recollection was perfectly recovered. I then reflected on the purpose that had led me to Welbeck's chamber. This purpose was yet unaccomplished. I desired Mervyn to linger a moment while I returned into the house. I once more enquired for the keeper, and told him I should leave to him the province of acquainting Welbeck with the necessity of sharing his apartment with a stranger. I speedily rejoined Mervyn in the street.

I lost no time in requiring an explanation of the scene that I had witnessed. How became you once more the companion of Welbeck? Why did you not inform me by letter of your arrival at Malverton, and of what occurred during your absence? What is the fate of Mr. Hadwin and of Wallace?

Alas! said he, I perceive, that, though I have written, you have never received my letters. The tale of what has occurred since we parted is long and various. I am not only willing but eager to communicate the story, but this is no suitable place. Have patience till we reach your house. I have involved myself in perils and embarrassments from which I depend upon your counsel and aid to release me.

I had scarcely reached my own door, when I was overtaken by a servant, whom I knew to belong to the family in which Carlton and his sisters resided. Her message, therefore, was readily guessed. She came, as I expected, to enquire for my friend, who had left his home in the morning with a stranger, and had not yet returned. His absence had occasioned some inquietude, and his sister had sent this message to me, to procure what information respecting the cause of his detention I was able to give.

My perplexity hindered me, for some time, from answering. I was willing to communicate the painful truth with my own mouth. I saw the necessity of putting an end to her suspence, and of preventing the news from reaching her with fallacious aggravations or at an unseasonable time.

I told the messenger, that I had just parted with Mr. Carlton, that he was well, and that I would speedily come and acquaint his sister with the cause of his absence.

Though burning with curiosity respecting Mervyn and Welbeck, I readily postponed its gratification till my visit to

Miss Carlton was performed. I had rarely seen this lady; my friendship for her brother, though ardent, having been lately formed, and chiefly matured by interviews at my house. I had designed to introduce her to my wife, but various accidents had hindered the execution of my purpose. Now consolation and counsel was more needed than ever, and delay or reluctance in bestowing it would have been, in an high degree, unpardonable.

I therefore parted with Mervyn, requesting him to await my return, and promising to perform the engagement which compelled me to leave him with the utmost dispatch. On entering Miss Carlton's apartment, I assumed an air of as much tranquillity as possible. I found the lady seated at a desk, with pen in hand and parchment before her. She greeted me with affectionate dignity, and caught from my countenance that cheerfulness of which on my entrance she was destitute.

You come, said she, to inform me what has made my brother a truant to-day. Till your message was received I was somewhat anxious. This day he usually spends in rambling through the fields, but so bleak and stormy an atmosphere I suppose would prevent his excursion. I pray, sir, what is it detains him?

To conquer my embarrassment, and introduce the subject by indirect and cautious means, I eluded her question, and casting an eye at the parchment, how now? said I; this is strange employment for a lady. I knew that my friend pursued this trade, and lived by binding fast the bargains which others made, but I knew not that the pen was ever usurped by his sister.

The usurpation was prompted by necessity. My brother's impatient temper and delicate frame unfitted him for this trade. He pursued it with no less reluctance than diligence, devoting to the task three nights in the week and the whole of each day. It would long ago have killed him, if I had not bethought myself of sharing his tasks. The pen was irksome and toilsome at first, but use has made it easy, and far more eligible than the needle, which was formerly my only tool.

This arrangement affords my brother opportunities of exercise and recreation, without diminishing our profits;

and my time, though not less constantly, is more agreeably, as well as more lucratively, employed than formerly.

I admire your reasoning. By this means provision is made against untoward accidents. If sickness should disable him, you are qualified to pursue the same means of support.

At these words the lady's countenance changed. She put her hand on my arm, and said, in a fluttering and hurried accent, is my brother sick?

No. He is in perfect health. My observation was an harmless one. I am sorry to observe your readiness to draw alarming inferences. If I were to say, that your scheme is useful to supply deficiencies, not only when your brother is disabled by sickness, but when thrown, by some inhuman creditor, into jail, no doubt you would perversely and hastily infer that he is now in prison.

I had scarcely ended the sentence, when the piercing eyes of the lady were anxiously fixed upon mine. After a moment's pause, she exclaimed—The inference, indeed, is too plain. I know his fate. It has long been foreseen and expected, and I have summoned up my equanimity to meet it. Would to Heaven he may find the calamity as light as I should find it; but I fear his too irritable spirit.

When her fears were confirmed, she started out into no vehemence of exclamation. She quickly suppressed a few tears which would not be withheld, and listened to my narrative of what had lately occurred, with tokens of gratitude.

Formal consolation was superfluous. Her mind was indeed more fertile than my own in those topics which take away its keenest edge from affliction. She observed that it was far from being the heaviest calamity which might have happened. The creditor was perhaps vincible by arguments and supplications. If these should succeed, the disaster would not only be removed, but that security from future molestation, be gained, to which they had for a long time been strangers.

Should he be obdurate, their state was far from being hopeless. Carlton's situation allowed him to pursue his profession. His gains would be equal, and his expences would not be augmented. By their mutual industry they might hope to amass sufficient to discharge the debt at no very remote period.

What she chiefly dreaded was the pernicious influence of dejection and sedentary labor on her brother's health. Yet this was not to be considered as inevitable. Fortitude might be inspired by exhortation and example, and no condition precluded us from every species of bodily exertion. The less inclined he should prove to cultivate the means of deliverance and happiness within his reach, the more necessary it became for her to stimulate and fortify his resolution.

If I were captivated by the charms of this lady's person and carriage, my reverence was excited by these proofs of wisdom and energy. I zealously promised to concur with her in every scheme she should adopt for her own or her brother's advantage; and after spending some hours with her, took my leave.

I now regretted the ignorance in which I had hitherto remained respecting this lady. That she was, in an eminent degree, feminine and lovely, was easily discovered; but intellectual weakness had been rashly inferred from external frailty. She was accustomed to shrink from observation, and reserve was mistaken for timidity. I called on Carlton only when numerous engagements would allow, and when by some accident, his customary visits had been intermitted. On those occasions, my stay was short, and my attention chiefly confined to her brother. I now resolved to atone for my ancient negligence, not only by my own assiduities, but by those of my wife.

On my return home, I found Mervyn and my wife in earnest discourse. I anticipated the shock which the sensibility of the latter would receive from the tidings which I had to communicate respecting Carlton. I was unwilling, and yet perceived the necessity, of disclosing the truth. I desired to bring these women, as soon as possible, to the knowledge of each other, but the necessary prelude to this was an acquaintance with the disaster that had happened.

263

Scarcely had I entered the room, when Mervyn turned to me and said, with an air of anxiety and impatience—Pray, my friend, have you any knowledge of Francis Carlton?

The mention of this name by Mervyn, produced some surprize. I acknowledged my acquaintance with him.

Do you know in what situation he now is?

In answer to this question, I stated by what singular means his situation had been made known to me, and the purpose, from the accomplishment of which, I had just returned. I enquired, in my turn, whence originated this question?

He had overheard the name of Carlton in the prison. Two persons were communing in a corner, and accident enabled him to catch this name, though uttered by them in an half whisper, and to discover that the person talked about, had lately been conveyed thither.

This name was not now heard for the first time. It was connected with remembrances that made him anxious for the fate of him to whom it belonged. In discourse with my wife, this name chanced to be again mentioned, and his curiosity was roused afresh. I was willing to communicate all that I knew, but Mervyn's own destiny was too remarkable not to absorb all my attention, and I refused to discuss any other theme till that were fully explained. He postponed his own gratification to mine, and consented to relate the incidents that had happened from the moment of our separation till the present.

CHAPTER VI

AT parting with you, my purpose was to reach the abode of the Hadwins as speedily as possible. I travelled therefore with diligence. Setting out so early, I expected, though on foot, to reach the end of my journey before noon. The activity of muscles is no obstacle to thought. So far from being inconsistent with intense musing, it is, in my own case, propitious to that state of mind.

Probably no one had stronger motives for ardent meditation than I. My second journey to the city was prompted by reasons, and attended by incidents, that seemed to have a present existence. To think upon them, was to view, more deliberately and thoroughly, objects and persons that still hovered in my sight. Instead of their attributes being already seen, and their consequences at an end, it seemed as if a series of numerous years and unintermitted contemplation were requisite to comprehend them fully, and bring into existence their most momentous effects.

If men be chiefly distinguished from each other by the modes in which attention is employed, either on external and sensible objects, or merely on abstract ideas and the creatures of reflection, I may justly claim to be enrolled in the second class. My existence is a series of thoughts rather than of motions. Ratiocination and deduction leave my senses unemployed. The fulness of my fancy renders my eye vacant and inactive. Sensations do not precede and suggest, but follow and are secondary to the acts of my mind.

265

There was one motive, however, which made me less inattentive to the scene that was continually shifting before and without me than I am wont to be. The loveliest form which I had hitherto seen, was that of Clemenza Lodi. I recalled her condition as I had witnessed it, as Welbeck had described, and as you had painted it. The past was without remedy; but the future was, in some degree, within our power to create and to fashion. Her state was probably dangerous. She might already be forlorn, beset with temptation or with anguish; or danger might only be approaching her, and the worst evils be impending ones.

I was ignorant of her state. Could I not remove this ignorance? Would not some benefit redound to her from beneficent and seasonable interposition?

You had mentioned that her abode had lately been with Mrs. Villars, and that this lady still resided in the country. The residence had been sufficiently described, and I perceived that I was now approaching it. In a short time I spied its painted roof and five chimnies through an avenue of *catalpas.*

When opposite the gate which led into this avenue, I paused. It seemed as if this moment were to decide upon the liberty and innocence of this being. In a moment I might place myself before her, ascertain her true condition, and point out to her the path of honor and safety. This opportunity might be the last. Longer delay might render interposition fruitless.

But how was I to interpose? I was a stranger to her language, and she was unacquainted with mine. To obtain access to her, it was necessary only to demand it. But how should I explain my views and state my wishes when an interview was gained? And what expedient was it in my power to propose?

Now, said I, I perceive the value of that wealth which I have been accustomed to despise. The power of eating and drinking, the nature and limits of existence and physical enjoyment, are not changed or enlarged by the increase of wealth. Our corporeal and intellectual wants are supplied at little expence; but our own wants are the wants of others, and that which remains, after our own necessities are obviated, it is always easy and just to employ in relieving the necessities of others.

There are no superfluities in my store. It is not in my power to supply this unfortunate girl with decent rayment and honest bread. I have no house to which to conduct her. I have no means of securing her from famine and cold.

Yet, though indigent and feeble, I am not destitute of friends and of home. Cannot she be admitted to the same asylum to which I am now going? This thought was sudden and new. The more it was revolved, the more plausible it seemed. This was not merely the sole expedient, but the best that could have been suggested.

The Hadwins were friendly, hospitable, unsuspicious. Their board, though simple and uncouth, was wholesome and plenteous. Their residence was sequestered and obscure, and not obnoxious to impertinent enquiries and malignant animadversion. Their frank and ingenuous temper would make them easy of persuasion, and their sympathies were prompt and overflowing.

I am nearly certain, continued I, that they will instantly afford protection to this desolate girl. Why shall I not anticipate their consent, and present myself to their embraces and their welcomes in her company?

Slight reflection showed me, that this precipitation was improper. Whether Wallace had ever arrived at Malverton? Whether Mr. Hadwin had escaped infection? whether his house were the abode of security and quiet, or a scene of desolation? were questions yet to be determined. The obvious and best proceeding was to hasten forward, to afford the Hadwins, if in distress, the feeble consolations of my friendship; or, if their state were happy, to procure their concurrence to my scheme respecting Clemenza.

Actuated by these considerations, I resumed my journey. Looking forward, I perceived a chaise and horse standing by the left hand fence, at the distance of some hundred yards. This object was not uncommon or strange, and, therefore, it was scarcely noticed. When I came near, however, methought I recognized in this carriage the same in

267

which my importunities had procured a seat for the languishing Wallace, in the manner which I have formerly
related.

It was a crazy vehicle and old fashioned. When once seen
it could scarcely be mistaken or forgotten. The horse was
held by his bridle to a post, but the seat was empty. My
solicitude with regard to Wallace's destiny, of which he to
whom the carriage belonged might possibly afford me some
knowledge, made me stop and reflect on what measures it
was proper to pursue.

The rider could not be at a great distance from this spot.
His absence would probably be short. By lingering a few
minutes an interview might be gained, and the uncertainty
and suspence of some hours be thereby precluded. I therefore waited, and the same person whom I had formerly
encountered made his appearance, in a short time, from
under a copse that skirted the road.

He recognized me with more difficulty than attended my
recognition of him. The circumstances, however, of our
first meeting were easily recalled to his remembrance. I
eagerly enquired when and where he had parted with the
youth who had been, on that occasion, entrusted to his care.

He answered, that, on leaving the city and inhaling the
purer air of the fields and woods, Wallace had been, in a
wonderful degree, invigorated and refreshed. An instantaneous and total change appeared to have been wrought in
him. He no longer languished with fatigue or fear, but
became full of gaiety and talk.

The suddenness of this transition; the levity with which
he related and commented on his recent dangers and evils,
excited the astonishment of his companion, to whom he not
only communicated the history of his disease, but imparted
many anecdotes of a humorous kind. Some of these my
companion repeated. I heard them with regret and dissatisfaction. They betokened a mind vitiated by intercourse with
the thoughtless and depraved of both sexes, and particularly with infamous and profligate women.

My companion proceeded to mention, that Wallace's
exhiliration lasted but for a short time, and disappeared as

suddenly as it had appeared. He was seized with deadly sickness, and insisted upon leaving the carriage, whose movements shocked his stomach and head to an insupportable degree. His companion was not void of apprehensions on his own account, but was unwilling to desert him, and endeavored to encourage him. His efforts were vain. Though the nearest house was at the distance of some hundred yards, and though it was probable that the inhabitants of this house would refuse to accommodate one in his condition, yet Wallace could not be prevailed on to proceed; and, in spite of persuasion and remonstrance, left the carriage and threw himself on the grassy bank beside the road.

This person was not unmindful of the hazard which he incurred by contact with a sick man. He conceived himself to have performed all that was consistent with duty to himself and to his family; and Wallace, persisting in affirming that, by attempting to ride farther, he should merely hasten his death, was at length left to his own guidance.

These were unexpected and mournful tidings. I had fondly imagined, that his safety was put beyond the reach of untoward accidents. Now, however, there was reason to suppose him to have perished by a lingering and painful disease, rendered fatal by the selfishness of mankind, by the want of seasonable remedies, and exposure to inclement airs. Some uncertainty, however, rested on his fate. It was my duty to remove it, and to carry to the Hadwins no mangled and defective tale. Where, I asked, had Wallace and his companion parted?

It was about three miles further onward. The spot and the house within view from the spot, were accurately described. In this house it was possible that Wallace had sought an asylum, and some intelligence respecting him might be gained from its inhabitants. My informant was journeying to the city, so that we were obliged to separate.

In consequence of this man's description of Wallace's deportment, and the proofs of a dissolute and thoughtless temper which he had given, I began to regard his death as

269

an event less deplorable. Such an one was unworthy of a being so devoutly pure, so ardent in fidelity and tenderness as Susan Hadwin. If he loved, it was probable that in defiance of his vows, he would seek a different companion. If he adhered to his first engagements, his motives would be sordid, and the disclosure of his latent defects might produce more exquisite misery to his wife, than his premature death or treacherous desertion.

The preservation of this man, was my sole motive for entering the infected city, and subjecting my own life to the hazards, from which my escape may almost be esteemed miraculous. Was not the end disproportioned to the means? Was there arrogance in believing my life a price too great to be given for his?

I was not, indeed, sorry for the past. My purpose was just, and the means which I selected, were the best my limited knowledge applied. My happiness should be drawn from reflection on the equity of my intentions. That these intentions were frustrated by the ignorance of others, or my own, was the consequence of human frailty. Honest purposes, though they may not bestow happiness on others, will, at least, secure it to him who fosters them.

By these reflections my regrets were dissipated, and I prepared to rejoice alike, whether Wallace should be found to have escaped or to have perished. The house to which I had been directed was speedily brought into view. I enquired for the master or mistress of the mansion, and was conducted to a lady of a plain and housewifely appearance.

My curiosity was fully gratified. Wallace, whom my description easily identifed, had made his appearance at her door on the evening of the day on which he left the city. The dread of *the fever* was descanted on with copious and rude eloquence. I supposed her eloquence on this theme to be designed to apologize to me for her refusing entrance to the sick man. The peroration, however, was different. Wallace was admitted, and suitable attention paid to his wants.

Happily, the guest had nothing to struggle with but extreme weakness. Repose, nourishing diet, and salubrious airs restored him in a short time to health. He lingered under this roof for three weeks, and then, without any professions of gratitude, or offers of pecuniary remuneration, or information of the course which he determined to take, he left them.

These facts, added to that which I had previously known, threw no advantageous light upon the character of Wallace. It was obvious to conclude, that he had gone to Malverton, and thither there was nothing to hinder me from following him.

Perhaps, one of my grossest defects is a precipitate temper. I chuse my path suddenly, and pursue it with impetuous expedition. In the present instance, my resolution was conceived with unhesitating zeal, and I walked the faster that I might the sooner execute it. Miss Hadwin deserved to be happy. Love was in her heart the all-absorbing sentiment. A disappointment there was a supreme calamity. Depravity and folly must assume the guise of virtue before it can claim her affection. This disguise might be maintained for a time, but its detection must inevitably come, and the sooner this detection takes place the more beneficial it must prove.

I resolved to unbosom myself, with equal and unbounded confidence, to Wallace and his mistress. I would chuse for this end not the moment when they were separate, but that in which they were together. My knowledge, and the sources of my knowledge, relative to Wallace, should be unfolded to the lady with simplicity and truth. The lover should be present, to confute, to extenuate, or to verify the charges.

During the rest of the day these images occupied the chief place in my thoughts. The road was miry and dark, and my journey proved to be more tedious and fatiguing than I expected. At length, just as the evening closed, the well-known habitation appeared in view. Since my departure, winter had visited the world, and the aspect of nature was desolate and dreary. All around this house was vacant, negligent, forlorn. The contrast between these appearances and those which I had noticed on my first approach to it, when the ground and the trees were decked with the

271

luxuriance and vivacity of summer, was mournful, and seemed to foretoken ill. My spirits drooped as I noticed the general inactivity and silence.

I entered, without warning, the door that led into the parlour. No face was to be seen or voice heard. The chimney was ornamented, as in summer, with evergreen shrubs. Though it was now the second month of frost and snow, fire did not appear to have been lately kindled on this hearth.

This was a circumstance from which nothing good could be deduced. Had there been those to share its comforts, who had shared them on former years, this was the place and hour at which they commonly assembled. A door on one side led, through a narrow entry, into the kitchen. I opened this door, and passed towards the kitchen.

No one was there but an old man, squatted in the chimney-corner. His face, though wrinkled, denoted undecayed health and an unbending spirit. An homespun coat, leathern breeches wrinkled with age, and blue yarn hose, were well suited to his lean and shrivelled form. On his right knee was a wooden bowl, which he had just replenished from a pipkin of hasty-pudding still smoking on the coals; and in his left hand a spoon, which he had, at that moment, plunged into a bottle of molasses that stood beside him.

This action was suspended by my entrance. He looked up and exclaimed, hey day! who's this that comes into other people's houses without so much as saying "by your leave?" What's thee business? Who's thee want?

I had never seen this personage before. I supposed it to be some new domestic, and enquired for Mr. Hadwin.

Ah! replied he with a sigh, William Hadwin. Is it him thee wants? Poor man! He is gone to rest many days since.

My heart sunk within me at these tidings. Dead, said I, do you mean that he is dead?—This exclamation was uttered in a tone of some vehemence. It attracted the attention of some one who was standing without, who immediately entered the kitchen. It was Eliza Hadwin. The moment she beheld me she shrieked aloud, and, rushing into my arms, fainted away.

The old man dropped his bowl; and, starting from his

seat, stared alternately at me and at the breathless girl. My emotion, made up of joy, and sorrow, and surprize, rendered me for a moment powerless as she. At length, he said, I understand this. I know who thee is, and will tell her thee's come. So saying he hastily left the room.

CHAPTER VII

I N a short time this gentle girl recovered her senses. She did not withdraw herself from my sustaining arm, but, leaning on my bosom, she resigned herself to passionate weeping. I did not endeavor to check this effusion, believing that its influence would be salutary.

I had not forgotten the thrilling sensibility and artless graces of this girl. I had not forgotten the scruples which had formerly made me check a passion whose tendency was easily discovered. These new proofs of her affection were, at once, mournful and delightful. The untimely fate of her father and my friend pressed with new force upon my heart, and my tears, in spite of my fortitude, mingled with hers.

The attention of both was presently attracted by a faint scream, which proceeded from above. Immediately tottering footsteps were heard in the passage, and a figure rushed into the room, pale, emaciated, haggard, and wild. She cast a piercing glance at me, uttered a feeble exclamation, and sunk upon the floor without signs of life.

It was not difficult to comprehend this scene. I now conjectured, what subsequent enquiry confirmed, that the old man had mistaken me for Wallace, and had carried to the elder sister the news of his return. This fatal disappointment of hopes that had nearly been extinct, and which were now so powerfully revived, could not be endured by a frame verging to dissolution.

This object recalled all the energies of Eliza, and engrossed all my solicitude. I lifted the fallen girl in my arms; and, guided by her sister, carried her to her chamber. I had now leisure to contemplate the changes which a few months had made in this lovely frame. I turned away from the spectacle with anguish, but my wandering eyes were recalled by some potent fascination, and fixed in horror upon a form which evinced the last stage of decay. Eliza knelt on one side, and, leaning her face upon the bed, endeavored in vain to smother her sobs. I sat on the other motionless, and holding the passive and withered hand of the sufferer.

I watched with ineffable solicitude the return of life. It returned, at length, but merely to betray symptoms that it would speedily depart forever. For a time my faculties were palsied, and I was made an impotent spectator of the ruin that environed me. This pusillanimity quickly gave way to resolutions and reflections better suited to the exigencies of the time.

The first impulse was to summon a physician, but it was evident that the patient had been sinking by slow degrees to this state, and that the last struggle had begun. Nothing remained but to watch her while expiring, and perform for her, when dead, the rites of interment. The survivor was capable of consolation and of succour. I went to her and drew her gently into another apartment. The old man, tremulous and wonderstruck, seemed anxious to perform some service. I directed him to kindle a fire in Eliza's chamber. Meanwhile I persuaded my gentle friend to remain in this chamber, and resign to me the performance of every office which her sister's condition required. I sat beside the bed of the dying till the mortal struggle was past.

I perceived that the house had no inhabitant beside the two females and the old man. I went in search of the latter, and found him crouched as before, at the kitchen fire, smoking his pipe. I placed myself on the same bench, and entered into conversation with him.

I gathered from him that he had, for many years, been Mrs. Hadwin's servant. That lately he had cultivated a small farm in this neighborhood for his own advantage. Stopping one day in October, at the tavern, he heard that his old master had lately been in the city, had caught *the fever*, and after his return had died with it. The moment he became sick, his servants fled from the house, and the neighbors refused to approach it. The task of attending his sick bed, was allotted to his daughters, and it was by their hands that his grave was dug, and his body covered with earth. The same terror of infection existed after his death as before, and these hapless females were deserted by all mankind.

Old Caleb was no sooner informed of these particulars, than he hurried to the house, and had since continued in their service. His heart was kind, but it was easily seen that his skill extended only to execute the directions of another. Grief for the death of Wallace, and her father, preyed upon the health of the elder daughter. The younger became her nurse, and Caleb was always at hand to execute any orders, the performance of which was on a level with his understanding. Their neighbors had not withheld their good offices, but they were still terrified and estranged by the phantoms of pestilence.

During the last week Susan had been too weak to rise from her bed, yet such was the energy communicated by the tidings that Wallace was alive, and had returned, that she leaped upon her feet and rushed down stairs. How little did that man deserve so strenuous and immortal an affection.

I would not allow myself to ponder on the sufferings of these women. I endeavored to think only of the best expedients for putting an end to these calamities. After a moment's deliberation, I determined to go to an house at some miles distance; the dwelling of one, who, though not exempt from the reigning panic, had shewn more generosity towards these unhappy girls than others. During my former abode in this district, I had ascertained his character, and found him to be compassionate and liberal.

Overpowered by fatigue and watching, Eliza was no sooner relieved by my presence, of some portion of her cares, than she sunk into profound slumber. I directed Caleb to watch the house till my return, which should be before midnight, and then set out for the dwelling of Mr. Ellis.

The weather was temperate and moist, and rendered the footing of the meadows extremely difficult. The ground that had lately been frozen and covered with snow, was now changed into gullies and pools, and this was no time to be fastidious in the choice of paths. A brook, swelled by the recent *thaw*, was likewise to be passed. The rail which I had formerly placed over it by way of bridge, had disappeared, and I was obliged to wade through it. At length I approached the house to which I was going.

At so late an hour, farmers and farmers' servants are usually abed, and their threshold is entrusted to their watch-dogs. Two belonged to Mr. Ellis, whose ferocity and vigilance were truly formidable to a stranger, but I hoped that in me they would recognize an old acquaintance, and suffer me to approach. In this I was not mistaken. Though my person could not be distinctly seen by star-light, they seemed to scent me from afar, and met me with a thousand caresses.

Approaching the house, I perceived that its tenants were retired to their repose. This I expected, and hastened to awaken Mr. Ellis, by knocking briskly at the door. Presently he looked out of a window above, and in answer to his enquiries, in which impatience at being so unseasonably disturbed, was mingled with anxiety, I told him my name, and entreated him to come down and allow me a few minutes conversation. He speedily dressed himself, and opening the kitchen door, we seated ourselves before the fire.

My appearance was sufficiently adapted to excite his wonder; he had heard of my elopement from the house of Mr. Hadwin, he was a stranger to the motives that prompted my departure, and to the events that had befallen me, and no interview was more distant from his expectations than the present. His curiosity was written in his features, but this was no time to gratify his curiosity. The end that I now had in view, was to procure accommodation for Eliza Hadwin in this man's house. For this purpose it was my duty to describe with simplicity and truth, the inconveniences which at present surrounded her, and to relate all that had happened since my arrival.

I perceived that my tale excited his compassion, and I continued with new zeal to paint to him the helplessness of this girl. The death of her father and sister left her the property of this farm. Her sex and age disqualified her for superintending the harvest-field and the threshing-floor; and no expedient was left, but to lease the land to another, and, taking up her abode in the family of some kinsman or friend, to subsist, as she might easily do, upon the rent. Meanwhile her continuance in this house was equally useless and dangerous, and I insinuated to my companion the propriety of immediately removing her to his own.

Some hesitation and reluctance appeared in him, which I immediately ascribed to an absurd dread of infection. I endeavored, by appealing to his reason, as well as to his pity, to conquer this dread. I pointed out the true cause of the death of the elder daughter, and assured him the youngest knew no indisposition but that which arose from distress. I offered to save him from any hazard that might attend his approaching the house, by accompanying her hither myself. All that her safety required was that his doors should not be shut against her when she presented herself before them.

Still he was fearful and reluctant; and, at length, mentioned that her uncle resided not more than sixteen miles farther; that he was her natural protector, and he dared to say would find no difficulty in admitting her into his house. For his part, there might be reason in what I said, but he could not bring himself to think but that there was still some danger of *the fever*. It was right to assist people in distress, to be sure; but to risk his own life he did not think to be his duty. He was no relation of the family, and it was the duty of relations to help each other. Her uncle was the proper person to assist her, and no doubt he would be as willing as able.

The marks of dubiousness and indecision which accompanied these words, encouraged me in endeavoring to subdue his scruples. The increase of his aversion to my scheme kept pace with my remonstrances, and he finally declared that he would, on no account, consent to it.

278

Ellis was by no means hard of heart. His determination
did not prove the coldness of his charity, but merely the
strength of his fears. He was himself an object more of
compassion than of anger; and he acted like the man, whose
fear of death prompts him to push his companion from the
plank which saved him from drowning, but which is unable
to sustain both. Finding him invincible to my entreaties, I
thought upon the expedient which he suggested of seeking
the protection of her uncle. It was true, that the loss of
parents had rendered her uncle her legal protector. His
knowledge of the world; his house, and property, and influence would, perhaps, fit him for this office in a more
eminent degree than I was fitted. To seek a different
asylum might, indeed, be unjust to both, and, after some
reflection, I not only dismissed the regret which Ellis's refusal had given me, but even thanked him for the intelligence and counsel which he had afforded me. I took leave
of him, and hastened back to Hadwin's.

Eliza, by Caleb's report, was still asleep. There was no
urgent necessity for awakening her; but something was
forthwith to be done with regard to the unhappy girl that
was dead. The proceeding incumbent on us was obvious.
All that remained was to dig a grave, and to deposit the
remains with as much solemnity and decency as the time
would permit. There were two methods of doing this. I
might wait till the next day; till a coffin could be made and
conveyed hither; till the woman, whose trade it was to make
and put on the habiliments assigned by custom to the dead,
could be sought out and hired to attend; till kindred,
friends, and neighbors could be summoned to the obsequies; till a carriage were provided to remove the body to
a burying-ground, belonging to a meeting-house, and five
miles distant; till those, whose trade it was to dig graves, had
prepared one, within the sacred inclosure, for her reception; or, neglecting this toilsome, tedious, and expensive
ceremonial, I might seek the grave of Hadwin, and lay the
daughter by the side of her parent.

Perhaps I was wrong in my preference of the latter mode.
The customs of burial may, in most cases, be in themselves

279

proper. If the customs be absurd, yet it may be generally proper to adhere to them: but, doubtless, there are cases in which it is our duty to omit them. I conceived the present case to be such an one.

The season was bleak and inclement. Much time, labor, and expence would be required to go through the customary rites. There was none but myself to perform these, and I had not the suitable means. The misery of Eliza would only be prolonged by adhering to these forms; and her fortune be needlesly diminished, by the expences unavoidably to be incurred.

After musing upon these ideas for some time, I rose from my seat, and desired Caleb to follow me. We proceeded to an outer shed where farmers' tools used to be kept. I supplied him and myself with a spade, and requested him to lead me to the spot where Mr. Hadwin was laid.

He betrayed some hesitation to comply, and appeared struck with some degree of alarm, as if my purpose had been to molest, instead of securing, the repose of the dead. I removed his doubts by explaining my intentions, but he was scarcely less shocked, on discovering the truth, than he had been alarmed by his first suspicions. He stammered out his objections to my scheme. There was but one mode of burial he thought that was decent and proper, and he could not be free to assist me in pursuing any other mode.

Perhaps Caleb's aversion to the scheme might have been easily overcome, but I reflected that a mind like his was at once flexible and obstinate. He might yield to arguments and entreaties, and act by their immediate impulse; but the impulse passed away in a moment, old and habitual convictions were resumed, and his deviation from the beaten track would be merely productive of compunction. His aid, on the present occasion, though of some use, was by no means indispensible. I forbore to solicit his concurrence, or even to vanquish the scruples he entertained against directing me to the grave of Hadwin. It was a groundless superstition that made one spot more suitable for this purpose than another. I desired Caleb, in a mild tone, to return to the kitchen, and leave me to act as I thought proper. I then proceeded to the orchard.

One corner of this field was somewhat above the level of the rest. The tallest tree of the groupe grew there, and there I had formerly placed a bench, and made it my retreat at periods of leisure. It had been recommended by its sequestered situation, its luxuriant verdure, and profound quiet. On one side was a potatoe field, on the other a *melon-patch*; and before me, in rows, some hundreds of apple trees. Here I was accustomed to seek the benefits of contemplation, and study the manuscripts of Lodi. A few months had passed since I had last visited this spot. What revolutions had since occurred, and how gloomily contrasted was my present purpose with what had formerly led me hither!

In this spot I had hastily determined to dig the grave of Susan. The grave was dug. All that I desired was a cavity of sufficient dimensions to receive her. This being made, I returned to the house, lifted the corpse in my arms, and bore it without delay to the spot. Caleb seated in the kitchen, and Eliza asleep in her chamber, were wholly unapprised of my motions. The grave was covered, the spade reposited under the shed, and my seat by the kitchen fire resumed in a time apparently too short for so solemn and momentous a transaction.

I look back upon this incident with emotions not easily described. It seems as if I acted with too much precipitation; as if insensibility, and not reason, had occasioned that clearness of conceptions, and bestowed that firmness of muscles, which I then experienced. I neither trembled nor wavered in my purpose. I bore in my arms the being whom I had known and loved, through the whistling gale and intense darkness of a winter's night; I heaped earth upon her limbs, and covered them from human observation, without fluctuations or tremors, though not without feelings that were awful and sublime.

Perhaps some part of my stedfastness was owing to my late experience, and some minds may be more easily inured to perilous emergencies than others. If reason acquires strength only by the diminution of sensibility, perhaps it is just for sensibility to be diminished.

CHAPTER VIII

THE safety of Eliza was the object that now occupied my cares. To have slept, after her example, had been most proper, but my uncertainty with regard to her fate, and my desire to conduct her to some other home, kept my thoughts in perpetual motion. I waited with impatience till she should awake and allow me to consult with her on plans for futurity.

Her sleep terminated not till the next day had arisen. Having recovered the remembrance of what had lately happened, she enquired for her sister. She wanted to view once more the face, and kiss the lips, of her beloved Susan. Some relief to her anguish she expected to derive from this privilege.

When informed of the truth, when convinced that Susan had disappeared forever, she broke forth into fresh passion. It seemed as if her loss was not hopeless or compleat as long as she was suffered to behold the face of her friend and to touch her lips. She accused me of acting without warrant and without justice; of defrauding her of her dearest and only consolation; and of treating her sister's sacred remains with barbarous indifference and rudeness.

I explained in the gentlest terms the reasons of my conduct. I was not surprized or vexed, that she, at first, treated them as futile, and as heightening my offence. Such was the impulse of a grief, which was properly excited by her loss. To be tranquil and stedfast, in the midst of the usual causes of impetuosity and agony, is either the prerogative of wisdom that sublimes itself above all selfish considerations, or the badge of giddy and unfeeling folly.

The torrent was at length exhausted. Upbraiding was at an end; and gratitude, and tenderness, and implicit acquiescence in any scheme which my prudence should suggest, succeeded. I mentioned her uncle as one to whom it would be proper, in her present distress, to apply.

She started and betrayed uneasiness at this name. It was evident that she by no means concurred with me in my notions of propriety; that she thought with aversion of seeking her uncle's protection. I requested her to state her objections to this scheme, or to mention any other which she thought preferable.

She knew no body. She had not a friend in the world but myself. She had never been out of her father's house. She had no relation but her uncle Philip, and he—she could not live with him. I must not insist upon her going to his house. It was not the place for her. She should never be happy there.

I was, at first, inclined to suspect in my friend some capricious and groundless antipathy. I desired her to explain what in her uncle's character made him so obnoxious. She refused to be more explicit, and persisted in thinking that his house was no suitable abode for her.

Finding her, in this respect, invincible, I sought for some other expedient. Might she not easily be accommodated as a boarder in the city, or some village, or in a remote quarter of the country? Ellis, her nearest and most opulent neighbor, had refused to receive her; but there were others who had not his fears. There were others, within the compass of a day's journey, who were strangers to the cause of Hadwin's death; but would it not be culpable to take advantage of that ignorance? Their compliance ought not to be the result of deception.

While thus engaged, the incidents of my late journey recurred to my remembrance, and I asked, is not the honest woman, who entertained Wallace, just such a person as that of whom I am in search? Her treatment of Wallace shews her to be exempt from chimerical fears, proves that she has room in her house for an occasional inmate.

Encouraged by these views, I told my weeping companion, that I had recollected a family in which she would be kindly treated; and that, if she chose, we would not lose a moment in repairing thither. Horses, belonging to the farm, grazed in the meadows, and a couple of these would carry us in a few hours to the place which I had selected for her residence. On her eagerly assenting to this proposal, I enquired in whose care, and in what state, our present habitation should be left.

The father's property now belonged to the daughter. Eliza's mind was quick, active, and sagacious; but her total inexperience gave her sometimes the appearance of folly. She was eager to fly from this house, and to resign herself and her property, without limitation or condition, to my controul. Our intercourse had been short, but she relied on my protection and counsel as absolutely as she had been accustomed to do upon her father's.

She knew not what answer to make to my enquiry. Whatever I pleased to do was the best. What did I think ought to be done?

Ah! thought I, sweet, artless, and simple girl! how wouldst thou have fared, if Heaven had not sent me to thy succour? There are beings in the world who would make a selfish use of thy confidence; who would beguile thee at once of innocence and property. Such am not I. Thy welfare is a precious deposit, and no father or brother could watch over it with more solicitude than I will do.

I was aware that Mr. Hadwin might have fixed the destination of his property, and the guardianship of his daughters, by will. On suggesting this to my friend, it instantly reminded her of an incident that took place after his last return from the city. He had drawn up his will, and gave it into Susan's possession, who placed it in a drawer, whence it was now taken by my friend.

By this will his property was now found to be bequeathed to his two daughters; and his brother, Philip Hadwin, was named executor, and guardian to his daughters till they should be twenty years old. This name was no sooner heard by my friend, than she exclaimed, in a tone of affright, executor! My uncle! What is that? What power does that give him?

I know not exactly the power of executors. He will, doubtless, have possession of your property till you are twenty years of age. Your person will likewise be under his care till that time.

Must he decide where I am to live?

He is vested with all the power of a father.

This assurance excited the deepest consternation. She fixed her eyes on the ground, and was lost, for a time, in the deepest reverie. Recovering, at length, she said, with a sigh, what if my father had made no will?

In that case, a guardian could not be dispensed with, but the right of naming him would belong to yourself.

And my uncle would have nothing to do with my affairs?

I am no lawyer, said I; but I presume all authority over your person and property would devolve upon the guardian of your own choice.

Then I am free. Saying this, with a sudden motion, she tore in several pieces the will, which, during this dialogue, she had held in her hand, and threw the fragments into the fire.

No action was more unexpected to me than this. My astonishment hindered me from attempting to rescue the paper from the flames. It was consumed in a moment. I was at a loss in what manner to regard this sacrifice. It denoted a force of mind little in unison with that simplicity and helplessness which this girl had hitherto displayed. It argued the deepest apprehensions of mistreatment from her uncle. Whether his conduct had justified this violent antipathy, I had no means of judging. Mr. Hadwin's choice of him, as his executor, was certainly one proof of his integrity.

My abstraction was noticed by Eliza, with visible anxiety. It was plain, that she dreaded the impression which this act of seeming temerity had made upon me. Do not be angry with me, said she; perhaps I have been wrong, but I could not help it. I will have but one guardian and one protector.

The deed was irrevocable. In my present ignorance of the

domestic history of the Hadwins, I was unqualified to judge how far circumstances might extenuate or justify the act. On both accounts, therefore, it was improper to expatiate upon it.

It was concluded to leave the care of the house to honest Caleb; to fasten closets and drawers, and, carrying away the money which was found in one of them, and which amounted to no inconsiderable sum, to repair to the house formerly mentioned. The air was cold; an heavy snow began to fall in the night; the wind blew tempestuously; and we were compelled to confront it.

In leaving her dwelling, in which she had spent her whole life, the unhappy girl gave way afresh to her sorrow. It made her feeble and helpless. When placed upon the horse, she was scarcely able to maintain her seat. Already chilled by the cold, blinded by the drifting snow, and cut by the blast, all my remonstrances were needed to inspire her with resolution.

I am not accustomed to regard the elements, or suffer them to retard or divert me from any design that I have formed. I had overlooked the weak and delicate frame of my companion, and made no account of her being less able to support cold and fatigue than myself. It was not till we had made some progress in our way, that I began to view, in their true light, the obstacles that were to be encountered. I conceived it, however, too late to retreat, and endeavored to push on with speed.

My companion was a skilful rider, but her steed was refractory and unmanageable. She was able, however, to curb his spirit till we had proceeded ten or twelve miles from Malverton. The wind and the cold became too violent to be longer endured, and I resolved to stop at the first house which should present itself to my view, for the sake of refreshment and warmth.

We now entered a wood of some extent, at the termination of which I remembered that a dwelling stood. To pass this wood, therefore, with expedition, was all that remained before we could reach an hospitable asylum. I endeavored to sustain, by this information, the sinking spirits of my

286

companion. While busy in conversing with her, a blast of irresistible force twisted off the highest branch of a tree before us. It fell in the midst of the road, at the distance of a few feet from her horse's head. Terrified by this accident, the horse started from the path, and, rushing into the wood, in a moment threw himself and his rider on the ground, by encountering the rugged stock of an oak.

I dismounted and flew to her succour. The snow was already dyed with the blood which flowed from some wound in her head, and she lay without sense or motion. My terrors did not hinder me from anxiously searching for the hurt which was received, and ascertaining the extent of the injury. Her forehead was considerably bruised; but, to my unspeakable joy, the blood flowed from the nostrils, and was, therefore, to be regarded as no mortal symptom.

I lifted her in my arms, and looked around me for some means of relief. The house at which I proposed to stop was upwards of a mile distant. I remembered none that was nearer. To place the wounded girl on my own horse, and proceed gently to the house in question, was the sole expedient; but, at present, she was senseless, and might, on recovering, be too feeble to sustain her own weight.

To recall her to life was my first duty; but I was powerless, or unacquainted with the means. I gazed upon her features, and endeavored, by pressing her in my arms, to inspire her with some warmth. I looked towards the road, and listened for the wished-for sound of some carriage that might be prevailed on to stop and receive her. Nothing was more improbable than that either pleasure or business would induce men to encounter so chilling and vehement a blast. To be lighted on by some traveller was, therefore, an hopeless event.

Meanwhile, Eliza's swoon continued, and my alarm increased. What effect her half-frozen blood would have in prolonging this condition, or preventing her return to life, awakened the deepest apprehensions. I left the wood, still bearing her in my arms, and re-entered the road, from the desire of descrying, as soon as possible, the coming passenger. I looked this way and that, and again listened.

Nothing but the sweeping blast, rent and falling branches, and snow that filled and obscured the air, were perceivable. Each moment retarded the course of my own blood and stiffened my sinews, and made the state of my companion more desperate. How was I to act? To perish myself or see her perish, was an ignoble fate: courage and activity were still able to avert it. My horse stood near, docile and obsequious; to mount him and to proceed on my way, holding my lifeless burthen in my arms, was all that remained.

At this moment my attention was called by several voices, issuing from the wood. It was the note of gaiety and glee: presently a sleigh, with several persons of both sexes, appeared, in a road which led through the forest into that in which I stood. They moved at a quick pace, but their voices were hushed and they checked the speed of their horses on discovering us. No occurrence was more auspicious than this; for I relied with perfect confidence on the benevolence of these persons, and as soon as they came near, claimed their assistance.

My story was listened to with sympathy, and one of the young men, leaping from the sleigh, assisted me in placing Eliza in the place which he had left. A female, of sweet aspect and engaging manners, insisted upon turning back and hastening to the house, where it seems her father resided, and which the party had just left. I rode after the sleigh, which in a few minutes arrived at the house.

The dwelling was spacious and neat, and a venerable man and woman, alarmed by the quick return of the young people, came forth to know the cause. They received their guest with the utmost tenderness, and provided her with all the accommodations which her condition required. Their daughter relinquished the scheme of pleasure in which she had been engaged, and, compelling her companions to depart without her, remained to nurse and console the sick.

A little time shewed that no lasting injury had been suffered. Contusions, more troublesome than dangerous, and easily curable by such applications as rural and traditional wisdom has discovered, were the only consequences of the fall. My mind, being relieved from apprehensions on this

288

score, had leisure to reflect upon the use which might be made of the present state of things.

When I marked the structure of this house, and the features and deportment of its inhabitants, methought I discerned a powerful resemblance between this family and Hadwin's. It seemed as if some benignant power had led us hither as to the most suitable asylum that could be obtained; and in order to supply, to the forlorn Eliza, the place of those parents and that sister she had lost, I conceived, that, if their concurrence could be gained, no abode was more suitable than this. No time was to be lost in gaining this concurrence. The curiosity of our host and hostess, whose name was Curling, speedily afforded me an opportunity to disclose the history and real situation of my friend. There were no motives to reserve or prevarication. There was nothing which I did not faithfully and circumstantially relate. I concluded with stating my wishes that they would admit my friend as a boarder into their house.

The old man was warm in his concurrence. His wife betrayed some scruples; which, however, her husband's arguments and mine removed. I did not even suppress the tenor and destruction of the will, and the antipathy which Eliza had conceived for her uncle, and which I declared myself unable to explain. It presently appeared that Mr. Curling had some knowledge of Philip Hadwin, and that the latter had acquired the repute of being obdurate and profligate. He employed all means to accomplish his selfish ends, and would probably endeavor to usurp the property which his brother had left. To provide against his power and his malice would be particularly incumbent on us, and my new friend readily promised his assistance in the measures which we should take to that end.

CHAPTER IX

THE state of my feelings may be easily conceived to consist of mixed, but on the whole, of agreeable sensations. The death of Hadwin and his elder daughter could not be thought upon without keen regrets. These it were useless to indulge, and were outweighed by reflections on the personal security in which the survivor was now placed. It was hurtful to expend my unprofitable cares upon the dead, while there existed one to whom they could be of essential benefit, and in whose happiness they would find an ample compensation.

This happiness, however, was still incomplete. It was still exposed to hazard, and much remained to be done before adequate provision was made against the worst of evils, poverty. I now found that Eliza, being only fifteen years old, stood in need of a guardian, and that the forms of law required that some one should make himself her father's administrator. Mr. Curling being tolerably conversant with these subjects, pointed out the mode to be pursued, and engaged to act on this occasion as Eliza's friend.

There was another topic on which my happiness, as well as that of my friend, required us to form some decision. I formerly mentioned, that during my abode at Malverton, I had not been insensible to the attractions of this girl. An affection had stolen upon me, for which, it was easily discovered, that I should not have been denied a suitable return. My reasons for stifling these emotions, at that time, have been mentioned. It may now be asked, what effect subsequent events had produced on my feelings, and how far partaking and relieving her distresses, had revived a passion which may readily be supposed to have been, at no time, entirely extinguished.

The impediments which then existed, were removed. Our union would no longer risk the resentment or sorrow of her excellent parent. She had no longer a sister to divide with her the property of the farm, and make what was sufficient for both, when living together, too little for either separately. Her youth and simplicity required, beyond most others, a legal protector, and her happiness was involved in the success of those hopes which she took no pains to conceal.

As to me, it seemed at first view, as if every incident conspired to determine my choice. Omitting all regard to the happiness of others, my own interest could not fail to recommend a scheme by which the precious benefits of competence and independence might be honestly obtained. The excursions of my fancy had sometimes carried me beyond the bounds prescribed by my situation, but they were, nevertheless, limited to that field to which I had once some prospect of acquiring a title. All I wanted for the basis of my gaudiest and most dazzling structures, was an hundred acres of plough-land and meadow. Here my spirit of improvement, my zeal to invent and apply new maxims of household luxury and convenience, new modes and instruments of tillage, new arts connected with orchard, garden and cornfield, were supplied with abundant scope. Though the want of these would not benumb my activity, or take away content, the possession would confer exquisite and permanent enjoyments.

My thoughts have ever hovered over the images of wife and children with more delight than over any other images. My fancy was always active on this theme, and its reveries sufficiently extatic and glowing; but since my intercourse with this girl, my scattered visions were collected and concentered. I had now a form and features before me, a sweet and melodious voice vibrated in my ear, my soul was filled, as it were, with her lineaments and gestures, actions and

291

looks. All ideas, possessing any relation to beauty or sex, appeared to assume this shape. They kept an immoveable place in my mind, they diffused around them an ineffable complacency. Love is merely of value as a prelude to a more tender, intimate and sacred union. Was I not in love, and did I not pant after the irrevocable bonds, the boundless privileges of wedlock?

The question which others might ask, I have asked myself. Was I not in love? I am really at a loss for an answer. There seemed to be irresistible weight in the reasons why I should refuse to marry, and even forbear to foster love in my friend. I considered my youth, my defective education and my limited views. I had passed from my cottage into the world. I had acquired even in my transient sojourn among the busy haunts of men, more knowledge than the lucubrations and employments of all my previous years had conferred. Hence I might infer the childlike immaturity of my understanding, and the rapid progress I was still capable of making. Was this an age to form an irrevocable contract; to chuse the companion of my future life, the associate of my schemes of intellectual and benevolent activity?

I had reason to contemn my own acquisitions; but were not those of Eliza still more slender? Could I rely upon the permanence of her equanimity and her docility to my instructions? What qualities might not time unfold, and how little was I qualified to estimate the character of one, whom no vicissitude or hardship had approached before the death of her father? Whose ignorance was, indeed, great, when it could justly be said even to exceed my own.

Should I mix with the world; enrol myself in different classes of society; be a witness to new scenes, might not my modes of judging undergo essential variations? Might I not gain the knowledge of beings whose virtue was the gift of experience and the growth of knowledge? Who joined to the modesty and charms of woman, the benefits of education, the maturity and steadfastness of age, and with whose character and sentiments my own would be much more congenial than they could possibly be with the extreme youth, rustic simplicity and mental imperfections of Eliza Hadwin?

To say truth, I was now conscious of a revolution in my mind. I can scarcely assign its true cause. No tokens of it appeared during my late retreat to Malverton. Subsequent incidents, perhaps, joined with the influence of meditation, had generated new views. On my first visit to the city, I had met with nothing but scenes of folly, depravity and cunning. No wonder that the images connected with the city, were disastrous and gloomy; but my second visit produced somewhat different impressions. Maravegli, Estwick, Medlicote and you, were beings who inspired veneration and love. Your residence appeared to beautify and consecrate this spot, and gave birth to an opinion that if cities are the chosen seats of misery and vice, they are likewise the soil of all the laudable and strenuous productions of mind.

My curiosity and thirst of knowledge had likewise received a new direction. Books and inanimate nature were cold and lifeless instructors. Men, and the works of men, were the objects of rational study, and our own eyes only could communicate just conceptions of human performances. The influence of manners, professions and social institutions, could be thoroughly known only by direct inspection.

Competence, fixed property and a settled abode, rural occupations and conjugal pleasures, were justly to be prized; but their value could be known, and their benefits fully enjoyed only by those who have tried all scenes; who have mixed with all classes and ranks; who have partaken of all conditions; and who have visited different hemispheres and climates and nations. The next five or eight years of my life, should be devoted to activity and change: it should be a period of hardship, danger and privation: it should be my apprenticeship to fortitude and wisdom, and be employed to fit me for the tranquil pleasures and steadfast exertions of the remainder of my life.

In consequence of these reflections, I determined to suppress that tenderness which the company of Miss Hadwin produced, to remove any mistakes into which she had fallen, and to put it out of my power to claim from her more than the dues of friendship. All ambiguities, in a case like this, and all delays were hurtful. She was not exempt from passion, but this passion I thought was young, and easily extinguished.

In a short time her health was restored, and her grief melted down into a tender melancholy. I chose a suitable moment, when not embarrassed by the presence of others, to reveal my thoughts. My disclosure was ingenuous and perfect. I laid before her the whole train of my thoughts, nearly in the order, though in different and more copious terms than those in which I have just explained them to you. I concealed nothing. The impression which her artless lovelines had made upon me at Malverton; my motives for estranging myself from her society; the nature of my present feelings with regard to her, and my belief of the state of her heart; the reasonings into which I had entered; the advantages of wedlock and its inconveniences; and, finally, the resolution I had formed of seeking the city, and perhaps, of crossing the ocean, were minutely detailed.

She interrupted me not, but changing looks, blushes, flutterings and sighs, shewed her to be deeply and variously affected by my discourse. I paused for some observation or comment. She seemed conscious of my expectation, but had no power to speak. Overpowered, at length, by her emotions, she burst into tears.

I was at a loss in what manner to construe these symptoms. I waited till her vehemence was somewhat subsided, and then said—what think you of my schemes? Your approbation is of some moment: do you approve of them or not?

This question excited some little resentment, and she answered—you have left me nothing to say. Go and be happy: no matter what becomes of me. I hope I shall be able to take care of myself.

The tone in which this was said, had something in it of upbraiding. Your happiness, said I, is too dear to me to leave it in danger. In this house you will not need my protection, but I shall never be so far from you, as to be disabled from hearing how you fared, by letter, and of being active for your good. You have some money which

294

you must husband well. Any rent from your farm cannot be soon expected; but what you have got, if you remain with Mr. Curling, will pay your board and all other expences for two years: but you must be a good economist. I shall expect, continued I, with a serious smile, a punctual account of all your sayings and doings. I must know how every minute is employed, and every penny is expended, and if I find you erring, I must tell you so in good round terms.

These words did not dissipate the sullenness which her looks had betrayed. She still forebore to look at me, and said—I do not know how I should tell you every thing. You care so little about me that—I should only be troublesome. I am old enough to think and act for myself, and shall advise with no body but myself.

That is true, said I. I shall rejoice to see you independent and free. Consult your own understanding, and act according to its dictates. Nothing more is wanting to make you useful and happy. I am anxious to return to the city; but, if you will allow me, will go first to Malverton, see that things are in due order, and that old Caleb is well. From thence, if you please, I will call at your uncle's, and tell him what has happened. He may, otherwise, entertain pretensions and form views, erroneous in themselves and injurious to you. He may think himself entitled to manage your estate. He may either suppose a will to have been made, or may actually have heard from your father, or from others, of that which you burnt, and in which he was named executor. His boisterous and sordid temper may prompt him to seize your house and goods, unless seasonably apprised of the truth; and, when he knows the truth, he may start into rage, which I shall be more fitted to encounter than you. I am told that anger transforms him into a ferocious madman. Shall I call upon him?

She shuddered at the picture which I had drawn of her uncle's character; but this emotion quickly gave place to self-upbraiding, for the manner in which she had repelled my proffers of service. She melted once more into tears and exclaimed:

295

I am not worthy of the pains you take for me. I am unfeeling and ungrateful. Why should I think ill of you for despising me, when I despise myself?

You do yourself injustice, my friend. I think I see your most secret thoughts; and these, instead of exciting anger or contempt, only awaken compassion and tenderness. You love; and must, therefore, conceive my conduct to be perverse and cruel. I counted on your harboring such thoughts. Time only and reflection will enable you to see my motives in their true light. Hereafter you will recollect my words, and find them sufficient to justify my conduct. You will acknowledge the propriety of my engaging in the cares of the world, before I sit down in retirement and ease.

Ah! how much you mistake me! I admire and approve of your schemes. What angers and distresses me is, that you think me unworthy to partake of your cares and labors; that you regard my company as an obstacle and incumbrance; that assistance and counsel must all proceed from you; and that no scene is fit for me, but what you regard as slothful and inglorious.

Have I not the same claims to be wise, and active, and courageous as you? If I am ignorant and weak, do I not owe it to the same cause that has made you so; and will not the same means which promote your improvement be likewise useful to me? You desire to obtain knowledge, by travelling and conversing with many persons, and studying many scenes; but you desire it for yourself alone. Me, you think poor, weak, and contemptible; fit for nothing but to spin and churn. Provided I exist, am screened from the weather, have enough to eat and drink, you are satisfied. As to strengthening my mind and enlarging my knowledge, these things are valuable to you, but on me they are thrown away. I deserve not the gift.

This strain, simple and just as it was, was wholly unexpected. I was surprized and disconcerted. In my previous reasonings I had certainly considered her sex as utterly unfitting her for those scenes and pursuits, to which I had destined myself. Not a doubt of the validity of my conclusion had insinuated itself; but now my belief was shaken,

296

though it was not subverted. I could not deny, that human ignorance was curable by the same means in one sex as in the other; that fortitude and skill was of no less value to one than to the other.

Questionless, my friend was rendered, by her age and inexperience, if not by sex, more helpless and dependent that I; but had I not been prone to overrate the difficulties which I should encounter? Had I not deemed unjustly of her constancy and force of mind? Marriage would render her property joint, and would not compel me to take up my abode in the woods, to abide forever in one spot, to shackle my curiosity, or limit my excursions.

But marriage was a contract awful and irrevocable. Was this the woman with whom my reason enjoined me to blend my fate, without the power of dissolution? Would not time unfold qualities in her which I did not at present suspect, and which would evince an incurable difference in our minds? Would not time lead me to the feet of one who more nearly approached that standard of ideal excellence which poets and romancers had exhibited to my view?

These considerations were powerful and delicate. I knew not in what terms to state them to my companion, so as to preclude the imputation of arrogance or indecorum. It became me, however, to be explicit, and to excite her resentment rather than mislead her judgment. She collected my meaning from a few words, and, interrupting me, said:

How very low is the poor Eliza in your opinion! We are, indeed, both too young to be married. May I not see you, and talk with you, without being your wife? May I not share your knowledge, relieve your cares, and enjoy your confidence, as a sister might do? May I not accompany you in your journeys and studies, as one friend accompanies another? My property may be yours; you may employ it for your benefit and mine; not because you are my husband, but my friend. You are going to the city. Let me go along with you. Let me live where you live. The house that is large enough to hold you, will hold me. The fare that is good enough for you will be luxury to me. Oh! let it be so, will you? You cannot think how studious, how thoughtful, how inquisitive I will be. How tenderly I will nurse you when sick: it is possible you may be sick, you know, and no one in the world will be half so watchful and affectionate as I shall be. Will you let me?

In saying this, her earnestness gave new pathos to her voice. Insensibly she put her face close to mine, and, transported beyond the usual bounds of reserve, by the charms of that picture which her fancy contemplated, she put her lips to my cheek, and repeated, in a melting accent, will you let me?

You, my friends, who have not seen Eliza Hadwin, cannot conceive what effect this entreaty was adapted to produce in me. She has surely the sweetest voice, the most speaking features, and most delicate symetry, that ever woman possessed. Her guileless simplicity and tenderness made her more enchanting. To be the object of devotion to an heart so fervent and pure, was, surely, no common privilege. Thus did she tender me herself; and was not the gift to be received with eagerness and gratitude?

No. I was not so much a stranger to mankind as to acquiesce in this scheme. As my sister or my wife, the world would suffer us to reside under the same roof; to apply, to common use, the same property; and daily to enjoy the company of each other: but she was not my sister, and marriage would be an act of the grossest indiscretion. I explained to her, in few words, the objections to which her project was liable.

Well, then, said she, let me live in the next house, in the neighborhood, or, at least, in the same city. Let me be where I may see you once a day, or once a week, or once a month. Shut me not wholly from your society, and the means of becoming, in time, less ignorant and foolish than I now am.

After a pause, I replied, I love you too well not to comply with this request. Perhaps the city will be as suitable a residence as any other for you, as it will, for some time, be most convenient to me. I shall be better able to watch over your welfare, and supply you with the means of improvement, when you are within a small distance. At present, you must consent to remain here, while I visit your uncle, and afterwards go to the city. I shall look out for you a suitable lodging, and inform you when it is found. If you then continue in the same mind, I will come, and, having gained the approbation of Mr. Curling, will conduct you to town. Here ended our dialogue.

CHAPTER X

THOUGH I had consented to this scheme, I was conscious that some hazards attended it. I was afraid of calumny, which might trouble the peace or destroy the reputation of my friend. I was afraid of my own weakness, which might be seduced into an indiscreet marriage, by the charms or sufferings of this bewitching creature. I felt that there was no price too dear to save her from slander. A fair fame is of the highest importance to a young female, and the loss of it but poorly supplied by the testimony of her own conscience. I had reason for tenfold solicitude on this account, since I was her only protector and friend. Hence, I cherished some hopes, that time might change her views, and suggest less dangerous schemes. Meanwhile, I was to lose no time in visiting Malverton and Philip Hadwin.

About ten days had elapsed since we had deserted Malverton. These were days of successive storms, and travelling had been rendered inconvenient. The weather was now calm and clear, and, early in the morning that ensued the dialogue which I have just related, I set out on horseback.

Honest Caleb was found, eating his breakfast, nearly in the spot where he had been first discovered. He answered my enquiries by saying, that, two days after our departure, several men had come to the house, one of whom was Philip Hadwin. They had interrogated him as to the condition of the farm, and the purpose of his remaining on it. William Hadwin they knew to have been sometime dead, but where were the girls, his daughters?

300

Caleb answered that Susy, the eldest, was likewise dead. These tidings excited astonishment. When died she, and how, and where was she buried?

It happened two days before, and she was buried, he believed, but could not tell where.

Not tell where? By whom then was she buried?

Really, he could not tell. Some strange man came there just as she was dying. He went to the room, and when she was dead, took her away, but what he did with the body, was more than he could say, but he had a notion that he buried it. The man staid till the morning, and then went off with Lizzy, leaving him to keep house by himself. He had not seen either of them, nor indeed, a single soul since.

This was all the information that Caleb could afford the visitants. It was so lame and incredible, that they began to charge the man with falsehood, and to threaten him with legal animadversion. Just then, Mr. Ellis entered the house, and being made acquainted with the subject of discourse, told all that he himself knew. He related the midnight visit which I had paid him, explained my former situation in the family, and my disappearance in September. He stated the advice he had given me to carry Eliza to her uncle's, and my promise to comply with his counsel. The uncle declared he had seen nothing of his niece, and Caleb added, that when she set out, she took the road that led to town.

These hints afforded grounds for much conjecture and suspicion. Ellis now mentioned some intelligence that he had gathered respecting me in a late journey to ———. It seems I was the son of an honest farmer in that quarter, who married a tidy girl of a milk maid, that lived with him. My father had detected me in making some atrocious advances to my mother-in-law, and had turned me out of doors. I did not go off, however, without rifling his drawer of some hundreds of dollars, which he had laid up against a rainy day. I was noted for such pranks, and was hated by all the neighbors for my pride and laziness. It was easy by comparison of circumstances, for Ellis to ascertain that Hadwin's servant Mervyn, was the same against whom such hearty charges were laid.

301

Previously to this journey, he had heard of me from Hadwin, who was loud in praise of my diligence, sobriety and modesty. For his part, he had always been cautious of giving countenance to vagrants, that came from nobody knew where, and worked their way with a plausible tongue. He was not surprised to hear it whispered that Betsey Hadwin had fallen in love with the youth, and now, no doubt, he had persuaded her to run away with him. The heiress of a fine farm was a prize not to be met with every day.

Philip broke into rage at this news; swore that if it turned out so, his niece should starve upon the town, and that he would take good care to baulk the lad. His brother he well knew had left a will, to which he was executor, and that this will, would in good time, be forth coming. After much talk and ransacking the house, and swearing at his truant niece, he and his company departed, charging Caleb to keep the house and its contents for his use. This was all that Caleb's memory had retained of that day's proceedings.

Curling had lately commented on the character of Philip Hadwin. This man was totally unlike his brother, was a noted brawler and bully, a tyrant to his children, a plague to his neighbors, and kept a rendezvous for drunkards and idlers, at the sign of the Bull's Head, at ———. He was not destitute of parts, and was no less dreaded for cunning than malignity. He was covetous, and never missed an opportunity of overreaching his neighbor. There was no doubt that his niece's property would be embezzled, should it ever come into his hands, and any power which he might obtain over her person, would be exercised to her destruction. His children were tainted with the dissoluteness of their father, and marriage had not repaired the reputation of his daughters, or cured them of depravity: this was the man whom I now proposed to visit.

I scarcely need to say that the calumny of Betty Lawrence gave me no uneasiness. My father had no doubt been deceived, as well as my father's neighbors, by the artifices of this woman. I passed among them for a thief and a profligate, but their error had hitherto been harmless to me. The time might come which should confute the tale, without my

302

efforts. Betty, sooner or later would drop her mask, and afford the antidote to her own poisons, unless some new incident should occur to make me hasten the catastrophe.

I arrived at Hadwin's house. I was received with some attention as a guest. I looked among the pimpled visages that filled the piazza, for that of the landlord, but found him in an inner apartment with two or three more, seated round a table. On intimating my wish to speak with him alone, the others withdrew.

Hadwin's visage had some traces of resemblance to his brother; but the meek, placid air, pale cheeks and slender form of the latter, were powerfully contrasted with the bloated arrogance, imperious brow and robust limbs of the former. This man's rage was awakened by a straw; it impelled him in an instant to oaths and buffetings, and made his life an eternal brawl. The sooner my interview with such a personage should be at an end, the better. I therefore explained the purpose of my coming as fully and in as few words as possible.

Your name, Sir, is Philip Hadwin. Your brother William, of Malverton, died lately and left two daughters. The youngest only is now alive, and I come, commissioned from her, to inform you, that as no will of her father's is extant, she is preparing to administer to his estate. As her father's brother, she thought you entitled to this information.

The change which took place in the countenance of this man, during this address, was remarkable, but not easily described. His cheeks contracted a deeper crimson, his eyes sparkled, and his face assumed an expression in which curiosity was mingled with rage. He bent forwards and said, in an hoarse and contemptuous tone, pray, is your name Mervyn?

I answered, without hesitation, and as if the question were wholly unimportant, yes: my name is Mervyn.

God damn it! You then are the damn'd rascal—(but permit me to repeat his speech without the oaths, with which it was plentifully interlarded. Not three words were uttered without being garnished with a—God damn it! damnation! I'll be damn'd to hell if—and the like energetic

303

expletives.) You then are the rascal that robbed Billy's house; that ran away with the fool his daughter; persuaded her to burn her father's will, and have the hellish impudence to come into this house! But I thank you for it. I was going to look for you—youv'e saved me trouble. I'll settle all accounts with you here. Fair and softly, my good lad! If I don't bring you to the gallows—If I let you escape without such a dressing! Damned impudence! Fellow! I've been at Malverton. I've heard of your tricks: so! finding the will not quite to your mind, knowing that the executor would baulk your schemes, you threw the will into the fire; you robbed the house of all the cash, and made off with the girl!—The old fellow saw it all, and will swear to the truth.

These words created some surprize. I meant not to conceal from this man the tenor and destruction of the will, nor even the measures which his niece had taken or intended to take. What I supposed to be unknown to him, appeared to have been communicated by the talkative Caleb, whose mind was more inquisitive and less sluggish than first appearances had led me to imagine. Instead of moping by the kitchen fire, when Eliza and I were conversing in an upper room, it now appeared that he had reconnoitred our proceedings through some key hole or crevice, and had related what he had seen to Hadwin.

Hadwin proceeded to exhaust his rage in oaths and menaces. He frequently clenched his fist, and thrust it in my face, drew it back as if to render his blow more deadly; ran over the same series of exclamations on my impudence and villainy, and talked of the gallows and the whipping-post; enforced each word by the epithets—*damnable* and *hellish*—closed each sentence with—and be curst to you!

There was but one mode for me to pursue: all forcible opposition to a man of his strength was absurd. It was my province to make his anger confine itself to words, and patiently to wait till the paroxism should end or subside of itself. To effect this purpose, I kept my seat, and carefully excluded from my countenance every indication of timidity and panick on the one hand, and of scorn and defiance on the other. My look and attitude were those of a man who expected harsh words, but who entertained no suspicion that blows would be inflicted.

I was indebted for my safety to an inflexible adherence to this medium. To have strayed, for a moment, to either side, would have brought upon me his blows. That he did not instantly resort to violence, inspired me with courage, since it depended on myself whether food should be supplied to his passion. Rage must either progress or decline, and since it was in total want of provocation, it could not fail of gradually subsiding.

My demeanor was calculated to damp the flame, not only by its direct influence, but by diverting his attention from the wrongs which he had received, to the novelty of my behaviour. The disparity in size and strength between us, was too evident to make him believe that I confided in my sinews for my defence; and since I betrayed neither contempt nor fear, he could not but conclude that I trusted to my own integrity or to his moderation. I seized the first pause in his rhetorick to enforce this sentiment.

You are angry, Mr. Hadwin, and are loud in your threats, but they do not frighten me. They excite no apprehension or alarm, because I know myself able to convince you that I have not injured you. This is an inn, and I am your guest. I am sure I shall find better entertainment than blows. Come, continued I, smiling, it is possible that I am not so mischievous a wretch as your fancy paints me. I have no claims upon your niece but that of friendship, and she is now in the house of an honest man, Mr. Curling, where she proposes to continue as long as is convenient.

It is true that your brother left a will, which his daughter burnt in my presence, because she dreaded the authority which that will gave you, not only over her property, but person. It is true that on leaving the house, she took away the money which was now her own, and which was necessary to subsistence. It is true that I bore her company, and have left her in an honest man's keeping. I am answerable for nothing more. As to you, I meant not to injure you; I advised not the burning of the will. I was a stranger till after that event, to your character. I knew neither good nor ill of you. I came to tell you all this, because, as Eliza's uncle, you had a right to the information.

So! you come to tell me that she burnt the will, and is going to administer—to what, I beseech you? To her father's property? Aye, I warrant you; but take this along with you, that property is mine; land, house, stock, every thing. All is safe and snug under cover of a mortgage, to which Billy was kind enough to add a bond. One was sued, and the other *entered up*, a week ago. So that all is safe under my thumb, and the girl may whistle or starve for me. I shall give myself no concern about the strumpet. You thought to get a prize; but, damn me, you've met with your match in me. Phil. Haddin's not so easily choused, I promise you. I intended to give you this news, and a drubbing into the bargain; but you may go, and make haste. She burnt the will, did she; because I was named in it—and sent you to tell me so? Good souls! It was kind of you, and I am bound to be thankful. Take her back news of the mortgage; and, as for you, leave my house. You may go scot free this time; but I pledge my word for a sound beating when you next enter these doors. I'll pay it you with interest. Leave my house, I say!

A mortgage, said I, in a low voice, and affecting not to hear his commands, that will be sad news for my friend. Why, sir, you are a fortunate man. Malverton is an excellent spot; well watered and manured; newly and completely fenced: not a larger barn in the county: oxen, and horses, and cows in the best order: I never sat eyes on a finer orchard. By my faith, sir, you are a fortunate man. But, pray, what have you for dinner? I am hungry as a wolf. Order me a beef-steak, and some potation or other. The bottle there—it is cyder, I take it; pray, push it to this side. Saying this, I stretched out my hand towards the bottle which stood before him.

I confided in the power of a fearless and sedate manner. Methought that as anger was the food of anger, it must unavoidably subside in a contest with equability. This opinion was intuitive, rather than the product of experience, and perhaps, I gave no proof of my sagacity in hazarding my safety on its truth. Hadwin's character made him dreaded and obeyed by all. He had been accustomed to ready and tremulous submission from men far more brawny and robust than I was, and to find his most vehement menaces and gestures, totally ineffectual on a being so slender and diminutive, at once wound up his rage and excited his astonishment. One motion counteracted and suspended the other. He lifted his hand, but delayed to strike. One blow, applied with his usual dexterity, was sufficient to destroy me. Though seemingly careless, I was watchful of his motions, and prepared to elude the stroke by shrinking or stooping. Meanwhile, I stretched my hand far enough to seize the bottle, and pouring its contents into a tumbler, put it to my lips.

Come, sir, I drink your health, and wish you speedy possession of Malverton. I have some interest with Eliza, and will prevail on her to forbear all opposition and complaint. Why should she complain? While I live, she shall not be a beggar. No doubt, your claim is legal, and therefore ought to be admitted. What the law gave, the law has taken away. Blessed be the dispensers of law—excellent cyder! open another bottle, will you, and I beseech hasten dinner, if you would not see me devour the table.

It was just, perhaps, to conjure up the demon avarice to fight with the demon anger. Reason alone, would, in such a contest, be powerless, but, in truth, I spoke without artifice or disguise. If his claim were legal, opposition would be absurd and pernicious. I meant not to rely upon his own assertions, and would not acknowledge the validity of his claim, till I had inspected the deed. Having instituted suits, this was now in a public office, and there the inspection should be made. Meanwhile, no reason could be urged why I should part from him in anger, while his kindred to Eliza, and his title to her property, made it useful to secure his favor. It was possible to obtain a remission of his claims, even when the law enforced them: it would be imprudent at least to diminish the chances of remission by fostering his wrath and provoking his enmity.

What, he exclaimed, in a transport of fury, a'n't I master of my own house? Out, I say!

These were harsh terms, but they were not accompanied

by gestures and tones so menacing as those which had before been used. It was plain that the tide, which so lately threatened my destruction, had begun to recede. This encouraged me to persist.

Be not alarmed, my good friend, said I, placidly and smiling. A man of your bone need not fear a pigmy like me. I shall scarcely be able to dethrone you in your own castle, with an army of hostlers, tapsters, and cooks at your beck. You shall still be master here, provided you use your influence to procure me a dinner.

His acquiescence in a pacific system, was extremely reluctant and gradual. He laid aside one sullen tone and wrathful look after the other; and, at length, consented not only to supply me with a dinner, but to partake of it with me. Nothing was more a topic of surprize to himself, than his forbearance. He knew not how it was. He had never been treated so before. He was not proof against entreaty and submission; but I had neither supplicated nor submitted. The stuff that I was made of was at once damnably tough and devilishly pliant. When he thought of my impudence, in staying in his house after he had bade me leave it, he was tempted to resume his passion. When he reflected on my courage, in making light of his anger, notwithstanding his known impetuosity and my personal inferiority, he could not withhold his esteem. But my patience under his rebukes, my unalterable equanimity, and my ready consent to the validity of his claims, soothed and propitiated him.

An exemption from blows and abuse was all that I could gain from this man. I told him the truth, with regard to my own history, so far as it was connected with the Hadwins. I exhibited, in affecting colours, the helpless condition of Eliza; but could extort from him nothing but his consent, that, if she chose, she might come and live with him. He would give her victuals and clothes for so much house-work as she was able to do. If she chose to live elsewhere, he promised not to molest her, or intermeddle in her concerns. The house and land were his by law, and he would have them.

308

It was not my province to revile, or expostulate with him. I stated what measures would be adopted by a man who regarded the interest of others more than his own; who was anxious for the welfare of an innocent girl, connected with him so closely by the ties of kindred, and who was destitute of what is called natural friends. If he did not cancel, for her sake, his bond and mortgage, he would, at least, afford her a frugal maintainance. He would extend to her, in all emergences, his counsel and protection.

All that, he said, was sheer nonsense. He could not sufficiently wonder at my folly, in proposing to him to make a free gift of an hundred rich acres, to a girl too who scarcely knew her right hand from her left; whom the first cunning young rogue, like myself, would *chouse* out of the whole, and take herself into the bargain. But my folly was even surpassed by my impudence, since, as the *friend* of this girl, I was merely petitioning on my own account. I had come to him, whom I never saw before, on whom I had no claim, and who, as I well knew, had reason to think me a sharper, and modestly said—"Here's a girl who has no fortune. I am greatly in want of one. Pray, give her such an estate that you have in your possession. If you do, I'll marry her, and take it into my own hands." I might be thankful that he did not answer such a petition with an horse-whipping. But if he did not give her his estate, he might extend to her, forsooth, his counsel and protection. That I've offered to do, continued he. She may come and live in my house, if she will. She may do some of the family work. I'll discharge the chamber-maid to make room for her. Lizzy, if I remember right, has a pretty face. She can't have a better market for it than as chamber-maid to an inn. If she minds her p's and q's she may make up a handsome sum at the year's end.

I thought it time to break off the conference; and, my dinner being finished, took my leave; leaving behind me the character of *a queer sort of chap.* I speeded to the prothonotary's office, which was kept in the village, and quickly ascertained the truth of Hadwin's pretensions. There existed a mortgage, with bond and warrant of attorney, to so great an

309

amount as would swallow up every thing at Malverton. Furnished with these tidings, I prepared, with a drooping heart, to return to Mr. Curling's.

CHAPTER XI

THIS incident necessarily produced a change in my views with regard to my friend. Her fortune consisted of a few hundreds of dollars, which, frugally administered, might procure decent accommodation in the country. When this was consumed, she must find subsistence in tending the big-wheel or the milk-pail, unless fortune should enable me to place her in a more favorable situation. This state was, in some respects, but little different from that in which she had spent the former part of her life; but, in her father's house, these employments were dignified by being, in some degree, voluntary, and relieved by frequent intervals of recreation and leisure. Now they were likely to prove irksome and servile, in consequence of being performed for hire, and imposed by necessity. Equality, parental solicitudes, and sisterly endearments would be wanting to lighten the yoke.

These inconveniences, however, were imaginary. This was the school in which fortitude and independence were to be learned. Habit, and the purity of rural manners, would, likewise, create a-new those ties which death had dissolved. The affections of parent and sister would be supplied by the fonder and more rational attachments of friendship. These toils were not detrimental to beauty or health. What was to be dreaded from them, was, their tendency to quench the spirit of liberal curiosity; to habituate the person to bodily, rather than intellectual, exertions; to supersede, and create indifference or aversion to the only instruments of rational improvement, the pen and the book.

311

This evil, however, was at some distance from Eliza. Her present abode was quiet and serene. Here she might enjoy domestic pleasures and opportunities of mental improvement, for the coming twelvemonth at least. This period would, perhaps, be sufficient for the formation of studious habits. What schemes should be adopted, for this end, would be determined by the destiny to which I myself should be reserved.

My path was already chalked out, and my fancy now pursued it with uncommon pleasure. To reside in your family; to study your profession; to pursue some subordinate or casual mode of industry, by which I might purchase leisure for medical pursuits, for social recreations, and for the study of mankind on your busy and thronged stage, was the scope of my wishes. This destiny would not hinder punctual correspondence and occasional visits to Eliza. Her pen might be called into action, and her mind be awakened by books, and every hour be made to add to her stores of knowledge and enlarge the bounds of her capacity.

I was spiritless and gloomy when I left ———, but reflections on my future lot, and just views of the situation of my friend, insensibly restored my cheerfulness. I arrived at Mr. Curling's in the evening, and hastened to impart to Eliza the issue of my commission. It gave her uneasiness, merely as it frustrated the design, on which she had fondly mused, of residing in the city. She was somewhat consoled by my promises of being her constant correspondent and occasional visitor.

Next morning I set out on my journey hither, on foot. The way was not long; the weather, though cold, was wholesome and serene. My spirits were high, and I saw nothing in the world before me but sunshine and prosperity. I was conscious that my happiness depended not on the revolutions of nature or the caprice of man. All without was, indeed, vicissitude and uncertainty; but within my bosom was a centre not to be shaken or removed. My purposes were honest and steadfast. Every sense was the inlet of pleasure, because it was the avenue to knowledge; and my soul brooded over the world of ideas, and glowed with exultation at the grandeur and beauty of its own creations.

This felicity was too rapturous to be of long duration. I gradually descended from these heights; and the remembrance of past incidents, connected with the images of your family, to which I was returning, led my thoughts into a different channel. Welbeck and the unhappy girl whom he had betrayed; Mrs. Villars and Wallace were recollected a-new. The views which I had formed, for determining the fate and affording assistance to Clemenza, were recalled. My former resolutions, with regard to her, had been suspended by the uncertainty in which the fate of the Hadwins was, at that time, wrapped. Had it not become necessary wholly to lay aside these resolutions?

That, indeed, was an irksome conclusion. No wonder that I struggled to repel it: that I fostered the doubt whether money was the only instrument of benefit: whether caution, and fortitude, and knowledge were not the genuine preservatives from evil. Had I not the means in my hands of dispelling her fatal ignorance of Welbeck and of those with whom she resided? Was I not authorized by my previous, though slender, intercourse, to seek her presence?

Suppose I should enter Mrs. Villars' house, desire to be introduced to the lady, accost her with affectionate simplicity, and tell her the truth? Why be anxious to smooth the way; why deal in apologies, circuities and inuendoes? All these are feeble and perverse refinements, unworthy of an honest purpose and an erect spirit. To believe her inaccessible to my visit, was absurd. To wait for the permission of those whose interest it might be to shut out visitants, was cowardice. This was an infringement of her liberty, which equity and law equally condemned. By what right could she be restrained from intercourse with others? Doors and passages may be between her and me. With a purpose such as mine, no one had a right to close the one or obstruct the other. Away with cowardly reluctances and clownish scruples, and let me hasten this moment to her dwelling.

Mrs. Villars is the portress of the mansion. She will prob-

313

ably present herself before me, and demand the reason of my visit. What shall I say to her? The truth. To faulter, or equivocate, or dissemble to this woman, would be wicked. Perhaps her character has been misunderstood and maligned. Can I render her a greater service than to apprize her of the aspersions that have rested on it, and afford her the opportunity of vindication? Perhaps she is indeed selfish and profligate; the betrayer of youth and the agent of lasciviousness. Does she not deserve to know the extent of her errors and the ignominy of her trade? Does she not merit the compassion of the good and the rebukes of the wise? To shrink from the task, would prove me cowardly and unfirm. Thus far, at least, let my courage extend.

Alas! Clemenza is unacquainted with my language. My thoughts cannot make themselves apparent but by words, and to my words she will be able to affix no meaning. Yet is not that an hasty decision? The version from the dramas of Zeno which I found in her toilet, was probably hers, and proves her to have a speculative knowledge of our tongue. Near half a year has since elapsed, during which she has dwelt with talkers of English, and consequently could not fail to have acquired it. This conclusion is somewhat dubious, but experiment will give it certainty.

Hitherto I had strolled along the path at a lingering pace. Time enough, methought, to reach your threshold between sun-rise and moonlight, if my way had been three times longer than it was. Yon were the pleasing phantoms that hovered before me, and beckoned me forward. What a total revolution had occurred in the course of a few seconds, for thus long did my reasonings with regard to Clemenza and the Villars require to pass through my understanding, and escape, in half muttered soliloquy, from my lips. My muscles trembled with eagerness, and I bounded forward with impetuosity. I saw nothing but a visto of catalpas, leafless, loaded with icicles, and terminating in four chimneys and a painted roof. My fancy outstripped my footsteps, and was busy in picturing faces and rehearsing dialogues. Presently I reached this new object of my pursuit, darted through the avenue, noticed that some windows of the house were unclosed, drew thence an hasty inference that the house was not without inhabitants, and knocked, quickly and loudly, for admission.

Some one within crept to the door, opened it with seeming caution, and just far enough to allow the face to be seen. It was the timid, pale and unwashed face of a girl who was readily supposed to be a servant, taken from a cottage, and turned into a bringer of wood and water, and a scourer of tubs and trenchers. She waited in timorous silence the delivery of my message. Was Mrs. Villars at home?

No: she was gone to town.

Were any of her daughters within?

She could not tell; she believed—she thought—which did I want? Miss Hetty or Miss Sally?

Let me see Miss Hetty. Saying this, I pushed gently against the door. The girl, half reluctant, yielded way: I entered the passage, and putting my hand on the lock of a door that seemed to lead into a parlour—is Miss Hetty in this room?

No: there was nobody there.

Go call her then. Tell her there is one who wishes to see her on important business. I will wait for her coming in this room. So saying, I opened the door, and entered the apartment, while the girl withdrew to perform my message.

The parlour was spacious and expensively furnished, but an air of negligence and disorder was every where visible. The carpet was wrinkled and unswept; a clock on the table, in a glass frame, so streaked and spotted with dust as scarcely to be transparent, and the index motionless, and pointing at four instead of nine; embers scattered on the marble hearth, and tongs lying on the fender with the handle in the ashes; an harpsicord, uncovered, one end loaded with *scores,* tumbled together in a heap, and the other with volumes of novels and plays, some on their edges, some on their backs, gaping open by the scorching of their covers; rent; blurred; stained; blotted; dog-eared; tables awry; chairs crouding each other; in short, no object but indicated the neglect or ignorance of domestic neatness and economy.

My leisure was employed in surveying these objects, and in listening for the approach of Miss Hetty. Some minutes

315

elapsed, and no one came. A reason for delay was easily imagined, and I summoned patience to wait. I opened a book; touched the instrument; surveyed the vases on the mantle-tree; the figures on the hangings, and the print of Apollo and the Sybil, taken from Salvator, and hung over the chimney. I eyed my own shape and garb in the mirror, and asked how my rustic appearance would be regarded by that supercilious and voluptuous being, to whom I was about to present myself.

Presently the latch of the door was softly moved, it opened, and the simpleton, before described, appeared. She spoke, but her voice was so full of hesitation, and so near a whisper, that much attention was needed to make out her words: Miss Hetty was not at home—she was gone to town with her *mistiss*.

This was a tale not to be credited. How was I to act? She persisted in maintaining the truth of it.—Well then, said I, at length, tell Miss Sally that I wish to speak with her. She will answer my purpose just as well.

Miss Sally was not at home neither. She had gone to town too. They would not be back, she did not know when: not till night, she supposed. It was so indeed, none of them wasn't at home: none but she and Nanny in the kitchen—indeed'n there wasn't.

Go tell Nanny to come here—I will leave my message with her. She withdrew, but Nanny did not receive the summons, or thought proper not to obey it. All was vacant and still.

My state was singular and critical. It was absurd to prolong it; but to leave the house with my errand unexecuted, would argue imbecility and folly. To ascertain Clemenza's presence in this house, and to gain an interview, were yet in my power. Had I not boasted of my intrepidity in braving denials and commands, when they endeavored to obstruct my passage to this woman? But here were no obstacles nor prohibitions. Suppose the girl had said truth, that the matron and her daughters were absent, and that Nanny and herself were the only guardians of the mansion. So much

316

the better. My design will not be opposed. I have only to mount the stair, and go from one room to another, till I find what I seek.

There was hazard, as well as plausibility, in this scheme. I thought it best once more to endeavor to extort information from the girl, and persuade her to be my guide to whomsoever the house contained. I put my hand to the bell and rung a brisk peal. No one came. I passed into the entry, to the foot of a stair-case, and to a back window. Nobody was within hearing or sight.

Once more I reflected on the rectitude of my intentions, on the possibility that the girl's assertions might be true, on the benefits of expedition, and of gaining access to the object of my visit without interruption or delay. To these considerations was added a sort of charm, not easily explained, and by no means justifiable, produced by the very temerity and hazardness accompanying this attempt. I thought, with scornful emotions, on the bars and hindrances which pride and caprice, and delusive maxims of decorum, raise in the way of human intercourse. I spurned at these semblances and substitutes of honesty, and delighted to shake such fetters into air, and trample such impediments to dust. I wanted to see an human being, in order to promote her happiness. It was doubtful whether she was within twenty paces of the spot where I stood. The doubt was to be solved. How? By examining the space. I forthwith proceeded to examine it. I reached the second story. I approached a door that was closed. I knocked: after a pause, a soft voice said, who is there?

The accents were as musical as those of Clemenza, but were in other respects, different. I had no topic to discuss with this person. I answered not, yet hesitated to withdraw. Presently the same voice was again heard: what is it you want? Why don't you answer? Come in!—I complied with the command, and entered the room.

It was deliberation and foresight that led me hither, and not chance or caprice. Hence, instead of being disconcerted or vanquished by the objects that I saw, I was tranquil and

317

firm. My curiosity, however, made me a vigilant observer. Two females, arrayed with voluptuous negligence, in a manner adapted to the utmost seclusion, and seated in a careless attitude, on a sofa, were now discovered.

Both darted glances at the door. One, who appeared to be the youngest, no sooner saw me, than she shrieked, and starting from her seat, betrayed, in the looks which she successively cast upon me, on herself and on the chamber, whose apparatus was in no less confusion than that of the apartment below, her consciousness of the unseasonableness of this meeting.

The other shrieked likewise, but on her it seemed to be the token of surprize, rather than that of terror. There was, probably, somewhat in my aspect and garb that suggested an apology for this intrusion, as arising from simplicity and mistake. She thought proper, however, to assume the air of one offended, and looking sternely—How now, fellow, said she, what is this? Why come you hither?

This questioner was of mature age, but had not passed the period of attractiveness and grace. All the beauty that nature had bestowed was still retained, but the portion had never been great. What she possessed was so modelled and embellished by such a carriage and dress, as to give it most power over the senses of the gazer. In proportion, however, as it was intended and adapted to captivate those, who know none but physical pleasures, it was qualified to breed distaste and aversion in me.

I am sensible how much error may have lurked in this decision. I had brought with me the belief of their being unchaste; and seized, perhaps, with too much avidity, any appearance that coincided with my prepossessions. Yet the younger by no means inspired the same disgust; though I had no reason to suppose her more unblemished than the elder. Her modesty seemed unaffected, and was by no means satisfied, like that of the elder, with defeating future curiosity. The consciousness of what had already been exposed filled her with confusion, and she would have flown away, if her companion had not detained her by some degree of force. What ails the girl? There's nothing to be frightened at. Fellow! she repeated, what brings you here?

I advanced and stood before them. I looked steadfastly, but, I believe, with neither effrontery nor anger, on the one who addressed me. I spoke in a tone serious and emphatical. I come for the sake of speaking to a woman, who formerly resided in this house, and probably resides here still. Her name is Clemenza Lodi. If she be here, I request you to conduct me to her instantly.

Methought I perceived some inquietude, a less imperious and more inquisitive air, in this woman, on hearing the name of Clemenza. It was momentary, and gave way to peremptory looks. What is your business with her? And why did you adopt this mode of enquiry? A very extraordinary intrusion! Be good enough to leave the chamber. Any questions proper to be answered, will be answered below.

I meant not to intrude or offend. It was not an idle or impertinent motive that led me hither. I waited below for some time after soliciting an audience of you, through the servant. She assured me you were absent, and laid me under the necessity of searching for Clemenza Lodi myself, and without a guide. I am anxious to withdraw, and request merely to be directed to the room which she occupies.

I direct you, replied she in a more resolute tone, to quit the room and the house.

Impossible, madam, I replied, still looking at her earnestly, leave the house without seeing her! You might as well enjoin me to pull the Andes on my head! To walk barefoot to Peking! Impossible!

Some solicitude was now mingled with her anger. This is strange insolence! unaccountable behaviour!—be gone from my room! will you compel me to call the gentlemen?

Be not alarmed, said I, with augmented mildness. There was indeed compassion and sorrow at my heart, and these must have somewhat influenced my looks. Be not alarmed—I came to confer a benefit, not to perpetrate an injury. I came not to censure or expostulate with you, but merely to counsel and aid a being that needs both: all I want

319

is to see her. In this chamber I sought not you, but her. Only lead me to her, or tell me where she is. I will then rid you of my presence.

Will you compel me to call those who will punish this insolence as it deserves?

Dearest madam! I compel you to nothing. I merely supplicate. I would ask you to lead me to these gentlemen, if I did not know that there are none but females in the house. It is you who must receive and comply with my petition. Allow me a moment's interview with Clemenza Lodi. Compliance will harm you not, but will benefit her. What is your objection?

This is the strangest proceeding! the most singular conduct! Is this a place fit to parley with you? I warn you of the consequence of staying a moment longer. Depend upon it, you will sorely repent it.

You are obdurate, said I, and turned towards the younger, who listened to this discourse in tremors and panick. I took her hand with an air of humility and reverence. Here, said I, there seems to be purity, innocence and condescension. I took this house to be the temple of voluptuousness. Females, I expected to find in it, but such only as traded in licentious pleasures: specious, perhaps not destitute of talents, beauty and address, but dissolute and wanton; sensual and avaricious; yet, in this countenance and carriage there are tokens of virtue. I am born to be deceived, and the semblance of modesty is readily assumed. Under this veil, perhaps, lurk a tainted heart and depraved appetites. Is it so?

She made me no answer, but somewhat in her looks seemed to evince that my favorable prepossessions were just. I noticed likewise that the alarm of the elder was greatly increased by this address to her companion. The thought suddenly occurred that this girl might be in circumstances not unlike those of Clemenza Lodi; that she was not apprized of the character of her associates, and might by this meeting be rescued from similar evils.

This suspicion filled me with tumultuous feelings. Clemenza was for a time forgotten. I paid no attention to the looks or demeanor of the elder, but was wholly occupied in gazing on the younger. My anxiety to know the truth, gave pathos and energy to my tones, while I spoke:

Who, where, what are you? Do you reside in this house? Are you a sister or daughter in this family, or merely a visitant? Do you know the character, profession and views of your companions? Do you deem them virtuous, or know them to be profligate? Speak! tell me, I beseech you!

The maiden confusion which had just appeared in the countenance of this person, now somewhat abated. She lifted her eyes, and glanced by turns at me and at her who sat by her side. An air of serious astonishment overspread her features, and she seemed anxious for me to proceed. The elder, meanwhile, betrayed the utmost alarm, again upbraided my audacity, commanded me to withdraw, and admonished me of the danger I incurred by lingering.

I noticed not her interference, but again entreated to know of the younger her true state. She had no time to answer me, supposing her not to want the inclination, for every pause was filled by the clamorous importunities and menaces of the other. I began to perceive that my attempts were useless to this end, but the chief, and most estimable purpose, was attainable. It was in my power to state the knowledge I possessed, through your means, of Mrs. Villars and her daughters. This information might be superfluous, since she to whom it was given, might be one of this licentious family. The contrary, however, was not improbable, and my tidings, therefore, might be of the utmost moment to her safety.

A resolute, and even impetuous manner, reduced my incessant interruptor to silence. What I had to say I compressed in a few words, and adhered to perspicuity and candor with the utmost care. I still held the hand that I had taken, and fixed my eyes upon her countenance with a steadfastness that hindered her from lifting her eyes.

I know you not; whether you be dissolute or chaste, I cannot tell. In either case, however, what I am going to say will be useful. Let me faithfully repeat what I have heard. It is mere rumor, and I vouch not for its truth. Rumor as it is, I submit it to your judgment, and hope that it may guide you into paths of innocence and honor.

Mrs. Villars and her three daughters are English women, who supported for a time an unblemished reputation, but who, at length, were suspected of carrying on the trade of prostitution. This secret could not be concealed forever. The profligates who frequented their house, betrayed them. One of them who died under their roof, after they had withdrawn from it into the country, disclosed to his kinsman, who attended his death bed, their genuine character.

The dying man likewise related incidents in which I am deeply concerned. I have been connected with one by name Welbeck. In his house I met an unfortunate girl, who was afterwards removed to Mrs. Villars's. Her name was Clemenza Lodi. Residence in this house, under the controul of a woman like Mrs. Villars and her daughters, must be injurious to her innocence, and from this controul I now come to rescue her.

I turned to the elder, and continued: By all that is sacred, I adjure you to tell me whether Clemenza Lodi be under this roof! if she be not, whither has she gone? To know this, I came hither, and any difficulty or reluctance in answering, will be useless; till an answer be obtained, I will not go hence.

During this speech, anger had been kindling in the bosom of this woman. It now burst upon me in a torrent of opprobrious epithets. I was a villain, a calumniator, a thief. I had lurked about the house, till those whose sex and strength enabled them to cope with me, had gone. I had entered these doors by fraud. I was a wretch, guilty of the last excesses of insolence and insult.

To repel these reproaches, or endure them, was equally useless. The satisfaction that I sought was only to be gained by searching the house. I left the room without speaking. Did I act illegally in passing from one story and one room to another? Did I really deserve the imputations of rashness and insolence? My behaviour, I well know, was ambiguous and hazardous, and perhaps wanting in discretion, but my motives were unquestionably pure. I aimed at nothing but the rescue of an human creature from distress and dishonor.

I pretend not to the wisdom of experience and age; to the praise of forethought or subtlety. I chuse the obvious path, and pursue it with headlong expedition. Good intentions, unaided by knowledge, will, perhaps, produce more injury than benefit, and therefore, knowledge must be gained, but the acquisition is not momentary; is not bestowed unasked and untoil'd for: meanwhile, we must not be unactive because we are ignorant. Our good purposes must hurry to performance, whether our knowledge be greater or less.

CHAPTER XII

TO explore the house in this manner was so contrary to ordinary rules, that the design was probably wholly unsuspected by the women whom I had just left. My silence, at parting, might have been ascribed by them to the intimidating influence of invectives and threats. Hence I proceeded in my search without interruption.

Presently I reached a front chamber in the third story. The door was ajar. I entered it on tiptoe. Sitting on a low chair by the fire, I beheld a female figure, dressed in a negligent, but not indecent manner. Her face in the posture in which she sat was only half seen. Its hues were sickly and pale, and in mournful unison with a feeble and emaciated form. Her eyes were fixed upon a babe, that lay stretched upon a pillow at her feet. The child, like its mother, for such she was readily imagined to be, was meagre and cadaverous. Either it was dead, or could not be very distant from death.

The features of Clemenza were easily recognized, though no contrast could be greater, in habit and shape, and complexion, than that which her present bore to her former appearance. All her roses had faded, and her brilliances vanished. Still, however, there was somewhat fitted to awaken the tenderest emotions. There were tokens of inconsolable distress.

Her attention was wholly absorbed by the child. She lifted not her eyes, till I came close to her, and stood before her. When she discovered me, a faint start was perceived. She looked at me for a moment, then putting one spread hand before her eyes, she stretched out the other towards the door, and waving it in silence, as if to admonish me to depart.

This motion, however emphatical, I could not obey. I wished to obtain her attention, but knew not in what words to claim it. I was silent. In a moment she removed her hand from her eyes, and looked at me with new eagerness. Her features bespoke emotions, which, perhaps, flowed from my likeness to her brother, joined with the memory of my connection with Welbeck.

My situation was full of embarrassment. I was by no means certain that my language would be understood. I knew not in what light the policy and dissimulation of Welbeck might have taught her to regard me. What proposal, conducive to her comfort and her safety, could I make to her?

Once more she covered her eyes, and exclaimed in a feeble voice, go away! be gone!

As if satisfied with this effort, she resumed her attention to her child. She stooped and lifted it in her arms, gazing, meanwhile, on its almost lifeless features with intense anxiety. She crushed it to her bosom, and again looking at me, repeated, go away! go away! be gone!

There was somewhat in the lines of her face, in her tones and gestures, that pierced to my heart. Added to this, was my knowledge of her condition; her friendlessness; her poverty; the pangs of unrequited love; and her expiring infant. I felt my utterance choaked, and my tears struggling for passage. I turned to the window, and endeavored to regain my tranquillity.

What was it, said I, that brought me hither? The perfidy of Welbeck must surely have long since been discovered. What can I tell her of the Villars which she does not already know, or of which the knowledge will be useful? If their treatment has been just, why should I detract from their merit? If it has been otherwise, their own conduct will have disclosed their genuine character. Though voluptuous themselves, it does not follow that they have labored to

325

debase this creature. Though wanton, they may not be inhuman.

I can propose no change in her condition for the better. Should she be willing to leave this house, whither is it in my power to conduct her? O that I were rich enough to provide food for the hungry, shelter for the housless, and raiment for the naked.

I was roused from these fruitless reflections by the lady, whom some sudden thought induced to place the child in its bed, and rising to come towards me. The utter dejection which her features lately betrayed, was now changed for an air of anxious curiosity. Where, said she, in her broken English, where is Signior Welbeck?

Alas! returned I, I know not. That question might, I thought, with more propriety be put to you than me.

I know where he be; I fear where he be.

So saying, the deepest sighs burst from her heart. She turned from me, and going to the child, took it again into her lap. Its pale and sunken cheek was quickly wet with the mother's tears, which, as she silently hung over it, dropped fast from her eyes.

This demeanor could not but awaken curiosity, while it gave a new turn to my thoughts. I began to suspect that in the tokens which I saw, there was not only distress for her child, but concern for the fate of Welbeck. Know you, said I, where Mr. Welbeck is? Is he alive? Is he near? Is he in calamity?

I do not know if he be alive. He be sick. He be in prison. They will not let me go to him. And—Here her attention and mine was attracted by the infant, whose frame, till now motionless, began to be tremulous. Its features sunk into a more ghastly expression. Its breathings were difficult, and every effort to respire produced a convulsion harder than the last.

The mother easily interpreted these tokens. The same mortal struggle seemed to take place in her feature as in those of her child. At length her agony found way in a piercing shriek. The struggle in the infant was past. Hope looked in vain for a new motion in its heart or its eyelids. The lips were closed, and its breath was gone, forever!

The grief which overwhelmed the unhappy parent, was of that outrageous and desperate kind which is wholly incompatible with thinking. A few incoherent motions and screams, that rent the soul, were followed by a deep swoon. She sunk upon the floor, pale and lifeless as her babe.

I need not describe the pangs which such a scene was adapted to produce in me. These were rendered more acute by the helpless and ambiguous situation in which I was placed. I was eager to bestow consolation and succour, but was destitute of all means. I was plunged into uncertainties and doubts. I gazed alternately at the infant and its mother. I sighed. I wept. I even sobbed. I stooped down and took the lifeless hand of the sufferer. I bathed it with my tears, and exclaimed, Ill-fated woman! unhappy mother! what shall I do for thy relief? How shall I blunt the edge of this calamity, and rescue thee from new evils?

At this moment the door of the apartment was opened, and the youngest of the women whom I had seen below, entered. Her looks betrayed the deepest consternation and anxiety. Her eyes in a moment were fixed by the decayed form and the sad features of Clemenza. She shuddered at this spectacle, but was silent. She stood in the midst of the floor, fluctuating and bewildered. I dropped the hand that I was holding, and approached her.

You have come, said I, in good season. I know you not, but will believe you to be good. You have an heart, it may be, not free from corruption, but it is still capable of pity for the miseries of others. You have an hand that refuses not its aid to the unhappy. See; there is an infant dead. There is a mother whom grief has, for a time, deprived of life. She has been oppressed and betrayed; been robbed of property and reputation—but not of innocence. She is worthy of relief. Have you arms to receive her? Have you sympathy, protection, and a home to bestow upon a forlorn, betrayed and unhappy stranger? I know not what this house is; I suspect it to be no better than a brothel. I know not what treatment

327

this woman has received. If, when her situation and wants are ascertained, will you supply her wants? Will you rescue her from evils that may attend her continuance here?

She was disconcerted and bewildered by this address. At length she said—All that has happened, all that I have heard and seen is so unexpected, so strange, that I am amazed and distracted. Your behaviour I cannot comprehend, nor your motive for making this address to me. I cannot answer you, except in one respect. If this woman has suffered injury, I have had no part in it. I knew not of her existence, nor her situation till this moment; and whatever protection or assistance she may justly claim, I am both able and willing to bestow. I do not live here, but in the city. I am only an occasional visitant in this house.

What then, I exclaimed, with sparkling eyes and a rapturous accent, you are not profligate; are a stranger to the manners of this house, and a detester of these manners? Be not a deceiver, I entreat you. I depend only on your looks and professions, and these may be dissembled.

These questions, which indeed argued a childish simplicity, excited her surprize. She looked at me, uncertain whether I was in earnest or in jest. At length she said, your language is so singular, that I am at a loss how to answer it. I shall take no pains to find out its meaning, but leave you to form conjectures at leisure. Who is this woman, and how can I serve her? After a pause, she continued—I cannot afford her any immediate assistance, and shall not stay a moment longer in this house. There (putting a card in my hand) is my name and place of abode. If you shall have any proposals to make, respecting this woman, I shall be ready to receive them in my own house. So saying, she withdrew.

I looked wistfully after her, but could not but assent to her assertion, that her presence here would be more injurious to her than beneficial to Clemenza. She had scarcely gone, when the elder woman entered. There was rage, sullenness, and disappointment in her aspect. These, however, were suspended by the situation in which she discovered the mother and child. It was plain that all the sentiments of woman were not extinguished in her heart. She summoned the servants and seemed preparing to take

328

such measures as the occasion prescribed. I now saw the folly of supposing that these measures would be neglected, and that my presence could not essentially contribute to the benefit of the sufferer. Still, however, I lingered in the room, till the infant was covered with a cloth, and the still senseless parent was conveyed into an adjoining chamber. The woman then, as if she had not seen me before, fixed scowling eyes upon me, and exclaimed, thief! villain! why do you stay here?

I mean to go, said I, but not till I express my gratitude and pleasure, at the sight of your attention to this sufferer. You deem me insolent and perverse, but I am not such; and hope that the day will come when I shall convince you of my good intentions.

Begone! interrupted she, in a more angry tone. Begone this moment, or I will treat you as a thief. She now drew forth her hand from under her gown, and shewed a pistol. You shall see, she continued, that I will not be insulted with impunity. If you do not vanish, I will shoot you as a robber.

This woman was far from wanting a force and intrepidity worthy of a different sex. Her gestures and tones were full of energy. They denoted an haughty and indignant spirit. It was plain that she conceived herself deeply injured by my conduct; and was it absolutely certain that her anger was without reason? I had loaded her house with atrocious imputations, and these imputations might be false. I had conceived them upon such evidence as chance had provided, but this evidence, intricate and dubious as human actions and motives are, might be void of truth.

Perhaps, said I, in a sedate tone, I have injured you; I have mistaken your character. You shall not find me less ready to repair, than to perpetrate, this injury. My error was without malice, and ——

I had not time to finish the sentence, when this rash and enraged woman thrust the pistol close to my head and fired it. I was wholly unaware that her fury would lead her to this excess. It was a sort of mechanical impulse that made me raise my hand, and attempt to turn aside the weapon. I did this deliberately and tranquilly, and without conceiving that any thing more was intended by her movement than to intimidate me. To this precaution, however, I was indebted for life. The bullet was diverted from my forehead to my left ear, and made a slight wound upon the surface, from which the blood gushed in a stream.

The loudness of this explosion, and the shock which the ball produced in my brain, sunk me into a momentary stupor. I reeled backward, and should have fallen had not I supported myself against the wall. The sight of my blood instantly restored her reason. Her rage disappeared, and was succeeded by terror and remorse. She clasped her hands, and exclaimed—Oh! what, what have I done? My frantic passion has destroyed me.

I needed no long time to shew me the full extent of the injury which I had suffered and the conduct which it became me to adopt. For a moment I was bewildered and alarmed, but presently perceived that this was an incident more productive of good than of evil. It would teach me caution in contending with the passions of another, and shewed me that there is a limit which the impetuosities of anger will sometimes overstep. Instead of reviling my companion, I addressed myself to her thus:

Be not frighted. You have done me no injury, and I hope will derive instruction from this event. Your rashness had like to have sacrificed the life of one who is your friend, and to have exposed yourself to infamy and death, or, at least, to the pangs of eternal remorse. Learn, from hence, to curb your passions, and especially to keep at a distance from every murderous weapon, on occasions when rage is likely to take place of reason.

I repeat that my motives in entering this house were connected with your happiness as well as that of Clemenza Lodi. If I have erred, in supposing you the member of a vile and pernicious trade, that error was worthy of being rectified, but violence and invective tend only to confirm it. I am incapable of any purpose that is not beneficent; but, in the means that I use and in the evidence on which I proceed, I am liable to a thousand mistakes. Point out to me the road by which I can do you good, and I will cheerfully pursue it.

330

Finding that her fears had been groundless, as to the consequences of her rashness, she renewed, though with less vehemence than before, her imprecations on my intermeddling and audacious folly. I listened till the storm was nearly exhausted, and then, declaring my intention to revisit the house, if the interest of Clemenza should require it, I resumed my way to the city.

CHAPTER XIII

W HY, said I, as I hasted forward, is my fortune so abundant in unforeseen occurrences? Is every man, who leaves his cottage and the impressions of his infancy behind him, ushered into such a world of revolutions and perils as have trammelled my steps? or, is my scene indebted for variety and change to my propensity to look into other people's concerns, and to make their sorrows and their joys mine?

To indulge an adventurous spirit, I left the precincts of the barn-door, enlisted in the service of a stranger, and encountered a thousand dangers to my virtue under the disastrous influence of Welbeck. Afterwards my life was set at hazard in the cause of Wallace, and now am I loaded with the province of protecting the helpless Eliza Hadwin and the unfortunate Clemenza. My wishes are fervent, and my powers shall not be inactive in their defence, but how slender are these powers!

In the offers of the unknown lady there is, indeed, some consolation for Clemenza. It must be my business to lay before my friend Stevens the particulars of what has befallen me, and to entreat his directions how this disconsolate girl may be most effectually succoured. It may be wise to take her from her present abode, and place her under some chaste and humane guardianship, where she may gradually lose remembrance of her dead infant and her specious betrayer. The barrier that severs her from Welbeck must be high as heaven and insuperable as necessity.

But, soft! Talked she not of Welbeck? Said she not that he was in prison and was sick? Poor wretch! I thought thy course was at an end; that the penalty of guilt no longer weighed down thy heart. That thy misdeeds and thy remorses were buried in a common and obscure grave; but it seems thou art still alive.

Is it rational to cherish the hope of thy restoration to innocence and peace? Thou art no obdurate criminal; hadst thou less virtue, thy compunctions would be less keen. Wert thou deaf to the voice of duty, thy wanderings into guilt and folly would be less fertile of anguish. The time will perhaps come, when the measure of thy transgressions and calamities will overflow, and the folly of thy choice will be too conspicuous to escape thy discernment. Surely, even for such transgressors as thou, there is a salutary power in the precepts of truth and the lessons of experience.

But, thou art imprisoned and art sick. This, perhaps, is the crisis of thy destiny. Indigence and dishonour were the evils, to shun which thy integrity and peace of mind have been lightly forfeited. Thou hast found that the price was given in vain; that the hollow and deceitful enjoyments of opulence and dignity were not worth the purchase; and that, frivolous and unsubstantial as they are, the only path that leads to them is that of honesty and diligence. Thou art in prison and art sick; and there is none to cheer thy hour with offices of kindness, or uphold thy fainting courage by the suggestions of good counsel. For such as thou the world has no compassion. Mankind will pursue thee to the grave with execrations. Their cruelty will be justified or palliated, since they know thee not. They are unacquainted with the goadings of thy conscience and the bitter retributions which thou art daily suffering: they are full of their own wrongs, and think only of those tokens of exultation and complacency which thou wast studious of assuming in thy intercourse with them. It is I only that thoroughly know thee, and can rightly estimate thy claims to compassion.

I have somewhat partaken of thy kindness, and thou meritest some gratitude at my hands. Shall I not visit and endeavor to console thee in thy distress? Let me, at least, ascertain thy condition, and be the instrument in repairing the wrongs which thou hast inflicted. Let me gain, from contemplation of thy misery, new motives to sincerity and rectitude.

While occupied by these reflections, I entered the city. The thoughts which engrossed my mind related to Welbeck. It is not my custom to defer till to-morrow what can be done to-day. The destiny of man frequently hangs upon the lapse of a minute. I will stop, said I, at the prison; and, since the moment of my arrival may not be indifferent, I will go thither with all possible haste. I did not content myself with walking, but, regardless of the comments of passengers, hurried along the way at full speed.

Having enquired for Welbeck, I was conducted through a dark room, crouded with beds, to a stair-case. Never before had I been in a prison. Never had I smelt so noisome an odour, or surveyed faces so begrimed with filth and misery. The walls and floors were alike squallid and detestable. It seemed that in this house existence would be bereaved of all its attractions; and yet those faces, which could be seen through the obscurity that encompassed them, were either void of care or distorted with mirth.

This, said I, as I followed my conductor, is the residence of Welbeck. What contrasts are these to the repose and splendor, pictured walls, glossy hangings, gilded sofas, mirrors that occupied from cieling to floor, carpets of Tauris, and the spotless and transcendent brilliancy of coverlets and napkins, in thy former dwelling? Here brawling and the shuffling of rude feet are eternal. The air is loaded with the exhalations of disease and the fumes of debauchery. Thou art cooped up in airless space, and, perhaps, compelled to share thy narrow cell with some stupid ruffian. Formerly, the breezes were courted by thy lofty windows. Aromatic shrubs were scattered on thy hearth. Menials, splendid in apparel, shewed their faces with diffidence in thy apartment, trod lightly on thy marble floor, and suffered not the sanctity of silence to be troubled by a whisper. Thy lamp shot its rays through the transparency of alabaster, and thy fragrant lymph flowed from vases of porcelain. Such were formerly the decorations of thy hall, the embellishments of thy existence; but now—alas!—

We reached a chamber in the second story. My conductor knocked at the door. No one answered. Repeated knocks were unheard or unnoticed by the person within. At length, lifting a latch, we entered together.

The prisoner lay upon the bed, with his face turned from the door. I advanced softly, making a sign to the keeper to withdraw. Welbeck was not asleep, but merely buried in reverie. I was unwilling to disturb his musing, and stood with my eyes fixed upon his form. He appeared unconscious that any one had entered.

At length, uttering a deep sigh, he changed his posture, and perceived me in my motionless and gazing attitude. Recollect in what circumstances we had last parted. Welbeck had, no doubt, carried away with him, from that interview, a firm belief, that I should speedily die. His prognostic, however, was fated to be contradicted.

His first emotions were those of surprize. These gave place to mortification and rage. After eyeing me for some time, he averted his glances, and that effort which is made to dissipate some obstacle to breathing, shewed me that his sensations were of the most excruciating kind. He laid his head upon the pillow, and sunk into his former musing. He disdained, or was unable, to utter a syllable of welcome or contempt.

In the opportunity that had been afforded me to view his countenance, I had observed tokens of a kind very different from those which used to be visible. The gloomy and malignant were more conspicuous. Health had forsaken his cheeks, and taken along with it those flexible parts, which formerly enabled him to cover his secret torments and insidious purposes, beneath a veil of benevolence and cheerfulness. Alas! said I, loud enough for him to hear me, here is a monument of ruin. Despair and mischievous passions are too deeply rooted in this heart for me to tear them away.

These expressions did not escape his notice. He turned

335

once more and cast sullen looks upon me. There was somewhat in his eyes that made me shudder. They denoted that his reverie was not that of grief, but of madness. I continued, in a less steadfast voice than before:

Unhappy Clemenza! I have performed thy message. I have visited him that is sick and in prison. Thou hadst cause for anguish and terror, even greater cause than thou imaginedst. Would to God that thou wouldst be contented with the report which I shall make; that thy misguided tenderness would consent to leave him to his destiny, would suffer him to die alone; but that is a forbearance which no eloquence that I possess will induce thee to practise. Thou must come, and witness for thyself.

In speaking thus, I was far from foreseeing the effects which would be produced on the mind of Welbeck. I was far from intending to instil into him a belief that Clemenza was near at hand, and was preparing to enter his apartment: yet no other images but these would, perhaps, have roused him from his lethargy, and awakened that attention which I wished to awaken. He started up, and gazed fearfully at the door.

What! he cried. What! Is she here? Ye powers, that have scattered woes in my path, spare me the sight of her! But from this agony I will rescue myself. The moment she appears I will pluck out these eyes and dash them at her feet.

So saying, he gazed with augmented eagerness upon the door. His hands were lifted to his head, as if ready to execute his frantic purpose. I seized his arm, and besought him to lay aside his terror, for that Clemenza was far distant. She had no intention, and besides was unable, to visit him.

Then I am respited. I breathe again. No; keep her from a prison. Drag her to the wheel or to the scaffold; mangle her with stripes; torture her with famine; strangle her child before her face, and cast it to the hungry dogs that are howling at the gate; but—keep her from a prison. Never let her enter these doors.—There he stopped; his eyes being fixed on the floor, and his thoughts once more buried in reverie. I resumed:

She is occupied with other griefs than those connected with the fate of Welbeck. She is not unmindful of you: she knows you to be sick and in prison; and I came to do for you whatever office your condition might require, and I came at her suggestion. She, alas! has full employment for her tears in watering the grave of her child.

He started. What! dead? Say you that the child is dead?

It is dead. I witnessed its death. I saw it expire in the arms of its mother; that mother whom I formerly met under your roof blooming and gay, but whom calamity has tarnished and withered. I saw her in the rayment of poverty, under an accursed roof; desolate; alone; unsolaced by the countenance or sympathy of human beings; approached only by those who mock at her distress, set snares for her innocence, and push her to infamy. I saw her leaning over the face of her dying babe.

Welbeck put his hands to his head and exclaimed: curses on thy lips, infernal messenger! Chant elsewhere thy rueful ditty! Vanish! if thou wouldst not feel in thy heart fangs red with blood less guilty than thine.

Till this moment the uproar in Welbeck's mind appeared to hinder him from distinctly recognizing his visitant. Now it seemed as if the incidents of our last interview suddenly sprung up in his remembrance.

What! This is the villain that rifled my cabinet, the maker of my poverty and of all the evils which it has since engendered! That has led me to a prison! Execrable fool! you are the author of the scene that you describe, and of horrors without number and name. To whatever crimes I have been urged since that interview, and the fit of madness that made you destroy my property, they spring from your act; they flowed from necessity, which, had you held your hand at that fateful moment, would never have existed.

How dare you thrust yourself upon my privacy? Why am I not alone? Fly! and let my miseries want, at least, the aggravation of beholding their author. My eyes loathe the sight of thee! My heart would suffocate thee with its own bitterness! Begone!

I know not, I answered, why innocence should tremble at

337

the ravings of a lunatic; why it should be overwhelmed by unmerited reproaches! Why it should not deplore the errors of its foe, labor to correct those errors, and ——

Thank thy fate, youth, that my hands are tied up by my scorn; thank thy fate that no weapon is within reach. Much has passed since I saw thee, and I am a new man. I am no longer inconstant and cowardly. I have no motives but contempt to hinder me from expiating the wrongs which thou hast done me in thy blood. I disdain to take thy life. Go; and let thy fidelity, at least, to the confidence which I have placed in thee, be inviolate. Thou hast done me harm enough, but canst do, if thou wilt, still more. Thou canst betray the secrets that are lodged in thy bosom, and rob me of the comfort of reflecting that my guilt is known but to one among the living.

This suggestion made me pause, and look back upon the past. I had confided this man's tale to you. The secrecy, on which he so fondly leaned, was at an end. Had I acted culpably or not?

But why should I ruminate, with anguish and doubt, upon the past? The future was within my power, and the road of my duty was too plain to be mistaken. I would disclose to Welbeck the truth, and cheerfully encounter every consequence. I would summon my friend to my aid, and take his counsel in the critical emergency in which I was placed. I ought not to rely upon myself alone in my efforts to benefit this being, when another was so near whose discernment, and benevolence, and knowledge of mankind, and power of affording relief were far superior to mine.

Influenced by these thoughts, I left the apartment without speaking; and, procuring pen and paper, dispatched to you the billet which brought about our meeting.

CHAPTER XIV

MERVYN'S auditors allowed no pause in their attention to this story. Having ended, a deep silence took place. The clock which stood upon the mantle, had sounded twice the customary *larum*, but had not been heard by us. It was now struck a third time. It was *one*. Our guest appeared somewhat startled at this signal, and looked, with a mournful sort of earnestness, at the clock. There was an air of inquietude about him, which I had never observed in an equal degree before.

I was not without much curiosity respecting other incidents than those which had just been related by him; but after so much fatigue as he had undergone, I thought it improper to prolong the conversation.

Come, said I, my friend, let us to bed. This is a drowsy time, and after so much exercise of mind and body, you cannot but need some repose. Much has happened in your absence, which is proper to be known to you, but our discourse will be best deferred till to-morrow. I will come into your chamber by day-dawn, and unfold to you my particular.

Nay, said he, withdraw not on my account. If I go to my chamber, it will not be to sleep, but to meditate, especially after your assurance that something of moment has occurred in my absence. My thoughts, independently of any cause of sorrow or fear, have received an impulse which solitude and darkness will not stop. It is impossible to know too much for our safety and integrity, or to know it too soon. What has happened?

I did not hesitate to comply with his request, for it was not difficult to conceive that, however tired the limbs might be, the adventures of this day would not be easily expelled from the memory at night. I told him the substance of the conversation with Mrs. Althorpe. He smiled at those parts of the narrative which related to himself; but when his father's depravity and poverty were mentioned, he melted into tears.

Poor wretch! I that knew thee in thy better days, might have easily divined this consequence. I foresaw thy poverty and degradation in the same hour that I left thy roof. My soul drooped at the prospect, but I said, it cannot be prevented, and this reflection was an antidote to grief, but now that thy ruin is complete, it seems as if some of it were imputable to me, who forsook thee when the succour and counsel of a son were most needed. Thou art ignorant and vicious, but thou art my father still. I see that the sufferings of a better man than thou art would less afflict me than thine. Perhaps it is still in my power to restore thy liberty and good name, and yet—that is a fond wish. Thou art past the age when the ignorance and groveling habits of a human being are susceptible of cure——There he stopt, and after a gloomy pause, continued:

I am not surprized or afflicted at the misconceptions of my neighbors, with relation to my own character. Men must judge from what they see: they must build their conclusions on their knowledge. I never saw in the rebukes of my neighbors, any thing but laudable abhorrence of vice. They were not eager to blame, to collect materials of censure rather than of praise. It was not me whom they hated and despised. It was the phantom that passed under my name, which existed only in their imagination, and which was worthy of all their scorn and all their enmity.

What I appeared to be in their eyes, was as much the object of my own disapprobation as of theirs. Their reproaches only evinced the rectitude of their decisions, as well as of my own. I drew from them new motives to complacency. They fortified my perseverance in the path which I had chosen as best; they raised me higher in my own esteem; they hightened the claims of the reproachers themselves to my respect and my gratitude.

They thought me slothful, incurious, destitute of knowledge, and of all thirst of knowledge, insolent and profligate. They say that in the treatment of my father, I have been ungrateful and inhuman. I have stolen his property, and deserted him in his calamity. Therefore they hate and revile me. It is well: I love them for these proofs of their discernment and integrity. Their indignation at wrong is the truest test of their virtue.

It is true that they mistake me, but that arises from the circumstances of our mutual situation. They examined what was exposed to their view: they grasped at what was placed within their reach. To decide contrary to appearances; to judge from what they know not, would prove them to be brutish and not rational, would make their decision of no worth, and render them, in their turn, objects of neglect and contempt.

It is true that I hated school; that I sought occasions of absence, and finally, on being struck by the master, determined to enter his presence no more. I loved to leap, to run, to swim, to climb trees, and to clamber up rocks, to shroud myself in thickets, and stroll among woods, to obey the impulse of the moment, and to prate or be silent, just as my humor prompted me. All this I loved more than to go to and fro in the same path, and at stated hours, to look off and on a book, to read just as much, and of such a kind, to stand up and be seated, just as another thought proper to direct. I hated to be classed, cribbed, rebuked and feruled at the pleasure of one, who, as it seemed to me, knew no guide in his rewards but caprice, and no prompter in his punishments but passion.

It is true that I took up the spade and the hoe as rarely, and for as short a time, as possible. I preferred to ramble in the forest and loiter on the hill: perpetually to change the scene; to scrutinize the endless variety of objects; to compare one leaf and pebble with another; to pursue those trains of thought which their resemblances and differences suggested; to enquire what it was that gave them this place, structure, and form, were more agreeable employments than plowing and threshing.

My father could well afford to hire labor. What my age and my constitution enabled me to do could be done by a sturdy boy, in half the time, with half the toil, and with none of the reluctance. The boy was a bond servant, and the cost of his clothing and food was next to nothing. True it is, that my service would have saved him even this expence, but my motives for declining the effort were not hastily weighed or superficially examined. These were my motives:

My frame was delicate and feeble. Exposure to wet blasts and vertical suns was sure to make me sick. My father was insensible to this consequence; and no degree of diligence would please him, but that which would destroy my health. My health was dearer to my mother than to me. She was more anxious to exempt me from possible injuries than reason justified; but anxious she was, and I could not save her from anxiety, but by almost wholly abstaining from labor. I thought her peace of mind was of some value, and that, if the inclination of either of my parents must be gratified at the expence of the other, the preference was due to the woman who bore me; who nursed me in disease; who watched over my safety with incessant tenderness; whose life and whose peace were involved in mine. I should have deemed myself brutish and obdurately wicked to have loaded her with fears and cares merely to smooth the brow of a froward old man, whose avarice called on me to sacrifice my ease and my health, and who shifted to other shoulders the province of sustaining me when sick, and of mourning for me when dead.

I likewise believed, that it became me to reflect upon the influence of my decision on my own happiness; and to weigh the profits flowing to my father from my labor, against the benefits of mental exercise, the pleasures of the woods and streams, healthful sensations, and the luxury of musing. The pecuniary profit was petty and contemptible. It obviated no necessity. It purchased no rational enjoyment. It merely provoked, by furnishing the means of indulgence, an appetite from which my father was not exempt. It cherished the seeds of depravity in him, and

342

lessened the little stock of happiness belonging to my mother.

I did not detain you long, my friends, in pourtraying my parents, and recounting domestic incidents, when I first told you my story. What had no connection with the history of Welbeck and with the part that I have acted upon this stage, I thought it proper to omit. My omission was likewise prompted by other reasons. My mind is ennervated and feeble like my body. I cannot look upon the sufferings of those I love without exquisite pain. I cannot steel my heart by the force of reason, and by submission to necessity; and, therefore, too frequently employ the cowardly expedient of endeavoring to forget what I cannot remember without agony.

I told you that my father was sober and industrious by habit, but habit is not uniform. There were intervals when his plodding and tame spirit gave place to the malice and fury of a demon. Liquors were not sought by him, but he could not withstand entreaty, and a potion that produced no effect upon others changed him into a maniac.

I told you that I had a sister, whom the arts of a villain destroyed. Alas! the work of her destruction was left unfinished by him. The blows and contumelies of a misjudging and implacable parent, who scrupled not to thrust her, with her new-born infant, out of doors; the curses and taunts of unnatural brothers left her no alternative but death—But I must not think of this; I must not think of the wrongs which my mother endured in the person of her only and darling daughter.

My brothers were the copyists of the father, whom they resembled in temper and person. My mother doated on her own image in her daughter and in me. This daughter was ravished from her by self-violence, and her other children by disease. I only remained to appropriate her affections and fulfil her hopes. This alone had furnished a sufficient reason why I should be careful of my health and my life, but my father's character supplied me with a motive infinitely more cogent.

It is almost incredible, but, nevertheless, true, that the only being whose presence and remonstrances had any

343

influence on my father, at moments when his reason was extinct, was myself. As to my personal strength, it was nothing; yet my mother's person was rescued from brutal violence: he was checked, in the midst of his ferocious career, by a single look or exclamation from me. The fear of my rebukes had even some influence in enabling him to resist temptation. If I entered the tavern, at the moment when he was lifting the glass to his lips, I never weighed the injunctions of decorum, but, snatching the vessel from his hand, I threw it on the ground. I was not deterred by the presence of others; and their censures, on my want of filial respect and duty, were listened to with unconcern. I chose not to justify myself by expatiating on domestic miseries, and by calling down that pity on my mother, which I knew would only have increased her distress.

The world regarded my deportment as insolent and perverse to a degree of insanity. To deny my father an indulgence which they thought harmless, and which, indeed, was harmless in its influence on other men; to interfere thus publicly with his social enjoyments, and expose him to mortification and shame, was loudly condemned; but my duty to my mother debarred me from eluding this censure on the only terms on which it could have been eluded. Now it has ceased to be necessary to conceal what passed in domestic retirements, and I should willingly confess the truth before any audience.

At first my father imagined, that threats and blows would intimidate his monitor. In this he was mistaken, and the detection of this mistake impressed him with an involuntary reverence for me, which set bounds to those excesses which disdained any other controul. Hence, I derived new motives for cherishing a life which was useful, in so many ways, to my mother.

My condition is now changed. I am no longer on that field to which the law, as well as reason, must acknowledge that I had some right, while there was any in my father. I must hazard my life, if need be, in the pursuit of the means of honest subsistence. I never spared myself while in the service of Mr. Hadwin; and, at a more inclement season, should probably have incurred some hazard by my diligence.

These were the motives of my *idleness*—for, my abstaining from the common toils of the farm passed by that name among my neighbors; though, in truth, my time was far from being wholly unoccupied by manual employments, but these required less exertion of body or mind, or were more connected with intellectual efforts. They were pursued in the seclusion of my chamber or the recesses of a wood. I did not labor to conceal them, but neither was I anxious to attract notice. It was sufficient that the censure of my neighbors was unmerited, to make me regard it with indifference.

I sought not the society of persons of my own age, not from sullen or unsociable habits, but merely because those around me were totally unlike myself. Their tastes and occupations were incompatible with mine. In my few books, in my pen, in the vegetable and animal existences around me, I found companions who adapted their visits and intercourse to my convenience and caprice, and with whom I was never tired of communing.

I was not unaware of the opinion which my neighbors had formed of my being improperly connected with Betty Lawrence. I am not sorry that I fell into company with that girl. Her intercourse has instructed me in what some would think impossible to be attained by one who had never haunted the impure recesses of licentiousness in a city. The knowledge, which residence in this town for ten years gave her audacious and inquisitive spirit, she imparted to me. Her character, profligate and artful, libidinous and impudent, and made up of the impressions which a city life had produced on her coarse but active mind, was open to my study, and I studied it.

I scarcely know how to repel the charge of illicit conduct, and to depict the exact species of intercourse subsisting between us. I always treated her with freedom, and sometimes with gaiety. I had no motives to reserve. I was so formed that a creature like her had no power over my senses. That species of temptation adapted to entice me from the true path, was widely different from the artifices of Betty. There was no point at which it was possible for her to get possession of my fancy. I watched her while she practised all her tricks and blandishments, just as I regarded a similar deportment in the *animal salax ignavumque* who inhabits the stye. I made efforts to pursue my observations unembarrassed; but my efforts were made, not to restrain desire, but to suppress disgust. The difficulty lay, not in withholding my caresses, but in forbearing to repulse her with rage.

Decorum, indeed, was not outraged, and all limits were not overstept, at once. Dubious advances were employed; but, when found unavailing, were displaced by more shameless and direct proceedings. She was too little versed in human nature to see that her last expedient was always worse than the preceding; and that, in proportion as she lost sight of decency, she multiplied the obstacles to her success.

Betty had many enticements in person and air. She was ruddy, smooth, and plump. To these she added—I must not say what, for it is strange to what lengths a woman destitute of modesty will sometimes go. But all her artifices availing her not at all in the contest with my insensibilities, she resorted to extremes which it would serve no good purpose to describe in this audience. They produced not the consequences she wished, but they produced another which was by no means displeasing to her. An incident one night occurred, from which a sagacious observer deduced the existence of an intrigue. It was useless to attempt to rectify his mistake, by explaining appearances, in a manner consistent with my innocence. This mode of explication implied a *continence* in me which he denied to be possible. The standard of possibilities, especially in vice and virtue, is fashioned by most men after their own character. A temptation which this judge of human nature knew that *he* was unable to resist, he sagely concluded to be irresistible by any other man, and quickly established the belief among my neighbors, that the woman who married the father had been prostituted to the son. Though I never admitted the truth of this aspersion, I believe it useless to deny, because no one would credit my denial, and because I had no power to disprove it.

CHAPTER XV

WHAT other enquiries were to be resolved by our young friend, we were now, at this late hour, obliged to postpone till the morrow. I shall pass over the reflections which a story like this would naturally suggest, and hasten to our next interview.

After breakfast next morning, the subject of last night's conversation was renewed. I told him that something had occurred in his absence, in relation to Mrs. Wentworth and her nephew, that had perplexed us not a little. My information is obtained, continued I, from Wortley; and it is nothing less, than that young Clavering, Mrs. Wentworth's nephew, is, at this time, actually alive.

Surprise, but none of the embarrassment of guilt, appeared in his countenance at these tidings. He looked at me as if desirous that I should proceed.

It seems, added I, that a letter was lately received by this lady from the father of Clavering, who is now in Europe. This letter reports that this son was lately met with in Charleston, and relates the means which old Mr. Clavering had used to prevail upon his son to return home; means, of the success of which he entertained well grounded hopes. What think you?

I can only reject it, said he, after some pause, as untrue. The father's correspondent may have been deceived. The father may have been deceived, or the father may conceive it necessary to deceive the aunt, or some other supposition, as to the source of the error, may be true; but an error it surely is. Clavering is not alive. I know the chamber where he died, and the withered pine under which he lies buried.

If she be deceived, said I, it will be impossible to rectify her error.

I hope not. An honest front and a straight story will be sufficient.

How do you mean to act?

Visit her without doubt, and tell her the truth. My tale will be too circumstantial and consistent to permit her to disbelieve.

She will not hearken to you. She is too strongly prepossessed against you to admit you even to an hearing.

She cannot help it. Unless she lock her door against me, or stuff her ears with wool, she must hear me. Her prepossessions are reasonable, but are easily removed by telling the truth. Why does she suspect me of artifice? Because I seemed to be allied to Welbeck, and because I disguised the truth. That she thinks ill of me is not her fault, but my misfortune; and, happily for me, a misfortune easily removed.

Then you will try to see her.

I will see her, and the sooner the better. I will see her to-day; this morning; as soon as I have seen Welbeck, whom I shall immediately visit in his prison.

There are other embarrassments and dangers of which you are not aware. Welbeck is pursued by many persons whom he has defrauded of large sums. By these persons you are deemed an accomplice in his guilt, and a warrant is already in the hands of officers for arresting you wherever you are found.

In what way, said Mervyn, sedately, do they imagine me a partaker of his crime?

I know not. You lived with him. You fled with him. You aided and connived at his escape.

Are these crimes?

I believe not, but they subject you to suspicion.

To arrest and to punishment?

To detention for a while, perhaps. But these alone cannot expose you to punishment.

349

I thought so. Then I have nothing to fear.

You have imprisonment and obloquy, at least, to dread.

True; but they cannot be avoided but by my exile and skulking out of sight—evils infinitely more formidable. I shall, therefore, not avoid them. The sooner my conduct be subjected to scrutiny, the better. Will you go with me to Welbeck?

I will go with you.

Enquiring for Welbeck of the keeper of the prison, we were informed that he was in his own apartment very sick. The physician, attending the prison, had been called, but the prisoner had preserved an obstinate and scornful silence; and had neither explained his condition, nor consented to accept any aid.

We now went, alone, into his apartment. His sensibility seemed fast ebbing, yet an emotion of joy was visible in his eyes at the appearance of Mervyn. He seemed likewise to recognize in me his late visitant, and made no objection to my entrance.

How are you this morning? said Arthur, seating himself on the bed-side, and taking his hand. The sick man was scarcely able to articulate his reply—I shall soon be well. I have longed to see you. I want to leave with you a few words. He now cast his languid eyes on me. You are his friend, he continued. You know all. You may stay.—

There now succeeded a long pause, during which he closed his eyes, and resigned himself as if to an oblivion of all thought. His pulse under my hand was scarcely perceptible. From this in some minutes he recovered, and fixing his eyes on Mervyn, resumed, in a broken and feeble accent:

Clemenza! You have seen her. Weeks ago, I left her in an accursed house: yet she has not been mistreated. Neglected and abandoned indeed, but not mistreated. Save her Mervyn. Comfort her. Awaken charity for her sake.

I cannot tell you what has happened. The tale would be too long—too mournful. Yet, in justice to the living, I must tell you something. My woes and my crimes will be buried with me. Some of them, but not all.

Ere this, I should have been many leagues upon the

ocean, had not a newspaper fallen into my hands while on the eve of embarkation. By that I learned that a treasure was buried with the remains of the ill-fated Watson. I was destitute. I was unjust enough to wish to make this treasure my own. Prone to think I was forgotten, or numbered with the victims of pestilence, I ventured to return under a careless disguise. I penetrated to the vaults of that deserted dwelling by night. I dug up the bones of my friend, and found the girdle and its valuable contents, according to the accurate description that I had read.

I hastened back with my prize to Baltimore, but my evil destiny overtook me at last. I was recognized by emissaries of Jamieson, arrested and brought hither, and here shall I consummate my fate and defeat the rage of my creditors by death. But first——

Here Welbeck stretched out his left hand to Mervyn, and, after some reluctance, shewed a roll of lead.

Receive this, said he. In the use of it, be guided by your honesty and by the same advertisement that furnished me the clue by which to recover it. That being secured, the world and I will part forever. Withdraw, for your presence can help me nothing.

We were unwilling to comply with his injunction, and continued some longer time in his chamber, but our kind intent availed nothing. He quickly relapsed into insensibility, from which he recovered not again, but next day expired. Such, in the flower of his age, was the fate of Thomas Welbeck.

Whatever interest I might feel in accompanying the progress of my young friend, a sudden and unforeseen emergency compelled me again to leave the city. A kinsman, to whom I was bound by many obligations, was suffering a lingering disease, and imagining, with some reason, his dissolution to be not far distant, he besought my company and my assistance, to sooth, at least, the agonies of his last hour. I was anxious to clear up the mysteries which Arthur's conduct had produced, and to shield him, if possible, from the evils which I feared awaited him. It was impossible, however, to decline the invitation of my kinsman, as

351

his residence was not a day's journey from the city. I was obliged to content myself with occasional information, imparted by Mervyn's letters, or those of my wife.

Meanwhile, on leaving the prison, I hasted to inform Mervyn of the true nature of the scene which had just passed. By this extraordinary occurrence, the property of the Maurices was now in honest hands. Welbeck, stimulated by selfish motives, had done that which any other person would have found encompassed with formidable dangers and difficulties. How this attempt was suggested or executed, he had not informed us, nor was it desirable to know. It was sufficient that the means of restoring their own to a destitute and meritorious family, were now in our possession.

Having returned home, I unfolded to Mervyn all the particulars respecting Williams and the Maurices, which I had lately learned from Wortley. He listened with deep attention, and my story being finished, he said: In this small compass, then, is the patrimony and subsistence of a numerous family. To restore it to them is the obvious proceeding—but how? Where do they abide?

Williams and Watson's wife live in Baltimore, and the Maurices live near that town. The advertisements alluded to by Wortley, and which are to be found in any newspaper, will inform us; but first, are we sure that any or all of these bills are contained in this covering?

The lead was now unrolled, and the bills which Williams had described, were found inclosed. Nothing appeared to be deficient. Of this, however, we were scarcely qualified to judge. Those that were the property of Williams might not be entire, and what would be the consequence of presenting them to him, if any had been embezzled by Welbeck?

This difficulty was obviated by Mervyn, who observed that the advertisement, describing these bills, would afford us ample information on this head. Having found out where the Maurices and Mrs. Watson live, nothing remains but to visit them, and put an end, as far as lies in my power, to their inquietudes.

What! Would you go to Baltimore?

Certainly. Can any other expedient be proper? How shall I otherwise insure the safe conveyance of these papers?

You may send them by post.

But why not go myself?

I can hardly tell, unless your appearance on such an errand, may be suspected likely to involve you in embarrassments.

What embarrassments? If they receive their own, ought they not to be satisfied?

The enquiry will naturally be made as to the manner of gaining possession of these papers. They were lately in the hands of Watson, but Watson has disappeared. Suspicions are awake respecting the cause of his disappearance. These suspicions are connected with Welbeck, and Welbeck's connection with you is not unknown.

These are evils, but I see not how an ingenuous and open conduct is adapted to increase these evils. If they come, I must endure them.

I believe your decision is right. No one is so skilful an advocate in a cause, as he whose cause it is. I rely upon your skill and address, and shall leave you to pursue your own way. I must leave you for a time, but shall expect to be punctually informed of all that passes. With this agreement we parted, and I hastened to perform my intended journey.

CHAPTER XVI

I AM glad, my friend, thy nimble pen has got so far upon its journey. What remains of my story may be dispatched in a trice. I have just now some vacant hours, which might possibly be more usefully employed, but not in an easier manner or more pleasant. So, let me carry on thy thread.

First, let me mention the resolutions I had formed at the time I parted with my friend. I had several objects in view. One was a conference with Mrs. Wentworth: another was an interview with her whom I met with at Villars's. My heart melted when I thought upon the desolate condition of Clemenza, and determined me to direct my first efforts for her relief. For this end I was to visit the female who had given me a direction to her house. The name of this person is Achsa Fielding, and she lived, according to her own direction, at No. 40, Walnut-street.

I went thither without delay. She was not at home. Having gained information from the servant, as to when she might be found, I proceeded to Mrs. Wentworth's. In going thither my mind was deeply occupied in meditation; and, with my usual carelessness of forms, I entered the house and made my way to the parlour, where an interview had formerly taken place between us.

Having arrived, I began, though somewhat unseasonably, to reflect upon the topics with which I should introduce my conversation, and particularly the manner in which I should introduce myself. I had opened doors without warning, and traversed passages without being noticed. This had arisen from my thoughtlessness. There was no one within hearing or sight. What was next to be done? Should I not return softly to the outer door, and summon the servant by knocking?

Preparing to do this, I heard a footstep in the entry which suspended my design. I stood in the middle of the floor, attentive to these movements, when presently the door opened, and there entered the apartment Mrs. Wentworth herself! She came, as it seemed, without expectation of finding any one there. When, therefore, the figure of a man caught her vagrant attention, she started and cast an hasty look towards me.

Pray! (in a peremptory tone) how came you here, sir? and what is your business?

Neither arrogance, on the one hand; nor humility, upon the other, had any part in modelling my deportment. I came not to deprecate anger, or exult over distress. I answered, therefore, distinctly, firmly, and erectly.

I came to see you, madam, and converse with you; but, being busy with other thoughts, I forgot to knock at the door. No evil was intended by my negligence, though propriety has certainly not been observed. Will you pardon this intrusion, and condescend to grant me your attention?

To what? What have you to say to me? I know you only as the accomplice of a villain in an attempt to deceive me. There is nothing to justify your coming hither, and I desire you to leave the house with as little ceremony as you entered it.

My eyes were lowered at this rebuke, yet I did not obey the command. Your treatment of me, madam, is such as I appear to you to deserve. Appearances are unfavorable to me, but those appearances are false. I have concurred in no plot against your reputation or your fortune. I have told you nothing but the truth. I came hither to promote no selfish or sinister purpose. I have no favor to entreat, and no petition to offer, but that you will suffer me to clear up those mistakes which you have harbored respecting me.

I am poor. I am destitute of fame and of kindred. I have

355

nothing to console me in obscurity and indigence, but the approbation of my own heart and the good opinion of those who know me as I am. The good may be led to despise and condemn me. Their aversion and scorn shall not make me unhappy; but it is my interest and my duty to rectify their error if I can. I regard your character with esteem. You have been mistaken in condemning me as a liar and impostor, and I came to remove this mistake. I came, if not to procure your esteem, at least, to take away hatred and suspicion.

But this is not all my purpose. You are in an error in relation not only to my character, but to the situation of your nephew Clavering. I formerly told you, that I saw him die; that I assisted at his burial; but my tale was incoherent and imperfect, and you have since received intelligence to which you think proper to trust, and which assures you that he is still living. All I now ask is your attention, while I relate the particulars of my knowledge.

Proof of my veracity or innocence may be of no value in your eyes, but the fate of your nephew ought to be known to you. Certainty, on this head, may be of much importance to your happiness, and to the regulation of your future conduct. To hear me patiently can do you no injury, and may benefit you much. Will you permit me to go on?

During this address, little abatement of resentment and scorn was visible in my companion.

I will hear you, she replied. Your invention may amuse if it does not edify. But, I pray you, let your story be short.

I was obliged to be content with this ungraceful concession, and proceeded to begin my narration. I described the situation of my father's dwelling. I mentioned the year, month, day, and hour of her nephew's appearance among us. I expatiated minutely on his form, features, dress, sound of his voice, and repeated his words. His favorite gestures and attitudes were faithfully described.

I had gone but a little way in my story, when the effects were visible in her demeanor which I expected from it. Her knowledge of the youth, and of the time and manner of his disappearance, made it impossible for me, with so minute a narrative, to impose upon her credulity. Every word, every incident related, attested my truth, by their agreement with what she herself previously knew.

Her suspicions and angry watchfulness was quickly exchanged for downcast looks, and stealing tears, and sighs difficultly repressed. Meanwhile, I did not pause, but described the treatment he received from my mother's tenderness, his occupations, the freaks of his insanity, and, finally, the circumstances of his death and funeral.

Thence I hastened to the circumstances which brought me to the city; which placed me in the service of Welbeck, and obliged me to perform so ambiguous a part in her presence. I left no difficulty to be solved and no question unanticipated.

I have now finished my story, I continued, and accomplished my design in coming hither. Whether I have vindicated my integrity from your suspicions, I know not. I have done what in me lay to remove your error; and, in that, have done my duty.—What more remains? Any enquiries you are pleased to make, I am ready to answer. If there be none to make, I will comply with your former commands, and leave the house with as little ceremony as I entered it.

Your story, she replied, has been unexpected. I believe it fully, and am sorry for the hard thoughts which past appearances have made me entertain concerning you.

Here she sunk into mournful silence. The information, she at length resumed, which I have received from another quarter respecting that unfortunate youth, astonishes and perplexes me. It is inconsistent with your story, but it must be founded on some mistake, which I am, at present, unable to unravel. Welbeck, whose connection has been so unfortunate to you——

Unfortunate! Dear Madam! How unfortunate? It has done away a part of my ignorance of the world in which I live. It has led me to the situation in which I am now placed. It has introduced me to the knowledge of many good people. It has made me the witness and the subject of many acts of beneficence and generosity. My knowledge of Welbeck has been useful to me. It has enabled me to be useful to others. I look back upon that allotment of my destiny which first led me to his door, with gratitude and pleasure.

Would to Heaven, continued I, somewhat changing my tone, intercourse with Welbeck had been as harmless to all others as it has been to me: that no injury to fortune and fame, and innocence and life, had been incurred by others greater than has fallen upon my head. There is one being, whose connection with him has not been utterly dissimilar in its origin and circumstances to mine, though the catastrophe has, indeed, been widely and mournfully different.

And yet, within this moment, a thought has occurred from which I derive some consolation and some hope. You, dear madam, are rich. These spacious apartments, this plentiful accommodation are yours. You have enough for your own gratification and convenience, and somewhat to spare. Will you take to your protecting arms, to your hospitable roof, an unhappy girl whom the arts of Welbeck have robbed of fortune, reputation and honor, who is now languishing in poverty, weeping over the lifeless remains of her babe, surrounded by the agents of vice, and trembling on the verge of infamy?

What can this mean? replied the lady. Of whom do you speak?

You shall know her. You shall be apprized of her claims to your compassion. Her story, as far as is known to me, I will faithfully repeat to you. She is a stranger; an Italian; her name is Clemenza Lodi.—

Clemenza Lodi! Good Heaven! exclaimed Mrs. Wentworth; why, surely—it cannot be. And yet—Is it possible that you are that person?

I do not comprehend you, madam.

A friend has related a transaction of a strange sort. It is scarcely an hour since she told it me. The name of Clemenza Lodi was mentioned in it, and a young man of most singular deportment was described.—But tell me how you were engaged on Thursday morning?

I was coming to this city from a distance. I stopped ten minutes at the house of——

Mrs. Villars?

The same. Perhaps you know her and her character. Perhaps you can confirm or rectify my present opinions concerning her. It is there that the unfortunate Clemenza abides. It is thence that I wish her to be speedily removed.

I have heard of you; of your conduct upon that occasion.

Of me? answered I eagerly. Do you know that woman? So saying, I produced the card which I had received from her, and in which her name was written.

I know her well. She is my countrywoman and my friend.

Your friend? Then she is good—she is innocent—she is generous. Will she be a sister, a protectress to Clemenza? Will you exhort her to a deed of charity? Will you be, yourself, an example of beneficence? Direct me to Miss Fielding, I beseech you. I have called on her already, but in vain, and there is no time to be lost.

Why are you so precipitate? What would you do?

Take her away from that house instantly—bring her hither—place her under your protection—give her Mrs. Wentworth for a counsellor—a friend—a mother. Shall I do this? Shall I hie thither to-day, this very hour—now? Give me your consent, and she shall be with you before noon.

By no means, replied she, with earnestness. You are too hasty. An affair of so much importance cannot be dispatched in a moment. There are many difficulties and doubts to be first removed.

Let them be reserved for the future. Withhold not your helping hand till the struggler has disappeared forever. Think on the gulph that is already gaping to swallow her. This is no time to hesitate and faulter. I will tell you her story, but not now; we will postpone it till to-morrow; and first secure her from impending evils. She shall tell it you herself. In an hour I will bring her hither, and she herself shall recount to you her sorrows. Will you let me?

Your behaviour is extraordinary. I can scarcely tell whether this simplicity be real or affected. One would think that your common sense would shew you the impropriety of your request. To admit under my roof a woman, notoriously dishonoured, and from an infamous house——

359

My dearest madam! How can you reflect upon the situation without irresistible pity? I see that you are thoroughly aware of her past calamity and her present danger. Do not these urge you to make haste to her relief? Can any lot be more deplorable than hers? Can any state be more perilous? Poverty is not the only evil that oppresses, or that threatens her. The scorn of the world, and her own compunction, the death of the fruit of her error and the witness of her shame, are not the worst. She is exposed to the temptations of the profligate; while she remains with Mrs. Villars, her infamy accumulates; her further debasement is facilitated; her return to reputation and to virtue is obstructed by new bars.

How know I that her debasement is not already complete and irremediable? She is a mother but not a wife. How came she thus? Is her being Welbeck's prostitute no proof of her guilt?

Alas! I know not. I believe her not very culpable; I know her to be unfortunate; to have been robbed and betrayed. You are a stranger to her history. I am myself imperfectly acquainted with it.

But let me tell you the little that I know. Perhaps my narrative may cause you to think of her as I do.

She did not object to this proposal, and I immediately recounted all that I had gained from my own observations, or from Welbeck himself, respecting this forlorn girl. Having finished my narrative, I proceeded thus:—

Can you hesitate to employ that power which was given you for good ends, to rescue this sufferer? Take her to your home; to your bosom; to your confidence. Keep aloof those temptations which beset her in her present situation. Restore her to that purity which her desolate condition, her ignorance, her misplaced gratitude and the artifices of a skilful dissembler, have destroyed, if it be destroyed; for how know we under what circumstances her ruin was accomplished? With what pretences or appearances, or promises she was won to compliance?

True. I confess my ignorance; but ought not that ignorance to be removed before she makes a part of my family?

O no! It may be afterwards removed. It cannot be re-

360

moved before. By bringing her hither you shield her, at least, from future and possible evils. Here you can watch her conduct and sift her sentiments conveniently and at leisure. Should she prove worthy of your charity, how justly may you congratulate yourself on your seasonable efforts in her cause? If she prove unworthy, you may then demean yourself according to her demerits.

I must reflect upon it. —To-morrow——

Let me prevail on you to admit her at once, and without delay. This very moment may be the critical one. To-day, we may exert ourselves with success, but to-morrow, all our efforts may be fruitless. Why fluctuate, why linger, when so much good may be done, and no evil can possibly be incurred? It requires but a word from you; you need not move a finger. Your house is large. You have chambers vacant and convenient. Consent only that your door shall not be barred against her; that you will treat her with civility; to carry your kindness into effect; to persuade her to attend me hither and to place herself in your care, shall be my province.

These, and many similar entreaties and reasonings, were ineffectual. Her general disposition was kind, but she was unaccustomed to strenuous or sudden exertions. To admit the persuasions of such an advocate to so uncommon a scheme as that of sharing her house with a creature, thus previously unknown to her, thus loaded with suspicion and with obloquy, was not possible.

I at last forbore importunity, and requested her to tell me when I might expect to meet with Miss Fielding at her lodgings? Enquiry was made to what end I sought an interview? I made no secret of my purpose.

Are you mad, young man? she exclaimed. Mrs. Fielding has already been egregiously imprudent. On the faith of an ancient slight acquaintance with Mrs. Villars in Europe, she suffered herself to be decoyed into a visit. Instead of taking warning by numerous tokens of the real character of that woman, in her behaviour, and in that of her visitants, she consented to remain there one night. The next morning took place that astonishing interview with you which she has since described to me. She is now warned against the like indiscretion. And pray, what benevolent scheme would you propose to her?

Has she property? Is she rich?

She is. Unhappily, perhaps, for her, she is absolute mistress of her fortune, and has neither guardian nor parent to controul her in the use of it.

Has she virtue? Does she know the value of affluence and a fair fame? And will not she devote a few dollars to rescue a fellow-creature from indigence and infamy and vice? Surely she will. She will hazard nothing by the boon. I will be her almoner. I will provide the wretched stranger with food and raiment and dwelling, I will pay for all, if Miss Fielding, from her superfluity will supply the means. Clemenza shall owe life and honor to your friend, till I am able to supply the needful sum from my own stock.

While thus speaking, my companion gazed at me with steadfastness—I know not what to make of you. Your language and ideas are those of a lunatic. Are you acquainted with Mrs. Fielding?

Yes. I have seen her two days ago, and she has invited me to see her again.

And on the strength of this acquaintance, you expect to be her almoner? To be the medium of her charity?

I desire to save her trouble; to make charity as light and easy as possible. 'Twill be better if she perform those offices herself. 'Twill redound more to the credit of her reason and her virtue. But I solicit her benignity only in the cause of Clemenza. For her only do I wish at present to call forth her generosity and pity.

And do you imagine she will entrust her money to one of your age and sex, whom she knows so imperfectly, to administer to the wants of one whom she found in such an house as Mrs. Villars's? She never will. She mentioned her imprudent engagement to meet you, but she is now warned against the folly of such confidence.

You have told me plausible stories of yourself and of this Clemenza. I cannot say that I disbelieve them, but I know the ways of the world too well to bestow implicit faith so

362

easily. You are an extraordinary young man. You may possibly be honest. Such an one as you, with your education and address, may possibly have passed all your life in an hovel; but it is scarcely credible, let me tell you. I believe most of the facts respecting my nephew, because my knowledge of him before his flight, would enable me to detect your falsehood; but there must be other proofs besides an innocent brow and a voluble tongue, to make me give full credit to your pretensions.

I have no claim upon Welbeck which can embarrass you. On that score, you are free from any molestation from me or my friends. I have suspected you of being an accomplice in some vile plot, and am now inclined to acquit you, but that is all that you must expect from me, till your character be established by other means than your own assertions. I am engaged at present, and must therefore request you to put an end to your visit.

This strain was much unlike the strain which preceded it. I imagined, by the mildness of her tone and manners, that her unfavorable prepossessions were removed, but they seemed to have suddenly regained their pristine force. I was somewhat disconcerted by this unexpected change. I stood for a minute silent and irresolute.

Just then a knock was heard at the door, and presently entered that very female whom I had met with at Villars's. I caught her figure as I glanced through the window. Mrs. Wentworth darted at me many significant glances, which commanded me to withdraw; but with this object in view, it was impossible.

As soon as she entered, her eyes were fixed upon me. Certain recollections naturally occurred at that moment, and made her cheeks glow. Some confusion reigned for a moment, but was quickly dissipated. She did not notice me, but exchanged salutations with her friend.

All this while I stood near the window, in a situation not a little painful. Certain tremors which I had not been accustomed to feel, and which seemed to possess a mystical relation to the visitant, disabled me at once from taking my leave, or from performing any useful purpose by staying. At

363

length, struggling for composure, I approached her, and shewing her the card she had given me, said: —

Agreeably to this direction, I called, an hour ago, at your lodgings. I found you not. I hope you will permit me to call once more. When shall I expect to meet you at home?

Her eyes were cast on the floor. A kind of indirect attention was fixed on Mrs. Wentworth, serving to intimidate and check her. At length she said, in an irresolute voice, I shall be at home this evening.

And this evening, replied I, I will call to see you. So saying, I left the house.

This interval was tedious; but was to be endured with equanimity. I was impatient to be gone to Baltimore, and hoped to be able to set out by the dawn of next day. Meanwhile, I was necessarily to perform something with respect to Clemenza.

After dinner I accompanied Mrs. Stevens to visit Miss Carlton. I was eager to see a woman who could bear adversity in the manner which my friend had described.

She met us at the door of her apartment. Her seriousness was not abated by her smiles of affability and welcome.—My friend! whispered I, How truly lovely is this Miss Carlton! Are the heart and the intelligence within worthy of these features? Yes, they are. Your account of her employments; of her resignation to the ill fate of the brother whom she loves, proves that they are.

My eyes were rivetted to her countenance and person. I felt uncontroulable eagerness to speak to her, and to gain her good opinion.

You must know this young man, my dear Miss Carlton, said my friend, looking at me: He is my husband's friend, and professes a great desire to be yours. You must not treat him as a mere stranger, for he knows your character and situation already, as well as that of your brother.

She looked at me with benignity.—I accept his friendship willingly and gratefully, and shall endeavor to convince him that his good opinion is not misplaced.

There now ensued a conversation somewhat general, in which this young woman shewed a mind vigorous from exercise and unembarrassed by care. She affected no concealment of her own condition, of her wants, or her comforts. She laid no stress upon misfortunes, but contrived to deduce some beneficial consequence to herself, and some motive for gratitude to Heaven, from every wayward incident that had befallen her.

This demeanor emboldened me, at length, to enquire into the cause of her brother's imprisonment, and the nature of his debt.

She answered frankly and without hesitation. It is a debt of his father's, for which he made himself responsible during his father's life. The act was generous but imprudent, as the event has shewn; though, at the time, the unhappy effects could not be foreseen.

My father, continued she, was arrested by his creditor, at a time when the calmness and comforts of his own dwelling were necessary to his health. The creditor was obdurate, and would release him upon no condition but that of receiving a bond from my brother, by which he engaged to pay the debt at several successive times and in small portions. All these instalments were discharged with great difficulty indeed, but with sufficient punctuality, except the last, to which my brother's earnings were not adequate.

How much is the debt?

Four hundred dollars.

And is the state of the creditor such as to make the loss of four hundred dollars of more importance to him than the loss of liberty to your brother?

She answered, smiling, that is a very abstract view of things. On such a question, you and I might, perhaps, easily decide in favor of my brother; but would there not be some danger of deciding partially? His conduct is a proof of his decision, and there is no power to change it.

Will not argument change it? Methinks in so plain a case I should be able to convince him. You say he is rich and childless. His annual income is ten times more than this sum. Your brother cannot pay the debt while in prison; whereas, if at liberty, he might slowly and finally discharge it. If his humanity would not yield, his avarice might be brought to acquiesce.

But there is another passion which you would find it

somewhat harder to subdue, and that is his vengeance. He thinks himself wronged, and imprisons my brother, not to enforce payment, but to inflict misery. If you could persuade him, that there is no hardship in imprisonment, you would speedily gain the victory; but that could not be attempted consistently with truth. In proportion to my brother's suffering is his gratification.

You draw an odious and almost incredible portrait.

And yet such an one as would serve for the likeness of almost every second man we meet.

And is such your opinion of mankind? Your experience must surely have been of a rueful tenor to justify such hard thoughts of the rest of your species.

By no means. It has been what those whose situation disables them from looking further than the surface of things, would regard as unfortunate; but if my goods and evils were equitably balanced, the former would be the weightiest. I have found kindness and goodness in great numbers, but have likewise met prejudice and rancor in many. My opinion of Farquhar is not lightly taken up. I have seen him yesterday, and the nature of his motives in the treatment of my brother was plain enough.

Here this topic was succeeded by others, and the conversation ceased not till the hour had arrived on which I had preconcerted to visit Mrs. Fielding. I left my two friends for this purpose.

I was admitted to Mrs. Fielding's presence without scruple or difficulty. There were two females in her company, and one of the other sex, well dressed, elderly, and sedate persons. Their discourse turned upon political topics, with which, as you know, I have but slight acquaintance. They talked of fleets and armies, of Robespierre and Pitt, of whom I had only a newspaper knowledge.

In a short time the women rose, and, huddling on their cloaks, disappeared, in company with the gentleman. Being thus left alone with Mrs. Fielding, some embarrassment was mutually betrayed. With much hesitation, which, however, gradually disappeared, my companion, at length, began the conversation.

You met me lately, in a situation, sir, on which I look back with trembling and shame, but not with any self-condemnation. I was led into it without any fault, unless a too hasty confidence may be stiled a fault. I had known Mrs. Villars in England, where she lived with an untainted reputation, at least; and the sight of my countrywoman, in a foreign land, awakened emotions, in the indulgence of which I did not imagine there was either any guilt or any danger. She invited me to see her at her house with so much urgency and warmth, and solicited me to take a place immediately in a chaise in which she had come to the city, that I too incautiously complied.

You are a stranger to me, and I am unacquainted with your character. What little I have seen of your deportment, and what little I have lately heard concerning you from Mrs. Wentworth, do not produce unfavorable impressions; but the apology I have made was due to my own reputation, and should have been offered to you whatever your character had been. There she stopped.

I came not hither, said I, to receive an apology. Your demeanor, on our first interview, shielded you sufficiently from any suspicions or surmises that I could form. What you have now mentioned was likewise mentioned by your friend, and was fully believed upon her authority. My purpose, in coming, related not to you but to another. I desired merely to interest your generosity and justice on behalf of one, whose destitute and dangerous condition may lay claim to your compassion and your succour.

I comprehend you, said she, with an air of some perplexity. I know the claims of that person.

And will you comply with them?

In what manner can I serve her?

By giving her the means of living.

Does she not possess them already?

She is destitute. Her dependence was wholly placed upon one that is dead, by whom her person was dishonored and her fortune embezzled.

But she still lives. She is not turned into the street. She is not destitute of home.

367

But what an home!

Such as she may chuse to remain in.

She cannot chuse it. She must not chuse it. She remains through ignorance, or through the incapacity of leaving it.

But how shall she be persuaded to a change?

I will persuade her. I will fully explain her situation. I will supply her with a new home.

You would persuade her to go with you, and to live at a home of your providing, and on your bounty?

Certainly.

Would that change be worthy of a cautious person? Would it benefit her reputation? Would it prove her love of independence?

My purposes are good. I know not why she should suspect them. But I am only anxious to be the instrument. Let her be indebted to one of her own sex, of unquestionable reputation. Admit her into this house. Invite her to your arms. Cherish and console her as your sister.

Before I am convinced that she deserves it? And even then, what regard shall I, young, unmarried, independent, affluent, pay to my own reputation in harboring a woman in these circumstances?

But you need not act yourself. Make me your agent and almoner. Only supply her with the means of subsistence through me.

Would you have me act a clandestine part? Hold meetings with one of your sex, and give him money for a purpose which I must hide from the world? Is it worth while to be a dissembler and impostor? And will not such conduct incur more dangerous surmises and suspicions, than would arise from acting openly and directly? You will forgive me for reminding you likewise, that it is particularly incumbent upon those in my situation, to be circumspect in their intercourse with men and with strangers. This is the second time that I have seen you. My knowledge of you is extremely dubious and imperfect, and such as would make the conduct you prescribe to me, in an high degree, rash and culpable. You must not, therefore, expect me to pursue it.

These words were delivered with an air of firmness and

dignity. I was not insensible to the truth of her representations. I confess, said I, what you have said makes me doubt the propriety of my proposal: yet I would fain be of service to her. Cannot you point out some practicable method?

She was silent and thoughtful, and seemed indisposed to answer my question.

I had set my heart upon success in this negociation, continued I, and could not imagine any obstacle to its success; but I find my ignorance of the world's ways much greater than I had previously expected. You defraud yourself of all the happiness redounding from the act of making others happy. You sacrifice substance to shew, and are more anxious to prevent unjust aspersions from lighting on yourself, than to rescue a fellow-creature from guilt and infamy.

You are rich, and abound in all the conveniences and luxuries of life. A small portion of your superfluity would obviate the wants of a being not less worthy than yourself. It is not avarice or aversion to labor that makes you withhold your hand. It is dread of the sneers and surmises of malevolence and ignorance.

I will not urge you further at present. Your determination to be wise should not be hasty. Think upon the subject calmly and sedately, and form your resolution in the course of three days. At the end of that period I will visit you again. So saying, and without waiting for comment or answer, I withdrew.

CHAPTER XVII

I MOUNTED the stage-coach at day-break the next day, in company with a sallow Frenchman from Saint Domingo, his fiddle-case, an ape, and two female blacks. The Frenchman, after passing the suburbs, took out his violin and amused himself with humming to his own *tweedle-tweedle*. The monkey now and then mounched an apple, which was given to him from a basket by the blacks, who gazed with stupid wonder, and an exclamatory *La! La!* upon the passing scenery; or chattered to each other in a sort of open-mouthed, half-articulate, monotonous, and sing-song jargon.

The man looked seldom either on this side or that; and spoke only to rebuke the frolics of the monkey, with a Tenez! Dominique! Prenez garde! Diable noir!

As to me my thought was busy in a thousand ways. I sometimes gazed at the faces of my *four* companions, and endeavored to discern the differences and samenesses between them. I took an exact account of the features, proportions, looks, and gestures of the monkey, the Congolese, and the Creole-Gaul. I compared them together, and examined them apart. I looked at them in a thousand different points of view, and pursued, untired and unsatiated, those trains of reflections which began at each change of tone, feature, and attitude.

I marked the country as it successively arose before me, and found endless employment in examining the shape and substance of the fence, the barn and the cottage, the aspect of earth and of heaven. How great are the pleasures of health and of mental activity.

My chief occupation, however, related to the scenes into which I was about to enter. My imaginations were, of course, crude and inadequate; and I found an uncommon gratification in comparing realities, as they successively occurred, with the pictures which my wayward fancy had depicted.

I will not describe my dreams. My proper task is to relate the truth. Neither shall I dwell upon the images suggested by the condition of the country through which I passed. I will confine myself to mentioning the transactions connected with the purpose of my journey.

I reached Baltimore at night. I was not so fatigued, but that I could ramble through the town. I intended, at present, merely the gratification of a stranger's curiosity. My visit to Mrs. Watson and her brother I designed should take place on the morrow. The evening of my arrival I deemed an unseasonable time.

While roving about, however, it occurred to me, that it might not be impolitic to find the way to their habitation even now. My purposes of general curiosity would equally be served whichever way my steps were bent; and, to trace the path to their dwelling, would save me the trouble of enquiries and interrogations to-morrow.

When I looked forward to an interview with the wife of Watson, and to the subject which would be necessarily discussed at that interview, I felt a trembling and misgiving at my heart. Surely, thought I, it will become me to exercise immeasurable circumspection and address; and yet how little are these adapted to the impetuosity and candor of my nature.

How am I to introduce myself? What am I to tell her? That I was a sort of witness to the murder of her husband? That I received from the hand of his assassin the letter which I afterwards transmitted to her? and, from the same hands, the bills contained in his girdle?

How will she start and look aghast? What suspicions will she harbor? What enquiries shall be made of me? How shall

371

they be disarmed and eluded, or answered? Deep consideration will be necessary before I trust myself to such an interview. The coming night shall be devoted to reflection upon this subject.

From these thoughts I proceeded to enquiries for the street mentioned in the advertisement, where Mrs. Watson was said to reside. The street, and, at length, the habitation, was found. Having reached a station opposite, I paused and surveyed the mansion. It was a wooden edifice of two stories; humble, but neat. You ascended to the door by several stone steps. Of the two lower windows, the shutters of one were closed, but those of the other were open. Though late in the evening, there was no appearance of light or fire within.

Beside the house was a painted fence, through which was a gate leading to the back of the building. Guided by the impulse of the moment, I crossed the street to the gate, and, lifting the latch, entered the paved alley, on one side of which was a paled fence, and on the other the house, looking through two windows into the alley.

The first window was dark like those in front; but at the second a light was discernible. I approached it, and, looking through, beheld a plain but neat apartment, in which parlour, kitchen, and nursery seemed to be united. A fire burnt cheerfully in the chimney, over which was a tea-kettle. On the hearth sat a smiling and playful cherub of a boy, tossing something to a black girl who sat opposite, and whose innocent and regular features wanted only a different hue to make them beautiful. Near it, in a rocking-chair, with a sleeping babe in her lap, sat a female figure in plain but neat and becoming attire. Her posture permitted half her face to be seen, and saved me from any danger of being observed.

This countenance was full of sweetness and benignity, but the sadness that veiled its lustre was profound. Her eyes were now fixed upon the fire and were moist with the tears of remembrance, while she sung, in low and scarcely audible strains, an artless lullaby.

This spectacle exercised a strange power over my feelings. While occupied in meditating on the features of the

372

mother, I was unaware of my conspicuous situation. The black girl having occasion to change her situation, in order to reach the ball which was thrown at her, unluckily caught a glance of my figure through the glass. In a tone of half surprize and half terror she cried out—O! see dare! a man!

I was tempted to draw suddenly back, but a second thought shewed me the impropriety of departing thus abruptly, and leaving behind me some alarm. I felt a sort of necessity for apologizing for my intrusion into these precincts, and hastened to a door that led into the same apartment. I knocked. A voice somewhat confused bade me enter. It was not till I opened the door and entered the room, that I fully saw in what embarrassments I had incautiously involved myself.

I could scarcely obtain sufficient courage to speak, and gave a confused assent to the question—"Have you business with me, sir?" She offered me a chair, and I sat down. She put the child, not yet awakened, into the arms of the black, who kissed it and rocked it in her arms with great satisfaction, and, resuming her seat, looked at me with inquisitiveness mingled with complacency.

After a moment's pause, I said—I was directed to this house as the abode of Mr. Ephraim Williams. Can he be seen, madam?

He is not in town at present. If you will leave a message with me, I will punctually deliver it.

The thought suddenly occurred, whether any more was needful than merely to leave the bills suitably enclosed, as they already were, in a pacquet. Thus all painful explanations might be avoided, and I might have reason to congratulate myself on his seasonable absence. Actuated by these thoughts, I drew forth the pacquet, and put it into her hand, saying, I will leave this in your possession, and must earnestly request you to keep it safe until you can deliver it into his own hands.

Scarcely had I said this before new suggestions occurred. Was it right to act in this clandestine and mysterious manner? Should I leave these persons in uncertainty respecting the fate of an husband and a brother? What perplexities, misunderstandings, and suspences might not grow out of this uncertainty; and ought they not to be precluded at any hazard to my own safety or good name?

These sentiments made me involuntarily stretch forth my hand to retake the pacquet. This gesture, and other significances in my manners, joined to a trembling consciousness in herself, filled my companion with all the tokens of confusion and fear. She alternately looked at me and at the paper. Her trepidation increased, and she grew pale. These emotions were counteracted by a strong effort.

At length she said faulteringly, I will take good care of them, and will give them to my brother.

She rose and placed them in a drawer, after which she resumed her seat.

On this occasion all my wariness forsook me. I cannot explain why my perplexity and the trouble of my tho'ts were greater upon this than upon similar occasions. However it be, I was incapable of speaking, and fixed my eyes upon the floor. A sort of electrical sympathy pervaded my companion, and terror and anguish were strongly manifested in the glances which she sometimes stole at me. We seemed fully to understand each other without the aid of words.

This imbecility could not last long. I gradually recovered my composure and collected my scattered thoughts. I looked at her with seriousness, and steadfastly spoke—Are you the wife of Amos Watson?

She started.—I am, indeed. Why do you ask? Do you know any thing of——? There her voice failed.

I replied with quickness, yes. I am fully acquainted with his destiny.

Good God! she exclaimed in a paroxysm of surprize, and bending eagerly forward, my husband is then alive. This pacquet is from him. Where is he? When have you seen him?

'Tis a long time since.

But where, where is he now? Is he well? Will he return to me?

Never.

Merciful Heaven! looking upwards and clasping her

374

hands, I thank thee at least for his life! But why has he forsaken me? Why will he not return?

For a good reason, said I with augmented solemnity, he will never return to thee. Long ago was he laid in the cold grave.

She shrieked; and, at the next moment, sunk in a swoon upon the floor. I was alarmed. The two children shrieked, and ran about the room terrified and unknowing what they did. I was overwhelmed with somewhat like terror, yet I involuntarily raised the mother in my arms, and cast about for the means of recalling her from this fit.

Time to effect this had not elapsed, when several persons, apparently Mrs. Watson's neighbors, and raised by the out-cries of the girls, hastily entered the room. They looked at me with mingled surprize and suspicion; but my attitude, being that not of an injurer but helper; my countenance, which shewed the pleasure their entrance, at this critical moment, afforded me; and my words, in which I besought their assistance, and explained, in some degree, and briefly, the cause of those appearances, removed their ill thoughts.

Presently, the unhappy woman, being carried by the new-comers into a bed-room adjoining, recovered her sensibility. I only waited for this. I had done my part. More information would be useless to her, and not to be given by me, at least, in the present audience, without embarrassment and peril. I suddenly determined to withdraw, and this, the attention of the company being otherwise engaged, I did without notice. I returned to my inn, and shut myself up in my chamber. Such was the change which, undesigned, unforeseen, an half an hour had wrought in my situation. My cautious projects had perished in their conception. That which I had deemed so arduous, to require such cir-cumspect approaches, such well concerted speeches, was done.

I had started up before this woman as if from the pores of the ground. I had vanished with the same celerity, but had left her in possession of proofs sufficient that I was neither spectre nor demon. I will visit her, said I, again. I will see her brother, and know the full effect of my disclosure. I will tell them all that I myself know. Ignorance would be no less injurious to them than to myself; but, first, I will see the Maurices.

CHAPTER XVIII

NEXT morning I arose betimes, and equipped myself without delay. I had eight or ten miles to walk, so far from the town being the residence of these people; and I forthwith repaired to their dwelling. The persons whom I desired to see were known to me only by name, and by their place of abode. It was a mother and her three daughters to whom I now carried the means not only of competence but riches; means which they, no doubt, had long ago despaired of regaining, and which, among all possible messengers, one of my age and guise would be the least suspected of being able to restore.

I arrived, through intricate ways, at eleven o'clock, at the house of Mrs. Maurice. It was a neat dwelling, in a very fanciful and rustic style, in the bosom of a valley, which, when decorated by the verdure and blossoms of the coming season, must possess many charms. At present it was naked and dreary.

As I approached it, through a long avenue, I observed two female figures, walking arm-in-arm and slowly to and fro, in the path in which I now was. These, said I, are daughters of the family. Graceful, well-dressed, fashionable girls they seem at this distance. May they be deserving of the good tidings which I bring.—Seeing them turn towards the house, I mended my pace, that I might overtake them and request their introduction of me to their mother.

As I more nearly approached, they again turned; and, perceiving me, they stood as if in expectation of my message. I went up to them.

A single glance, cast at each, made me suspect that they were not sisters; but, somewhat to my disappointment, there was nothing highly prepossessing in the countenance of either. They were what is every day met with, though less embellished by brilliant drapery and turban, in markets and streets. An air, somewhat haughty, somewhat supercilious, lessened still more their attractions. These defects, however, were nothing to me.

I enquired, of her that seemed to be the elder of the two, for Mrs. Maurice.

She is indisposed, was the cold reply.

That is unfortunate. Is it not possible to see her?

No—with still more gravity.

I was somewhat at a loss how to proceed. A pause ensued. At length, the same lady resumed—What's your business? You can leave your message with me.

With no body but her. If she be not *very* indisposed——

She is very indisposed, interrupted she peevishly. If you cannot leave your message, you may take it back again, for she must not be disturbed.

This was a singular reception. I was disconcerted and silent. I knew not what to say. Perhaps, I at last observed, some other time——

No, with increasing heat, no other time. She is more likely to be worse than better. Come, Betsy, said she, taking hold of her companion's arm; and, hieing into the house, shut the door after her, and disappeared. I stood, at the bottom of the steps, confounded at such strange and unexpected treatment. I could not withdraw till my purpose was accomplished. After a moment's pause, I stepped to the door, and pulled the bell. A Negro came, of a very unpropitious aspect, and opening the door, looked at me in silence. To my question, was Mrs. Maurice to be seen? he made some answer, in a jargon which I could not understand; but his words were immediately followed by an unseen person within the house—Mrs. Maurice can't be seen by any body. Come in, Cato, and shut the door. This injunction was obeyed by Cato without ceremony.

Here was a dilemma! I came with ten thousand pounds in my hands, to bestow freely on these people, and such was the treatment I received. I must adopt, said I, a new mode.

I lifted the latch, without a second warning, and, Cato having disappeared, went into a room, the door of which chanced to be open, on my right hand. I found within the two females whom I had accosted in the portico. I now addressed myself to the younger—This intrusion, when I have explained the reason of it, will, I hope, be forgiven. I come, madam——

Yes, interrupted the other, with a countenance suffused by indignation, I know very well whom you come from, and what it is that prompts this insolence, but your employer shall see that we have not sunk so low as he imagines. Cato! Bob! I say.

My employer, madam! I see you labor under some great mistake. I have no employer. I come from a great distance. I come to bring intelligence of the utmost importance to your family. I come to benefit and not to injure you.

By this time, Bob and Cato, two sturdy blacks, entered the room. Turn this person, said the imperious lady, regardless of my explanations, out of the house. Don't you hear me? she continued, observing that they looked one upon the other and hesitated.

Surely, madam, said I, you are precipitate. You are treating like an enemy one who will prove himself your mother's best friend.

Will you leave the house? she exclaimed, quite beside herself with anger. Villains! why don't you do as I bid you?

The blacks looked upon each other, as if waiting for an example. Their habitual deference for every thing *white*, no doubt, held their hands from what they regarded as a profanation. At last Bob said, in a whining, beseeching tone—Why, missee, massa buckra wanna go for doo, dan he wanna go fo' wee.

The lady now burst into tears of rage. She held out her hand, menacingly. Will you leave the house?

Not willingly, said I, in a mild tone. I came too far to

379

return with the business that brought me unperformed. I am persuaded, madam, you mistake my character and my views. I have a message to deliver your mother which deeply concerns her and your happiness, if you are her daughter. I merely wished to see her, and leave with her a piece of important news; news in which her fortune is deeply interested.

These words had a wonderful effect upon the young lady. Her anger was checked. Good God! she exclaimed, are you Watson?

No: I am only Watson's representative, and come to do all that Watson could do if he were present.

She was now importunate to know my business.

My business lies with Mrs. Maurice. Advertisements, which I have seen, direct me to her, and to this house, and to her only shall I deliver my message.

Perhaps, said she, with a face of apology, I have mistaken you. Mrs. Maurice is my mother. She is really indisposed, but I can stand in her place on this occasion.

You cannot represent her in this instance. If I cannot have access to her now, I must go; and shall return when you are willing to grant it.

Nay, replied she, she is not, perhaps, so very sick but that—I will go, and see if she will admit you.—So saying, she left me for three minutes; and returning said, her mother wished to see me.

I followed up stairs, at her request; and, entering an ill-furnished chamber, found, seated in an arm-chair, a lady seemingly in years, pale and visibly infirm. The lines of her countenance were far from laying claim to my reverence. It was too much like the daughter's.

She looked at me, at my entrance, with great eagerness, and said, in a sharp tone, pray, friend, what is it you want with me? Make haste; tell your story, and begone.

My story is a short one, and easily told. Amos Watson was your agent in Jamaica. He sold an estate belonging to you, and received the money.

He did, said she, attempting ineffectually to rise from her seat, and her eyes beaming with a significance that shocked me—He did, the villain, and purloined the money, to the ruin of me and my daughters. But if there be justice on earth it will overtake him. I trust, I shall have the pleasure one day—I hope to hear he's hanged. Well, but go on, friend. He *did* sell it, I tell you.

He sold it for ten thousand pounds, I resumed, and invested this sum in bills of exchange. Watson is dead. These bills came into my hands. I was lately informed, by the public papers, who were the real owners, and have come from Philadelphia with no other view than to restore them to you. There they are, continued I, placing them in her lap, entire and untouched.

She seized the papers, and looked at me and at her daughter, by turns, with an air of one suddenly bewildered. She seemed speechless, and growing suddenly more ghastly pale, leaned her head back upon the chair. The daughter screamed, and hastened to support the languid parent, who difficultly articulated—O! I am sick; sick to death. Put me on the bed.

I was astonished and affrighted at this scene. Some of the domestics, of both colours, entered, and gazed at me with surprize. Involuntarily I withdrew, and returned to the room below into which I had first entered, and which I now found deserted.

I was for some time at a loss to guess at the cause of these appearances. At length it occurred to me, that joy was the source of the sickness that had seized Mrs. Maurice. The abrupt recovery of what had probably been deemed irretrievable, would naturally produce this effect upon a mind of a certain texture.

I was deliberating, whether to stay or go, when the daughter entered the room, and, after expressing some surprize at seeing me, whom she supposed to have retired, told me that her mother wished to see me again before my departure. In this request there was no kindness. All was cold, supercilious, and sullen. I obeyed the summons without speaking.

I found Mrs. Maurice seated in her arm-chair, much in her former guise. Without desiring me to be seated, or relaxing ought in her asperity of looks and tones—Pray, friend, how did you *come by* these papers?

I assure you, madam, they were honestly *come by*, answered I, sedately and with half a smile; but, if the whole is there that was missing, the mode and time in which they came to me is matter of concern only to myself. Is there any deficiency?

I'm not sure. I don't know much of these matters. There may be less. I dare say there is. I shall know that soon. I expect a friend of mine every minute who will look them over. I don't doubt you can give a good account of yourself.

I doubt not but I can—to those who have a right to demand it. In this case, curiosity must be very urgent indeed, before I shall consent to gratify it.

You must know this is a suspicious case. Watson, to be sure, embezzled the money: to be sure, you are his accomplice.

Certainly, said I, my conduct, on this occasion, proves that. What I have brought to you, of my own accord; what I have restored to you, fully and unconditionally, it is plain Watson embezzled, and that I was aiding in the fraud. To restore what was never stolen always betrays the thief. To give what might be kept without suspicion, is, without doubt, arrant knavery.—To be serious, madam, in coming thus far, for this purpose, I have done enough; and must now bid you farewel.

Nay, don't go yet. I have something more to say to you. My friend I'm sure will be here presently. There he is, noticing a peal upon the bell. Polly, go down, and see if that's Mr. Somers. If it is, bring him up. The daughter went.

I walked to the window absorbed in my own reflections. I was disappointed and dejected. The scene before me was the unpleasing reverse of all that my fancy, while coming hither, had foreboded. I expected to find virtuous indigence and sorrow lifted, by my means, to affluence and exultation. I expected to witness the tears of gratitude and the caresses of affection. What had I found? Nothing but sordidness, stupidity, and illiberal suspicion.

The daughter staid much longer than the mother's patience could endure. She knocked against the floor with her heel. A servant came up.—Where's Polly, you slut? It was not you, hussey, that I wanted. It was her.

She is talking in the parlour with a gentleman.

Mr. Somers, I suppose; hay! fool! Run with my compliments to him, wench. Tell him, please walk up.

It is not Mr. Somers, ma'am.

No! Who then, saucebox? What gentleman can have any thing to do with Polly?

I don't know, ma'am.

Who said you did, impertinence? Run, and tell her I want her this instant.

The summons was not delivered, or Polly did not think proper to obey it. Full ten minutes of thoughtful silence on my part, and of muttered vexation and impatience on that of the old lady, elapsed before Polly's entrance. As soon as she appeared, the mother began to complain bitterly of her inattention and neglect; but Polly, taking no notice of her, addressed herself to me, and told me, that a gentleman below wished to see me. I hastened down, and found a stranger, of a plain appearance, in the parlour. His aspect was liberal and ingenuous; and I quickly collected from his discourse, that this was the brother-in-law of Watson, and the companion of his last voyage.

CHAPTER XIX

MY eyes sparkled with pleasure at this unexpected interview, and I willingly confessed my desire to communicate all the knowledge of his brother's destiny which I possessed. He told me, that, returning late to Baltimore on the last evening, he found his sister in much agitation and distress, which, after a time, she explained to him. She likewise put the pacquets I had left into his hands.

I leave you to imagine, continued he, my surprize and curiosity at this discovery. I was, of course, impatient to see the bearer of such extraordinary tidings. This morning, enquiring for one of your appearance at the taverns, I was, at length, informed of your arrival yesterday in the stage; of your going out alone in the evening; of your subsequent return; and of your early departure this morning. Accidentally I lighted on your footsteps; and, by suitable enquiries on the road, have finally traced you hither.

You told my sister her husband was dead. You left with her papers that were probably in his possession at the time of his death. I understand from Miss Maurice that the bills belonging to her mother, have just been delivered to her. I presume you have no objection to clear up this mystery.

To you I am anxious to unfold every thing. At this moment, or at any time, but the sooner, the more agreeable to me, I will do it.

This, said he, looking around him, is no place; there is an inn not an hundred yards from this gate, where I have left my horse; will you go thither? I readily consented, and calling for a private apartment, I laid before this man every incident of my life connected with Welbeck and Watson; my full, circumstantial and explicit story, appeared to remove every doubt which he might have entertained of my integrity.

In Williams, I found a plain good man, of a temper confiding and affectionate. My narration being finished, he expressed, by unaffected tokens, his wonder and his grief on account of Watson's destiny. To my enquiries, which were made with frankness and fervor, respecting his own and his sister's condition, he said, that the situation of both was deplorable till the recovery of this property. They had been saved from utter ruin, from beggary and a jail, only by the generosity and lenity of his creditors, who did not suffer the suspicious circumstances attending Watson's disappearance to outweigh former proofs of his probity. They had never relinquished the hopes of receiving some tidings of their kinsman.

I related what had just passed in the house of Mrs. Maurice, and requested to know from him the history and character of this family.

They have treated you, he answered, exactly as any one who knew them would have predicted. The mother is narrow, ignorant, bigotted, and avaricious. The eldest daughter, whom you saw, resembles the old lady in many things. Age, indeed, may render the similitude complete. At present, pride and ill-humor are her chief characteristics.

The youngest daughter has nothing in mind or person in common with her family. Where they are irrascible, she is patient; where they are imperious, she is humble; where they are covetous, she is liberal; where they are ignorant and indolent, she is studious and skilful. It is rare, indeed, to find a young lady more amiable than Miss Fanny Maurice, or who has had more crosses and afflictions to sustain.

The eldest daughter always extorted the supply of her wants, from her parents, by threats and importunities; but the younger could never be prevailed upon to employ the same means, and, hence, she suffered inconveniences which, to any other girl, born to an equal rank, would have been, to the last degree, humiliating and vexatious. To her they only afforded new opportunities for the display of her most shining virtues—fortitude and charity. No instance of their sordidness or tyranny ever stole a murmur from her. For what they had given, existence and a virtuous education, she said they were entitled to gratitude. What they withheld was their own, in the use of which they were not accountable to her. She was not ashamed to owe her subsistence to her own industry, and was only held, by the pride of her family—in this instance their pride was equal to their avarice—from seeking out some lucrative kind of employment. Since the shock which their fortune sustained, by Watson's disappearance, she has been permitted to pursue this plan, and she now teaches music in Baltimore for a living. No one, however, in the highest rank, can be more generally respected and caressed than she is.

But will not the recovery of this money make a favorable change in her condition?

I can hardly tell; but I am inclined to think it will not. It will not change her mother's character. Her pride may be awakened anew, and she may oblige Miss Fanny to relinquish her new profession, and that will be a change to be deplored.

What good has been done, then, by restoring this money?

If pleasure be good, you must have conferred a great deal on the Maurices; upon the mother and two of the daughters, at least. The only pleasure, indeed, which their natures can receive. It is less than if you had raised them from absolute indigence, which has not been the case, since they had wherewithal to live upon beside their Jamaica property. But how, continued Williams, suddenly recollecting himself, have you claimed the reward promised to him who should restore these bills?

What reward?

No less than a thousand dollars. It was publicly promised under the hands of Mrs. Maurice and of Hemming, her husband's executor.

Really, said I, that circumstance escaped my attention, and I wonder that it did; but is it too late to repair the evil?

Then you have no scruple to accept the reward?

Certainly not. Could you suspect me of so strange a punctilio as that?

Yes; but I know not why. The story you have just finished taught me to expect some unreasonable refinement upon that head.—To be hired, to be bribed to do our duty is supposed by some to be degrading.

This is no such bribe to me. I should have acted just as I have done, had no recompence been promised. In truth, this has been my conduct, for I never once thought of the reward; but now that you remind me of it, I would gladly see it bestowed. To fulfil their engagements, in this respect, is no more than justice in the Maurices. To one, in my condition, the money will be highly useful. If these people were poor, or generous and worthy, or if I myself were already rich, I might less repine at their withholding it; but, things being as they are with them and with me, it would, I think, be gross injustice in them to withhold, and in me to refuse.

That injustice, said Williams, will, on their part, I fear, be committed. 'Tis pity you first applied to Mrs. Maurice. Nothing can be expected from her avarice, unless it be wrested from her by a lawsuit.

That is a force which I shall never apply.

Had you gone first to Hemming's, you might, I think, have looked for payment. He is not a mean man. A thousand dollars he must know is not much to give for forty thousand. Perhaps, indeed, it may not yet be too late. I am well known to him, and if you please, will attend you to him in the evening, and state your claim.

I thankfully accepted this offer, and went with him accordingly. I found that Hemmings had been with Mrs. Maurice in the course of the day; had received from her intelligence of this transaction, and had entertained the expectation of a visit from me for this very purpose.

While Williams explained to him the nature of my claim, he scanned me with great intentness. His austere and inflexible brow, afforded me little room to hope for success, and this hopelessness was confirmed by his silence and perplexity, when Williams had made an end.

To be sure, said he, after some pause, the contract was

explicit. To be sure, the conditions on Mr. Mervyn's side have been performed. Certain it is, the bills are entire and complete, but Mrs. Maurice will not consent to do her part, and Mrs. Maurice, to whom the papers were presented, is the person, by whom, according to the terms of the contract, the reward must be paid.

But Mrs. Maurice, you know, sir, may be legally compelled to pay, said Williams.

Perhaps she may; but I tell you plainly, that she never will do the thing without compulsion. Legal process, however, in this case, will have other inconveniences besides delay. Some curiosity will naturally be excited, as to the history of these papers. Watson disappeared a twelve month ago. Who can avoid asking, where have these papers been deposited all this while, and how came this person in possession of them?

That kind of curiosity, said I, is natural and laudable, and gladly would I gratify it. Disclosure or concealment in that case, however, would no wise affect my present claim. Whether a bond, legally executed, shall be paid, does not depend upon determining whether the payer is fondest of boiled mutton or roast beef. Truth, in the first case, has no connection with truth in the second. So far from eluding this curiosity; so far from studying concealment, I am anxious to publish the truth.

You are right, to be sure, said Hemmings. Curiosity is a natural, but only an incidental consequence in this case. I have no reason for desiring that it should be an unpleasant consequence to you.

Well, sir, said Williams, you think that Arthur Mervyn has no remedy in this case but the law.

Mrs. Maurice, to be sure, will never pay but on compulsion. Mervyn should have known his own interest better. While his left hand was stretched out to give, his right should have been held forth to receive. As it is, he must be contented with the aid of law. Any attorney will prosecute on condition of receiving *half the sum* when recovered.

We now rose to take our leave, when, Hemmings desiring us to pause a moment, said, to be sure, in the utmost strictness of the terms of our promise, the reward was to be paid by the person who received the papers; but it must be owned that your claim, at any rate, is equitable. I have money of the deceased Mr. Maurice in my hands. These very bills are now in my possession. I will therefore pay you your due, and take the consequences of an act of justice on myself. I was prepared for you. Sign that receipt, and there is a *check* for the amount.

CHAPTER XX

THIS unexpected and agreeable decision was accompanied by an invitation to supper, at which we were treated by our host with much affability and kindness. Finding me the author of Williams's good fortune, as well as Mrs. Maurice's, and being assured by the former of his entire conviction of the rectitude of my conduct, he laid aside all reserve and distance with regard to me. He enquired into my prospects and wishes, and professed his willingness to serve me.

I dealt with equal unreserve and frankness. I am poor, said I. Money for my very expences hither, I have borrowed from a friend, to whom I am, in other respects, much indebted, and whom I expect to compensate only by gratitude and future services.

In coming hither, I expected only an increase of my debts; to sink still deeper into poverty; but happily the issue has made me rich. This hour has given me competence, at least.

What! call you a thousand dollars competence?

More than competence. I call it an abundance. My own ingenuity, while I enjoy health, will enable me to live. This I regard as a fund, first to pay my debts, and next to supply deficiencies occasioned by untoward accidents or ill health, during the ensuing three or four years, at least.

We parted with this new acquaintance at a late hour, and I accepted Williams's invitation to pass the time I should spend at Baltimore, under his sister's roof. There were several motives for prolonging this stay. What I had heard of Miss Fanny Maurice, excited strong wishes to be personally acquainted with her. This young lady was affectionately attached to Mrs. Watson, by whose means my wishes were easily accomplished.

I never was in habits of reserve, even with those whom I had no reason to esteem. With those who claimed my admiration and affection, it was impossible to be incommunicative. Before the end of my second interview, both these women were mistresses of every momentous incident of my life, and of the whole chain of my feelings and opinions, in relation to every subject, and particularly in relation to themselves. Every topic disconnected with these, is comparatively lifeless and inert.

I found it easy to win their attention, and to render them communicative in their turn. As full disclosures as I had made without condition or request, my enquiries and example easily obtained from Mrs. Watson and Miss Maurice. The former related every event of her youth, and the circumstances leading to her marriage. She depicted the character of her husband, and the whole train of suspences and inquietudes occasioned by his disappearance. The latter did not hide from me her opinions upon any important subject, and made me thoroughly acquainted with her actual situation.

This intercourse was strangely fascinating. My heart was buoyed up by a kind of intoxication. I now found myself exalted to my genial element, and began to taste the delights of existence. In the intercourse of ingenious and sympathetic minds, I found a pleasure which I had not previously conceived.

The time flew swiftly away, and a fortnight passed almost before I was aware that a day had gone by. I did not forget the friends whom I had left behind, but maintained a punctual correspondence with Stevens, to whom I imparted all occurrences.

The recovery of my friend's kinsman, allowed him in a few days to return home. His first object was the consolation and relief of Carlton, whom, with much difficulty, he persuaded to take advantage of the laws in favor of insolvent debtors. Carlton's only debt was owing to his uncle, and by rendering up every species of property, except his clothes and the implements of his trade, he obtained a full discharge. In conjunction with his sister, he once more assumed the pen, and being no longer burthened with debts he was unable to discharge, he resumed, together with his pen, his cheerfulness. Their mutual industry was sufficient for their decent and moderate subsistence.

The chief reason for my hasty return, was my anxiety respecting Clemenza Lodi. This reason was removed by the activity and benevolence of my friend. He paid this unfortunate stranger a visit at Mrs. Villars's. Access was easily obtained, and he found her sunk into the deepest melancholy. The recent loss of her child, the death of Welbeck, of which she was soon apprized, her total dependence upon those with whom she was placed, who, however, had always treated her without barbarity or indecorum, were the calamities that weighed down her spirit.

My friend easily engaged her confidence and gratitude, and prevailed upon her to take refuge under his own roof. Mrs. Wentworth's scruples, as well as those of Mrs. Fielding, were removed by his arguments and entreaties, and they consented to take upon themselves, and divide between them, the care of her subsistence and happiness. They condescended to express much curiosity respecting me, and some interest in my welfare, and promised to receive me on my return, on the footing of a friend.

With some reluctance, I at length bade my new friends farewel, and returned to Philadelphia. Nothing remained, before I should enter on my projected scheme of study and employment, under the guidance of Stevens, but to examine the situation of Eliza Hadwin with my own eyes, and if possible, to extricate my father from his unfortunate situation.

My father's state had given me the deepest concern. I figured to myself his condition, besotted by brutal appetites, reduced to beggary, shut up in a noisome prison, and condemned to that society which must foster all his de-

praved propensities. I revolved various schemes for his
relief. A few hundreds would take him from prison, but
how should he be afterwards disposed of? How should he
be cured of his indolent habits? How should he be screened
from the contagion of vicious society? By what means, consistently with my own wants, and the claims of others,
should I secure to him an acceptable subsistence?

Exhortation and example were vain. Nothing but restraint would keep him at a distance from the haunts of
brawling and debauchery. The want of money would be no
obstacle to prodigality and waste. Credit would be resorted
to as long as it would answer his demand. When that failed,
he would once more be thrown into a prison; the same
means to extricate him would be to be repeated, and money
be thus put into the pockets of the most worthless of mankind, the agents of drunkenness and blasphemy, without
any permanent advantage to my father, the principal object
of my charity.

Though unable to fix on any plausible mode of proceeding, I determined, at least, to discover his present condition.
Perhaps, something might suggest itself, upon the spot,
suited to my purpose. Without delay I proceeded to the
village of Newtown, and alighting at the door of the prison,
enquired for my father.

Sawny Mervyn you want, I suppose, said the keeper. Poor
fellow! He came into limbo in a crazy condition, and has
been a burthen on my hands ever since. After lingering
along for some time, he was at last kind enough to give us
the slip. It is just a week since he drank his last pint—and
died.

I was greatly shocked at this intelligence. It was some time
before my reason came to my aid, and shewed me that this
was an event, on the whole, and on a disinterested and
dispassionate view, not unfortunate. The keeper knew not
my relation to the deceased, and readily recounted the
behaviour of the prisoner and the circumstances of his last
hours.

I shall not repeat the narrative. It is useless to keep alive
the sad remembrance. He was now beyond the reach of my

charity or pity; and since reflection could answer no beneficial end to him, it was my duty to divert my thoughts into different channels, and live henceforth for my own happiness and that of those who were within the sphere of my influence.

I was now alone in the world, so far as the total want of kindred creates solitude. Not one of my blood, nor even of my name, were to be found in this quarter of the world. Of my mother's kindred I knew nothing. So far as friendship or service might be claimed from them, to me they had no existence. I was destitute of all those benefits which flow from kindred, in relation to protection, advice or property. My inheritance was nothing. Not a single relique or trinket in my possession constituted a memorial of my family. The scenes of my childish and juvenile days were dreary and desolate. The fields which I was wont to traverse, the room in which I was born, retained no traces of the past. They were the property and residence of strangers, who knew nothing of the former tenants, and who, as I was now told, had hastened to new-model and transform every thing within and without the habitation.

These images filled me with melancholy, which, however, disappeared in proportion as I approached the abode of my beloved girl. Absence had endeared the image of my *Bess* —I loved to call her so—to my soul. I could not think of her without a melting softness at my heart, and tears in which pain and pleasure were unaccountably mingled. As I approached Curling's house, I strained my sight, in hopes of distinguishing her form through the evening dusk.

I had told her of my purpose, by letter. She expected my approach at this hour, and was stationed, with a heart throbbing with impatience, at the road side, near the gate. As soon as I alighted, she rushed into my arms.

I found my sweet friend less blithsome and contented than I wished. Her situation, in spite of the parental and sisterly regards which she received from the Curlings, was mournful and dreary to her imagination. Rural business was irksome, and insufficient to fill up her time. Her life was tiresome, and uniform and heavy.

I ventured to blame her discontent, and pointed out the advantages of her situation. Whence, said I, can these dissatisfactions and repinings arise?

I cannot tell, said she; I don't know how it is with me. I am always sorrowful and thoughtful. Perhaps, I think too much of my poor father and of Susan, and yet that can't be it neither, for I think of them but seldom; not half as much as I ought, perhaps. I think of nobody almost, but you. Instead of minding my business, or chatting and laughing with Peggy Curling, I love to get by myself—to read, over and over, your letters, or to think how you are employed just then, and how happy I should be if I were in Fanny Maurice's place.

But it is all over now; this visit rewards me for every thing. I wonder how I could ever be sullen or mopeful. I will behave better, indeed I will, and be always, as now, a most happy girl.

The greater part of three days was spent in the society of my friend, in listening to her relation of all that had happened during my absence, and in communicating, in my turn, every incident which had befallen myself. After this I once more returned to the city.

CHAPTER XXI

I NOW set about carrying my plan of life into effect. I began with ardent zeal and unwearied diligence the career of medical study. I bespoke the counsels and instructions of my friend; attended him on his professional visits, and acted, in all practicable cases, as his substitute. I found this application of time more pleasurable than I had imagined. My mind gladly expanded itself, as it were, for the reception of new ideas. My curiosity grew more eager, in proportion as it was supplied with food, and every day added strength to the assurance that I was no insignificant and worthless being; that I was destined to be *something* in this scene of existence, and might sometime lay claim to the gratitude and homage of my fellow-men.

I was far from being, however, monopolized by these pursuits. I was formed on purpose for the gratification of social intercourse. To love and to be loved; to exchange hearts, and mingle sentiments with all the virtuous and amiable, whom my good fortune had placed within the circuit of my knowledge, I always esteemed my highest enjoyment and my chief duty.

Carlton and his sister, Mrs. Wentworth and Achsa Fielding, were my most valuable associates beyond my own family. With all these my correspondence was frequent and unreserved, but chiefly with the latter. This lady had dignity and independence, a generous and enlightened spirit beyond what her education had taught me to expect. She was circumspect and cautious in her deportment, and was not prompt to make advances or accept them. She withheld her esteem and confidence until she had full proof of their being deserved.

I am not sure that her treatment of me was fully conformable to her rules. My manners, indeed, as she once told me, she had never met with in another. Ordinary rules were so totally overlooked in my behaviour, that it seemed impossible for any one who knew me to adhere to them. No option was left but to admit my claims to friendship and confidence, instantly, or to reject them altogether.

I was not conscious of this singularity. The internal and undiscovered character of another, weighed nothing with me in the question, whether they should be treated with frankness or reserve. I felt no scruple on any occasion, to disclose every feeling and every event. Any one who could listen, found me willing to talk. Every talker found me willing to listen. Every one had my sympathy and kindness, *without* claiming it, but I *claimed* the kindness and sympathy of every one.

Achsa Fielding's countenance bespoke, I thought, a mind worthy to be known and to be loved. The first moment I engaged her attention, I told her so. I related the little story of my family, spread out before her all my reasonings and determinations, my notions of right and wrong, my fears and wishes. All this was done with sincerity and fervor, with gestures, actions and looks, in which I felt as if my whole soul was visible. Her superior age, sedateness and prudence, gave my deportment a filial freedom and affection, and I was fond of calling her "*mamma.*"

I particularly dwelt upon the history of my dear country girl; painted her form and countenance; recounted our dialogues, and related all my schemes for making her wise and good and happy. On these occasions my friend would listen to me with the mutest attention. I shewed her the letters I received, and offered her for her perusal, those which I wrote in answer, before they were sealed and sent.

On these occasions she would look by turns on my face

and away from me. A varying hue would play upon her cheek, and her eyes were fuller than was common of meaning.

Such and such, I once said, are my notions; now what do *you* think?

Think! emphatically, and turning somewhat aside, she answered, that you are the most—*strange* of human creatures.

But tell me, I resumed, following and searching her averted eyes, am I right; would you do thus? Can you help me to improve my girl? I wish you knew the bewitching little creature. How would that heart overflow with affection and with gratitude towards you. She should be your daughter. No—you are too nearly of an age for that. A sister: her *elder* sister you should be. *That*, when there is no other relation, includes them all. Fond sisters you would be, and I the fond brother of you both.

My eyes glistened as I spoke. In truth, I am in that respect, a mere woman. My friend was more powerfully moved. After a momentary struggle, she burst into tears.

Good Heaven! said I, what ails you? Are you not well?

Her looks betrayed an unaccountable confusion, from which she quickly recovered—it was folly to be thus affected. Something ailed me I believe, but it is past—But come; you want some lines of finishing the description of the *Boa* in Lacepede.

True. And I have twenty minutes to spare. Poor Franks is very ill indeed, but he cannot be seen till nine. We'll read till then.

Thus on the wings of pleasure and improvement past my time; not without some hues, occasionally of a darker tinct. My heart was now and then detected in sighing. This occurred when my thoughts glanced at the poor Eliza, and measured, as it were, the interval between us. We are too—*too* far apart, thought I.

The best solace on these occasions was the company of Mrs. Fielding; her music, her discourse, or some book which she set me to rehearsing to her. One evening, when preparing to pay her a visit, I received the following letter from my Bess.

To A. Mervyn.

Curling's, May 6, 1794.

WHERE does this letter you promised me, stay all this while? Indeed, Arthur, you torment me more than I deserve, and more than I could ever find it in my heart to do you. You treat me cruelly. I must say so, though I offend you. I must write, though you do not deserve that I should, and though I fear I am in a humor not very fit for writing. I had better go to my chamber and weep: weep at your— *unkindness*, I was going to say; but, perhaps, it is only forgetfulness: and yet what can be more unkind than forgetfulness? I am sure I have never forgotten you. Sleep itself, which wraps all other images in forgetfulness, only brings you nearer, and makes me see you more distinctly.

But where can this letter stay?—O! that—hush! foolish girl! If a word of that kind escape thy lips, Arthur will be angry with thee; and then, indeed, thou mightst weep in earnest. *Then* thou wouldst have some cause for thy tears. More than once already has he almost broken thy heart with his reproaches. Sore and weak as it now is, any new reproaches would assuredly break it quite.

I *will* be content. I will be as good an housewife and dairy-woman, stir about as briskly, and sing as merrily as Peggy Curling. Why not? I am as young, as innocent, and enjoy as good health.—Alas! she has reason to be merry. She has father, mother, brothers; but I have none.—And he that was all these, and more than all these, to me, has— *forgotten* me.

But, perhaps, it is some accident that hinders. Perhaps Oliver left the market earlier than he used to do; or you mistook the house; or, perhaps, some poor creature was sick, was taken suddenly ill, and you were busy in chafing his clay-cold limbs; it fell to you to wipe the clammy drops from his brow. Such things often happen; don't they, Arthur, to people of your trade, and some such thing has happened now; and that was the reason you did not write.

And if so, shall I repine at your silence? O no! At such a time the poor Bess might easily be, and ought to be forgotten. She would not deserve your love, if she could repine at a silence brought about this way.

And O! May it be so! May there be nothing worse than this. If the sick man—see, Arthur, how my hand trembles. Can you read this scrawl? What is always bad, my fears make worse than ever.

I must not think that. And yet, if it be so, if my friend himself be sick, what will become of me? Of me, that ought to cherish you and comfort you; that ought to be your nurse. Endure for you your sickness, when she cannot remove it.

O! that—I *will* speak out—O! that this strange scruple had never possessed you. Why should I *not* be with you? Who can love you and serve you as well as I? In sickness and health, I will console and assist you. Why will you deprive yourself of such a comforter, and such an aid as I would be to you?

Dear Arthur, think better of it. Let me leave this dreary spot, where, indeed, as long as I am thus alone, I can enjoy no comfort. Let me come to you. I will put up with any thing for the sake of seeing you, tho' it be but once a day. Any garret or cellar in the dirtiest lane or darkest alley, will be good enough for me. I will think it a palace, so that I can *but* see you now and then.

Do not refuse—do not argue with me, so fond you always are of arguing! My heart is set upon your compliance. And yet, dearly as I prize your company, I would not ask it, if I thought there was any thing improper. You say there is, and you talk about it in a way that I do not understand. For my sake, you tell me, you refuse, but let me entreat you to comply for my sake.

Your pen cannot teach me like your tongue. You write me long letters, and tell me a great deal in them, but my soul droops when I call to mind your voice and your looks, and think how long a time must pass before I see you and hear you again. I have no spirit to think upon the words and paper before me. My eye and my thought wander far away.

I bethink me how many questions I might ask you; how many doubts you might clear up if you were but within hearing. If you were but close to me; but I cannot ask them here. I am too poor a creature at the pen, and, some how or another, it always happens, I can only write about myself or about you. By the time I have said all this, I have tired my fingers, and when I set about telling you how this poem and that story have affected me, I am at a loss for words; I am bewildered and bemazed as it were.

It is not so when we talk to one another. With your arm about me, and your sweet face close to mine, I can prattle forever. Then my heart overflows at my lips. After hours thus spent, it seems as if there were a thousand things still to be said. Then I can tell you what the book has told me. I can repeat scores of verses by heart, though I heard them only once read, but it is because *you* have read them to me.

Then there is nobody here to answer my questions. They never look into books. They hate books. They think it waste of time to read. Even Peggy, who you say has naturally a strong mind, wonders what I can find to amuse myself in a book. In her playful mood, she is always teazing me to lay it aside.

I do not mind her, for I like to read; but if I did not like it before, I could not help doing so ever since you told me that nobody could gain your love who was not fond of books. And yet, though I like it on that account, more than I did, I don't read somehow so earnestly, and understand so well as I use to do, when my mind was all at ease; always frolicksome, and ever upon *tiptoe*, as I may say.

How strangely, (have you not observed it?) I am altered of late; I that was ever light of heart, the very soul of gaiety, brim full of glee—am now, demure as our old *tabby*—and not half as wise. Tabby had wit enough to keep her paws out of the coals, whereas poor I have—but no matter what. It will never come to pass, I see that. So many reasons for every thing! Such looking forward! Arthur, are not men sometimes too *wise* to be happy?

I am now *so* grave. Not one smile can Peggy sometimes get from me, though she tries for it the whole day. But I know how it comes. Strange, indeed, if losing father and sister, and thrown upon the wide world, pennyless and *friendless*

401

too, now that *you* forget me, I should continue to smile. No. I never shall smile again. At least, while I stay here, I never shall, I believe.

If a certain somebody suffer me to live with him—*near* him, I mean: perhaps the sight of him as he enters the door, perhaps the sound of his voice, asking—"where is my Bess?"—might produce a smile. Such a one as the very thought produces now—yet not, I hope, so transient, and so quickly followed by a tear. Women are born, they say, to trouble, and tears are given them for their relief. 'Tis all very true.

Let it be as I wish, will you? If Oliver bring not back good tidings, if he bring not a letter from thee, or thy letter still refuses my request—I don't know what may happen. Consent, if you love your poor girl.

E. H.

CHAPTER XXII

THE reading of this letter, though it made me mournful, did not hinder me from paying the visit I intended. My friend noticed my discomposure.

What, Arthur, thou art quite the "penseroso" to night. Come, let me cheer thee with a song. Thou shalt have thy favorite ditty:—She stepped to the instrument, and with more than airy lightness, touched and sung:

> Now knit hands and beat the ground
> In a light, fantastic round,
> Till the tell-tale sun descry
> Our conceal'd solemnity.

Her music, though blithsome and aerial, was not sufficient for the end. My cheerfulness would not return even at her bidding. She again noticed my sedateness, and enquired into the cause.

This girl of mine, said I, has infected me with her own sadness. There is a letter I have just received—she took it and began to read.

Meanwhile, I placed myself before her, and fixed my eyes steadfastly upon her features. There is no book in which I read with more pleasure, than the face of woman. *That* is generally more full of meaning, and of better meaning too, than the hard and inflexible lineaments of man, and *this* woman's face has no parallel.

She read it with visible emotion. Having gone through it,

403

she did not lift her eye from the paper, but continued silent, as if buried in thought. After some time, for I would not interrupt the pause, she addressed me thus:

This girl seems to be very anxious to be with you.

As much as I am that she should be so.—My friend's countenance betrayed some perplexity. As soon as I perceived it, I said, why are you thus grave? Some little confusion appeared as if she would not have her gravity discovered. There again, said I, new tokens in your face, my good mamma, of something which you will not mention. Yet, sooth to say, this is not your first perplexity. I have noticed it before, and wondered. It happens only when my *Bess* is introduced. Something in relation to her it must be, but what I cannot imagine. Why does *her* name, particularly, make you thoughtful; disturbed; dejected?—There now—but I must know the reason. You don't agree with me in my notions of this girl, I fear, and you will not disclose your thoughts.

By this time, she had gained her usual composure, and without noticing my comments on her looks, said: Since you are both of one mind, why does she not leave the country?

That cannot be, I believe. Mrs. Stevens says it would be disreputable. I am no proficient in etiquette, and must, therefore, in affairs of this kind, be guided by those who are. But would to Heaven, I were truly her father or brother. Then all difficulties would be done away.

Can you seriously wish that?

Why no. I believe it would be more rational to wish that the world would suffer me to act the fatherly or brotherly part, without the relationship.

And is that the only part you wish to act towards this girl?

Certainly, the only part.

You surprize me. Have you not confessed your love for her?

I *do* love her. There is nothing upon earth more dear to me than my *Bess*.

But love is of different kinds. She was loved by her father——

Less than by me. He was a good man, but not of lively feelings. Besides, he had another daughter, and they

404

shared his love between them, but she has no sister to share *my* love. Calamity too, has endeared her to me; I am all her consolation, dependence and hope, and nothing, surely, can induce me to abandon her.

Her reliance upon you, for happiness, replied my friend, with a sigh, is plain enough.

It is: but why that sigh? And yet I understand it. It remonstrates with me on my incapacity for her support. I know it well, but it is wrong to be cast down. I have youth, health and spirits, and ought not to despair of living for my own benefit and hers; but you sigh again, and it is impossible to keep my courage when *you* sigh. Do tell me what you mean by it?

You partly guessed the cause. She trusts to you for happiness, but I somewhat suspect she trusts in vain.

In vain! I beseech you tell me why you think so.

You say you love her—why then not make her your wife?

My wife! Surely her extreme youth, and my destitute condition, will account for that.

She is fifteen: the age of delicate fervor; of inartificial love, and suitable enough for marriage. As to your condition, you may live more easily together than apart. She has no false taste or perverse desires to gratify. She has been trained in simple modes and habits. Besides, that objection can be removed another way. But are these all your objections?

Her youth I object to, merely in connection with her mind. She is too little improved to be my wife. She wants that solidity of mind; that maturity of intelligence which ten years more may possibly give her, but which she cannot have at this age.

You are a very prudential youth; then you are willing to wait ten years for a wife?

Does that follow? Because my Bess will not be qualified for wedlock, in less time, does it follow that I must wait for her?

I spoke on the supposition that you loved her.

And that is true; but love is satisfied with studying her happiness as her father or brother. Some years hence, perhaps in half a year, for this passion, called wedded, or *marriage-wishing* love, is of sudden growth, my mind may change, and nothing may content me but to have Bess for my wife. Yet I do not expect it.

Then you are determined against marriage with this girl.

Of course; until that love comes which I feel not now; but which, no doubt, will come, when Bess has had the benefit of five or eight years more, unless previously excited by another.

All this is strange, Arthur. I have heretofore supposed that you actually loved (I mean with the *marriage-seeking* passion) your *Bess*.

I believe I once did; but it happened at a time when marriage was improper; in the life of her father and sister, and when I had never known in what female excellence consisted. Since that time my happier lot has cast me among women so far above Eliza Hadwin; so far above, and so widely different from any thing which time is likely to make her, that I own, nothing appears more unlikely than that I shall ever love her.

Are you not a little capricious in that respect, my good friend? You have praised your *Bess* as rich in natural endowments; as having an artless purity and rectitude of mind, which somewhat supersedes the use of formal education; as being full of sweetness and tenderness, and in her person a very angel of loveliness.

All that is true. I never saw features and shape so delicately beautiful; I never knew so young a mind so quick sighted and so firm; but, nevertheless, she is not the creature whom I would call my *wife*. My bosom slave; counsellor; friend; the mother; the pattern; the tutress of my children must be a different creature.

But what are the attributes of this *desirable* which Bess wants?

Every thing she wants. Age, capacity, acquirements, person, features, hair, complexion, all, all are different from this girl's.

And pray of what kind may they be?

I cannot pourtray them in words—but yes, I can:—The creature whom I shall worship:—it sounds oddly, but, I verily believe, the sentiment which I shall feel for my wife, will be more a kin to worship than any thing else. I shall never love, but such a creature as I now image to myself, and *such* a creature will deserve, or almost deserve, worship—but this creature, I was going to say, must be the exact counterpart, my good mamma—of *yourself*.

This was said very earnestly, and with eyes and manners that fully expressed my earnestness: perhaps my expressions were unwittingly strong and emphatic, for she started and blushed, but the cause of her discomposure, whatever it was, was quickly removed, and she said:

Poor Bess! This will be sad news to thee!

Heaven forbid! said I, of what moment can my opinions be to her?

Strange questioner that thou art. Thou knowest that her gentle heart is touched with love. See how it shews itself in the tender and inimitable strain of this epistle. Does not this sweet ingenuousness bewitch you?

It does so, and I love, beyond expression, the sweet girl; but my love is in some inconceivable way, different from the passion which that *other* creature will produce. She is no stranger to my thoughts. I will impart every thought over and over to her. I question not but I shall make her happy without forfeiting my own.

Would marriage with her, be a forfeiture of your happiness?

Not absolutely, or forever, I believe. I love her company. Her absence for a long time is irksome. I cannot express the delight with which I see and hear her. To mark her features, beaming with vivacity; playful in her pleasures; to hold her in my arms, and listen to her prattle; always musically voluble; always sweetly tender, or artlessly intelligent—and this you will say is the dearest privilege of marriage: and so it is; and dearly should I prize it; and yet, I fear my heart would droop as often as that *other* image should occur to my fancy. For then, you know, it would occur as something never to be possessed by me.

Now this image might, indeed, seldom occur. The intervals, at least, would be serene. It would be my interest to prolong these intervals as much as possible, and my endeavors to this end, would, no doubt, have some effect.

Besides, the bitterness of this reflection would be lessened by contemplating, at the same time, the happiness of my beloved girl.

I should likewise have to remember, that to continue unmarried, would not necessarily secure me the possession of the *other* good——

But these reflections, my friend (broke she in upon me) are of as much force to induce you to marry, as to reconcile you to marriage already contracted.

Perhaps they are. Assuredly, I have not a hope that the *fancied* excellence will ever be mine. Such happiness is not the lot of humanity, and is, least of all, within my reach.

Your diffidence, replied my friend, in a timorous accent, has not many examples; but your character, without doubt, is all your own; possessing all and disclaiming all, is, in few words, your picture.

I scarcely understand you. Do you think I ever shall be happy to that degree which I have imagined. Think you I shall ever meet with an exact copy of *yourself*!

Unfortunate you will be, if you do not meet with many better. Your Bess, in personals, is, beyond measure, *my* superior, and in mind, allowing for difference in years, quite as much so.

But that, returned I, with quickness and fervor, is not the object. The very counterpart of *you* I want; neither worse nor better, nor different in any thing. Just such form, such features, such hues. Just that melting voice, and above all, the same habits of thinking and conversing. In thought, word and deed; gesture, look and form, that rare and precious creature whom I shall love, must be your resemblance. Your——

Have done with these comparisons, interrupted she, in some hurry, and let us return to the country girl, thy Bess.

You once, my friend, wished me to treat this girl of yours as my sister. Do you know what the duties of a sister are?

They imply no more kindness or affection than you already feel toward my Bess. Are you not her sister?

I ought to have been so. I ought to have been proud of the relation you ascribe to me, but I have not performed any of its duties. I blush to think upon the coldness and perverseness of my heart. With such means as I possess, of giving happiness to others, I have been thoughtless and inactive to a strange degree; perhaps, however, it is not yet too late. Are you still willing to invest me with all the rights of an elder sister over this girl? And will she consent, think you?

Certainly, she will; she has.

Then the first act of sistership, will be to take her from the country; from persons on whose kindness she has no natural claim, whose manners and characters are unlike her own, and with whom no improvement can be expected, and bring her back to her sister's house and bosom, to provide for her subsistence and education, and watch over her happiness.

I will not be a nominal sister. I will not be a sister by halves. *All* the rights of that relation I will have, or none. As for you, you have claims upon her, on which I must be permitted to judge, as becomes the elder sister, who, by the loss of all other relations, must occupy the place, possess the rights, and fulfil the duties of father, mother and brother.

She has now arrived at an age, when longer to remain in a cold and churlish soil, will stunt her growth and wither her blossoms. We must hasten to transplant her to a genial element, and a garden well enclosed. Having so long neglected this charming plant, it becomes me henceforth to take her wholly to myself.

And now, for it is no longer in her or your power to take back the gift, since she is fully mine, I will charge you with the office of conducting her hither. I grant it to you as a favor. Will you go?

Go! I will fly! I exclaimed, in an extacy of joy, on pinions swifter than the wind. Not the lingering of an instant will I bear. Look! one, two, three—thirty minutes after nine. I will reach Curling's gate by the morn's dawn. I will put my girl into a chaise, and by noon, she shall throw herself into the arms of her sister. But first, shall I not, in some way, manifest my gratitude?

My senses were bewildered, and I knew not what I did. I intended to kneel, as to my mother or my deity, but, instead of that, I clasped her in my arms, and kissed her lips fervently. I staid not to discover the effects of this insanity, but

409

left the room and the house, and calling for a moment at Stevens's, left word with the servant, my friend being gone abroad, that I should not return till the morrow.

Never was a lighter heart, a gaiety more overflowing, and more buoyant than mine. All cold from a boisterous night, at a chilly season, all weariness from a rugged and miry road, were charmed away. I might have ridden, but I could not brook delay, even the delay of enquiring for and equipping an horse. I might thus have saved myself fatigue, and have lost no time, but my mind was in too great a tumult for deliberation and forecast. I saw nothing but the image of my girl, whom my tidings would render happy.

The way was longer than my fond imagination had foreseen. I did not reach Curling's till an hour after sun-rise. The distance was full thirty-five miles. As I hastened up the green lane leading to the house, I spied my Bess passing through a covered way, between the dwelling and kitchen. I caught her eye. She stopped and held up her hands, and then ran into my arms.

What means my girl? Why this catching of the breath? Why this sobbing? Look at me my love. It is Arthur, he who has treated you with forgetfulness, neglect and cruelty.

O! do not, she replied, hiding her face with her hand. One single reproach, added to my own, will kill me. That foolish, wicked letter—I could tear my fingers for writing it.

But, said I, I will kiss them—and put them to my lips. They have told me the wishes of my girl. They have enabled me to gratify her wishes. I have come to carry thee this very moment to town.

Lord bless me, Arthur—said she, lost in a sweet confusion, and her cheeks, always glowing, glowing still more deeply—indeed, I did not mean—I meant only—I will stay here—I would rather stay——

It grieves me to hear that, said I, with earnestness, I thought I was studying our mutual happiness.

It grieves you? Don't say so. I would not grieve you for the world—but, indeed, indeed, it is too soon. Such a girl as I, am not yet fit to—live in your city. Again she hid her glowing face in my bosom.

Sweet consciousness! Heavenly innocence! thought I;

may Achsa's conjectures prove false!—You have mistaken my design, for I do not intend to carry you to town with such a view as you have hinted—but merely to place you with a beloved friend; with Achsa Fielding, of whom already you know so much, where we shall enjoy each other's company without restraint or intermission.

I then proceeded to disclose to her the plan suggested by my friend, and to explain all the consequences that would flow from it. I need not say that she assented to the scheme. She was all rapture and gratitude. Preparations for departure were easily and speedily made. I hired a chaise of a neighboring farmer, and, according to my promise, by noon the same day, delivered the timid and bashful girl into the arms of her new sister.

She was received with the utmost tenderness, not only by Mrs. Fielding, but by all my friends. Her affectionate heart was encouraged to pour forth all its feeling as into the bosom of a mother. She was reinspired with confidence. Her want of experience was supplied by the gentlest admonitions and instructions. In every plan for her improvement, suggested by her new *mamma*, for she never called her by any other name, she engaged with docility and eagerness; and her behaviour and her progress exceeded the most sanguine hopes that I had formed, as to the softness of her temper and the acuteness of her genius.

Those graces which a polished education, and intercourse with the better classes of society, are adapted to give, my girl possessed, in some degree, by a native and intuitive refinement and sagacity of mind. All that was to be obtained from actual observation and instruction, was obtained without difficulty; and in a short time, nothing but the affectionate simplicity and unperverted feelings of the country girl, bespoke the original condition.—

What art so busy about, Arthur? Always at thy pen of late. Come, I must know the fruit of all this toil and all this meditation. I am determined to scrape acquaintance with Haller and Lineus. I will begin this very day. All one's friends you know should be our's. Love has made many a patient, and let me see if it cannot, in my case, make a physician. But first, what is all this writing about?

411

Mrs. Wentworth has put me upon a strange task—not disagreeable, however, but such as I should, perhaps, have declined, had not the absence of my Bess, and her mamma, made the time hang somewhat heavy. I have, oftener than once, and far more circumstantially than now, told her my adventures, but she is not satisfied. She wants a written narrative, for some purpose which she tells me she will disclose to me hereafter.

Luckily, my friend Stevens has saved me more than half the trouble. He has done me the favor to compile much of my history with his own hand. I cannot imagine what could prompt him to so wearisome an undertaking; but he says that adventures and a destiny so singular as mine, ought not to be abandoned to forgetfulness like any vulgar and *every-day* existence. Besides, when he wrote it, he suspected that it might be necessary to the safety of my reputation and my life, from the consequences of my connection with Welbeck. Time has annihilated that danger. All enmities and all suspicions are buried with that ill-fated wretch. Wortley has been won by my behaviour, and confides in my integrity now as much as he formerly suspected it. I am glad, however, that the task was performed. It has saved me a world of writing. I had only to take up the broken thread, and bring it down to the period of my present happiness, and this was done, just as you tripped along the entry this morning.

To bed, my friend, it is late, and this delicate frame is not half so able to encounter fatigue as a youth spent in the hay-field and the dairy might have been expected to be.

I will, but let me take these sheets along with me. I will read them, that I am determined, before I sleep, and watch if you have told the whole truth.

Do so, if you please; but remember one thing. Mrs. Wentworth requested me to write not as if it were designed for her perusal, but for those who have no previous knowledge of her or of me. 'Twas an odd request. I cannot imagine what she means by it, but she never acts without good reason, and I have done so. And now withdraw, my dear, and farewel.

CHAPTER XXIII

MOVE on, my quill! wait not for my guidance. Reanimated with thy master's spirit, all-airy light! An hey day rapture! A mounting impulse sways him: lifts him from the earth.

I must, cost what it will, rein in this upward-pulling, forward-urging—what shall I call it? But there are times, and now is one of them, when words are poor.

It will not do—Down this hill, up that steep; thro' this thicket, over that hedge—I have *labored* to fatigue myself: To reconcile me to repose; to lolling on a sofa; to poring over a book; to any thing that might win for my heart a respite from these throbs; to deceive me into a few *tolerable* moments of forgetfulness.

Let me see: they tell me this is Monday night. Only three days yet to come! If thus restless to day; if my heart thus bounds till its mansion scarcely can hold it, what must be my state to morrow! What next day! What as the hour hastens on; as the sun descends; as my hand touches her in sign of wedded unity, of love without interval; of concord without end.

I must quell these tumults. They will disable me else. They will wear out all my strength. They will drain away life itself. But who could have thought! So soon! Not three months since I first set eyes upon her. Not three weeks since our plighted love, and only three days to terminate suspense and give me *all*.

I must compel myself to quiet: to sleep. I must find some

refuge from anticipations so excruciating. All extremes are agonies. A joy like this is too big for this narrow tenement. I must thrust it forth; I must bar and bolt it out for a time, or these frail walls will burst asunder. The pen is a pacifyer. It checks the mind's career; it circumscribes her wanderings. It traces out, and compels us to adhere to one path. It ever was my friend. Often it has blunted my vexations; hushed my stormy passions; turned my peevishness to soothing; my fierce revenge to heart-dissolving pity.

Perhaps it will befriend me now. It may temper my impetuous wishes; lull my intoxication; and render my happiness supportable: And, indeed, it has produced partly this effect already. My blood, within the few minutes thus employed, flows with less destructive rapidity. My thoughts range themselves in less disorder—And now that the conquest is effected, what shall I say? I must continue at the pen, or shall immediately relapse.

What shall I say? Let me look back upon the steps that led me hither. Let me recount preliminaries. I cannot do better.

And first as to Achsa Fielding—to describe this woman.

To recount, in brief, so much of her history as has come to my knowledge, will best account for that zeal, almost to idolatry, with which she has, ever since I thoroughly knew her, been regarded by me.

Never saw I one to whom the term *lovely* more truly belonged: And yet, in stature she is too low; in complection, dark and almost sallow; and her eyes, though black and of piercing lustre, has a cast, which I cannot well explain. It lessens without destroying their lustre and their force to charm; but all personal defects are outweighed by her heart and her intellect. There is the secret of her power to entrance the soul of the listener and beholder. It is not only when she sings that her utterance is musical. It is not only when the occasion is urgent and the topic momentous that her eloquence is rich and flowing. They are always so.

I had vowed to love her and serve her, and been her frequent visitant, long before I was acquainted with her past life. I had casually picked up some intelligence, from others, or from her own remarks. I knew very soon that she

414

was English by birth, and had been only a year and an half in America; that she had scarcely passed her twenty-fifth year, and was still embellished with all the graces of youth; that she had been a wife; but was uninformed whether the knot had been untied by death or divorce: That she possessed considerable, and even splendid fortune; but the exact amount, and all beside these particulars, were unknown to me till some time after our acquaintance was begun.

One evening, she had been talking very earnestly on the influence annexed, in Great Britain, to birth, and had given me some examples of this influence. Meanwhile, my eyes were fixed steadfastly on hers. The peculiarity in their expression never before affected me so strongly. A vague resemblance to something seen elsewhere, on the same day, occurred, and occasioned me to exclaim, suddenly in a pause of her discourse—

As I live, my good mamma, those eyes of yours have told me a secret. I almost think they spoke to me; and I am not less amazed at the strangeness than at the distinctness of their story.

And pry'thee what have they said?

Perhaps I was mistaken. I might have been deceived by a fancied voice, or have confounded one word with another near akin to it; but let me die, if I did not think they said that you were—*a Jew*.

At this sound, her features were instantly veiled with the deepest sorrow and confusion. She put her hand to her eyes, the tears started and she sobbed. My surprise at this effect of my words, was equal to my contrition. I besought her to pardon me, for having thus unknowingly, alarmed and grieved her.

After she had regained some composure, she said, you have not offended, Arthur. Your surmise was just and natural, and could not always have escaped you. Connected with that word are many sources of anguish, which time has not, and never will, dry up; and the less I think of past events, the less will my peace be disturbed. I was desirous that you should know nothing of me, but what you see; nothing but the present and the future, merely that no

415

allusions might occur in our conversation, which will call up sorrows and regrets that will avail nothing.

I now perceive the folly of endeavoring to keep you in ignorance, and shall therefore, once for all, inform you of what has befallen me, that your enquiries and suggestions may be made, and fully satisfied at once, and your curiosity have no motive for calling back my thoughts to what I ardently desire to bury in oblivion.

My father was indeed a *jew*, and one of the most opulent of his nation in London. A Portuguese by birth, but came to London when a boy. He had few of the moral or external qualities of jews. For I suppose there is some justice in the obloquy that follows them so closely. He was frugal without meanness, and cautious in his dealings, without extortion. I need not fear to say this, for it was the general voice.

Me, an only child, and of course, the darling of my parents, they trained up in the most liberal manner. My education was purely English. I learned the same things and of the same masters with my neighbors. Except frequenting their church and repeating their creed, and partaking of the same food, I saw no difference between them and me. Hence I grew more indifferent, perhaps, than was proper to the distinctions of religion. They were never enforced upon me. No pains were taken to fill me with scruples and antipathies. They never stood, as I may say, upon the threshold: They were often thought upon but were vague, and easily eluded or forgotten.

Hence it was that my heart too readily admitted impressions, that more zeal and more parental caution would have saved me from. They could scarcely be avoided, as my society was wholly English; and my youth, my education and my father's wealth made me an object of much attention. And the same causes that lulled to sleep my own watchfulness, had the same effect upon that of others. To regret or to praise this remissness, is now too late. Certain it is, that my destiny, and not a happy destiny, was fixed by it.

The fruit of this remissness was a passion for one, who fully returned it. Almost as young as I, who was only sixteen, he knew as little as myself, what obstacles the difference of our births was likely to raise between us. His father, Sir Ralph Fielding, a man nobly born, high in office, splendidly allied, could not be expected to consent to the marriage of his eldest son, in such green youth, to the daughter of an alien, a Portuguese, a Jew; but these impediments were not seen by my ignorance, and were overlooked by the youth's passion.

But strange to tell, what common prudence would have so confidently predicted, did not happen. Sir Ralph had a numerous family, likely to be still more so; had but slender patrimony: the income of his offices nearly made up his all. The young man was head-strong, impetuous, and would probably disregard the inclinations of his family. Yet the father would not consent but on one condition, that of my admission to the English church.

No very strenuous opposition to these terms could be expected from me. At so thoughtless an age, with an education so unfavorable to religious impressions; swayed likewise, by the strongest of human passions; made somewhat impatient by the company I kept, of the disrepute and scorn to which the Jewish nation are every where condemned, I could not be expected to be very averse to the scheme.

My fears, as to what my father's decision would be, were soon at an end. He loved his child too well to thwart her wishes in so essential a point. Finding in me no scruples, no unwillingness, he thought it absurd to be scrupulous for me. My own heart having abjured my religion, it was absurd to make any difficulty about a formal renunciation. These were his avowed reasons for concurrence, but time shewed that he had probably other reasons, founded, indeed, in his regard for my happiness, but such as, if they had been known, would probably have strengthened into invincible, the reluctance of my lover's family.

No marriage was ever attended with happier presages. The numerous relations of my husband, admitted me with the utmost cordiality, among them. My father's tenderness was unabated by this change, and those humiliations to which I had before been exposed, were now no more; and every tie was strengthened, at the end of a year, by the feelings of a *mother*. I had need, indeed, to know a season of happiness, that I might be fitted to endure the sad reverses that succeeded. One after the other my disasters came, each one more heavy than the last, and in such swift succession, that they hardly left me time to breathe.

I had scarcely left my chamber, I had scarcely recovered my usual health, and was able to press with true fervor, the new and precious gift to my bosom, when melancholy tidings came—I was in the country, at the seat of my father-in-law, when the messenger arrived.

A shocking tale it was! and told abruptly, with every unpitying aggravation. I hinted to you once, my father's death. The *kind* of death—O! my friend! It was horrible. He was then a placid venerable old man; though many symptoms of disquiet had long before been discovered by my mother's watchful tenderness. Yet none could suspect him capable of such a deed; for none, so carefully had he conducted his affairs, suspected the havock that mischance had made of his property.

I, that had so much reason to love my father—I will leave you to imagine how I was affected by a catastrophe so dreadful, so unlooked-for. Much less could I suspect the cause of his despair; yet he had foreseen his ruin before my marriage; had resolved to defer it for his daughter's and his wife's sake, as long as possible, but had still determined not to survive the day that should reduce him to indigence. The desperate act was thus preconcerted—thus deliberate.

The true state of his affairs was laid open by his death. The failure of great mercantile houses at Frankfort and Liege was the cause of his disasters. Thus were my prospects shut in. That wealth, which no doubt, furnished the chief inducement with my husband's family to concur in his choice, was now suddenly exchanged for poverty.

Bred up, as I had been, in pomp and luxury; conscious that my wealth was my chief security from the contempt of the proud and bigotted, and my chief title to the station to which I had been raised, and which I the more delighted in because it enabled me to confer so great obligations on my husband, what reverse could be harder than this, and how much bitterness was added by it to the grief, occasioned by the violent end of my father!

Yet, loss of fortune, though it mortified my pride, did not prove my worst calamity. Perhaps it was scarcely to be ranked with evils, since it furnished a touchstone by which my husband's affections were to be tried; especially as the issue of the trial was auspicious; for my misfortune seemed only to heighten the interest which my character had made for me in the hearts of all that knew me. The paternal regards of Sir Ralph had always been tender, but that tenderness seemed now to be redoubled.

New events made this consolation still more necessary. My unhappy mother!—She was nearer to the dreadful scene when it happened. Had no surviving object to beguile her sorrow; was rendered, by long habit, more dependent upon fortune than her child.

A melancholy always mute was the first effect upon my mother. Nothing could charm her eye, or her ear. Sweet sounds that she once loved, and especially when her darling child was the warbler, were heard no longer. How, with streaming eyes, have I sat and watched the dear lady, and endeavored to catch her eye, to rouse her attention!—But I must not think of these things.

But even this distress was little in comparison with what was to come. A frenzy thus mute, motionless and vacant, was succeeded by fits, talkative, outrageous, requiring incessant superintendance, restraint, and even violence.

Why led you me thus back to my sad remembrances? Excuse me for the present. I will tell you the rest some other time; to-morrow.

To-morrow, accordingly, my friend resumed her story.

Let me now make an end, said she, of my mournful narrative, and never, I charge you, do any thing to revive it again.

Deep as was my despondency, occasioned by these calamities, I was not destitute of some joy. My husband and my child were lovely and affectionate. In their caresses, in their welfare, I found peace; and might still have found it, had there not been—But why should I open afresh, wounds which time has imperfectly closed? But the story must have sometime been told to you, and the sooner it is told and dismissed to forgetfulness, the better.

My ill fate led me into company with a woman too well known in the idle and dissipated circles. Her character was not unknown to me. There was nothing in her features or air to obviate disadvantageous prepossessions. I sought not her intercourse; I rather shunned it, as unpleasing and discreditable, but she would not be repulsed. Self invited, she made herself my frequent guest; took unsolicited part in my concerns; did me many kind offices; and, at length, in spite of my counter inclination, won upon my sympathy and gratitude.

No one in the world, did I fondly think, had I less reason to fear than Mrs. Waring. Her character excited not the slightest apprehension for my own safety. She was upwards of forty, no wise remarkable for grace or beauty; tawdry in her dress; accustomed to render more conspicuous the traces of age by her attempts to hide them; the mother of a numerous family, with a mind but slenderly cultivated; always careful too to save appearances; studiously preserving distance with my husband, and he, like myself, enduring, rather than wishing her society. What could I fear from the arts of such an one?

But alas! the woman had consummate address.— Patience too, that nothing could tire. Watchfulness that none could detect. Insinuation the wiliest and most subtle. Thus wound she herself into my affections, by an unexampled perseverance in seeming kindness; by tender confidence; by artful glosses of past misconduct; by self-rebukes and feigned contritions.

Never were stratagems so intricate, dissimulation so profound! But still, that such an one should seduce my husband; young; generous; ambitious; impatient of contumely and reproach, and surely not indifferent; before this fatal intercourse, not indifferent to his wife and child!—Yet, so it was!

I saw his discontents; his struggles; I heard him curse this

420

woman, and the more deeply for my attempts, unconscious as I was of her machinations, to reconcile them to each other, to do away what seemed a causeless indignation, or antipathy against her. How little I suspected the nature of the conflict in his heart, between a new passion and the claims of pride; of conscience and of humanity; the claims of a child and a wife; a wife already in affliction, and placing all that yet remained of happiness, in the firmness of his virtue; in the continuance of his love; a wife, at the very hour of his meditated flight, full of terrors at the near approach of an event, whose agonies demand a double share of an husband's supporting, encouraging love—

Good Heaven! For what evils are some of thy creatures reserved! Resignation to thy decree, in the last, and most cruel distress, was, indeed, an hard task.

He was gone. Some unavoidable engagement calling him to Hamburgh was pleaded. Yet to leave me at such an hour! I dared not upbraid, nor object. The tale was so specious! The fortunes of a friend depended on his punctual journey. The falsehood of his story too soon made itself known. He was gone, in company with his detested paramour!

Yet, though my vigilance was easily deceived, it was not so with others. A creditor, who had his bond for three thousand pounds, pursued, and arrested him at Harwich. He was thrown into prison, but his companion, let me, at least, say that in her praise, would not desert him. She took lodging near the place of his confinement, and saw him daily. That, had she not done it, and had my personal condition allowed, should have been my province.

Indignation and grief hastened the painful crisis with me. I did not weep that the second fruit of this unhappy union saw not the light. I wept only that this hour of agony, was not, to its unfortunate mother, the last.

I felt not anger; I had nothing but compassion for Fielding. Gladly would I have recalled him to my arms and to virtue: I wrote, adjuring him by all our past joys, to return; vowing only gratitude for his new affection, and claiming only the recompence of seeing him restored to his family; to liberty; to reputation.

421

But alas! Fielding had a good, but a proud, heart. He looked upon his error with remorse, with self-detestation, and with the fatal belief that it could not be retrieved; shame made him withstand all my reasonings and persuasions, and in the hurry of his feelings, he made solemn vows that he would, in the moment of restored liberty, abjure his country and his family forever. He bore indignantly the yoke of his new attachment, but he strove in vain to shake it off. Her behaviour, always yielding, doating, supplicative, preserved him in her fetters. Though upbraided, spurned and banished from his presence, she would not leave him, but by new efforts and new artifices, soothed, appeased, and won again, and kept his tenderness.

What my entreaties were unable to effect, his father could not hope to accomplish. He offered to take him from prison; the creditor offered to cancel the bond, if he would return to me; but this condition he refused. All his kindred, and one who had been his bosom friend from childhood, joined in beseeching his compliance with these conditions; but his pride, his dread of my merited reproaches, the merits and dissuasions of his new companion, whose sacrifices for his sake had not been small, were obstacles which nothing could subdue.

Far, indeed, was I from imposing these conditions. I waited only till, by certain arrangements, I could gather enough to pay his debts, to enable him to execute his vow; empty would have been my claims to his affection, if I could have suffered, with the means of his deliverance in my hands, my husband to remain a moment in prison.

The remains of my father's vast fortune, was a jointure of a thousand pounds a year, settled on my mother, and after her death, on me. My mother's helpless condition put this revenue into my disposal. By this means was I enabled, without the knowledge of my father-in-law, or my husband, to purchase the debt, and dismiss him from prison. He set out instantly, in company with his paramour, to France.

When somewhat recovered from the shock of this calamity, I took up my abode with my mother. What she had was enough, as you, perhaps, will think, for plentiful subsistence, but to us, with habits of a different kind, it was little better than poverty. That reflection, my father's memory, my mother's deplorable state, which every year grew worse, and the late misfortune, were the chief companions of my thoughts.

The dear child, whose smiles were uninterrupted by his mother's afflictions, was some consolation in my solitude. To his instruction and to my mother's wants, all my hours were devoted. I was sometimes not without the hope of better days. Full as my mind was of Fielding's merits, convinced by former proofs of his ardent and generous spirit, I trusted that time and reflection would destroy that spell by which he was now bound.

For some time, the progress of these reflections was not known. In leaving England, Fielding dropped all correspondence and connection with his native country. He parted with the woman at Rouen, leaving no trace behind him by which she might follow him, as she wished to do. She never returned to England, but died a twelve month afterwards in Switzerland.

As to me, I had only to muse day and night upon the possible destiny of this beloved fugitive. His incensed father cared not for him. He had cast him out of his paternal affections, ceased to make enquiries respecting him, and even wished never to hear of him again. My boy succeeded to my husband's place in his grand-father's affections, and in the hopes and views of the family; and his mother wanted nothing which their compassionate and respectful love could bestow.

Three long and tedious years passed away, and no tidings were received. Whether he were living or dead, nobody could tell. At length, an English traveller, going out of the customary road from Italy, met with Fielding, in a town in the Venaissin. His manners, habit and language, had become French. He seemed unwilling to be recognized by an old acquaintance, but not being able to avoid this, and becoming gradually familiar, he informed the traveller of many particulars in his present situation. It appeared that he had made himself useful to a neighboring *Seigneur*, in whose *chateau* he had long lived on the footing of a brother. France he had resolved to make his future country, and among other changes for that end, he had laid aside his English name, and taken that of his patron, which was *Perrin*. He had endeavored to compensate himself for all other privations, by devoting himself to rural amusements and to study.

He carefully shunned all enquiries respecting me, but when my name was mentioned by his friend, who knew well all that had happened, and my general welfare, together with that of his son, asserted, he shewed deep sensibility, and even consented that I should be made acquainted with his situation.

I cannot describe the effect of this intelligence on me. My hopes of bringing him back to me, were suddenly revived. I wrote him a letter, in which I poured forth my whole heart; but his answer contained avowals of all his former resolutions, to which time had only made his adherence more easy. A second and third letter were written, and an offer made to follow him to his retreat, and share his exile; but all my efforts availed nothing. He solemnly and repeatedly renounced all the claims of an husband over me, and absolved me from every obligation as a wife.

His part in this correspondence, was performed without harshness or contempt. A strange mixture there was of pathos and indifference; of tenderness and resolution. Hence I continually derived hope, which time, however, brought no nearer to certainty.

At the opening of the revolution, the name of Perrin appeared among the deputies to the constituent assembly, for the district in which he resided. He had thus succeeded in gaining all the rights of a French citizen; and the hopes of his return became almost extinct; but that, and every other hope, respecting him, has since been totally extinguished by his marriage with Marguerite D'Almont, a young lady of great merit and fortune, and a native of Avignon.

A long period of suspence was now at an end, and left me in a state almost as full of anguish as that which our first separation produced. My sorrows were increased by my mother's death, and this incident freeing me from those restraints upon my motions which before existed, I determined to come to America.

My son was now eight years old, and his grandfather claiming the province of his instruction, I was persuaded to part with him, that he might be sent to a distant school. Thus was another tie removed, and in spite of the well meant importunities of my friends, I persisted in my scheme of crossing the ocean.

I could not help, at this part of her narration, expressing my surprise, that any motives were strong enough to recommend this scheme.

It was certainly a freak of despair. A few months would, perhaps, have allayed the fresh grief, and reconciled me to my situation; but I would not pause or deliberate. My scheme was opposed by my friends, with great earnestness. During my voyage, affrighted by the dangers which surrounded me, and to which I was wholly unused, I heartily repented of my resolution; but now, methinks, I have reason to rejoice at my perseverance. I have come into a scene and society so new, I have had so many claims made upon my ingenuity and fortitude, that my mind has been diverted in some degree from former sorrows. There are even times when I wholly forget them, and catch myself indulging in cheerful reveries.

I have often reflected with surprise on the nature of my own mind. It is eight years since my father's violent death. How few of my hours since that period, have been blessed with serenity! How many nights and days, in hateful and lingering succession, have been bathed in tears and tormented with regrets! That I am still alive with so many causes of death, and with such a slow consuming malady, is surely to be wondered at.

I believe the worst foes of man, at least of men in grief, are solitude and idleness. The same eternally occurring round of objects, feeds his disease, and the effects of mere vacancy and uniformity, is sometimes mistaken for those of grief. Yes, I am glad I came to America. My relations are importunate for my return, and till lately, I had some thoughts of

425

it; but I think now, I shall stay where I am, for the rest of my days.

Since I arrived, I am become more of a student than I used to be. I always loved literature, but never, till of late, had a mind enough at ease, to read with advantage. I now find pleasure in the occupation which I never expected to find.

You see in what manner I live. The letters which I brought secured me a flattering reception from the best people in your country; but scenes of gay resort had nothing to attract me, and I quickly withdrew to that seclusion in which you now find me. Here, always at leisure, and mistress of every laudable means of gratification, I am not without the belief of serene days yet to come.

I now ventured to enquire what were her latest tidings of her husband.

At the opening of the revolution, I told you he became a champion of the people. By his zeal and his efforts he acquired such importance as to be deputed to the National Assembly. In this post he was the adherent of violent measures, till the subversion of monarchy; and then, when too late for his safety, he checked his career.

And what has since become of him?

She sighed deeply. You were yesterday reading a list of the proscribed under Robespierre. I checked you. I had good reason. But this subject grows too painful, let us change it.

Some time after I ventured to renew this topic; and discovered that Fielding, under his new name of Perrin d'Almont, was among the outlawed deputies of last year*, and had been slain in resisting the officers, sent to arrest him. My friend had been informed that his *wife* Philippine d'Almont, whom she had reason to believe, a woman of great merit, had eluded persecution, and taken refuge in some part of America. She had made various attempts, but in vain, to find out her retreat. Ah! said I, you must commission me to find her. I will hunt her through the continent from Penobscot to Savanna. I will not leave a nook unsearched.

*1793.

426

CHAPTER XXIV

NONE will be surprized, that to a woman thus unfortunate and thus deserving, my heart willingly
rendered up all its sympathies; that as I partook of
all her grief, I hailed, with equal delight, those omens of
felicity which now, at length, seemed to play in her fancy.

I saw her often, as often as my engagements would permit, and oftener than I allowed myself to visit any other. In
this I was partly selfish. So much entertainment, so much of
the best instruction did her conversation afford me, that I
never had enough of it.

Her experience had been so much larger than mine, and
so wholly different, and she possessed such unbounded
facility of recounting all she had seen and felt, and absolute
sincerity and unreserve in this respect, were so fully established between us, that I can imagine nothing equally instructive and delightful with her conversation.

Books are cold, jejune, vexatious in their sparingness of
information at one time, and their impertinent loquacity
at another. Besides, all they chuse to give, they give at once;
they allow no questions; offer no further explanations, and
bend not to the caprices of our curiosity. They talk to us
behind a screen. Their tone is lifeless and monotonous.
They charm not our attention by mute significances of
gesture and looks. They spread no light upon their meaning by cadences and emphasis and pause.

How different was Mrs. Fielding's discourse! So versatile;
so bending to the changes of occasion; so obsequious to my

427

curiosity, and so abundant in that very knowledge in which I was most deficient, and on which I set the most value, the knowledge of the human heart; of society as it existed in another world, more abundant in the varieties of customs and characters, than I had ever had the power to witness.

Partly selfish I have said my motives were, but not wholly so, as long as I saw that my friend derived pleasure, in her turn, from my company. Not that I could add directly to her knowledge or pleasure, but that expansion of heart, that ease of utterance and flow of ideas which always were occasioned by my approach, were sources of true pleasure of which she had been long deprived, and for which her privation had given her a higher relish than ever.

She lived in great affluence and independence, but made use of her privileges of fortune chiefly to secure to herself the command of her own time. She had been long ago tired and disgusted with the dull and fulsome uniformity and parade of the play-house and ball-room. Formal visits were endured as mortifications and penances, by which the delights of privacy and friendly intercourse were by contrast increased. Music she loved, but never sought it in place of public resort, or from the skill of mercenary performers, and books were not the least of her pleasures.

As to me, I was wax in her hand. Without design and without effort, I was always of that form she wished me to assume. My own happiness became a secondary passion, and her gratification the great end of my being. When with her, I thought not of myself. I had scarcely a separate or independent existence, since my senses were occupied by her, and my mind was full of those ideas which her discourse communicated. To meditate on her looks and words, and to pursue the means suggested by my own thoughts, or by her, conducive, in any way, to her good, was all my business.

What a fate, said I, at the conclusion of one of our interviews, has been yours. But, thank Heaven, the storm has disappeared before the age of sensibility has gone past, and without drying up every source of happiness. You are still young: all your powers unimpaired; rich in the compassion and esteem of the world; wholly independent of the claims and caprices of others; amply supplied with that mean of usefulness, called money; wise in that experience which only adversity can give. Past evils and sufferings, if incurred and endured without guilt, if called to view without remorse, make up the materials of present joy. They cheer our most dreary hours with the whispered accents of "well done," and they heighten our pleasures into somewhat of celestial brilliancy, by furnishing a deep, a ruefully deep contrast.

From this moment, I will cease to weep for you. I will call you the happiest of women. I will share with you your happiness by witnessing it—but that shall not content me. I must someway contribute to it. Tell me how I shall serve you? What can I do to make you happier? Poor am I in every thing but zeal, but still I may do something. What—pray tell me what can I do?

She looked at me with sweet and solemn significance. What it was exactly, I could not divine, yet I was strangely affected by it. It was but a glance, instantly withdrawn. She made me no answer.

You must not be silent; you *must* tell me what I can do for you. Hitherto I have done nothing. All the service is on your side. Your conversation has been my study, a delightful study, but the profit has only been mine. Tell me how I can be grateful—my voice and manner, I believe, seldom belye my feelings. At this time, I had almost done what a second thought made me suspect to be unauthorized. Yet I cannot tell why. My heart had nothing in it but reverence and admiration. Was she not the substitute of my lost mamma. Would I not have clasped that beloved shade? Yet the two beings were not just the same, or I should not, as now, have checked myself, and only pressed her hand to my lips.

Tell me, repeated I, what can I do to serve you? I read to you a little now, and you are pleased with my reading. I copy for you when you want the time. I guide the reins for you when you chuse to ride. Humble offices, indeed, though, perhaps, all that a raw youth like me can do for you; but I can be still more assiduous. I can read several hours in the day, instead of one. I can write ten times as much as now.

Are you not my lost mamma come back again? And yet,

not *exactly* her, I think. Something different; something better, I believe, if that be possible. At any rate, methinks I would be wholly yours. I shall be impatient and uneasy till every act, every thought, every minute, someway does you good.

How! said I—her eye still averted, seemed to hold back the tear with difficulty, and she made a motion as if to rise—have I grieved you? Have I been importunate? Forgive me if I have offended you.

Her eyes now overflowed without restraint. She articulated with difficulty—Tears are too prompt with me of late; but they did not upbraid you. Pain has often caused them to flow, but now it—is—*pleasure.*

What an heart must yours be, I resumed. When susceptible of such pleasures, what pangs must formerly have rent it!—But you are not displeased, you say, with my importunate zeal. You will accept me as your own in every thing. Direct me: prescribe to me. There must be *something* in which I can be of still more use to you: some way in which I can be wholly yours——

Wholly mine! she repeated, in a smothered voice, and rising—leave me, Arthur. It is too late for you to be here. It was wrong to stay so late.

I have been wrong, but how too late! I entered but this moment. It is twilight still: Is it not?

No—it is almost twelve. You have been here a long four hours; short ones, I would rather say—but indeed you must go.

What made me so thoughtless of the time! But I will go, yet not till you forgive me. I approached her with a confidence, and for a purpose at which, upon reflection, I am not a little surprized, but the being called Mervyn is not the same in her company and in that of another. What is the difference, and whence comes it? Her words and looks engross me. My mind wants room for any other object. But why enquire whence the difference? The superiority of her merits and attractions to all those whom I knew, would surely account for my fervor. Indifference, if I felt it, would be the only just occasion of wonder.

The hour was, indeed too late, and I hastened home.

Stevens was waiting my return with some anxiety. I apologized for my delay, and recounted to him what had just passed. He listened with more than usual interest. When I had finished,

Mervyn, said he, you seem not to be aware of your present situation. From what you now tell me, and from what you have formerly told me, one thing seems very plain to me.

Pry'thee, what is it?

Eliza Hadwin—do you wish—could you bear to see her the wife of another?

Five years hence I will answer you. Then my answer may be—"No: I wish her only to be mine." Till then, I wish her only to be my pupil, my ward, my sister.

But these are remote considerations: they are bars to marriage, but not to love. Would it not molest and disquiet you to observe in her a passion for another?

It would, but only on her own account: not on mine. At a suitable age it is very likely I may love her, because, it is likely, if she holds on in her present career, she will then be worthy, but, at present, though I would die to ensure her happiness, I have no wish to ensure it by marriage with her.

Is there no other whom you love?

No. There is one worthier than all others: one whom I wish the woman who shall be my wife to resemble in all things.

And who is this model?

You know I can only mean Achsa Fielding.

If you love her likeness, why not love herself?

I felt my heart leap.—What a thought is that! Love her I *do* as I love my God; as I love virtue. To love her in another sense, would brand me for a lunatic.

To love her as a woman, then, appears to you an act of folly.

In me it would be worse than folly. 'Twould be frenzy.

And why?

Why? Really, my friend, you astonish me. Nay, you startle me—for a question like that implies a doubt in you whether I have not actually harbored the tho't.

No, said he, smiling, presumtuous though you be, you

431

have not, to be sure, reached so high a pitch. But still, though I think you innocent of so heinous an offence, there is no harm in asking why you might not love her, and even seek her for a wife.

Achsa Fielding *my wife!* Good Heaven!—The very sound threw my soul into unconquerable tumults.—Take care, my friend, continued I, in beseeching accents, you may do me more injury than you conceive, by even starting such a thought.

True, said he, as long as such obstacles exist to your success; so many incurable objections; for instance, she is six years older than you——

That is an advantage. Her age is what it ought to be.

But she has been a wife and mother already.

That is likewise an advantage. She has wisdom, because she has experience. Her sensibilities are stronger, because they have been exercised and chastened. Her first marriage was unfortunate. The purer is the felicity she will taste in a second! If her second choice be propitious, the greater her tenderness and gratitude.

But she is a foreigner: independent of controul, and rich.

All which, are blessings to herself and to him for whom her hand is reserved; especially if like me, he is indigent.

But then she is unsightly as a *night-hag*, tawney as a moor, the eye of a gypsey, low in stature, contemptibly diminutive, scarcely bulk enough to cast a shadow as she walks, less luxuriance than a charred log, fewer elasticities than a sheet pebble.

Hush! hush! blasphemer!—and I put my hand before his mouth—have I not told you that in mind, person and condition, she is the type after which my enamored fancy has modelled my wife.

O ho! Then the objection does not lie with you. It lies with her, it seems. She can find nothing in you to esteem! And pray, for what faults do you think she would reject you?

I cannot tell. That she can ever balance for a moment, on such a question, is incredible. *Me! me!* That Achsa Fielding should think of me!

Incredible, indeed! You who are loathsome in your person, an ideot in your understanding, a villain in your morals! deformed! withered! vain, stupid and malignant. That such an one should chuse *you* for an idol!

Pray, my friend, said I, anxiously, jest not. What mean you by an hint of this kind?

I will not jest then, but will soberly enquire, what faults are they which make this lady's choice of you so incredible? You are younger than she, though no one, who merely observed your manners, and heard you talk, would take you to be under thirty. You are poor; are these impediments?

I should think not. I have heard her reason with admirable eloquence, against the vain distinctions of property and nation and rank. They were once of moment in her eyes; but the sufferings, humiliations and reflections of years, have cured her of the folly. Her nation has suffered too much by the inhuman antipathies of religious and political faction; she, herself, has felt so often the contumelies of the rich, the high-born, and the bigotted, that——

Pry'thee then, what dost imagine her objections to be?

Why—I don't know. The thought was so aspiring; to call her *my wife*, was an height of bliss, the very far-off view of which made my head dizzy.

An height, however, to attain which you suppose only her consent, her love, to be necessary?

Without doubt, her love is indispensible.

Sit down, Arthur, and let us no longer treat this matter lightly. I clearly see the importance of this moment to this lady's happiness and yours. It is plain that you love this woman. How could you help it? A brilliant skin is not her's; nor elegant proportions; nor majestic stature; yet no creature had ever more power to bewitch. Her manners have grace and dignity that flow from exquisite feeling, delicate taste, and the quickest and keenest penetration. She has the wisdom of men and of books. Her sympathies are enforced by reason, and her charities regulated by knowledge. She has a woman's age, fortune more than you wish, and a spotless fame. How could you fail to love her?

You, who are her chosen friend, who partake her pleasures, and share her employments, on whom she almost exclusively bestows her society and confidence, and to whom she thus affords the strongest of all indirect proofs of impassioned esteem. How could you, with all that firmness to love, joined with all that discernment of her excellence, how could you escape the enchantment?

You have not thought of marriage. You have not suspected your love. From the purity of your mind, from the idolatry with which this woman has inspired you, you have imaged no delight beyond that of enjoying her society as you now do, and have never fostered an hope beyond this privilege.

How quickly would this tranquillity vanish, and the true state of your heart be evinced, if a rival should enter the scene and be entertained with preference; then would the seal be removed, the spell be broken, and you would awaken to terror and to anguish.

Of this, however, there is no danger. Your passion is not felt by you alone. From her treatment of you, your diffidence disables you from seeing, but nothing can be clearer to me than, that she loves you.

I started on my feet. A flush of scorching heat flowed to every part of my frame. My temples began to throb like my heart. I was half delirious, and my delirium was strangely compounded of fear and hope, of delight and of terror.

What have you done, my friend? You have overturned my peace of mind. Till now the image of this woman has been followed by complacency and sober rapture; but your words have dashed the scene with dismay and confusion. You have raised up wishes and dreams and doubts, which possess me in spite of my reason, in spite of a thousand proofs.

Good God! You say she loves; loves *me!* me, a boy in age; bred in clownish ignorance; scarcely ushered into the world; more than childishly unlearned and raw; a barndoor simpleton; a plow-tail, kitchen-hearth, turnip-hoeing novice! She, thus splendidly endowed; thus allied to nobles; thus gifted with arts, and adorned with graces; that she should chuse me, me for the partner of her fortune; her affections; and her life! It cannot be. Yet, if it were; if your guesses should—prove—Oaf! madman! To indulge so fatal a chimera! So rash a dream!

My friend! my friend! I feel that you have done me an irreparable injury. I can never more look her in the face. I can never more frequent her society. These new thoughts will beset and torment me. My disquiet will chain up my tongue. That overflowing gratitude; that innocent joy, unconscious of offence, and knowing no restraint, which have hitherto been my titles to her favor, will fly from my features and manners. I shall be anxious, vacant and unhappy in her presence. I shall dread to look at her, or to open my lips lest my mad and unhallowed ambition should betray itself.

Well, replied Stevens, this scene is quite new. I could almost find it in my heart to pity you. I did not expect this; and yet from my knowledge of your character, I ought, perhaps, to have foreseen it. This is a necessary part of the drama. A joyous certainty, on these occasions, must always be preceded by suspenses and doubts, and the close will be joyous in proportion as the preludes are excruciating. Go to bed, my good friend, and think of this. Time and a few more interviews with Mrs. Fielding, will, I doubt not, set all to rights.

CHAPTER XXV

I WENT to my chamber, but what different sensations did I carry into it, from those with which I had left it a few hours before. I stretched myself on the mattress and put out the light; but the swarm of new images that rushed on my mind, set me again instantly in motion. All was rapid, vague and undefined, wearying and distracting my attention. I was roused as by a divine voice, that said:— "Sleep no more: Mervyn shall sleep no more."

What chiefly occupied me was a nameless sort of terror. What shall I compare it to? Methinks, that one falling from a tree, overhanging a torrent, plunged into the whirling eddy, and gasping and struggling while he sinks to rise no more, would feel just as I did then. Nay, some such image actually possessed me. Such was one of my reveries, in which suddenly I stretched my hand, and caught the arm of a chair. This act called me back to reason, or rather gave my soul opportunity to roam into a new track equally wild.

Was it the abruptness of this vision that thus confounded me! was it a latent error in my moral constitution, which this new conjuncture drew forth into influence? These were all the tokens of a mind lost to itself; bewildered; unhinged; plunged into a drear insanity.

Nothing less could have prompted so phantastically—for midnight as it was, my chamber's solitude was not to be supported. After a few turns across the floor, I left the room, and the house. I walked without design and in an hurried pace. I posted straight to the house of Mrs. Fielding. I lifted the latch, but the door did not open. It was, no doubt, locked.

How comes this, said I, and looked around me. The hour and occasion were unthought of. Habituated to this path, I had taken it spontaneously. How comes this? repeated I. Locked upon *me!* but I will summon them, I warrant me—and rung the bell, not timidly or slightly, but with violence. Some one hastened from above. I saw the glimmer of a candle through the key-hole.

Strange, thought I, a candle at noon day!—The door was opened, and my poor Bess, robed in a careless and a hasty manner, appeared. She started at sight of me, but merely because she did not, in a moment, recognize me.—Ah! Arthur, is it you? Come in. My mamma has wanted you these two hours. I was just going to dispatch Philip to tell you to come.

Lead me to her, said I.

She led the way into the parlor.—Wait a moment here: I will tell her you are come—and she tripped away.

Presently a step was heard. The door opened again, and then entered a man. He was tall, elegant, sedate to a degree of sadness: Something in his dress and aspect that bespoke the foreigner; the Frenchman.

What, said he, mildly, is your business with my wife? She cannot see you instantly, and has sent me to receive your commands.

Your *wife!* I want Mrs. Fielding.

True; and Mrs. Fielding is my wife. Thank Heaven I have come in time to discover her, and claim her as such.

I started back. I shuddered. My joints slackened, and I stretched my hand to catch something by which I might be saved from sinking on the floor. Meanwhile, Fielding changed his countenance into rage and fury. He called me villain! bad me avaunt! and drew a shining steel from his bosom, with which he stabbed me to the heart. I sunk upon the floor, and all, for a time, was darkness and oblivion! At length, I returned as it were to life. I opened my eyes. The mists disappeared, and I found myself stretched upon the bed in my own chamber. I remembered the fatal blow I had received. I put my hand upon my breast; the spot where the dagger entered. There were no traces of a wound. All was perfect and entire. Some miracle had made me whole.

I raised myself up. I re-examined my body. All around me was hushed, till a voice from the pavement below, proclaimed that it was "past three o'clock."

What, said I, has all this miserable pageantry, this midnight wandering, and this ominous interview, been no more than—*a dream*!

It may be proper to mention, in explanation of this scene, and to shew the thorough perturbation of my mind, during this night, intelligence gained some days after from Eliza. She said, that about two o'clock, on this night, she was roused by a violent ringing of the bell. She was startled by so unseasonable a summons. She slept in a chamber adjoining Mrs. Fielding's, and hesitated whether she should alarm her friend, but the summons not being repeated, she had determined to forbear.

Added to this, was the report of Mrs. Stevens, who, on the same night, about half an hour after I and her husband had retired, imagined that she heard the street-door opened and shut, but this being followed by no other consequence, she supposed herself mistaken. I have little doubt, that, in my feverish and troubled sleep, I actually went forth, posted to the house of Mrs. Fielding, rung for admission, and shortly after, returned to my own apartment.

This confusion of mind was somewhat allayed by the return of light. It gave way to more uniform, but not less rueful and despondent perceptions. The image of Achsa filled my fancy, but it was the harbinger of nothing but humiliation and sorrow. To outroot the conviction of my own unworthiness, to persuade myself that I was regarded with the tenderness that Stevens had ascribed to her, that the discovery of my thoughts would not excite her anger and grief, I felt to be impossible.

In this state of mind, I could not see her. To declare my feelings would produce indignation and anguish; to hide them from her scrutiny was not in my power: yet, what would she think of my estranging myself from her society?

438

What expedient could I honestly adopt to justify my absence, and what employments could I substitute for those precious hours hitherto devoted to her.

This afternoon, thought I, she has been invited to spend at Stedman's country house on Schuylkill. She consented to go, and I was to accompany her. I am fit only for solitude. My behaviour, in her presence, will be enigmatical, capricious and morose. I must not go: Yet, what will she think of my failure? Not to go will be injurious and suspicious.

I was undetermined. The appointed hour arrived. I stood at my chamber window, torn by variety of purposes, and swayed alternately by repugnant arguments. I several times went to the door of my apartment, and put my foot upon the first step of the stair-case, but as often paused, reconsidered and returned to my room.

In these fluctuations the hour passed. No messenger arrived from Mrs. Fielding, enquiring into the cause of my delay. Was she offended at my negligence? Was she sick and disabled from going, or had she changed her mind? I now remember her parting words at our last interview. Were they not susceptible of two constructions? She said my visit was too long, and bad me begone. Did she suspect my presumption, and is she determined thus to punish me?

This terror added anew to all my former anxieties. It was impossible to rest in this suspense. I would go to her. I would lay before her all the anguish of my heart: I would not spare myself. She shall not reproach me more severely than I will reproach myself. I will hear my sentence from her own lips, and promise unlimited submission to the doom of separation and exile, which she will pronounce.

I went forthwith to her house. The drawing-room and summer-house was empty. I summoned Philip the footman—his mistress was gone to Mr. Stedman's.

How?—To Stedman's?—In whose company?

Miss Stedman and her brother called for her in the carriage, and persuaded her to go with them.

Now my heart sunk, indeed! Miss Stedman's *brother*! A youth, forward, gallant and gay! Flushed with prosperity, and just returned from Europe, with all the confidence of

439

age, and all the ornaments of education! She has gone with him, though pre-engaged to me! Poor Arthur, how art thou despised!

This information only heightened my impatience. I went away, but returned in the evening. I waited till eleven, but she came not back. I cannot justly paint the interval that passed till next morning. It was void of sleep. On leaving her house, I wandered into the fields. Every moment increased my impatience. She will probably spend the morrow at Stedman's, said I, and possibly the next day. Why should I wait for her return? Why not seek her there, and rid myself at once of this agonizing suspense? Why not go thither now? This night, wherever I spend it, will be unacquainted with repose. I will go, it is already near twelve, and the distance is more than eight miles. I will hover near the house till morning, and then, as early as possible, demand an interview.

I was well acquainted with Stedman's Villa, having formerly been there with Mrs. Fielding. I quickly entered its precincts. I went close to the house; looked mournfully at every window. At one of them a light was to be seen, and I took various stations to discover, if possible, the persons within. Methought once I caught a glimpse of a female, whom my fancy easily imagined to be Achsa. I sat down upon the lawn, some hundred feet from the house, and opposite the window whence the light proceeded. I watched it, till at length some one came to the window, lifted it, and leaning on her arms, continued to look out.

The preceding day had been a very sultry one; the night, as usual after such a day, and the fall of a violent shower, was delightfully serene and pleasant. Where I stood, was enlightened by the moon. Whether she saw me or not, I could hardly tell, or whether she distinguished any thing but a human figure.

Without reflecting on what was due to decorum and punctilio, I immediately drew near the house. I quickly perceived that her attention was fixed. Neither of us spoke, till I had placed myself directly under her; I then opened my lips, without knowing in what manner to address her. She spoke first, and in a startled and anxious voice—

440

Who is that?

Arthur Mervyn: he that was two days ago your friend.

Mervyn! What is it that brings you here at this hour? What is the matter? What has happened? Is any body sick?

All is safe—all are in good health.

What then do you come hither for at such an hour?

I meant not to disturb you: I meant not to be seen.

Good Heavens! How you frighten me. What can be the reason of so strange——

Be not alarmed. I meant to hover near the house till morning, that I might see you as early as possible.

For what purpose?

I will tell you when we meet, and let that be at five o'clock; the sun will then be risen; in the cedar grove under the bank; till when, farewel.

Having said this, I prevented all expostulation, by turning the angle of the house, and hastening towards the shore of the river. I roved about the grove that I have mentioned. In one part of it is a rustic seat and table, shrouded by trees and shrubs, and an intervening eminence, from the view of those in the house. This I designed to be the closing scene of my destiny.

Presently, I left this spot and wandered upward through embarrassed and obscure paths, starting forward or checking my pace, according as my wayward meditations governed me. Shall I describe my thoughts?—Impossible! It was certainly a temporary loss of reason; nothing less than madness could lead into such devious tracts, drag me down to so hopeless, helpless, panickful a depth, and drag me down so suddenly; lay waste, as at a signal, all my flourishing structures, and reduce them in a moment to a scene of confusion and horror.

What did I fear? What did I hope? What did I design? I cannot tell; my glooms were to retire with the night. The point to which every tumultuous feeling was linked, was the coming interview with Achsa. That was the boundary of fluctuation and suspense. Here was the sealing and ratification of my doom.

I rent a passage through the thicket, and struggled upward till I reached the edge of a considerable precipice; I

441

laid me down at my length upon the rock, whose cold and hard surface I pressed with my bared and throbbing breast. I leaned over the edge; fixed my eyes upon the water and wept—plentifully; but why?

May *this* be my heart's last beat, if I can tell why.

I had wandered so far from Stedman's, that when roused by the light, I had some miles to walk before I could reach the place of meeting. Achsa was already there. I slid down the rock above, and appeared before her. Well might she be startled at my wild and abrupt appearance.

I placed myself, without uttering a word, upon a seat opposite to her, the table between, and crossing my arms upon the table, leaned my head upon them. While my face was turned towards and my eyes fixed upon hers, I seemed to have lost the power and the inclination to speak.

She regarded me, at first, with anxious curiosity; after examining my looks, every emotion was swallowed up in terrified sorrow. For God's sake!—what does all this mean? Why am I called to this place? What tidings, what fearful tidings do you bring?

I did not change my posture or speak. What, she resumed, could inspire all this woe? Keep me not in this suspense, Arthur; these looks and this silence shocks and afflicts me too much.

Afflict you? said I, at last: I come to tell you, what, now that I am here, I cannot tell——there I stopped.

Say what, I entreat you. You seem to be very unhappy— such a change—from yesterday!

Yes! From yesterday: all then was a joyous calm, and now all is—but then I knew not my infamy, my guilt——

What words are these, and from you Arthur? Guilt is to you impossible. If purity is to be found on earth, it is lodged in your heart. What have you done?

I have dared—how little you expect the extent of my daring. That such as I should look upwards with this ambition.

I now stood up, and taking her hands in mine, as she sat, looked earnestly in her face—I come only to beseech your pardon. To tell you my crime, and then disappear forever;

442

but first let me see if there be any omen of forgiveness. Your looks—they are kind; heavenly; compassionate still. I will trust them, I believe: and yet—letting go her hands, and turning away.—This offence is beyond the reach even of *your* mercy.

How beyond measure these words and this deportment distress me! Let me know the worst; I cannot bear to be thus perplexed.

Why, said I, turning quickly round, and again taking her hands, that Mervyn, whom you have honored and confided in, and blessed with your sweet regards, has been——

What has he been? Divinely amiable, heroic in his virtue, I am sure. What else has he been?

This Mervyn has imagined, has dared—Will you forgive him?

Forgive you what? Why don't you speak? Keep not my soul in this suspense.

He has dared—But do not think that I am he. Continue to look as now, and reserve your killing glances, the vengeance of those eyes as for one that is absent.—Why, what—You weep, then, at last. That is a propitious sign. When pity drops from the eyes of our judge, then should the suppliant approach. Now, in confidence of pardon, I will tell you: This Mervyn, not content with all you have hitherto granted him, has dared—to *love* you; nay, to think of you, as of *his wife!*

Her eye sunk beneath mine, and disengaging her hands, covered her face with them.

I see my fate, said I, in a tone of despair. Too well did I predict the effect of this confession; but I will go—*and unforgiven.*

She now partly uncovered her face. The hand withdrawn from her cheek, was stretched towards me. She looked at me.

Arthur! I *do* forgive thee.—With what accents was this uttered! With what looks! The cheek that was before pale with terror, was now crimsoned over by a different emotion, and delight swam in her eye.

Could I mistake? My doubts, my new-born fears made me tremble, while I took the offered hand.

Surely—faultered I, I am not—I cannot be—so blessed.

There was no need of words. The hand that I held, was sufficiently eloquent. She was still silent.

Surely, said I, my senses deceive me. A bliss like this cannot be reserved for me. Tell me, once more—set my doubting heart at rest.—

She now gave herself to my arms—I have not words—Let your own heart tell you, you have made your Achsa ——

At this moment, a voice from without, it was Miss Stedman's, called—Mrs. Fielding! where are you?

My friend started up, and in a hasty voice, bade me begone! You must not be seen by this giddy girl. Come hither this evening, as if by my appointment, and I will return with you.—She left me in a kind of trance. I was immoveable. My reverie was too delicious;—but let me not attempt the picture. If I can convey no image of my state, previous to this interview, my subsequent feelings are still more beyond the reach of my powers to describe.

Agreeably to the commands of my mistress, I hastened away, evading paths which might expose me to observation. I speedily made my friends partake of my joy, and passed the day in a state of solemn but confused rapture. I did not accurately pourtray the various parts of my felicity. The whole rushed upon my soul at once. My conceptions were too rapid, and too comprehensive to be distinct.

I went to Stedman's in the evening. I found in the accents and looks of my Achsa new assurances that all which had lately past, was more than a dream. She made excuses for leaving the Stedmans sooner than ordinary, and was accompanied to the city by her friend. We dropped Mrs. Fielding at her own house, and thither, after accompanying Miss Stedman to her own home, I returned, upon the wings of tremulous impatience.—

Now could I repeat every word of every conversation that has since taken place between us; but why should I do that on paper? Indeed it could not be done. All is of equal value, and all could not be comprized but in many volumes. There needs nothing more deeply to imprint it on my memory; and while thus reviewing the past, I should be iniquitously neglecting the present. What is given to the pen, would be taken from her; and that, indeed, would be—but no need of saying what it would be, since it is impossible.

I merely write to allay those tumults which our necessary separation produces; to aid me in calling up a little patience, till the time arrives, when our persons, like our minds, shall be united forever. That time—may nothing happen to prevent—but nothing can happen. But why this ominous misgiving just now? My love has infected me with these unworthy terrors, for she has them too.

This morning I was relating my dream to her. She started, and grew pale. A sad silence ensued the cheerfulness that had reigned before—why thus dejected, my friend?

I hate your dream. It is a horrid thought. Would to God it had never occurred to you.

Why surely you place no confidence in dreams.

I know not where to place confidence; not in my present promises of joy—and she wept. I endeavored to soothe or console her. Why, I asked, did she weep.

My heart is sore. Former disappointments were so heavy; the hopes which were blasted, were so like my present ones, that the dread of a like result, will intrude upon my thoughts. And now your dream! Indeed, I know not what to do. I believe I ought still to retract—ought, at least, to postpone an act so irrevocable.

Now was I obliged again to go over in my catalogue of arguments to induce her to confirm her propitious resolution to be mine within the week. I, at last, succeeded, even in restoring her serenity and beguiling her fears by dwelling on our future happiness.

Our houshold, while we staid in America—in a year or two we hie to Europe—should be *thus* composed. Fidelity and skill and pure morals, should be sought out, and enticed, by generous recompences, into our domestic service. Duties should be light and regular.—Such and such should be our amusements and employments abroad and at home, and would not this be true happiness?

O yes—If it may be so.

It shall be so; but this is but the humble outline of the scene; something is still to be added to complete our felicity.

What more can be added?

What more? Can Achsa ask what more? She who has not been *only* a wife——

But why am I indulging this pen-prattle? The hour she fixed for my return to her is come, and now take thyself away, quill. Lie there, snug in thy leathern case, till I call for thee, and that will not be very soon. I believe I will abjure thy company till all is settled with my love. Yes: I *will* abjure thee, so let *this* be thy last office, till Mervyn has been made the happiest of men.

THE END

Introduction to the Historical Essay

Over the years, critical perspectives vary, as do perceptions, but a survey of the secondary bibliography subsequent to publication of Norman Grabo's Historical Essay reveals that nothing has come forth regarding matters of conception, provenance, composition, influence, or concurrent history to require modification of anything Grabo has written. Much attention has centered on the irreconcilable elements in Mervyn's character and a correspondence between the revolutionary climate of the times and the yellow fever epidemic—discussion for which Grabo's narrative of fact provides a terminus ad quo, making his essay as relevant now as when originally published. (For a sampling of typical analysis, consult the appended bibliography.)

Some years ago, *Arthur Mervyn* was called Brown's "most ambitious work" (Elliott, 143), and, more recently, it has been indicated that "modern criticism has so upgraded" *Mervyn* that it vies with *Wieland* as "Brown's most highly praised novel" (Christophersen, 89)—reason enough to have it made more widely available for reconsideration.

Sydney J. Krause, 2001

HISTORICAL ESSAY

Nearly 2,500 died in that ghastly Philadelphia summer of 1793. Not suddenly and cleanly, but slowly, with fevers and chills, pain and enervation increasing over a week or ten days, culminating in hemorrhage and bilious vomit. Death's undignified stench mixed with the smell of fear, for no one knew its cause or what to do about it. Citizens burned fires in the streets to ward it off. They smoked, hoping tobacco would prevent it, so that by the middle of September even women and children seemed never without cigars in their mouths. All muffled their heads in vinegar-soaked kerchiefs to block out the disease as well as the noisomeness of quickly putrefying bodies. Physicians tried what they could— changes of air, bleeding, purgatives—all to no effect.

It was not that the yellow fever was unexpected; it occurred annually. And indeed those who could afford to—like the Brown family, or President Washington and Congressmen (the Federal government still sat at Philadelphia then)—usually planned to leave the city by mid-summer. In fact, so many prominent citizens were absent by the time of the first death of 19 August that the city was practically without government of any kind. But no one expected the pestilence to explode as it did that summer. Within two weeks so many were dying or dead that not even the makeshift facilities at the circus grounds were able to handle them. A spontaneously formed Committee of Health performed heroically to subdue public panic and attend to the ill and the dead. They stopped the constant ringing of death knells throughout the city, appointed a vigilance committee to guard against looting, borrowed money to pay for carts to haul the sick and the dead, and posted threats to prosecute those who inter- fered with the men hired to remove the bodies. They appropri- ated the Bushhill mansion (over the objections of its summer tenant), converting it into a 140-bed hospital, and found a staff to man it, though conditions there were deplorable until the middle of September, when two of the Committee undertook its management personally. The epidemic was stabilized by October, though rumors so exaggerated conditions that one newspaper printed correspondence to the effect that 15,000 workmen had expired. Neighboring communities refused to accept refugees from Philadelphia, stage and ferry lines were blocked, ports controlled, and private citizens severely cautioned not to admit Philadelphians to their homes. By mid-November the Committee urged Philadelphians to return, and by the end of the month all stores and shops had reopened—all that could.

For the physical terrors were only part of Philadelphia's distress that summer. Before the pestilence struck, the city was in many ways feverish. Bank policies were erratic and unreliable. Merchants and businessmen were investing wildly in exotic financial schemes that burst with uncommon regularity. Prices—especially rents—sky-rocketed. And businesses failed in startling numbers, with ruined bankrupts crowding the streets, the stock-piled wharves, the places of trade. It was a community demoralized, without confidence, without trust, and in no position to handle the stress of the epidemic that had descended upon it. In so charged an atmosphere the ensuing panic is understandable. The horrors to which it led quickly shocked and appalled all who viewed them. Children deserted their parents to save themselves. Parents fled their children, for fear. Women in labor were lucky to attract passers-by to help deliver their babies. And usually both mother and child died. Men who had spent their lives providing for their families were cast off to the care of black servants (their race supposedly being exceptionally immune to the pestilence), and left wives and daughters to support themselves by prostitution in the months to follow. (There was room for them; the previous *filles de joie*, as one eyewitness calls them, were more susceptible to the disease than solid citizens.) Friends passing on the street no longer shook hands in the City of Brotherly Love.

And when the great convulsion passed in November, there were the recriminations, the grief, the numb realization both of the suffering and of the mortifying moral failure, the empty thanks to those who died trying to help and to those who helped and survived, the congratulations of the selfless Committee of Health, and the final leaden numbering of the dead and their identification so that the distribution of their property might be lawful and orderly. And to those remaining, there was the shame and guilt. This was indeed a summer that tried men's souls, as Mathew Carey, one of the Committee of Health, wrote in his committee report, *A Short Account of the Malignant Fever* (13 November 1793).[1] Ten days later a second edition was necessary, a week after that yet a third, and six weeks later a fourth, before public demand to know what had indeed happened was glutted. Nine years before his death in 1839, Carey brought out a final edition, with the note, "The novel of *Arthur Mervyn*, by C. B. Brown, gives a vivid and terrifying picture, probably not too highly coloured, of the horrors of that period" (p. 25). By the time Carey wrote that, Charles Brockden Brown's fame was inseparable from his picture of that gruesome summer of 1793. Although there has been a rather general assumption that Brown was not present during the horrors of the 1793 epidemic, there is evidence which places him in Philadelphia at least through August and likely into the first part of September, and some validation therefore for his remarking in the "Preface" to the *First Part* that the incidents described "came within the sphere of his own observation."[2] Obviously a corruscating image of a city sick in soul and body had sunk deeply into Brown's consciousness.

[1] All the preceding details of that summer are from Carey's *A Short Account of the Malignant Fever which prevailed in Philadelphia, in the year 1793: with a statement of the proceedings that took place on the subject, in different parts of the United States.* Fifth Edition, improved (Philadelphia: Clark & Raser, 1830).

[2] P. 3. Among those who place Brown out of town during the late summer of 1793 is Warfel, who has him visiting Smith and traveling through Connecticut with him (Harry R. Warfel, *Charles Brockden Brown: American Gothic Novelist* [Gainesville: Univ. of Florida Press, 1949], p. 44). However, the record shows that while Brown had visited Smith in April and was in Hartford during June and July, by 29 July he was back in Philadelphia and still there by 16 August when he was writing his friend Joseph Bringhurst (Daniel Edwards Kennedy, "Charles Brockden Brown: His Life and Works," pp. 631, 633, 636, 647, 648, 655. Kennedy's unpublished manuscript—hereafter referred to as Kennedy—is in the Kent State Brown collection). Concerning his whereabouts thereafter, we have very little definite evidence, except that he is supposed to have gone to be with Smith in New York, a meeting that could not have occurred, however, earlier than 5 September, when Smith is supposed to have arrived in New York (*The Diary of Elihu Hubbard Smith (1771–1798)*, ed. James E. Cronin [Philadelphia: American Philosophical Society, 1973], p. 290. Hereafter, Smith, *Diary*). He is thought to have returned to Philadelphia in the late fall (David Lee Clark, *Charles Brockden Brown, Pioneer Voice of America* [Durham, N.C.: Duke Univ. Press, 1952], p. 107).

Within two years Brown was working on a novel, apparently with the image of the city foremost. A year later, in 1796, Brown moved to New York and found his work on the novel interrupted by projects and interests connected with his new associates and their activities. But in February of 1797, Dr. Smith noted that Brown had "recommenced his Phila. novel; so fiercely undertaken in the Autumn of 1795."[3] Was this the beginning of *Arthur Mervyn*? The answer can only be speculative, for much of Brown's fiction is set in Philadelphia and its environs. But neither *Wieland* nor "Sky-Walk" (some of the contents of which would become incorporated in *Edgar Huntly*) uses the city in such a way that Brown or his friends would refer to it as "his Phila. novel"; and with *Ormond* not only does the city not figure quite so prominently as it does in *Arthur Mervyn*, but we have a novel which was begun much later than the time in question. Possibly the novel referred to by Smith was simply abandoned, unfinished, and uncannibalized. But Brown was not a writer to leave ideas entirely unused, and if any of his fictions deserve such a description as Smith's, it is surely *Arthur Mervyn*, wherein the city itself takes on nearly the aspect of a character whose conditions generate the actions of most of the other characters, and whose contagions infect all. Indeed, nowhere else in Brown's fiction are the problems of personal psychic identity so obviously and extensively explored in social circumstances as they are in *Arthur Mervyn*. When the countrified Arthur stumbles off the farm to be bilked in the city and to confront those corruptions so poignantly depicted by Carey, we have a situation unique in Brown's fiction. But it is in the circumstantial details of city life—inns and hospitals and toll-takers, investors, swindlers, lawyers, and scriveners, physicians, and jails and the ominous rumbling of burial carts—that

Since Carey has the first death from the yellow fever occurring on 19 August (p. 19) and has the city in a crisis state shortly thereafter (p. 24), there seems good reason to believe that Brown did indeed draw upon personal observation for the plague scenes he described in his novel. By Paul Allen's account, incidentally, Brown "saw the desolation of his native city by [the] pestilence" though he fled with the rest of his family "in time to avoid its influence" (William Dunlap, *The Life of Charles Brockden Brown*, 2 vols. [Philadelphia: James P. Parke, 1815], II, [3]. Hereafter, *Life*). (Though initially written by Allen, the biography was given to Dunlap for editing when it was being prepared for publication.)

[3]Entry for Monday, 13 February 1797. Smith, *Diary*, p. 290. I take Warfel's transcription of "recommenced" in preference to Cronin's "recommended"; clearly the former makes better sense. A photocopy of Warfel's typescript is in the Kent State Brown collection.

Arthur Mervyn makes its claim as the most likely consequence of that early "Philadelphia novel."

If by 1795, then, Brown likely had the setting and occasion—a moral matrix for a major fiction—it is not clear that he had either a firm conception of his characters or their story. Indeed, his first attempt to handle the yellow fever matter of 1793 appeared in a series of thirteen loosely organized sketches and essays that appeared weekly in the Philadelphia *Weekly Magazine* from 23 February to 28 April 1798. Called "The Man at Home," the series recounts the ruminations of a man ruined financially by trusting his business partner. Hiding from his creditors, the sixty-year-old Man has virtually imprisoned himself in a house deserted by its former occupants who suffered inordinately from the pestilence that summer. Those occupants consisted of an elderly French botanist and his daughter, who had taken refuge from the French Revolution in Philadelphia. M. De Moivre takes great interest in the progress of the yellow fever, observing the city's reactions to it so closely that he himself contracts the disease and dies.[4] His daughter buries him crudely in the garden, observed by a neighbor, Baxter, one of the nightwatch set to ward off looters. The bulk of this sketch Brown incorporated wholesale into Chapter VII of *Ormond*, which he composed later in 1798, changing the name from De Moivre to Monrose. In that later telling, Baxter is the sole witness to Miss De Moivre's ghastly act, but in "The Man at Home" there is another witness, a curious and concerned young man who sounds very much like Arthur Mervyn and may be considered the first appearance of that character in print.[5]

The eleventh sketch (14 April, pp. 320–323) approaches the yellow fever from a very different perspective. The Man describes to a group of friends an act of ruthless political terrorism that silently and dreadfully destroys its enemies in silence, terror, and dread—a social allegory of the yellow fever itself. Clearly, Brown is indicating his awareness that the epidemic is social and

[4]It is questionable whether De Moivre (Monrose) has actually died of the yellow fever. ("There was no *proof* that Monrose had fallen a victim to the reigning disease," p. 81. My italics. [*Ormond; or the Secret Witness* (New York: H. Caritat, 1799), p. 81.]) Brown cites this case as "an example of the force of imagination" (*Ormond*, p. 81)—i.e., as a sign of the effect of the hysteria psychology of the times.

[5]"The Man at Home," *Weekly Magazine*, 1 (3, 10 March 1798), 133–136, 167–170. These are reprinted in *The Rhapsodist and Other Uncollected Writings by Charles Brockden Brown*, ed. Harry R. Warfel (New York: Scholars' Facsimiles & Reprints, 1943), pp. 51–56.

moral as well as physical. But the Man's dolorous views are refuted by one of his auditors, named Wallace, who claims to have been driven from his business and the city to Lancaster, where he "formed an acquaintance with a young lady, who added three hundred pounds a year, to youth, beauty, and virtue. This acquaintance soon ripened into love, and now you see me one of the happiest of men. A lovely wife, a plentiful fortune, health, and leisure are the ingredients of my present lot, and for all these I am indebted to the yellow fever" (*Rhapsodist*, p. 85). The pestilence, then, can reward as well as destroy. Four days before that sketch appeared, on 10 April, Brown's friend William Dunlap arrived from New York for a visit. Brown informed him of having completed yet another novel, one turning on somnambulism and then called "Sky-Walk," and he read to Dunlap the opening pages of a new novel, *Wieland*.[6] By 16 June the first chapter of *Arthur Mervyn* was carried in number 20 of the *Weekly Magazine*, to be succeeded by a chapter a week for the next four weeks, Chapter 5 appearing on 14 July.

But by 3 July Brown had moved to New York (Dunlap, *Diary*, I, 305), apparently to avoid what the *Weekly Magazine* would report on 18 August as the "alarming" increase in "the malignant fever" (p. 95). In the issue of 21 July the editor, James Watters, gave notice that the serialization of Arthur Mervyn's adventures was suspended because of the indisposition and distance of some of his correspondents (p. 384). If Brown was distant, he was not indisposed in those weeks; he was rather actively socializing, especially with the Dunlaps, with whom he stayed in the company of Elihu Hubbard Smith and William Johnson, writing steadily at *Wieland* and thinking about a projected weekly magazine to be published in New York.[7] Dunlap, who was Brown's daily companion, makes no mention of *Arthur Mervyn*, even though he was presumably reading it in issues of the *Weekly Magazine* forwarded

[6]*Diary of William Dunlap (1766–1839)* (New York: The New York Historical Society, 1930), I, 240–242. Hereafter, Dunlap, *Diary*.
[7]Brown lived with the Dunlaps till they left town on 29 July 1798 (*Diary*, I, 319) and thereafter stayed with Smith and Johnson. The thought of a magazine project which he mentioned to his brother James in August (*Life*, II, [3]) had evidently been brewing for some time and may actually have originated with Dunlap, who in June spoke to Smith of their doing a weekly magazine in New York, to be printed by the Swordses, on the model of Watters' Philadelphia journal (*Diary*, I, 276). Back in the city again briefly on 7 August, Dunlap once more talked about the proposed magazine with Smith, Johnson, and Brown (*Diary*, I, 323).

from Philadelphia. Watters must simply not have had any copy in hand past Chapter 5 when he published his notice of suspension. Two weeks later, however, publication was resumed in the *Weekly Magazine* with Chapter 6 on 4 August, and it was continued through Chapter 9 on 23 August. At that point Watters himself succumbed to the annual epidemic, and the *Weekly Magazine* as a whole discontinued publication until 2 February 1799.

By the time of this serialization, the character of Arthur had assumed a firm and clear shape from its cloudy anticipations in the benevolent benefactor of Miss De Moivre in the tenth number of "The Man at Home" (7 April), and it would seem that Brown must have had the story firmly in mind—at least conceptually, if not on paper—through Chapter 12. The death of Watters ended the serialization at the end of Chapter 9, recording Arthur's fifth tumultuous day in Philadelphia, and containing the discovery that Thomas Welbeck has killed Amos Watson, and the beginning of Welbeck's story of how this came about. Welbeck's confession of his progressive moral corruption seems in full flight at this point, and Chapter 10 picks up the narrative with no conclusive marks of interruption. Chapter 12 concludes that confession, and with the burial of Watson's body and Welbeck's apparent suicide in Chapter 12, Arthur's first incursion into the city ends, as does his own narrative. Chapter 13 resumes Stevens' frame narrative, reintroduces the yellow fever epidemic, and begins a wholly new series of episodes and characters that will postpone any continuation of the Mervyn-Welbeck relationship until Welbeck's surprising reappearance at the end of Chapter 20. The nature of this break at the end of Chapter 12, and especially the new material introduced in what follows, suggests a later period of writing than the first twelve chapters.

Three aspects of the latter segment of the *First Part* support the probability of later composition: the earliest possible date of Chapter 16, the intensification of the pestilence itself, and the arrangements between Brown and publisher Hugh Maxwell. The first of these is firmest. Arthur, seeking Wallace (whose name and whose initial fortune may both derive from the "Wallace" mentioned in that eleventh number of "The Man at Home," 14 April), enters the Thetford house, where, after several misadventures and misunderstandings he learns of the selfless behavior and bitter fate of Maravegli. Maravegli's circumstances and death correspond closely to those of Joseph B. Scandella, an Italian physician who arrived in New York on 12 September from

455

Philadelphia, already showing symptoms of the fever. Dr. Smith, with whom Brown was then staying after the Dunlaps had removed to Perth Amboy, brought Scandella to his lodgings, hoping to arrest the disease. Scandella died in Smith's apartment on Sunday, 17 September, to be followed three days later by Smith himself. The information Dunlap records about Scandella very strongly suggests that he is the model for Maravegli.[8] That establishes 17 September as the earliest date by which Chapter 16—or at least the Maravegli episode in it—could have been written. Of course it could be a later interpolation, for it is introduced into the narrative only by a conscious delay on the narrator's part, but we know at least that this portion of the novel could not have been in Watters' hands prior to the time of his death in August.

Scandella's death—and more significantly, Smith's—literally brought the gruesomeness of the epidemic home to Brown with a vividness he tried to blot out. "My labour," he wrote to Dunlap, "is to forget and exclude surrounding scenes and recent incidents" (*Life*, II, 9). Almost at once he too contracted a mild form of the disease, as did his other close companion, attorney William Johnson; both fled as soon as strength permitted to the reviving country airs of Perth Amboy and the invigorating company of the Dunlaps. On 21 September Brown wrote to Dunlap:

> Most ardently do I long to shut out this City from my view but my strength has been, within these few days, so totally & unaccountably subverted, that I can scarcely flatter myself with being able, very shortly, to remove. I do not understand my own case, but see enough to discover that the combination of bodily & mental causes have made such deep inroads on the vital energies of brain & stomach, I am afraid I canot [sic] think of departing before Monday at the least. (Dunlap, *Diary*, I, 341)

[8]See *First Part*, Chapter 16 (pp. 151–154) and Dunlap, *Life*, II, 5–8. Maravegli and Scandella were respectively described as Venetian physicians, belonging to distinguished families, and both died of the yellow fever during a short visit to America just as they were getting ready to return home. In each case it was a delayed departure that resulted in their contracting the disease, and the reason for the delay was that both men had "concern for the welfare of an amiable family of helpless females, a widowed mother and her daughters" (*Life*, II, 6)—an "English" family in each instance. Scandella, like Maravegli, had the misfortune of witnessing "the death of every individual of the family" before falling victim to the disease himself; and in both accounts mention is also made of the witnessing of the Venetian physician's dying agonies.

Nevertheless, by 24 September Brown and Johnson were in the country with Dunlap, bearing a printed copy of *Wieland* and the opening pages of another novel, *Stephen Calvert*. On receiving them that day, Dunlap reported in his diary: "Brown has quite recovered but is pale & so is William. They say the change of air & exhiliaration [sic] of spirits they have experienced on leaving ye city is inconceivable" (p. 342). The next month (until his departure from the Dunlaps on 21 October) seems to have been a steady round of walks, hunting, playing with the Dunlap children, and conversing as Brown's body and mind regained strength. News of the terrific devastations of the epidemic in New York reached them daily and must have heightened Brown's sense of the immediate horror he himself had just endured. He talked to Dunlap of Scandella's and Smith's deaths. Considering his habits, then, the state of his mind, his recent experiences, and his enforced leisure, the vivid and morbid descriptions of the epidemic that dominate *Arthur Mervyn* after Chapter 13 may well have been composed during this period of recuperation. We know that by November he had thrown himself into the writing of *Ormond*, and that this would primarily occupy him to the end of the year (*Life*, II, 15, 93). It may very well be then that his freest time to work on this portion of *Arthur Mervyn* would be October and early November of 1798, when the ravages of the yellow fever were still quite fresh in his mind.

But the third item of evidence—while it too supports a later state of composition for the second portion of the *First Part*—seems to rule out this period. On 20 December Brown wrote to his brother Armit informing him that Hugh Maxwell (printer of the still-suspended *Weekly Magazine*) had written, "proposing the publication of Mervyn on the terms and in the manner mentioned by you." It is not clear whether Armit broached the subject of book publication or whether Brown had proposed the scheme himself. In either case, the letter from Maxwell got Brown's immediate agreement. He adds to Armit, "I wrote him an immediate answer, assenting, perhaps, too hastily to the publication, and promising, when my present engagements were fulfilled to finish the adventures of A. Mervyn" (*Life*, II, 93). Those "present engagements" must refer almost exclusively to *Ormond*, which he was pushing to finish by the end of the month, a goal he likely achieved. Copyright for *Ormond* was secured on 16 January 1799, and Caritat announced it for sale on 21 January in the New York *Commercial Advertiser*. The amount of work that suddenly had to be poured into *Ormond* suggests that Brown would not have had time to turn to the completion of *Arthur Mervyn* for Maxwell until after the first of January 1799.

How much still remained to be finished of the *First Part* is uncertain. But, however much there was, the volume was complete by early February. A letter from Brown to his brother James indicates that James, in Philadelphia, had seen all the material through the final Chapter 23, had raised objections to it, and had communicated these to Brown sufficiently before 15 February to require Brown's opening this letter by saying, "I know not why I suffered your last letter to remain so long unanswered" (*Life*, II, 97). How long "so long" was he does not specify, but circumstances suggest that Brown must have completed the volume by 10 February at the latest. That would mean it had taken roughly five or six weeks to compose the final fourteen chapters, if we suppose him to have written nothing on the novel since the publication of Chapter 9 in the *Weekly Magazine*—a rate not beyond Brown's powers. That rate is even greater if we take literally Brown's remark to his brother that, "instead of industriously employing the last fortnight, it has been whiled away in desultory reading" (*Life*, II, 98). That would mean that he had completed the manuscript by 1 February.

The continuation of the adventures of Arthur probably did not come to mind until near the completion of the *First Part*. Perhaps Brown saw that there was simply no time in which to tie up many of the loose ends of what he had so far written—the Clemenza affair, the budding romance between Arthur and Eliza, the fate of Wallace—as well as bring the first great contest between Arthur and Welbeck to an appropriate conclusion in the scope of a single volume—or in the framework of Maxwell's printing schedule. There is also an enthusiastic air in Brown's announcing to brother James in the 15 February 1799 letter, "I have purposely left an opening for the publication of a second part or sequel" to the book. That purpose sounds much more conscious and intentional in the "Preface" published with the *First Part*, whose brief concluding paragraph reads,

> In the following tale a particular series of adventures is brought to a close; but these are necessarily connected with the events which happened subsequent to the period here described. These events are not less memorable than those which form the subject of the present volume, and may hereafter be published either separately or in addition to this. (p. 3)

What these statements tell us, I believe, is that the continuation was a late development in the composition of the story, that it necessitated leaving some problems unsolved (the most obvious being the escape in Chapter 23 of Welbeck, whose function in the story is essentially exhausted by this time), and that Brown had some definite ideas concerning the direction his story would take. This last is at least clear from the same letter to James cited above:

> The destiny of Wallace and of Mr. Hadwin is not mentioned in the present work. I intended that Mr. Hadwin, on returning to his family, should be seized with the fatal disease. That the task of nursing him, while struggling with the malady, and of interring him when dead, should, by the fears of their neighbours, be assigned to his daughters. Wallace, by his unseasonable journey, is thrown into a relapse, and dies upon the road. Mervyn, preparing to leave the city, is accidentally detained, and his fortitude and virtue, subjected to severer trials than any hitherto related.
>
> The character of Wallace is discovered to have been essentially defective. Marriage with this youth is proved to be highly dangerous to the happiness of Susan. To prevent this union, and to ascertain the condition of this family, he speeds, at length, after the removal of various impediments, to Hadwin's residence, where he discovers the catastrophe of Wallace and his uncle, and by his presence and succour, relieves the two helpless females from their sorrows and their fears. Marriage with the youngest; the death of the elder by a consumption and grief, leaves him in possession of competence, and the rewards of virtue. (*Life*, II, 98)

With some significant changes, this scenario would finally occupy Chapters 6 through 9, when Arthur next resumes his tale to Stevens. Meanwhile, Brown's interest in Mervyn seems to have undergone some serious changes. The "severer trials than any hitherto related" seem not to have been envisaged as finally presented, and the whole conception of Arthur as both guardian (with respect to Eliza) and ward, lover, and husband (with respect to Mrs. Fielding) is nowhere evident.

Before these changes occurred, Brown as usual had much to distract him. Printing of the *First Part* moved apace, appearing from Maxwell's press sometime between 7 March and 21 May 1799.[9] There is no evidence of revisions subsequent to 15 February; Brown apparently left it to James to see the book through the

---

[9] See Jacob Blanck, *Bibliography of American Literature* (New Haven: Yale Univ. Press, 1955), I, 302, and Warfel, *Charles Brockden Brown*, p. 243.

press and to read proof, while Brown remained in New York developing other projects. The year-old notion of a New York weekly magazine had by now been realized as a *Monthly Magazine and American Review* under Brown's editorship. While getting it started, Brown evidently had gotten *Edgar Huntly* underway, reaching back to the lost "Sky-Walk" for some of its materials, and offered a selection from *Huntly* in the first issue (April) of his new magazine. By June, copy for the whole of that novel was probably complete and in Hugh Maxwell's hands for printing, for it was announced as "In the Press" in *The Philadelphia Gazette & Universal Daily Advertiser* for 30 July–15 August.[10] It is interesting to note that by that time Brown had had sufficient response to the success of the *First Part* of *Arthur Mervyn* to express his satisfaction in the preface to *Edgar Huntly*. Part of June was spent on a jaunt of several days to Middletown, Connecticut (*Life*, II, 47), and on 26 July, anticipating another return of the "pestilence," he was preparing for a new trip, this time probably north to Albany with William Johnson (*Life*, II, 97).

No further information on the progress of Arthur's adventures exists until spring of 1800. By that time *Arthur Mervyn* was, in the minds of some, a book with which Brown's reputation was to be notably connected. On 5 February 1800 John Davis, sometime tutor, traveller, poet, and translator, landed in New York. Among his first memorable acts was a meeting with "the author of *Arthur Mervyn*, living at *New-York*"; in Brown, he said, "I sought acquaintance with a man who had acquired so much intellectual renown."[11] How this renown should have come to Davis is probably explained by Davis' friendship with one of Brown's major professional connections in New York. When Davis first arrived in New York in the spring of 1798, he was quickly taken up by another recent arrival in America, the Frenchman, Hocquet Caritat. Caritat had opened a Circulating Library in New York, trying several locations before settling into the City Hotel, where his rooms became a regular retreat and gathering place for New Yorkers of intellectual and literary bent until 1804, when Caritat returned to France. Caritat sold as well as lent books, encouraging ambitious literary talent, making space available for browsing and

[10] Blanck, I, 304.

[11] John Davis, *Travels of Four Years and a Half in the United States of America; During 1798, 1799, 1800, 1801, and 1802* (London, 1803); citations refer to the New York edition of A. J. Morrison (Henry Holt and Co., 1909), pp. 161–163.

talking, and increasingly stocking his tables with the most current European, and especially French, books. It seems most likely that Brown frequented Caritat's Library from 1799 to 1801, while he edited the *Monthly Magazine*, to pick up materials for his reviews and staple column of "Miscellaneous Articles of Literary and Philosophical Intelligence." And we must remember that it was Caritat who secured the copyrights—and was indeed publisher—for both *Wieland* and *Ormond*, Brown's two New York publications up to this time. Davis would remember in 1803 that it was Caritat who "was my only friend at *New York*, when the energies of my mind were depressed by the chilling prospects of poverty" (*Travels*, p. 204). That Caritat acted as go-between for his two protégés, Davis and Brown, seems very probable.[12]

The important matter is that Davis claims that Brown, on this first meeting in the late winter or early spring of 1800, dressed in great coat and worn-down shoes, was busy "embodying virtue in a new novel, and making his pen fly before him" (*Travels*, p. 163). This may indeed point to the *Second Part* of *Arthur Mervyn*, but the evidence is vague at best and, considering Davis' generally arch tone, could apply to anything Brown may have been working on at the time. In April of that year, however, Brown himself gives us further evidence about this volume. He wrote then to brother James, indicating, first, his dissatisfaction with Hugh Maxwell's dilatoriness; second, his acquiescence in James's suggestion that a new publisher be sought in New York—"I know not whether the advantageous publication of Mervyn (the sequel of it) can be brought about in this city, but shall have it done in the way you mention"; and third, his delight that Caritat is busy promoting his novels abroad—"The salelibility [sic] of my works will much depend upon their popularity in England, whither Caritat has carried a considerable number of Wieland, Ormond and Mervyn" (*Life*, II, 100). How long Caritat was in England negotiating with the Minerva Press to secure English publication is not certain, though it is probable that Brown made satisfactory arrangements with the printer George F. Hopkins in Caritat's absence.

[12] For a fuller view of Caritat's New York activities, see LeRoy Elwood Kimball, "An Account of Hocquet Caritat, XVIII Century New York Circulating Librarian, Bookseller, and Publisher of the First Two Novels of Charles Brockden Brown, 'America's First Professional Man of Letters'" *Colophon*, 5 (September 1934), n. pag., and George Gates Raddin, Jr., *Hocquet Caritat and the Early New York Literary Scene* (Dover, N.J.: The Dover Advance Press, 1953).

Evidence of the exact date on which Hopkins issued the *Second Part* varies from as early as 4 July to as late as 3 September.[13] If we accept a date closer to September than to July—as perforce we must, given Brown's own statement in the August issue of the *Monthly Magazine* (pp. 156–157) that the *Second Part* "has just been published"—we face a question of Brown's attitude toward the sequel. His having turned the proofreading of the *First Part* over to his brother James is understandable, considering his distance from Philadelphia and his pressing obligations in New York. But with the *Second Part* just freshly out, Brown was again away, this time in Philadelphia, writing on 1 September, "I had no engagements that detained me in New York, and so I came hither, . . . merely to see a different set of faces. I staid in Jersey, at Newark, Brunswick and Princeton half a week . . . " (*Life*, II, 101). The letter makes no mention of the volume, expressing not even relief that the final rigors of seeing the book through the press are behind him nor joy at its appearance. Either the book was well off Brown's mind by that time, or it held rather little importance for him.

A year prior, and with unmistakable reference to the *First Part* of *Arthur Mervyn*, completed eight months earlier, Brown had written in "Walstein's School of History" of the primary importance of marriage as the occasion that brings together the primary grounds of all human happiness and misery—property and sex.[14] Clearly that concern had occupied Brown in the *First Part*, especially with respect to Clemenza and Eliza Hadwin. And it is precisely that subject that prompted Brown's most inventive incidents in the continuation of his story—Arthur's love and eventual marriage to Achsa Fielding, his concern for Eliza's financial as well as her amorous security, his return of Mrs. Watson's money, and his restoration of their property to the ungrateful Maurices. In "Walstein's School" Brown imagines a distinguished and high-minded historian dedicated to promoting human happiness by presenting models for virtuous behavior in his lives of Cicero and the Marquis de Pombal. This model for Brown's own work has gathered about him a coterie of nine favored students, one of whom—Engel—has written a "fictitious history" called "Olivo

[13] Warfel cites a Washington, D.C. newspaper announcement for the earlier date; Blanck (I, 304) opts for the later date on the basis of advertisements in New York newspapers, supposing the local press to be more accurate.

[14] *Monthly Magazine,* 1 (September 1799), 408–409.

Ronsica," based on his mentor's principles. Brown gives us a summary of that history, which is essentially the story of the *First Part* of *Arthur Mervyn*—including even the appearance of "a pestilential disease . . . in the city." The summary ends thus: Olivo "resolves to become a physician, but is prompted by benevolence to return, for a time, to the farm which he had lately left. The series of ensuing events, are long, intricate, and congruous, and exhibit the hero of the tale in circumstances that task his fortitude, his courage, and his disinterestedness" (*Monthly Magazine*, p. 411). This last sentence is considerably vaguer than Brown's letter to his brother the preceding February about the exact shape of those "ensuing events," but it indicates that Brown's principles for the *Second Part* were clearly in mind. But the same essay also betrays a somewhat cavalier attitude towards the details that might embody those principles. Brown writes:

> Exact similitude is not required to render an imaginary portrait useful to those who survey it. The usefulness, undoubtedly, consists in suggesting a mode of reasoning and acting somewhat similar to that which is ascribed to a feigned person; and, for this end, some similitude is requisite between the real and imaginary situation; but that similitude is not hard to produce. Among the incidents which invention will set before us, those are to be culled out which afford most scope to wisdom and virtue, which are most analogous to facts, which most forcibly suggest to the reader the parallel between his state and that described, and most strongly excite his desire to act as the feigned personages act. These incidents must be so arranged as to inspire, at once, curiosity and belief, to fasten the attention, and thrill the heart. (*Monthly Magazine*, pp. 409–410)

Insofar as we may take these considerations to represent Brown's actual practice, we may assume that he operated from a too sanguine confidence in the ease with which similitudes and incidents are produced, and therefore did not himself appropriately evaluate the effect achieved by the new incidents that distinguish the *Second Part*.

Such considerations, however, help us only partially in determining Brown's sense of the relationship of the two parts of his novel, and help us not at all with the date and process of composition of the *Second Part*. They indicate, with almost equal weight, that Brown saw the *Second Part* (1) as logically and aesthetically necessitated by the incompletions of the *First Part*, (2) as a consistent adumbration of principles that lay at the heart of his didactic purposes, and (3) as a convenient way of exploiting the success of the *First Part*—that is, as a self-conscious "sequel," to use Brown's own term. Indeed, the closer one examines the evidence, the less certain Brown's artistic intentions regarding the relationship of the two parts become. There is no question that Brown at times saw Arthur's marriage as not just a structural and conventional convenience, but as a philosophical necessity. That warrants our considering the two parts as a conceptual whole. But there is also no arguing with the general critical consensus that the *Second Part*—no matter how intriguing its details—devolves into conventional patterns, strained solutions, and apparently hurried and unsatisfactory development. Philosophically both parts of *Arthur Mervyn* operate sympathetically; artistically, the *Second Part* is an afterthought, more interesting for its incidental perceptions than for its structural and emotional integrity.

In 1801 Hocquet Caritat made another visit to England, this time to deal with William Lane's new young partner, Anthony King Newman, under whose direction the Minerva Press would quickly gain preeminence in the field of cheap popular fiction. Having already established systematic outlets for English productions in America, Caritat became the authorized distributor of Minerva Press books. Perhaps through Caritat's influence, Newman saw enough value in *Arthur Mervyn* as a literary property to bring the two parts together for the first time in a three-decker selling for four shillings a volume—the standard price for Minerva fiction then—in 1803. Brown, however, had no hand in that edition; indeed, there is no sign of any further involvement with the text of *Arthur Mervyn* on Brown's part after the New York printing of the *Second Part*.

Serious critical response to *Arthur Mervyn* was slow in coming. The book was read and—though overshadowed by *Wieland*—remembered in the 1820s and 1830s. The story was even imitated twice by the time of Brown's death.[15] But it was not until 1815 and the appearance of Dunlap's *Life* that significant critical attention came to the novel. This was certainly not for any lack of trying to secure serious attention on Brown's part. Readers generally take

[15] See Henri Petter, *The Early American Novel* (Columbus: Ohio State Univ. Press, 1971), pp. 324–326.

at face value Brown's announced intention in the "Advertisement" to *Wieland* to illustrate "some important branches of the moral constitution of man." But in recent decades Brown's claims for *Arthur Mervyn*, perhaps because they do not skirt the miraculous, are taken skeptically, and ironically. Arthur's self-seeking undercuts his virtuous protestations, and even the structural complications of the narrative are seen as signals of Brown's ironic and satiric intentions. Attractive as such views have become, there is still value in seeing *Arthur Mervyn* as Brown himself apparently wanted his readers to see it.

He states his conscious intentions first in the "Preface," the most ambitious statement of purpose to accompany the first three novels. The story is primarily to memorialize a significant event—to be "a brief but faithful sketch of the condition" of Philadelphia during the epidemic of 1793. Second, it is to depict in "lively colours" the suffering, fortitude, and constancy of the victims of social calamity in order to move readers to compassion, charity, and reform. And third, it is to rouse readers to the emulation of virtue, defined as disinterested benevolence. This "humble narrative," Brown advises, is didactic, morally instructive, exemplary; he appeals to the reader as "moral observer" and, intentionally or not, directs attention away from the "particular series of adventures" to their moral end. That tack flatters the reader and perhaps justifies dealing in fiction at all—a common trope of eighteenth-century novelists—while it tends to divert attention from faults of execution. Given his concern with duplicity and illusions in the previous novels, and the sensational events and moral ambiguities to occupy this one, to suspect Brown of devious purposes here is not unreasonable.

But we must always remember that Brown insistently expressed himself with an extraordinary moral earnestness. His earlier letters to Joseph Bringhurst sport with the notion of living among allegories superior to dull realities. Even through the sportiveness, however, one senses a serious commitment to levels of truth unsullied by real experience. Allegory, he contends, is the "native region of the poet," whether in verse or prose.[16] This, of course, is long before *Arthur Mervyn*, but such convictions seem to be reinforced, after the production of the *First Part*, in his "Walstein's School of History," which in many ways supports the sincerity of Brown's intentions in *Arthur Mervyn*'s preface. Walstein,

[16]Letter to Bringhurst, 30 May 1792, Kennedy, pp. 553A–554.

remember, is the fictitious historian at Jena who has drawn to himself several disciples, one of whom—Engel—produces a history that is fictitious but is nonetheless as capable as any history of the highest instructive purposes. "To exhibit, in an eloquent narration, a model of right conduct, is the highest province of benevolence" and the guiding purpose of Engel's history, which exactly conforms to *Arthur Mervyn*.[17] Insofar as we grant Brown some degree of seriousness, then, we may suppose that *Arthur Mervyn* proceeded from principles similar to those that inspired Engel, and that these are embodied in Walstein's "School."

Walstein has written two imaginary histories of real persons, Cicero and the Marquis de Pombal (the enlightened chief minister of Portugal's King Joseph I from 1750 to 1777). Walstein's purpose is clearly the moral improvement of his readers: "By exhibiting a virtuous being in opposite conditions, and pursuing his end by means suited to his own condition, he believes himself displaying a model of right conduct, and furnishing incitements to imitate that conduct, supplying men not only with knowledge of just ends and just means, but with the love and the zeal of virtue" (*Monthly Magazine*, 1, 337). What attracts Walstein to the ancient Roman and the modern statesman is that both share his own desire to promote "the general happiness," and that both influence society by virtue of their "intellectual vigour." According to Brown, both the effort and the resulting works are entirely admirable. He especially celebrates Walstein's risking the imposture of imagined autobiography in order to observe the significance of events and ideas through the narrator's own passionate involvement in them. Clearly, Walstein stands behind Brown's own work in some vague way, less perhaps in *Wieland* and *Ormond* than in the curiosity, tenacity, and good intentions of *Edgar Huntly*.

Even more clearly Walstein stands behind Engel who, like Brown, sees no insuperable difficulty in making his "model of right conduct" totally fictitious. But Engel also reasons that his model need not be an eminent public figure, because all men exist in spheres of relationship and therefore of potential moral influence, even the simplest:

> The relations in which men, unendowed with political authority, stand to each other, are numerous. An extensive

[17]*Monthly Magazine*, 1 (September 1799), 408, 410–411.

source of these relations, is property. No topic can engage the attention of man more momentous than this. Opinions, relative to property, are the immediate source of nearly all the happiness and misery that exist among mankind. If men were guided by justice in the acquisition and disbursement, the brood of private and public evils would be extinguished.

To ascertain the precepts of justice, and exhibit these precepts reduced to practice, was, therefore, the favourite task of Engel. This, however, did not constitute his whole scheme. Every man is encompassed by numerous claims, and is the subject of intricate relations. Many of these may be comprised in a copious narrative, without infraction of simplicity or detriment to unity.

Next to property, the most extensive source of our relations is sex. On the circumstances which produce, and the principles which regulate the union between the sexes, happiness greatly depends. The conduct to be pursued by a virtuous man in those situations which arise from sex, it was thought useful to display. (*Monthly Magazine*, 1, 408–409)

According to the sketch of Engel's "Olivo Ronsica" which follows, however, Brown emphasizes relations of property rather than of sex. This may indeed be the clue to Brown's discovery of what his sequel should concentrate on. Readers of modern sensibility may feel uneasy with the notion of sex as only another form of property relations, but that is what Brown seems here to be saying, and we must remember the subtlety and complexity with which he explored that connection in *Alcuin*. Nonetheless, Brown's description of Engel's hero has a telling application to Arthur Mervyn:

He is destitute of property, of friends, and of knowledge of the world. These are to be acquired by his own exertions, and virtue and sagacity are to guide him in the choice and the use of suitable means.

Ignorance subjects us to temptation, and poverty shackles our beneficence. Olivo's conduct shews us how temptation may be baffled, in spite of ignorance, and benefits be conferred in spite of poverty. (*Monthly Magazine*, 1, 410)

Arthur or Olivo, is, like Richardson's Clarissa, a "being of uncommon virtue, bereaved of many external benefits by the vices of others." But he is no Clarissa: "Olivo is a different personage. His talents are exerted to reform the vices of others, to defeat their malice when exerted to his injury, to endure, without diminution of his usefulness or happiness, the injuries which he cannot shun" (*Monthly Magazine*, pp. 410, 411).

Some part of Brown, at least after completing the *First Part* of *Arthur Mervyn,* took Arthur's virtue quite seriously. What interests one now about Brown's review of his own work is where he put the emphases. Somewhat at odds with the "Preface," the "pestilential disease" of "Olivo Ronsica" is reduced to a mere occasion to display the hero's valor and ingenuity. And that hero shows for the first time in Brown's fiction an energetic, positive, assertive virtue, not merely the passive victimized virtue of Clara or Constantia, or the compulsive, forced heroics of Edgar—a decided advance upon previous presentations. This emphasis also suggests that the epidemic of *Arthur Mervyn* is not, as it has so often been taken to be, the equivalent of his earlier ventriloquism, disguises, and somnambulism, but that Arthur's virtue itself is the strange but true element Brown expected to dominate his readers' attention.

In the very last paragraph of "Walstein's School" Brown evaluates Engel's masterpiece, expressing what he must have hoped would be the judgment upon *Arthur Mervyn*:

> Engel has certainly succeeded in producing a tale, in which are powerful displays of fortitude and magnanimity; a work whose influence must be endlessly varied by varieties of character and situation of the reader, but, from which, it is not possible for any one to rise without some degree of moral benefit, and much of that pleasure which always attends the emotions of curiosity and sympathy. (*Monthly Magazine,* 1, 411)

Brown's hope was at best premature, for he still had no clear series of episodes, no full plot for the sequel of his story. He did have the controlling idea—the relationships of sex and their interrelationship with property—but how to lay out the story was not before him.

The *Second Part* falls into three main segments. The five opening chapters (with no apparent shift in time) are clearly designed to reinvigorate interest as most of Arthur's previous explanations are questioned. Stevens, the man of science, must steadily measure his faith in the truthfulness of his young friend against the testimony of honest and apparently disinterested witnesses who call Arthur's story and his character into very reasonable doubt. A second segment, beginning with Stevens' accidental discovery of Arthur at the debtors' prison (Chapter 5), relates what has happened to Stevens' young charge since the burning of the supposedly forged bank notes in the catastrophe of the *First Part.* This segment extends through Chapter 15, and both concludes and introduces some important matter. First, the original intention to marry Arthur to Eliza Hadwin has definitely altered. Second, Welbeck, directly faced with Arthur's killing virtue, expires. Third, Arthur meets Achsa Fielding, a totally new conception. And fourth, faced directly with the accusations against his character, Arthur dispells all (or most) of the suspicions. This segment ends with Arthur's setting out to Baltimore to redress all the proprietary injustices done to Mrs. Watson and to the Maurices. The third segment is in the form of a letter whose status is very vague and indefinite. It is apparently not written to Stevens, who is treated here as a character (see esp. p. 391). Indeed, Stevens fades as the narrative voice, and Arthur takes over his own story. The substance of this third segment is Arthur's increasing attachment to Achsa, in whom property and sex join in very complicated ways.

Some of these complications are the natural consequence of the yellow fever. Brown treats the shifts in time in his story very casually, but he has really worked them out with some concern for feasibility. The *First Part,* ended in September 1793, is thus set nicely into the very period when we know the epidemic to have been at its height. The action of the *Second Part* extends from September through the winter and into the spring of 1794. Clemenza has borne her baby, living since the previous July in Mrs. Villars' whorehouse, and it is in seeking her that Arthur meets Achsa in the spring, moving to his reward, as June approaches, even more ecstatically than did "Wallace" of "The Man at Home," who in the eleventh sketch—as previously cited—met and married the young lady to whose "youth, beauty, and virtue" were added "three hundred pounds a year" (Warfel, *Rhapsodist,* p. 85). Indeed, it seems that Brown went back to "The Man at Home" for several matters, some of major importance. Concern with debtors' prison lurks throughout the meditations of the Man, but I think we can see the emergence of the Arthur/Achsa marriage in the following episodes. The Man, under the pretext of encouraging Miss De Moivre to exploit her own adventurous life, sketches that life in Numbers IX and X. The life is incredibly packed with incident; it is not surprising that under Brown's imagination, Miss De Moivre could easily split into three or four characters: merely by changing her name she becomes Miss Monrose of *Ormond,* and her international background is incorporated with the political feelings of Martinette in the same work, but it is Miss De Moivre who meets the Man's young friend in circumstances that anticipate the meeting of Achsa and Arthur, Arthur's compulsive search through the Villars house, the pistol threat, and even the encounter with death (Clemenza's infant taking the role of Miss De Moivre's father). The Man concludes his description, "I do not despair of one day seeing her the wife of my young friend. Their sympathy of views and character, can scarcely fail of accomplishing their nuptial union" (*Rhapsodist,* pp. 79–80).

If Brown found Achsa's involvement with Arthur in some sense predestined by his handling of the same characters in "The Man at Home," his friend and first serious critic, William Dunlap, was infuriated by that turn in the story. Eliza he found "abandoned both by hero and author, in a manner as unexpected as disgusting" (*Life,* II, 40), and could barely contain his exasperation. Dunlap's attitude is especially important because his remarks in the biography have pretty much set the categories for critical comment on *Arthur Mervyn* ever since. Dunlap focused on three issues: the autobiographical origins of the story, its literary sources, and its formal deficiencies. By and large, Dunlap (along with Paul Allen, the original biographer) does not so much make capital of the autobiographical material he has at hand, as he sets it forth in recollections, samples of Brown's early moral opinions and legal judgments, and personal letters. Who could not see in the youthful Brown's love of long walks, bookishness, aversion to athletics, curiosity about property and money, and unorthodox opinions of social conventions the naïveté of Arthur Mervyn? Thus we are told " . . . he inherited from nature a frail, delicate, and a sickly constitution; a constitution which incapacitated him from athletic exercise. In another letter to one of his correspondents, he congratulates himself on this infirmity. He is by the benevolence of nature rendered in a manner an exile from many of the temptations that infest the minds of ardent youth. Possessing such a constitutional infirmity, he had nothing to apprehend from those enticements which usually sway the minds of young men" (*Life*, I, 49). If that were reliable, we would have additional evidence of Brown's sincere and straightforward intentions regarding Arthur's virtue, but Dunlap allows insufficiently for

Brown's youthful posings in his personal letters, especially those to Bringhurst and Wilkins in the early 1790s. More to the point, however, was Brown's personal experience of yellow fever, the topic with which Dunlap opens his second volume. We have commented on this already, but Dunlap is much more telling in hooking the epidemics of 1793 and 1798 together through Brown's letters, which register Brown's personal shock and wonder at the disease and its consequences, the "many moral incidents" surrounding the deaths of Scandella and Smith, and Brown's own personal discomfiture. Dunlap takes the horror, heroism, and humanity of Brown's observations so totally for granted in their immediate relevance to *Arthur Mervyn* that he does not comment on them explicitly.

Dunlap's citation of literary sources is limited to William Godwin's *Political Justice* and *Caleb Williams*; he notes that in 1798 Brown "was an avowed admirer of Godwin's style, and the effects of that admiration, may be discerned in many of his early compositions." And in describing Welbeck's secretiveness and Arthur's curiosity, he later exclaims: "The reader cannot but be again reminded of Caleb Williams, and Falkland, yet here is no servile copy, the characters of Mervyn and Welbeck are distinct in many circumstances from Williams and his master, and the situations in which they are placed are altogether new" (*Life,* II, 15, 21). Next to the plague itself, this Godwinian connection has haunted criticism of *Arthur Mervyn* from Dunlap on, though reviewers prove more inclined to register the connection between the two rather than the differences Dunlap noted. Godwin's very successful *Things As They Are; or, The Adventures of Caleb Williams* was written in 1793, published in England the following year, and reprinted in Philadelphia on 30 March 1795. By September of that year, Brown indicates that he knows the book and is working at a novel "equal in extent to Caleb Williams."[20] Like innumerable readers, Brown must have been intrigued by Godwin's intricate tale of young Caleb the servant, whose curiosity about the affairs of his benefactor Falkland and whose straightforward honesty lead him into a series of conflicts with social custom and law and into a world of complete lawlessness, until he reveals the secret culpability of his benefactor and persecutor—a revelation equal, in

[20] Brown to Dunlap, September 1795. William Dunlap, "Charles Brockden Brown," *The National Portrait Gallery of Distinguished Americans,* ed. James Herring and James B. Longacre (New York: Hermon Bancroft, 1836), III, 3.

Caleb's own conscience, to the enormities of Falkland himself. But Brown was not persuaded that these were "things as they are." Indeed, despite the close parallels between Caleb and Falkland in Godwin's novel and Arthur and Welbeck in Brown's, the differences are profound and extensive. Chief among them is young Arthur's (and we may also assume Brown's) supreme confidence that manly and noble actions proceeding from clear conscience and upright intentions will always prevail over their opposites, no matter how questionable they may appear from time to time. This confidence removes much of the moral complexity, irony, and ambivalence that distinguish Godwin's tale. It also shifts attention from personality or character to incident and complexity of plot and narration, to puzzles and false appearances, the untangling of which primarily occupies the reader.

Clearly, too, Brown saw the novel as a vehicle for ideas, some of them prominent in Godwin—for example, the concern with secrecy, curiosity, reputation, forthrightness, the fate of innocence in a sick world, and the relationships of individual morality with social institutions—ideas which Dunlap leaves unmentioned. But his observations proved sufficient for *Arthur Mervyn* to be labeled a Godwinian novel for more than a century.

Later critics also echo Dunlap's criticism of *Arthur Mervyn's* formal deficiencies. Throughout the *Life,* Dunlap depicts Brown as bewilderingly unsystematic in his thinking, slovenly in his personal habits, and downright sloppy about his stories.

> The faults which deform this interesting and eloquent narrative, are altogether owing to haste, both in composing and in publishing. The work was sent to the printer before the writer had fully determined its plot. But for this, we should not meet with such obvious errors, as making Mervyn perfectly resemble both Lodi and Clavering, without any necessity for his resembling either; exciting an interest in Mrs. Wentworth, and leaving her and her story, like Butler's bear and fiddle; keeping Welbeck's servants quietly asleep in the house, while pistols are discharged, murder committed, the dead body buried, &c. when they could have been so easily removed; not to mention the impropriety of crowding so many incidents into the short space of five days. Dramatists are supposed to be bound by time, and circumscribed in the scene of their action; not so novelists, and therefore probability should not be violated, when no advantage can be gained by it. These are venial faults, and the

472

beauties of Arthur Mervyn are splendid. But in proportion
to the talents displayed by the author, is our regret that he
did not do as much and as well, as he proved himself capable
of doing. (*Life*, II, 29–30)

What those beauties are Dunlap does not say, though he com-
mends the "style of elegance and force" of the Watson burial
episode and believes that Brown "exerted his powers to the utmost" in the final chapter of the *First Part* (*Life*, II, 24, 29).

With the *Second Part* Dunlap's exasperation makes him totally
impatient. The sequel, he complains, is planless and inconsistent,
tries to be funny and fails, excites our curiosity and then forgets to
satisfy it, and enlists our interest and sympathy in young Eliza
only to frustrate her and us disgustingly. Dunlap does acknowledge "passages eminently beautiful" but instead of identifying
them, reverts to autobiographical elements in the story, noting
that Arthur's mental habits (see pp. 265–266) perfectly describe
Brown's (*Life*, II, 41).[21]

The full impact of Dunlap's judgments came not so much upon
the biography's initial publication in Philadelphia as upon its
republication in London in 1822, issued there by Henry Colburn
in the course of his republishing several Brown novels in 1821
and 1822. It was in his financial interest, of course, to promote
both Dunlap and Brown, and the pages of his *Colburn's New
Monthly Magazine* were used for that purpose.[22] In a sense, however, Colburn was only one of a multitude of participants in the
general flurry of critical respect and attention accorded Brown in
the 1820s, following the increasingly testy and chauvinistic claims
for American culture in the *North American Review* and elsewhere,
the happy success of Washington Irving's elegant *Sketchbook,* and
the enthusiastic claims made for Cooper's new works, especially
The Spy and *The Pioneers.* Attentive—and often flattering—as the
reviews are, they generally ignore *Arthur Mervyn,* except to mention the realism of the plague descriptions. Indeed, there is often
an air of not having read *Arthur Mervyn* at all, of hearsay report-

[21] In a brief biography produced years later, Dunlap notes very specif-
ically that "the author has in this work fully expressed his conviction, that
he was to die early and by consumption." See *National Portrait Gallery,* III,
5.

[22] See William B. Cairns, *British Criticisms of American Writings,
1815–1833,* Univ. of Wisconsin Studies in Language and Literature,
No. 14 (Madison: Univ. of Wisconsin Press, 1922), pp. 192–200.

ing, mostly from Dunlap, which may account for the derivative judgments.

Occasionally, of course, the general remarks, or those proceeding primarily from considerations of *Wieland,* have special pertinence to *Arthur Mervyn.* Thus William H. Gardiner, in a long review of *The Spy,* concludes that Cooper is "the first who has deserved the appellation of a distinguished American novel writer. Brown, who is beginning to attain a merited distinction abroad as well as at home, although his scenes are laid in America, cannot be said with truth to have produced an American novel .... His works have nothing but American topography about them. We recognize the names of places that are familiar to us and nothing more."[23]

Two years earlier an anonymous British reviewer had made some very telling judgments. *Arthur Mervyn,* like other Brown novels, was a victim of Brown's and Caritat's eagerness for British publication. With nothing but scorn for Lane, Newman, and their Minerva Press, the reviewer complains: " ... it was the fate of those works, when first reprinted in this country, to issue from one of the common reservoirs of sentimental trash, and, consequently, (as we imagine) to share in the general contempt attached to those poor productions, which, like the redundant and needy members of a great house, have nothing but sounding titles to sustain them."[24] He makes the subtle and interesting observation that the distinguishing method of Brown's fiction—putting undistinguished persons into strange situations brought about by "a fatal series of untoward accidents"—parallels Godwin's method not from direct imitation but from their shared political and moral purposes. Discussing Caleb Williams very much as one might Arthur or any of Brown's first-person narrators, the reviewer says, " ... the external events he passed through, would never have obtained such a grasp of our imagination, had it not been for the deep conflict of passions within, to which they are made subservient, and of which the spirited and elaborate analysis forms the principal attraction of his story" (*New Monthly Magazine,* p. 610). Thus we have a "key" to Brown, as this reviewer says, which acknowledges the Godwin connection without making Brown a mere imitator. Moreover, he perceives in Arthur a

[23]*North American Review,* 15 (July 1822), 281–282.
[24]"On the Writings of Charles Brockden Brown, the American Novelist," *New Monthly Magazine and Universal Register,* 14 (December 1820), 609.

national symbol, much as recent critics have discovered anew: "In the language and conduct of Edgar Huntly and Arthur Mervyn there is a certain Colonial cast of frankness, frugality, and intelligent simplicity, mixed up with habits of steady, unostentatious benevolence, and patient self-denial, betokening the American notions of the qualities best befitting the youth of their republic—while in the occasional decision and physical energy that they display, we recognise the importance annexed to those more masculine attributes, by which the gigantic infant is destined one day to ascend to the heights of power and renown" (*New Monthly Magazine*, p. 611). Here indeed Brown found a rare reader of kindred spirit.

A long essay on "American Literature" appeared in the *Retrospective Review* in 1824, ostensibly a review of *Arthur Mervyn*.[25] But only six pages are given to Brown, most of them a summary of the *First Part* of *Mervyn*, apparently all the reviewer had seen. The reviewer concludes: "Brown was not without his faults. He was defective, generally speaking, in the construction of his plots. His story turns too entirely on one character, and the events are sometimes improbable; but he has redeeming points,—a stern masculine eloquence, and apparent sincerity of purpose, a plain dealing with events (if we may so speak), and occasionally scenes of overwhelming interest" (*Retrospective Review*, pp. 322–323). One hopes for better from the sprightly though quirky effusions of John Neal, but neither the remarks in his *Blackwood's Magazine* articles (1824–1825) nor those in his novel *Randolph* (1823)[26] warrant any attention, except, perhaps, the suggestion that Welbeck is the hero of Brown's tale, or the judgment that for all his arresting and exciting effects, Brown was essentially a writer out of control. That suggestion still haunts criticism of *Arthur Mervyn*.

Throughout the nineteenth and to nearly the middle of the twentieth century, *Arthur Mervyn* has served primarily to illustrate Brown's descriptive realism and to acknowledge the psychological force of such realism in the history of Gothic fiction in America.[27] The title of Warfel's important study, *Charles Brockden*

---

[25] Vol. 9, pp. 304–326.

[26] These are reprinted in John Neal, *American Writers: A Series of Papers Contributed to Blackwood's Magazine (1824–1825)*, ed. Fred Lewis Pattee (Durham, N.C.: Duke Univ. Press, 1937).

[27] The history of Brown criticism is admirably reviewed in Paul Witherington's "Charles Brockden Brown: A Bibliographical Essay," *Early American Literature*, 9 (Fall 1974), 164–187.

Brown: American Gothic Novelist, essentially sums up that Gothic context, while a present resurgence of interest in the dynamics of that genre both deepens and expands the interpretive possibilities in this novel. Thus Leslie Fiedler's swashbuckling romp through *Arthur Mervyn,* opening still unexhausted possibilities in terms of Freudian and Marxist analysis, launches itself from "The Invention of the American Gothic."[28] It is nonetheless worth noting that what Fiedler calls his own "balance between psychological and sociological insights" only extends, albeit in more vigorous and timely language, Brown's own perception in "Walstein's School" that the balance between sex and property was basic to *Arthur Mervyn.* It is no surprise, then, that Fiedler should see both parts of the novel as mutually necessary to Brown's creation.

Less profoundly, but still very powerfully, the sense that Brown consciously or unconsciously discovered in *Arthur Mervyn* an archetypal or eponymous American character and situation was developed in mythic terms by R. W. B. Lewis.[29] Despite the slightness of Lewis' treatment (he is eager to get on to Cooper), his view of *Arthur Mervyn* as "a muffled version of an adventure to be located by later fiction in the very heart of American life" (p. 98) tremendously broadened the cultural and literary significance of Brown's novel. To no small extent Lewis and Fiedler recalled serious attention to *Arthur Mervyn* and helped nurture a burgeoning critical interest in Brown. Warner Berthoff's Rinehart edition made the novel widely available for study after 1962, and the emergence of the journal *Early American Literature* has provided an arena for increasingly intelligent and sophisticated interpretations of Arthur's adventures. Various as recent interpretations are, they seem to circle constantly around a central issue in *Arthur Mervyn*—the issue of sincerity—addressed morally and aesthetically. Most conspicuously it takes the form of questioning Arthur's professed ideals in the light of what seems his shrewd and self-serving actions, but it also extends to other forms—the honesty of Brown's announced intentions and the degree of trust he himself put in Arthur's character; the functions of ambiguity, contradiction, irony, and even cynicism in the story; the purpose of the complicated narrative structure; the relative reliability of

[28] Leslie A. Fiedler, *Love and Death in the American Novel,* rev. ed. (New York: Stein and Day, 1966, originally 1960), pp. 98–161, 296–297.

[29] *The American Adam: Innocence, Tragedy and Tradition in the Nineteenth Century* (Chicago: Univ. of Chicago Press, 1955), pp. 92–98.

the several narrators; and even the question of Brown's artistic self-consciousness.[30]

So we are brought into an even more profound perplexity than that assaulting Dr. Stevens during Arthur's absence. Once again Arthur's character is plagued by doubt, distrust, suspicion. His actions look jaundiced to us. And like Stevens we have "nothing but his own narrative" by which to judge them. "A smooth exterior, a show of virtue, and a specious tale, are, a thousand times, exhibited in human intercourse by craft and subtlety," and whereas Stevens could soothe his anxieties by recalling that "the face of Mervyn is the index of an honest mind" (p. 229), we do not have that face before us to support our confidence. For us Mervyn is only his story. Dr. Stevens helped Arthur elude the yellow fever, but seems to have quickened in us something of that other Philadelphia fever of 1793. Our questions about Mervyn and Brown are deeper and sharper now than they were when the book was first published.

N.S.G.

---

[30]Warner Berthoff's disbelief in Arthur's virtuous protestations was announced in "Adventures of the Young Man: An Approach to Charles Brockden Brown," *American Quarterly,* 9 (Winter 1957), 421–434. By 1966, Donald A. Ringe feels obliged to warn his readers that Mervyn is probably not "a conscious fraud," despite the telling evidence to the contrary (*Charles Brockden Brown* [New York: Twayne Publishers, 1966], pp. 80–85). And by 1974 the fall issue of *Early American Literature* prints excellent and subtle studies by William Hedges and Michael Davitt Bell that extend duplicity, deception, contradiction, paradox, deceit, and masquerade into principles of artistic construction and even into strategies of artistic criticism.

SELECTED BIBLIOGRAPHY

Axelrod, Alan. *Charles Brockden Brown: An American Tale.* Austin: Univ. of Texas Press, 1983.

Christophersen, Bill. *The Apparition in the Glass: Charles Brockden Brown's American Gothic.* Athens: Univ. of Georgia Press, 1993. Chapter 5.

Cohen, Daniel A. "Arthur Mervyn and His Elders: The Ambivalence of Youth in the Early Republic." *William and Mary Quarterly* 43 (1986): 362–80.

Eiselein, Gregory. "Humanitarianism and Uncertainty in *Arthur Mervyn.*" *Essays in Literature* 22 (1995): 215–26.

Elliott, Emory. "Narrative Unity and Moral Resolution in *Arthur Mervyn.*" In *Critical Essays on Charles Brockden Brown.* Ed. Bernard Rosenthal. Boston: G. K. Hall, 1981. 142–63.

Feeney, Joseph J. "Modernized by 1800: The Portrait of Urban America, Especially Philadelphia, in the Novels of Charles Brockden Brown." *American Studies* 23 (1982): 23–38.

Ferguson, Robert A. "Yellow Fever and Charles Brockden Brown: The Context of the Emerging Novelist." *Early American Literature* 14 (1979–80): 293–305.

Grabo, Norman S. *The Coincidental Art of Charles Brockden Brown.* Chapel Hill: Univ. of North Carolina Press, 1981. Chapter 4.

Hinds, Elizabeth Jane Wall. *Charles Brockden Brown's Gendered Economics of Virtue.* Newark: Univ. of Delaware Press, 1997. Chapter 3.

Larson, David M. "*Arthur Mervyn, Edgar Huntly* and the Critics." *Essays in Literature* 15 (1988): 207–19.

Levine, Robert S. "Arthur Mervyn's Revolutions." *Studies in American Fiction* 12 (1984): 145–60.

Person, Leland S., Jr. "'My Good Mama': Women in *Edgar Huntly* and *Arthur Mervyn.*" *Studies in American Fiction* 9 (1981): 33–46.

Russo, James R. "The Chameleon of Convenient Vice: A Study of the Narrative of *Arthur Mervyn.*" *Studies in the Novel* 11 (1979): 381–405.

Samuels, Shirley. "Plague and Politics in 1793: *Arthur Mervyn.*" *Criticism* 27 (1985): 225–46.

Spangler, George M. "Charles Brockden Brown's *Arthur Mervyn:* A Portrait of the Young American Artist." *American Literature* 52 (1981): 578–92.

Tompkins, Jane: *Sensational Designs: The Cultural Works of American Fiction, 1790–1860.* New York: Oxford Univ. Press, 1985. Chapter 3.

Watts, Steven. *The Romance of Real Life: Charles Brockden Brown and the Origins of American Culture.* Baltimore: Johns Hopkins Univ. Press, 1994. Chapter 5.